A DEATH IN THE TIWI ISLANDS

A DEATH IN THE
TIWI ISLANDS
Conflict, Ritual and Social Life in an
Australian Aboriginal Community

ERIC VENBRUX

University of Nijmegen

CAMBRIDGE
UNIVERSITY PRESS

Published by the Press Syndicate of the University of Cambridge
The Pitt Building, Trumpington Street, Cambridge CB2 IRP, UK
40 West 20th Street, New York, NY 10011–4211, USA
10 Stamford Road, Oakleigh, Melbourne 3166, Australia

Printed in Hong Kong by Colorcraft

National Library of Australia cataloguing-in-publication data
Venbrux, Eric.
A death in the Tiwi islands: conflict, ritual and
social life in an Australian Aboriginal community.
Bibliography.
Includes index.
1. Homicide – Northern Territory – Garden Point.
2. Funeral rites and ceremonies – Northern Territory – Garden
Point. 3. Tiwi (Australian people) – Death. 4. Tiwi
(Australian people) – Mortuary customs. 5. Tiwi (Australian
people) – Social life and customs. I. Title.
364.152089915

Library of Congress cataloguing-in-publication data
Venbrux, Eric.
A death in the Tiwi islands: conflict, ritual and social life in
an Australian Aboriginal community/Eric Venbrux.
p.   cm.
Includes bibliographical references and index.
1. Tiwi (Australian people) – Funeral customs and rites. 2. Tiwi
(Australian people) – Social conditions. 3. Homicide – Australia –
Pularumpi (N.T.) 4. Death – Social aspects – Australia – Pularumpi
(N.T.) 5. Rites and ceremonies – Australia – Pularumpi (N.T.)
6. Pularumpi (N.T.) – Social life and customs.
DU125.T5V45 1995
994.2'95–dc20   95–7772

A catalogue record for this book is available from the British Library.

ISBN 0 521 47351 9 Hardback

Contents

Preface and Acknowledgements

'We cannot live other people's lives,
and it is a piece of bad faith to try.
We can but listen to what, in words,
in images, in actions, they say about
their lives.'

Clifford Geertz (1986: 373)

Tobias Arapi made me his friend. His tragic death has changed my life.

Sometimes it is as if I hear his voice or feel a gentle breeze and I remember how we sat under the mango tree in front of his hut, where Tobias shared his memories with me. I was shocked when I learned he had been killed. Why did it happen? How could his violent death be understood? Did the homicide make sense from his people's point of view? It remained unclear who had killed Tobias. How would people evaluate the killing and how would they deal with the matter?

The homicide took place some two months after I had arrived on Melville Island to conduct anthropological fieldwork. The aim of my research was to study Tiwi mortuary practice and ritual. With at least a year's stay on the island I decided to document all events connected with the homicide case as meticulously as possible. The killing puzzled me but over time it became an avenue to gain insight into late twentieth-century Tiwi society and culture.

This book, based on fieldwork conducted on Melville and Bathurst Islands between September 1988 and November 1989, and in October and November 1991, provides a detailed description and analysis of a single complex of events related to a homicide in a Tiwi community (northern Australia). It includes an account of the victim's life, his disputes with other people shortly before he met his death, the response of Tiwi people to the killing, the mortuary ritual cycle, the seasonal rituals, the police investigation of the homicide and the case in the criminal courts as well as how the Tiwi people involved perceived the proceedings and handled the matter.

The choice of representing a special case is a strategic one: things are out of proportion, and thus what we see is a magnification of what remains hidden, common sociocultural processes that underlie

behaviour in ordinary circumstances but that are difficult to detect in
other ways (cf. Ginzburg 1982; Thompson 1979; Davis 1985; Darnton
1985). Shore states, 'An alien culture is inevitably a mystery and its comprehension can aptly be described as a piece of detective work' (1982:
xiii). The case could help to illuminate something of contemporary Tiwi
culture (although it is not my intention here to reify 'culture', of course;
for a discussion of the concept of culture see, among others, Peacock
1989). I do not pretend to know who actually killed Tobias; the case is
unsolved. What is more important is that it opens up a range of cultural
possibilities (cf. Ginzburg 1984: 190, 210–13), represented by various
Tiwi points of view.

To protect people's privacy I have substituted pseudonyms for real
names. Tiwi people have 'a lot of names'; that is, they are important
people, and hope I have not been impudent in adding these names.

'Under the mango tree' was used as a label for the homicide case
(alluding to earlier events and violent occurrences) and as a post-
humous name for the victim by his kin and friends.

The tragic event of a homicide was reworked in a celebration of Tiwi
culture; above all, I hope readers will appreciate the creativity of Tiwi
people, the dynamics of their society, and the strength and vitality of
their culture amid change.

This book would never have been possible without the invaluable assistance of many people and institutions, in Australia as well as the
Netherlands, and, of course, it builds on the work of anthropologists
who previously conducted research in the Tiwi islands.

My chief debt is to the Tiwi people from Melville and Bathurst Islands.
I would like to express my gratitude to the delegates to the Tiwi Land
Council for the trust they placed in my companion Jeanette Deenen and
me, for the permission they granted me to attend land council meetings,
and for the hospitality we received. Tiwi people – in Pularumpi, our host
community, in particular – made us feel most welcome. My warmest
thanks go to all those fine people who 'looked after' Jeanette and me,
gave us their good company, took us out on hunting trips, provided us
with accommodation and transport, shared food and sleeping places
with us, took pains to answer our unremitting questions, and expressed
their sympathy in Tiwi fashion. The superb collaboration throughout of
my 'mother' has been invaluable; she not only took me under her wing
but also translated and interpreted the Tiwi songs for me. Our stay in the
Tiwi islands has enriched our lives enormously.

This work is based on my doctoral dissertation (1993c). I thank my
supervisors, Professor Albert Trouwborst and Ad Borsboom, and the
examiners of the dissertation, Professor Frans Hüsken, Lex van der

Leeden and Ian Keen, for their constructive comments. For their encouragement, support and helpful comments on my writing I am also indebted to a great many colleagues and friends: although I am unable to mention them all by name, I would like to acknowledge their contribution here. Jon Altman, Henk Driessen and Léon Buskens have been of crucial importance in this respect and it is to them that I am most heavily indebted. I received invaluable comments, in addition, from the participants in the seminar for PhD students convened by Albert Trouwborst, from Vallaurie Crawford, Ton Otto and Anton Ploeg, and from two anonymous readers for Cambridge University Press. For the Press Jean Cooney, Robin Derricourt and Jane Farago managed the work through the phases of production and improved it with their editorial skills.

I am grateful to the Netherlands Foundation for the Advancement of Tropical Research (WOTRO) in The Hague and the Department of Anthropology of the University of Nijmegen for funding my research. I also would like to thank the following institutions for their invaluable assistance: the Australian Institute of Aboriginal and Torres Strait Islander Studies, the Department of Archaeology and Anthropology (the Faculties) and the North Australia Research Unit of the Australian National University, the Roman Catholic Church on Melville and Bathurst Islands, the North Australian Aboriginal Legal Aid Service and the Northern Territory Police Force.

Thanks are due to Donna Burak for permission to reproduce her work of art on the cover and to Nicolas Peterson for allowing me to study the fieldnotes of C.W.M. Hart in his possession. To the Tiwi man charged with murder by the police and his counsel for defence I am indebted for permission to cite the court transcripts. An earlier version of chapter 7 (see Venbrux 1993a) was presented to the NICCOS Conference on the Politics of Ethnographic Reading and Writing in Plasmolen, The Netherlands (12–13 December, 1991).

For their material assistance and friendship in northern Australia I thank David and Elaine Benson, Annie Franklin, Susan Ostling, Celine Auton, Therese Fortier and Bob Dunbar. I am grateful for conversations with Gary Robinson, Jane Goodale, Maria Brandl, Andrée Grau and Arnold Pilling. Gary and I were able to compare observations of Tiwi society on several occasions.

From my parents, Jan and Toos Venbrux, I have received continual encouragement. Jeanette Deenen, my life companion and co-worker in the field, lent her generous personality to this work. Her love and faith in me, even when times were tough, kept me going. My deepest gratitude is to Jeanette.

Genealogies

Selected genealogies of significant relationships referred to in the text. See also Dramatis Personae, following section.

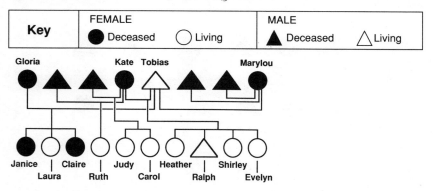

Figure 1 Tobias (Stone clan), his wives Gloria (Mosquito clan), Kate (Pandanus clan) and Marylou (Mosquito clan) and children.

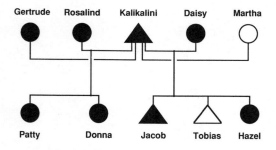

Figure 2 Kalikalini (Mosquito clan), his wives and children.

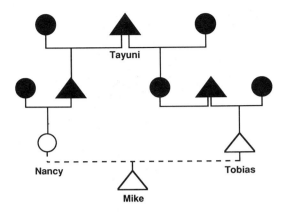

Figure 3   The relationship between Tobias (Stone clan) and Nancy (Mosquito clan).

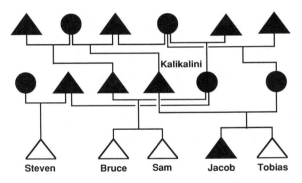

Figure 4   The genealogical relationship between the brothers Jacob and Tobias (Stone clan) and their classificatory brothers Bruce and Sam (Stone clan) and Steven (March Fly clan).

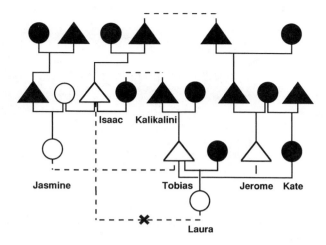

Figure 5 Tobias' marriage to Kate (Pandanus clan), Jerome's half-sister, his relationship with Jasmine (Pandanus clan), Isaac's stepdaughter; and the relationship Isaac (Stone clan) wanted with Laura (Mosquito clan), Tobias' daughter, which was refused by her.

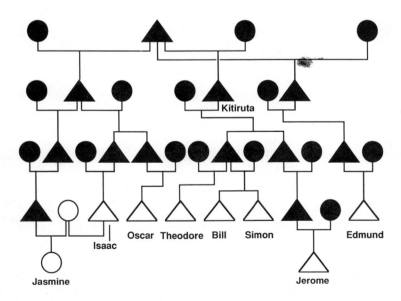

Figure 6 Some members of the Pamantari patrilineage: Jasmine (Pandanus clan), Isaac (Stone clan), Oscar, Theodore, Bill and Simon (Fire clan), Jerome (Pandanus clan) and Edmund (Honeyeater clan).

Dramatis Personæ

See also Genealogies, preceding section. (All names are pseudonyms, except for those of Jeanette and Eric.)

AGATHA TAMPAJANI, wife of Steven; mother of Max and Harold; clan sister of Jerome and Jasmine.
ALAN PAMANTARI, a health worker; son of Bill.
ALEC ADRANANGO, half-brother of Nancy; senior clan brother of Jasmine.
ANNA WANGITI, a widow; sister of Melanie; Mike's lover.
ANDREW MUNULUKA, husband of Jasmine; clan brother of Sally.
ARAMUKUWANI (†), son of Tayuni.
ARTHUR WANGITI, elder classificatory brother of Kevin.

BARRY PAMANTARI, son of Edmund.
BASIL MUNULUKA, Miputingkimi's son's son; classificatory father of Tobias.
BETTY KERIMERINI, daughter of Bruce.
BILL PAMANTARI, brother of Simon, Mabel, Theodore and Mary; father of Alan; classificatory brother of Isaac; died in 1990.
BRENDA PAMANTARI, sister of Reuben; daughter of Jerome.
BRUCE KERIMERINI, elder brother of Sam; father of Jim and Betty; classificatory brother of Tobias; died in 1992.

CAROL ARAPI, daughter of Kate; stepdaughter of Tobias.
CECIL JATUKWANI, former husband of Tobias' half-sister Patty.
CHARLES FISHER, J., judge in the Northern Territory Supreme Court.
CHRISTEL PAMANTARI, daughter of Jerome.
CLAIRE ARAPI (†), youngest daughter of Gloria and Tobias; died in 1952.
CLAUDIA CALLEY, daughter of Maud and Lester; granddaughter of Nancy and Sam.
CURT JAMESON, Kevin's solicitor from the Aboriginal Legal Aid Service during the murder trial.

DICK PAMANTARI, husband of Sally; elder brother of Jasmine and Rodney; stepson of Isaac; 'prisoner's friend' to Kevin.
DIMITRI PAPURULUWI, senior clan brother of Jasmine.
DON WANGITI, classificatory brother of Kevin.
DONNA ARAPI (†), sister of Tobias.
DOROTHY KILIMIRIKA, sister and former co-wife of Marylou.

EDGAR TAPALINGA, senior man from Nguiu.
EDMUND PAMANTARI, classificatory brother of Bill, Mary, Theodore, Mabel, Simon, Isaac and Oscar; died in 1991.
ELLA IMALU, wife of Simon; mother of Mildred and Rolf; half-sister of Roger; died in 1989.
EMMY JONES, Oscar's lover.
ERIC VENBRUX, the author, 'son' of Nancy.
EVELYN ARAPI, youngest daughter of Kate and Tobias.

FANNY GROVES (†), wife of Jacob.
FELICIA MUNULUKA, a widow who went to live with Kevin after he had been released on bail.

GEOFFREY ADRANANGO, classificatory brother of Nancy; friend and next door neighbour of Tobias.
GLADYS PAMANTARI, a health worker.
GLORIA PALURATI (†), first wife of Tobias; mother of Laura; died in 1959.

HAROLD TAMPAJANI, son of Agatha and Steven; classificatory son of Tobias.
HAZEL ARAPI (†), sister of Tobias.
HEATHER ARAPI, daughter of Kate and Tobias; sister of Ralph, Shirley and Evelyn; half-sister of Laura, Ruth, Judy, and Carol.
HELMUT BROWN, detective in charge of the homicide investigation.

ISAAC PAMANTARI, stepfather of Dick, Jasmine and Rodney; classificatory mother's brother of Tobias; died in 1992.

JACOB ARAPI (†), son of Kalikalini; brother of Tobias; speared by Tobias; died in 1976.
JACK MUNULUKA, brother of Mavis; classificatory father of Tobias.
JANICE ARAPI (†), first-born daughter of Gloria and Tobias, found dead in the Apsley Strait in 1952.
JASMINE MUNULUKA, wife of Andrew; sister of Dick and Rodney; clan sister of Jerome; stepdaughter of Isaac; Tobias's lover.
JEANETTE DEENEN, wife of Eric, 'daughter' of Jerome.
JEROME PAMANTARI, half-brother of Kate, classificatory brother of Jasmine and Nancy; father of Reuben; 'father' of Jeanette; classificatory son of Simon and Isaac; brother-in-law of Tobias.
JESSICA NEMANGERAU, a widow; sister of Nancy; former lover of Tobias.

JIM KERIMERINI, son of Bruce; brother of Betty; classificatory son of Tobias.

JUDY ARAPI, daughter of Kate; sister of Carol; stepdaughter of Tobias.

KALIKALINI (†), father of Jacob and Tobias; former husband of Martha.

KATE MARUWAKA (†), half-sister of Jerome; mother of Ruth, Judy, Carol, Heather, Ralph, Shirley and Evelyn; second wife of Tobias; died of a snake bite in 1976.

KAREN ADRANANGO, interpreter, daughter of Mary.

KARL HANSEN, a Norwegian sailor, living with Laura in 1988.

KEVIN WANGITI, the accused; clan brother of Mavis; classificatory father of Sally.

KITIRUTA (†), a 'magic man'; father's father of Bill, Theodore, Mary, Simon and Mabel; father's father's father of Jerome.

LAURA ARAPI, daughter of Gloria and Tobias.

LESTER CALLEY, husband of Maud.

LIONEL JATUKWANI, a ritual worker from Nguiu.

MABEL PAMANTARI, sister of Mary, Bill, Theodore, and Simon.

MARTHA ARAPI, only surviving wife of Kalikalini; died in 1989.

MARY ADRANANGO, sister of Bill, Theodore, Simon and Mabel; mother of Paul and Karen; and clan sister of Oscar; died in 1989.

MARYLOU KILIMIRIKA (†), third wife of Tobias; sister of Dorothy; died in a car accident in 1988.

MAUD CALLEY, a health worker; daughter of Nancy and Sam.

MAVIS PAMANTARI, sister of Jack; clan sister of Kevin; classificatory mother of Tobias.

MAX TAMPAJANI, son of Agatha and Steven; brother of Harold.

MELANIE WANGITI, a widow, sister of Anna; mother of Phillip; Roger's lover.

MIKE KERIMERINI, son of Sam and Nancy.

MILDRED PAMANTARI, daughter of Ella and Simon.

MIPUTINGKIMI (†), classificatory brother of Kalikalini; father's father of Jack, Mavis, Basil and Ryan.

NANCY KERIMERINI, wife of Sam; mother of Maud, Walter and Mike; 'mother' of Eric; sister of Jessica; half-sister of Alec; former lover of Tobias.

OSCAR PAMANTARI, classificatory brother of Isaac; classificatory father of Jasmine; clan brother of Mary; former lover of Ruth.

OWEN BERMAN, detective investigating the homicide.

PAMELA WURUKWATI, classificatory mother of Kevin; clan sister of Nancy and Marylou.

PAUL ADRANANGO, son's son of Miputingkimi; son of Mary.

PATRICK NORMAN, QC, barrister who undertook Kevin's defence during the murder trial.

PATTY JATUKWANI (†), half-sister of Tobias.

PETER SMITH, Crown prosecutor in the Northern Territory Supreme Court.

PHILLIP WANGITI, an interpreter; son of Melanie; died in 1989.

RALPH ARAPI, son of Kate and Tobias.

REUBEN PAMANTARI, son of Jerome; living with Laura from 1991 onwards.

RICHARD SIMPSON, prosecutor in the Court of Summary Jurisdiction.

RODNEY PAMANTARI, younger brother of Dick and Jasmine.

ROGER IMALU, husband of Vanessa; lover of Melanie; classificatory father of Tobias.

ROLF PAMANTARI, eldest son of Ella and Simon.

ROY MORNINGTON, adoptive brother of Dick, Jasmine and Rodney.

RYAN MUNULUKA, classificatory father of Tobias.

RUTH WAKITAPA, daughter of Kate; stepdaughter of Tobias; wife of Theodore.

SALLY PAMANTARI, wife of Dick; clan sister of Andrew; classificatory daughter of Kevin.

SAM KERIMERINI, younger brother of Bruce; husband of Nancy; father of Maud and Walter; elder classificatory brother of Tobias.

SHIRLEY ARAPI, daughter of Kate and Tobias.

SIMON PAMANTARI, husband of Ella; brother of Bill, Theodore, Mary and Mabel; father of Rolf and Mildred; lover of Ruth.

STANLEY FORD, the local senior police constable.

STEVEN TAMPAJANI, husband of Agatha; father of Max and Harold; and classificatory brother of Bruce, Sam and Tobias; died in 1989.

TAJAMINI (†), father of Bruce and Sam.

TAKAMPUNGA (†), father's father of Paul; father's brother of Alec, Jessica and Nancy.

TAMPAJANI (†), father of Steven.

TAYUNI (†), father's father of Nancy, Jessica and Alec.

THEODORE PAMANTARI, Simon's elder brother; and Ruth's husband.

TOBIAS ARAPI, the homicide victim, 'Under the Mango Tree'.

TREVOR KIRINGARRA, most senior man of Tobias' country.

VANESSA IMALU, wife of Roger.

WALTER KERIMERINI, son of Nancy and Sam; classificatory son of Tobias.

YINGKERLATI (†), victim of Tayuni's sons.

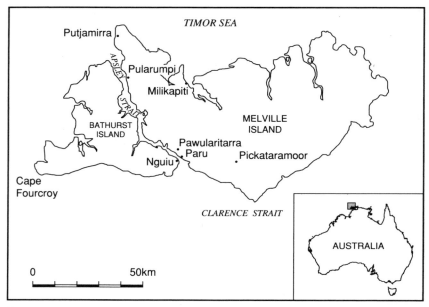

Map 1   Melville and Bathurst Islands

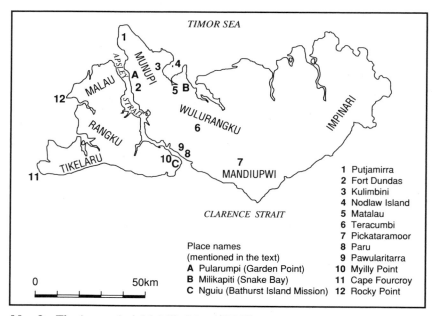

Map 2   The 'countries', Melville Island (1988)

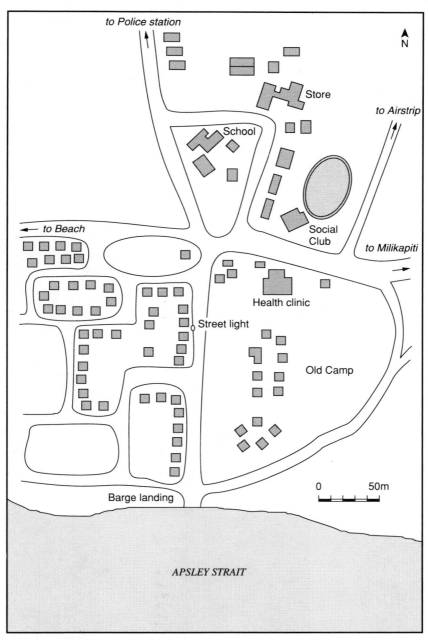

Map 3 Pularumpi, Melville Island

To the memory of
ngia ringani

CHAPTER 1

Under the Mango Tree

In the year Australia was celebrating its bicentennial of European invasion, the Tiwi Land Council, representing the Aboriginal people from Melville and Bathurst islands, gave me permission to conduct anthropological research in the islands. The research proposal focused on a study of Tiwi mortuary ritual and mortuary practices. The delegates to the land council who lived in Pularumpi on Melville Island had decided they wanted me and my wife, Jeanette Deenen, to stay in their community.

At the end of the 1980s, three predominantly Aboriginal townships, which had developed out of previous mission and government settlements, existed on the islands: Nguiu, with a population of over 1200, on Bathurst Island, and Milikapiti and Pularumpi on Melville Island (see map 1). In September 1988, about 300 people lived in Pularumpi, whereas Milikapiti had a somewhat larger population of about 400.[1] Near Pularumpi were the remains of Fort Dundas, the first British colonial settlement in northern Australia (1824–29), abandoned within five years (see Campbell 1834). It was not until 1937 that the Australian government founded a rations depot at the site of the present township, to be taken over by the Roman Catholic Mission of Bathurst Island (founded in 1911) three years later as a place where they would raise children of mixed descent. In 1968, the mission sold out to the government: Pularumpi, known as Garden Point at that time, became a predominantly Tiwi community (Pye 1985). Two decades passed before Jeanette and I would become acquainted with Tobias, the later homicide victim, who had spent most of his time during these years in Pularumpi.

The light aircraft that came in twice a day circled above Fort Dundas and then descended over huge mango and cashew trees, planted by the mission nearly fifty years earlier, before it landed on Pularumpi's unsealed airstrip. In the pre-wet, that is before the rains, the atmosphere

1

was hot and humid. Three tourists, bathed in sweat, left the cramped plane. They were taken to Putjamirra Safari Camp, about 20 km north of Pularumpi, in a Landrover. The African-style tourist resort was in its second year of operation. A Tiwi woman was greeted by her relatives who had come to the airstrip. Jeanette and I were expected too. For the first few days we stayed in the vacant presbytery, then we moved to a dilapidated little house in the heart of the community. Tiwi people helped us to fix up our Pularumpi home.

On the day of our arrival there was a dancing ceremony under the mango trees in an area locally known as the Old Camp (see map 3). Here I met two delegates to the Tiwi Land Council, Roger Imalu and Jerome Pamantari, and a senior woman called Nancy Kerimerini. These people told me I had come to study their 'culture'. The senior people in Pularumpi (who perceived their community as a stronghold of Tiwi culture) had decided, so I was told, to teach me. In the Social Club, a beer canteen, Jerome announced that my wife Jeanette was from then on his 'daughter', whereupon, following a discussion with Roger, Nancy made it known I would be her 'son'. She embraced us and kissed us. White people who were expected to stay in the community for a longish period were soon given a position in the kinship system, whether they knew it or not. Jerome told me the next day I had to 'support' him because he was my 'father-in-law'.

The initial days of fieldwork were overwhelming, I must admit. The morning after our arrival, Nancy took Jeanette and me with her into the mangrove swamps and wanted us to share in a feast of delicious mud crabs, mussels and whelks. In the afternoon, Jerome demonstrated his spear-making skills. He gave us a number of artifacts he had made, such as throwing sticks, a barbed spear, and miniature mortuary poles, while he said he would produce some better poles because these were only for 'bloody tourists'. Jerome presented himself to me as a knowledgeable person and almost immediately started to teach me words in the Tiwi language.[2]

Late at night, someone rattled at our door. A lean Aboriginal man with grey hair introduced himself as Tobias Arapi. He said he had heard about us, this was the reason that he had come to see us. Tobias said that he was concerned about the younger people losing their culture. According to him, even adult men did not know their language properly; they mixed things up. Tobias stressed that it was important that we 'get it straight' and what we would write down had to be correct, because after we left we would pass it on to other people. In this context he asked about the words we had already learned (from Jerome). He used these as a case in point: some of these words were wrong! 'This is what I mean', said Tobias, 'it is all mixed up in their heads.' He gave us the 'right' words and left no doubt that *he* was a better teacher. 'In my opinion', he phrased his proposal, we would have to start together with the smaller words and after much repetition proceed to the more difficult and larger ones. Tobias emphasised that he was a knowledgeable man. He had been to Canberra twice to record his comments which were a major part of the commentary in an ethnographic film about a Tiwi mortuary ritual. 'I explained the concepts and ideas', Tobias said. These were the first signs of rivalry between Tobias and his brother-in-law Jerome. At our first meeting, Tobias revealed much about himself and his life, speaking about his children and his deceased wives. His third and last wife, Marylou Kilimirika, had been killed in a car accident a few months earlier. Tears came to his eyes. 'The memories of a black man are different', said Tobias, 'I see her before my eyes all the time.' Tobias told us that he would leave Pularumpi that week to stay with his daughter, Heather, in the other township on Melville Island. Perhaps, he continued, he would return at the end of the wet season for the annual yam ritual.

Despite Tobias' intention to leave Pularumpi, we were to see each other often from then on until his death. We had long talks at our place and on the verandah of his hut or under the mango tree in front of it. Sometimes Tobias cried. Several times he showed us photographs of Marylou, saying that he did not need these to picture her. Tobias was the first to give me a sense of what death meant for a Tiwi person.

Tobias lived in the Old Camp, which was the focus of ceremonial activities (see map 3). The huge mango trees provided shade for the people beneath them. During the hottest times of the year it was considered one of the most pleasant places to be in the township, as there was always a gentle breeze. Lorikeets gathered in the trees, eating the ripening mangoes. By moonlight, Tiwi boys sometimes tried to shoot flying foxes in the mango and cashew trees with their catapults. Visitors to the Old Camp had to chase away the many camp dogs that roamed about there.

Tobias occupied one of the little houses or huts in the Old Camp. In the 1960s, these huts were built for the people of mixed descent who had been raised at the local mission. Tobias' fibro hut consisted of a single square room (approximately 2 by 2 metres) with a verandah in front, on a concrete slab; the hut had a tin roof, a door, and three small windows with glass louvres. Like his neighbours, Tobias did his cooking on a campfire outside. Water could be obtained from one of the few taps in the area. The Tiwi people in the Old Camp shared one toilet building.

In the hut opposite Tobias' lived his 'mother's brother' Isaac Pamantari.[3] Isaac was widely regarded as the most knowledgeable person in the township in matters of traditional lore. Next to Tobias, on the verandah of a somewhat larger house Geoffrey Adranango, a frail old man who had been a petty officer in the Australian navy in his youth, was staying. Geoffrey first camped under a tree, but he had moved to the verandah because of the rains. Tobias regarded this man as his friend. Geoffrey was very ill and Tobias often brought him bush food. Kevin Wangiti, a forty-year-old bachelor, lived in the hut next to Geoffrey. Behind these huts and passing behind the health clinic, a footpath led to the Social Club. People could drink beer here from 4 till 7 pm, except on Sundays. At the edge of the Old Camp, opposite the club, stood Simon Pamantari's hut.

The footpath went in the other direction to the camp of Tobias' classificatory brother, Sam Kerimerini, back in the Old Camp, which consisted of a semicircular grouping of five huts. The membership of this camp fluctuated, as visiting relatives from the other townships often stayed here. The more-or-less-steady occupants of the huts were Sam and his wife Nancy, their two adult sons Walter and Mike, and Tobias' daughter, Laura, and her white friend Karl Hansen. The white man, a Norwegian sailor, did not talk much. He cared for his pet lorikeets and experimented with tropical gardening, and in order to protect his plants from children and dogs he had put wire netting around them.

The only metalled road, which led from the barge landing to the community buildings (school, store, and council office), separated the Old Camp from the rest of the township. Late at night, people used to play cards under the street light on the other side of the road. Pre- and post-funeral rituals and the seasonal yam ritual were held at ceremonial grounds in the Old Camp. Local community meetings and outdoor Catholic masses took place in this location as well. The people in the Old Camp had many visitors during the day who preferred their company under the trees, chatting and playing cards. The elderly people in the Old Camp – Isaac, Simon, Nancy, Sam, and Geoffrey – received pensioner cheques every fortnight (A$219). Karl had a relatively well-paid job as a carpenter with the local housing association. Kevin also was paid by the local community council; he helped maintain the public gardens. The local Aboriginal police tracker had learned his tracking skills from Tobias, who had been in this job previously. Tobias and his daughter Laura participated in the Community Development Employment Projects scheme (CDEP, cf. Morony 1991) which had replaced government unemployment benefits in the townships on Melville Island. They did various cleaning jobs and, in accordance with CDEP regulations, worked a maximum of four hours a day for five days a week (earning A$5 per hour). Tobias obtained some additional income demonstrating his hunting skills as a tourist guide for Putjamirra Safari Camp. The Safari Camp would be temporarily closed during the wet season. When this was about to happen, Tobias was found dead under the mango tree in front of his hut in the Old Camp.

Early on the morning of 29 October 1988, Kevin, following his daily routine, left his hut to get a cup of tea and breakfast at Sam's camp from his 'mother' Nancy. Then, so he told me, his attention was caught by barking dogs which were around the body of one of his neighbours lying under the mango tree. Kevin signalled to another neighbour who was having tea at his campfire, which had been shifted and newly made. The man, Isaac Pamantari, indicated he did not know what Kevin was making a fuss about: 'What for? I don't know', he said to Kevin, and proceeded to ignore him. Kevin went nearer. He made signs to another man who was approaching, driving a loader behind Tobias' hut, indicating that there was something wrong. The man on the loader, Lester Calley, then drove to his house to tell his wife Maud about it, because Tobias was her 'father'. Kevin saw that Tobias' body was covered with blood. He decided to warn the health worker, Alan Pamantari, who was on call at that time. Kevin told Alan that there was something wrong with Tobias. Together they came back with the ambulance to have a look.

Alan, according to the account he gave me, soon found out that Tobias must have been dead for some time. He had bled from the mouth and there were flies crawling out of his mouth to which his body had not reacted. The time was about 6 am. Alan made a telephone call to the local police constable, as health workers had to report unnatural or sudden deaths.

In the meantime, Maud Calley, who had been informed by her husband and by Alan as well, had set out to enlighten Tobias' close relatives. She had sent her daughter Claudia to her parents, Sam and Nancy Kerimerini, in the Old Camp with the message. The girl caught her grandfather, Tobias' elder 'brother', asleep. She woke him up and told him, according to Nancy, that his 'brother' was dead. 'You stupid', she would have said to Sam, for he was considered 'deaf', that is, he could not understand in both senses of the word, and he was supposed to protect his 'brother'. Nancy informed Tobias' daughter, Laura Arapi, who lived with Karl in the hut next to her. Maud herself made her rounds through the township to tell the people concerned about Tobias' death. She also came to our house early that morning.

About 6.40 Maud knocked on the wall. She told us she had bad news. 'The old man is finished', she said. 'He died last night . . .' In response to our reaction of disbelief and grief she added that he had had a stroke. Jeanette and I hurried to the Old Camp.

Tobias' body was lying under the mango tree in front of his hut. More precisely, the corpse, facing Sam's camp, was located beside a tap about three steps from the verandah of Isaac's hut, from where it was around twelve steps to Tobias' verandah.[4] He lay naked except for a pair of shorts. Some fifteen Tiwi people stood at a little distance. The police

constable had come to the scene and decided to cordon off the area surrounding the body with a white and red tape.

Nancy walked over to us to tell what was going on: 'That old man died
yesterday night! Too much beer. He drunk too much, too much sugar
in his tea', she said, maintaining an explanation suggested by the
Aboriginal health workers. 'Doctor told him not to use sugar, his blood
pressure was too high.' A few days earlier Tobias and a number of other
Tiwi people had given blood to a medical team investigating diabetes.
Tobias, however, had neither diabetes nor high blood pressure. But at
this point a medical explanation of the cause of his death could not be
excluded as a possibility.

We went nearer and joined the close relatives of the deceased. When
the policeman covered the corpse with a sheet, the people present
started wailing loudly. They cried, bent over, and wiped their eyes with
their fingers. At this stage, many people from the township came to the
Old Camp. Some came to have a closer look, others remained at a
distance.

Jerome Pamantari, facing the body of his brother-in-law, said to us,
'Maybe someone killed him or he killed himself'. He made a sign with
his thumb on his side.[5] 'They had a fight last night', he told us. Although
Jerome's words were rather indecisive, I felt it inappropriate to elicit
further comment.

Several men walked up to Tobias' hut. They looked around his verandah and turned round. There were large patches of blood on the concrete floor of the verandah. The dead man's pipe lay carelessly to one
side. Obviously his shirt had been dropped at the entrance to the verandah. The recently re-elected community president was looking in the
grass around Tobias' hut. He later told me he had been trying to find a
knife. The town clerk also came to have a look. 'This is suspicious; there
is something wrong here', he remarked. Both men of mixed descent,
raised at the mission, represented the community government council.
The local Tiwi assigned some responsibility for maintaining law and
order in the township to the council. As the matter was already in the
hands of the police, they could contribute little here. Jasmine
Munuluka, who had been Tobias' lover, visited the Old Camp too. She
showed little emotion and remained at a distance. We left the Old Camp
accompanied by Jasmine's cousin, Ireen Pamantari, and her infant
daughter. 'Some people hated him', Ireen said.

About 7.45 am we had breakfast with Jerome at our place. Afterwards,
Jerome explained, he had to perform certain tasks as a ritual worker
(*ambaru*). He belonged to this category of people because his half-sister
Kate had been married to Tobias. Among other things he would have to
collect the dead man's clothes and personal belongings. These had

become taboo (*pukamani*) after Tobias' death and therefore had to be destroyed, buried, or thrown into the sea. The tasks of the ritual workers could not be carried out by the dead man's relatives in other categories of bereaved kin, who were restricted by mourning taboos.

Back in the Old Camp we passed Kevin's hut. He sat on his verandah reading a newspaper, the *Northern Territory News*. Roy Mornington, his friend, was leaning against the verandah. Kevin would assist Roy in skinning and roasting buffalo meat for the white headmaster's wedding that was to take place in the afternoon. When asked, they said that Kevin had found the dead man early in the morning. In front of the next house, the one next to Tobias' place (empty because its occupant was in Darwin Hospital), the police constable and the Aboriginal police tracker discussed the situation. The constable said that a post-mortem had to be done when a body was found under suspicious circumstances. He preferred a forensic pathologist to do it on the spot in order to minimise intrusion in Tiwi affairs and mourning. If this could not be done in this case, the corpse would have to be sent to Darwin. First the policeman wanted to talk with the close relatives of the deceased and have them to agree to a post-mortem.

Near the corpse, a senior man named Bill Pamantari approached us. 'He killed his elder brother with a spear', Bill said, pointing at the middle of his chest. 'Someone killed him', he said, 'He killed his brother, he killed his big brother with a spear . . . over there [Sam's camp].' Bill's gesture of pointing to his chest indicated in terms of Tiwi body symbolism his relationship to the deceased's late brother, his 'mother's brother'.

In the meantime Nancy performed a mourning song. She walked back and forth along the footpath between Tobias' and Sam's place making strokes, as if beating, with raising one arm in the air. Her conventional body posture and movements denoted a feature of her role, characterised by aggressiveness and sexual jealousy, as a ritual worker. Jerome instantly translated Nancy's mourning song: 'His father was a killer, now he is killed himself!'

In Sam's camp Tobias' 'daughter' Betty Kerimerini wanted to play cards. She was told off because she was restricted by mourning taboos and not allowed to play cards until a special cleansing rite with water had been performed. Some people were crying. Laura appeared to be in a state of shock. She sat silently and glared. Nancy continued her singing. According to her daughter Maud she sang about what had happened: 'Yesterday they had heard something and now they had found him.' Nancy's sister Jessica, who used to live in Milikapiti, happened to be staying in the Old Camp too. Tobias and Jessica had had an affair when both were young. When they were both widowed, Tobias composed a song saying he wanted her as his wife but she had refused. Like her sister, Jessica walked back and forth performing a song: 'You are singing long way now. You cannot come to sing with me.' Jessica stressed the physical distance Tobias' death had created between them. The singing (of love songs) in her text is an allusion to sexuality.

Nancy said that she herself sang about Tobias' father. 'He was a bad man. He killed a lot of people', she said. 'Someone killed him [Tobias].' She explained to other people that she and her husband were listening to their new music cassettes the previous night. Because the music was so loud they had heard nothing else. She said she would bring the two tapes (with Christian songs in Tiwi) back, one from her and one from Sam. Then to us: 'They had a fight over there, maybe they know. Someone must have walked around with a big crowbar, maybe Isaac, that he has done it, I don't know.' Moving with her head towards Isaac at a distance, 'Look that policeman is talking with him.' We saw the constable approaching Isaac and having some very brief communication with him. Isaac signalled with his head that he could not understand what the man was saying.

We all walked back from Sam's camp to Tobias' hut. At the back we sat down on a tarpaulin, waiting for the dead man's other children to come. The women were wailing. Betty dropped down and beat the ground with her fists. Her brother Jim wailed extremely loudly. Simon Pamantari arrived at the scene. He sat down, together with two grandchildren, on a bed beside the hut. In the corner of the verandah at the other side of the house lay a long iron bar. Nancy pointed out this piece of metal to me as the weapon with which Tobias would have been killed.

Just after nine o'clock a truck drove very fast up the main road towards the village. The small truck, laden with people, turned off in the direction of the Old Camp. About 150 metres from Tobias' hut, a girl dropped off the rear of the truck, landing on her front, wailing loudly. Another woman, Tobias' stepdaughter Ruth Wakitapa, threw herself from the fast-moving truck. She remained lying on her back, crying with loud screams. Heather, another daughter, jumped out of the cabin. She landed on a piece of corrugated iron. Her white husband brought the truck to a stand-still. Trembling, he took hold of her wrists to stop her from doing herself harm. Another young girl was wildly flailing around, hitting herself mainly. Nancy told her husband to hold on to her as one of his 'children bereaved of a parent'. Sam did not react. Nancy went to the girl and took her by the wrists. The wailing of Tobias' children continued for a while and the other women who were in the truck started wailing loudly as well when they saw the huddled body covered with a sheet.

Jerome walked backward and forward along the inside of the cordon. He held one hand in the air and performed another song. It was a mourning song that he would repeat several times. The constable wrote a short note. The police tracker went away with a blank piece of paper. He wore only track suit pants, a pair of plastic gloves in his belt.

Jerome entered Tobias' hut, the door of which had been closed until now. He came out with a Polaroid photo of Tobias which he showed to the dead man's daughters. They became upset immediately and started wailing and hitting themselves again. Heather's husband took the photo and put it away. Jerome and Nancy's half-brother Alec Adranango, another ritual worker, re-entered the hut to collect Tobias' personal belongings. Under the bed cowered the dead man's dog. A month before, Tobias had told me that he had raised this dog to protect him. Its long teeth would easily bite out part of a man's leg, he said. The dog, however, now seemed to be shivering in fear. On a little table near the bed was some paper and small coins which Tobias used to give to people who came to borrow money. Jerome found the photographs of Tobias' last wedding and his marriage certificate under the mattress. He dropped the certificate and went outside to give the photographs to Tobias' children. This time they did not look at the photographs but put them away immediately.

The tracker returned with the police car and gave the piece of paper, some kind of form, to the constable. Having formally identified the deceased and carried out his duties, the police tracker did not participate in the mourning sessions. Jeremy, the constable, had told him that he did not have to work if he did not want to. A lot of people from the township were seated at some distance from the dead man's hut; Roger Imalu and Edmund Pamantari sat under a cashew tree. The previous night the bar had been closed at eight o'clock, according to Roger. It had been quiet in the Social Club, Tobias must have been one of the last to leave, said Edmund. Jeanette, my wife, talked with Jasmine. She said that someone killed him, and went on to play cards with some other women.

From here we went to Sam's place. A special police plane flew over the Old Camp. The tracker put on a shirt to go to the airstrip to fetch the pathologist and the coroner from the plane.

The people at Sam's camp moved back to Tobias' hut, where a new episode was about to be added to the happenings. About 10.15 am the police car arrived at the scene. The tracker, wearing his police hat, got out of the car. The other passengers were two men in shorts, the coroner and the pathologist, accompanied by a police sergeant in uniform. Their luggage consisted of three suitcases carrying a number of instruments. They were briefed by the local constable, while the tracker remained at a distance, just outside the ribboned demarcation area and close to the large group of mourners. The coroner took a few pictures of the place where the body was; he also took a shot of Tobias' hut. The men took a large plastic body bag out of one of the suitcases and unfolded it. They had to put the corpse in it, and went towards the body. One of them pulled the sheet away.

Immediately loud wailing started. Heather screamed and hit herself. Judy, another of Tobias' daughters, threw herself with some force against the metal wall of the house next door. She tried to beat herself unconscious, slamming her head against the wall. Nancy grabbed the youngest daughter, Evelyn, and prevented her from doing herself more harm. Sam, her 'father', stood close by. Karl, on the scene for the first time, picked his girlfriend Laura up from the ground. He had taken a shower and combed his hair.

The coroner took a few additional photographs of the position of the body, and the forensic pathologist examined the body more closely. Then the people from Milikapiti were allowed to view the corpse. The women fell to the ground, prostrate next to their father's body. Wailing loudly, they hit themselves and the earth with their fists. Simon made a sign to me, placing his hand on the back of his head. 'He has a big cut there', he said. Simon, like Nancy, was of opinion that Tobias had been hit with the metal bar.

The policemen turned the body around so that Tobias was lying on his back now; his hands were tensed, his fingers outstretched. His arms lay stiff on his breast. While the policemen were handling the body, the onlookers wailed. The men put the body in the plastic bag and closed it with a zip. Then they left for the police station. They were waiting for Tobias' son Ralph and stepdaughter Carol, who had to come from Nguiu on Bathurst Island. The police wanted to give them the opportunity to view the corpse.

The demarcation ribbon had been taken away. Jerome walked back and forth near the body, first his left hand up in the air, then his right. He performed his song again: (Dead man saying to him) 'My brother-in-law, you did not sing properly for me./I am the one who married your sister!/And I made a big family with your sister.' Nancy took her turn and repeated her song too. She walked backward and forward, also with one hand lifted up. Then Jerome took the long iron bar (thought by Nancy and Simon to be the weapon) and stuck it in the earth in front of the body.

Heather yelled at the people from Pularumpi: 'You fucking coward, come out, you fucking . . . Who killed my father?'[6] Her half-sister Judy called out, 'If I was a man I would come by day, not at night!' While she was yelling she looked at Isaac, who sat motionless on his verandah opposite Tobias' hut.

When they quietened down, Simon told the people from Milikapiti about killings in an ambush carried out by Tobias' father. (This is discussed in detail in chapter 3.) Simon attempted, when the people were gathered around the corpse, to let his people from Pularumpi speak about what had happened. No one responded. When I asked him what he thought had happened, Simon said, 'Yeah, someone killed him. I think they know, but people are frightened to say . . . I was playing cards over there [he pointed at a street light approximately 150 metres away] . . . We heard a lot of noise . . . but nobody went to look.'

The mourners had a break. The people from Milikapiti prepared some wallaby meat they had brought with them. They did not share the prized meat with the local people nor did they accept food from them, which indicated that they did not trust the people from Pularumpi. The food was cooked at a distance from the corpse because that location had become taboo.

Around 12.15 pm the cattle truck with football players from Nguiu approached Pularumpi. A stepdaughter and son of Tobias were among the people in the back of the truck. The son, Ralph, came walking in the direction of the hut in the Old Camp, followed by four of his 'brothers'. Ralph had a green army bag over his shoulder. Laura went towards him. When he had reached the back of Kevin's house he took the sleeve of his shirt and with two fingers pressed it on his eyes. Rubbing his fingers over his eyes, he walked with his head bent down. With the boy in the lead, other people went back to the body. The bag was unzipped. Ralph burst into tears and threw himself flat on the ground. At the other side of the body his half-sister Carol fell to the ground too. They wailed loudly, bent over their father's body, and stared at his face. The expression of emotion by these two children triggered a new wave of wailing from the others.

The policemen came back; Tobias' corpse would be flown to Darwin for an autopsy and the bag with the body was loaded on the back of the truck from Milikapiti to the sound of more loud wailing and crying. The close relatives of the deceased jumped on the back of the truck. A few other cars, also carrying a full load of people, followed and some people went to the airstrip by foot. Nearly all the local people had come to the airstrip. Tobias' children had to be restrained by other people. The policemen from Darwin tried to fit Tobias' body in the plane's left wing cargo compartment, twice letting the lid drop on the body. The people wailed. As the corpse was too big to fit into the compartment, the policemen took a seat out of the plane and put the body bag in the passenger space. When the plane took off the mourners began wailing and crying again. Amongst them was Jack Munuluka, a 'father' of Tobias from Bathurst Island, who wove the lyrics of a mourning song into his wailing. (I did not obtain the text of his song, which was in the *mamanakuni* style.) Thereafter, the people went back from the airstrip to the township. Alan gave Jeanette and me a lift in the ambulance, saying, as he dropped us off near his own place, that he *hoped* that the post-mortem would establish that Tobias' death was caused by high blood pressure, a burst blood vessel, or a stroke.

In the afternoon people's attention was diverted by the football match. It seemed as if nothing unusual had taken place that morning. The audience – men, women and children – watched the match on the local oval. No one said a word about Tobias' violent death. Jerome paid us a visit before he went to the Social Club. He named Walter and Jim Kerimerini (the eldest sons of Tobias' 'brothers', Sam and Bruce), and me as the 'sons' of the dead man who had to kill his 'murderer' in the same way. Anyone could do it, he said, but in reality it was us who had to do it.

After sunset, people at the Social Club wailed. Alan went around to pick up his children. He had been busy the whole day, he said, 'but now I think, that fellow that died, I shall miss him'. And with tears in his eyes he said, 'He was a good man'. Tobias had supported Alan in the council election three days earlier. Gladys Pamantari, another health worker, said that card players had heard loud noises, a 'big fight', in the Old Camp the night before. No one went to look, she added. The health workers hoped something else would come out of the post-mortem. Tobias' daughters had sought help in asking around about who had done it, but nobody had given them help; they wanted a meeting but none of those present had opened their mouths. Once again, Gladys emphasised that she hoped that a cause of death other than homicide would be revealed by the autopsy. She then said, 'Seems punishment, tribal punishment, three times beaten on the back . . . It's the Law, old Law. We thought maybe it fades away, culture, but it still goes on. We hoped it might [have] stopped.' The health workers would try to find out who had done it, she stated. Maud Calley had gone to the health clinic to get some medicine. She had a string of pandanus leaves around her head, the traditional remedy for a headache. Her family was bereaved, she lived close to the Old Camp, and soon the mourners would come from the beer canteen to her home, all drunk and in a violent mood.

The next day, a Sunday, we went to Milikapiti for a post-funeral ritual to be directed by Simon. On arrival people expressed their condolences to Isaac and Sam because they had lost Tobias, their 'sister's son' and 'brother' respectively. Tobias' daughters were present in order to gain wider support for themselves. At the end of the ceremony Simon, the 'boss' of this ritual, at their request, tried to organise an inquest. He himself stood on the circular ceremonial ground. None of those present, however, came forward to participate in the meeting. Tobias' daughters only uttered their grievances. Just as in Pularumpi, nobody was prepared here to talk in public, although gossip had it that Sam had killed Tobias. Because of the lack of response, and in accordance with a dream of Tobias earlier that week, Simon asked 'What shall we do?'

Finding out who had killed Tobias would soon become a matter for the white police, as the results of the post-mortem were known. On Monday afternoon two police detectives and a coroner from Darwin came to Pularumpi to investigate the homicide. As the detectives were confronted with reluctance on the part of Tiwi people to speak about what had happened, and a search of the Old Camp did not produce the desired result, they started a series of interrogations, one person after the other, at the local police station.

As the investigation went, they charged Kevin (who had found the body) with murder, after his confession to having killed Tobias. At 10 pm on Tuesday the detectives concluded their investigation when Kevin was put in custody. More than nine months later he stood trial in the Supreme Court of the Northern Territory, but was acquitted. Many Tiwi people, from the outset, were adamant that the police had charged the wrong person. A year after Kevin's arrest, the detective in charge of the homicide investigation told me that as far as the police were concerned the case was 'over and done with'.

*   *   *

How can Tobias' violent death be understood? Maddock writes that in Aboriginal societies 'the most puzzling cases for an outsider concern death by violence' (1986: 151). Although the homicide case remained unsolved in terms of the Australian criminal justice system, a number of questions might be raised in looking at the case from an ethnographic angle: Does this homicide make sense from the Tiwi point of view? How does it fit, in the context of contemporary Tiwi society? Why did it happen? Can the event be related to underlying tensions in Tiwi social organisation? What was the meaning of statements made by some Tiwi people, such as that the victim's father was a 'killer' and that he himself had speared his elder brother? Did the killing then have its antecedents in histories of disputes and homicides? Why did a senior man and woman point out an iron bar as the lethal weapon? Why did another man stick this piece of metal into the earth next to the corpse? Could, as one woman suspected, a 'tribal punishment' have taken place? And if so, why? What made the victim's daughters state that their father had been killed? Why were Tiwi people from the victim's township, who in some cases had information, reluctant or frightened to speak about what had happened? For what reason was a Western medical explanation as to the cause of Tobias' death hoped for and supported by some people, who at the very same time were trying to figure out who might have killed him? Why did the victim's children fail to gain sufficient support to bring the matter into the open? What would happen next? What were the consequences, if any, of the homicide? How would Tiwi people evaluate the killing? And how would they deal with the matter? What would be the impact of the state's criminal justice system on the course of events?

In pursuing these questions and in order to obtain a better understanding of the homicide it is necessary, in my view, to show through detailed or thick description (Geertz 1973) how the case unfolded over time. The homicide case furthermore has to be placed in its broader cultural and historical context. From Tiwi people's responses to the finding of the corpse it follows that much of the situation was uncertain, and that people were looking for explanations and ways to deal with the matter. I see no reason why this element of uncertainty and, for that matter, other 'spontaneous human tendencies' (Malinowski 1940: 119) should have to be excluded from the analysis.

The approach I have adopted is known as processual analysis. Rosaldo describes it thus:

> This view stresses the case history method; it shows how ideas, events, and institutions interact and change through time. Such studies more nearly resemble the medical diagnosis of a particular patient than lawlike generalizations about a certain disease. . . . One thus tries to understand particular cases by showing how a number of factors come together, rather than separating them out, one by one, and showing their independent effects. (1989: 92–3)

The Manchester school in British anthropology represents a rich tradition in processual ethnography, including 'the extended-case method' or 'situational analysis' as described by Van Velsen (1967), Turner's concept of 'social drama' (1957, 1974) and Moore's recent proposal to study 'diagnostic events' (1987).

My treatment of the case derives its inspiration mainly from Moore, who starts from the assumption that 'social reality is fluid and indeterminate' (1975: 237). Even continuity is a manifestation of processes demanding the actors' efforts and therefore cannot be taken for granted (Moore 1975, 1987). Moore addresses the problem of the limitations of anthropological fieldwork in time and place: 'Can such an anthropology effectively analyze ongoing local affairs and at the same time connect the local scene with large-scale historical change?' (1987: 727). At issue is 'how to understand the fieldwork time as a moment in a sequence, how to understand the place of the small-scale event in the large historical process, how to look at part-structures being built and torn down' (ibid.: 730). In order to get at these issues, she suggests treating fieldwork as 'current history', with its inherent uncertainties about the future, and to study 'diagnostic events': 'events that are in no sense staged for the sake of the anthropologist are to be preferred, together with local commentaries on them'; further, 'the kind of event that should be privileged is one that reveals ongoing contests and conflicts and competitions and the effort to prevent, suppress, or repress these' (ibid.). The events to be selected very likely provide clues with regard to 'the making of history', an open-ended process, both showing contradictory meanings and local interpretations attached to these occurrences and how the events are linked to simultaneous processes beyond the local level (ibid.: passim). I take the events concerning the homicide case as 'diagnostic events' with regard to the complexity of contemporary Tiwi life.

In a dramatic incident such as a homicide one can expect things to become manifest that usually remain latent in ordinary life (cf. Turner 1974: 35, 37). People's statements in relation to the killing of Tobias Arapi, described above, already show heterogeneity and indeterminacy. The involvement of the state's criminal justice system plainly turned the matter into an extra-local affair as well. In addition, the mortuary rituals for the victim might offer good vantage points from which to view contemporary Tiwi society: as Metcalf and Huntington put it, '[T]he issue of death throws into relief the most important cultural values by which people live their lives and evaluate their experiences. Life becomes transparent against the background of death, and fundamental social and cultural issues are revealed' (1991: 25).

A homicide or 'murder' considered an indictable offence in Australian law is not necessarily wrong according to Aboriginal views (cf. Stanner 1987: 87, 93). Therefore, I use 'violence' (cf. Riches 1986, 1991), 'homicide' and 'killing' neutrally, as terms without negative connotations. In Western societies in which the infliction of violence is a well-established monopoly of the state, according to Blok, there exists a tendency to consider acts of violence in mainly negative terms, as behaviour that distorts or at least disrupts a presupposed order, often senseless or irrational. Consequently, research into violence is predominantly focused on the instrumental aspects of violent behaviour, the classification of acts of violence, and on composing statistics indicating increase or decrease of the incidence of violence, which in addition is closely linked to a preoccupation of public opinion concerned with its prevention and suppression (1991: 189, 192). Blok makes clear that the related sensitivities concerning the use of violence inhibit an adequate understanding of the phenomenon and strongly argues for a study of 'the culture of violence', the meaning accorded to it by the people most directly involved, by putting it in context; that is, to present thick descriptions of cases (ibid.: 190, 195, passim; with regard to homicide, see also Bohannan 1967: 230–1).

I tend more to a position in line with the processual paradigm than the opposed rule-centred paradigm, as distinguished within legal anthropology by Comaroff and Roberts; the processual approach 'envisions dispute as normal and inevitable', while the rule-centred one regards it as 'pathological or dysfunctional' (1981: 5, 5–17).[7]

Homicides have been ill-researched in contemporary Aboriginal societies (cf. Brandl 1971: 341; for a notable exception, see D. Rose 1992: 153–62). In his book *Black Death White Hands*, Wilson paints a bleak picture of these societies by relating Aboriginal homicide to 'the sense of hopelessness and futility that exists among Aborigines – born out of dispossession and exploitation' (1982: 9). The case of an Aboriginal man who killed his girlfriend is threaded through his book on violence in Aboriginal communities in Queensland. 'Whites have', in his view, '(. . .) created conditions which foster murder and assault in Aboriginal communities' (ibid.). Wilson considers cases of these types of violence 'the indices of [community] disintegration' (ibid.: 16). I do not want to deny the impact of colonisation on Aboriginal societies, an impact that in many cases has been detrimental, to say the least, and that may vary from one place to another. The view that Aboriginal violence is primarily related to anomie resulting from colonisation (including missionisation) and excessive state intervention, however, is problematic in a number of respects.

First, it denies Aboriginal people a commitment to their own deeds and strips them of their dignity. Second, it ignores the possibility that Aboriginal people might perceive their acts of violence differently. In many contexts, conflicts and fighting generate meaning; despite our moral judgements, these are meaningful activities for Aboriginal people (e.g., Macdonald 1988; Langton 1988). Finally, the enforcement of state law and the 'pacification' of Aboriginal societies have also been part of the history of colonisation. The ethnographic literature shows that before colonisation Aboriginal societies had high rates of violence and homicide (cf. Warner 1931, 1958; Pilling 1958, 1978; F. Rose 1987). Might the increase in violence which has been observed not also be related to the disappearance of the so-called Aboriginal reserves as 'total institutions', to borrow Goffman's term, tightly controlled by white government or mission superintendents (cf. Rowley 1986)?

In my opinion, the present homicide case cannot be separated from its cultural and historical context. Until the foundation of a Roman Catholic mission on Bathurst Island in 1911, the Tiwi institution of killings in sneak attacks (*kwampi*) was in full operation (Pilling 1958). To a much lesser extent, violent deaths also occurred in spear-throwing duels and pitched battles. Pilling, who in 1954 recorded Tiwi homicide cases of the pre-mission period from the reminiscences of elderly people, arrived at a figure of 45 victims (mainly at the hands of sneak attackers) for the 1890–1909 period. This, with a population of roughly 1,000 people, amounts to an overall average annual homicide rate of about 225 per 100,000 persons (1978: 35). In 1988–90, there were five Tiwi cases of homicide; in a population of about 1900, this represents an annual homicide rate (87.7 per 100,000 persons) about ten times that of the United States in 1986 (a rate of 8.6, cited in Kuschel 1992: 10).

Pilling (1958: 122, 142; 1962; 1978: 82, 86) and Brandl (1971: 477–8) have advanced the thesis that as a result of the enforcement of state law on the islands, Tiwi turned to killings by indirect means, 'poisonings', including actual poisonings as well as sorcery. 'Since the establishment of the Mission, "poisoning" has replaced outright killing as the means by which a group rids itself of an offender', according to Pilling (1958: 142). Cases of 'poisoning' were rarely if ever detected by white authorities (Brandl 1971: 478). In relation to one of the cases I recorded, I was told that two alleged 'poisoners' were 'taken to court' by Tiwi themselves; they admitted the offence and were punished, receiving a beating until blood flowed. My informants considered 'poisoning' still a realistic option in retaliation for a serious wrong.

Since the 1970s, when government policy concerning Aborigines changed from 'assimilation' to 'self-determination' or 'self-management', Aboriginal societies in northern Australia have seen a cultural renaissance (cf. Borsboom 1982; 1987). After the assimilation era, with its attempts to suppress traditional practices and to destroy Tiwi institutions, a cultural revival has also taken place on Melville and Bathurst Islands. The Tiwi are in formal possession of their own lands, their rituals no longer need to be hidden for the missionaries.

The cultural revival and the decline of supervision of Tiwi people's daily lives in the townships in the last two decades seem to have gone hand in hand with a re-emergence of killings by direct means. What these cases of homicide, say from 1974 until 1991, have in common with earlier cases is that my male and female informants related these to 'woman trouble': conflicts in which relationships with female partners are at stake. Disputes that revolve around relationships with women frequently occur and stand out as the most important reason given for killings in the literature (cf. Pilling 1958; Hiatt 1965; Brandl 1971; Burbank 1980; McKnight 1981; F. Rose 1987). Such 'women-related' disputes also might be the initial grievance leading to a series of killings (Pilling 1978: 10–11; see also R. Berndt 1965: 176). Hart notes that one of 'the main emphases in Tiwi culture [was] the enormous frequency of disputes, fights, duels, and war parties arising directly or indirectly out of cases of seduction. If we may call this area of life the legal area, then over 90 percent of legal affairs were matters in which women were in some way involved' (Hart and Pilling 1960: 80).

What I have to report is that as of the end of the 1980s, Tiwi society had seen little change in this regard. These matters were such an integral part of life and such frequent happenings that I do not expect I have recorded them all; sometimes I heard of and witnessed a handful of such occurrences in a single day.[8] Sexual jealousy, love affairs, and suspicions of infidelity were given as reasons for fights between marriage partners or lovers.[9] When these kinds of fights escalated, relatives of either sex assisted each other but men fought men and women fought women. Competition for spouses or lovers and love affairs could lead to fights between women on the one hand and men on the other. Throughout the century the issues over which people were killed seem to have remained the same ones.

The 1988 homicide on Melville Island which we are concerned with here, the case of Tobias Arapi, predictably led to the involvement of the criminal justice system of the state, had an impact on how Tiwi people could deal with the matter themselves, and was the result of the imposition of another legal system, declared some two centuries ago and gradually enforced in this area over the last eighty years.

Recent Tiwi homicides display outwardly somewhat modified characteristics when compared to the institution of sneak attacks which were common before outside intrusion. In these outright killings, knives have replaced spears as the most used weapon. Intra-community killings have emerged in contrast to the sneak attacks as extra-local affairs, and in addition the former seem to be alcohol-related. In two cases I know of women killed as well (in 1974 and 1988), which seems to have been without historical precedent, but in any event it indicates that homicidal actions by females were rare. Two of the five homicide cases in the three years 1988–90 remained unsolved as far as the national criminal justice system is concerned. Leaving aside the case in which the victim was a white man (who was said to have repeatedly assaulted his Tiwi wife of mixed descent), there was one case, in November 1989, of a man stabbing to death his wife, who had threatened to leave him. A planeload of police was flown in to prevent the husband from being lynched by his wife's relatives; this man got a life sentence. In April 1990, a man found another man in his bed and killed him. The killer was convicted of manslaughter. In October 1988, Tobias was stabbed to death. And the same happened to another man in January 1990. In both cases the actual killer remains unknown to the Australian police. My informants stated that these killings had to do with trouble related to the exchange of marriage partners between matriclans. After a killing, sneak attackers used to paint their bodies with white pipeclay and they pulled out their beards so they were identifiable by their fellows elsewhere. According to my informants this practice has ceased. When it was possible (in some cases it was too obvious), the actual killers remained hidden after the contemporary homicides, a strategy also employed by the 'poisoners' in the era in between the pre- and post-colonial times of outright killings. In this way they probably protected themselves against the close associates of their victims, who were more likely to be present in the larger-scale townships, and also against the investigating police.

I propose the hypothesis that the practice of homicide on the islands is still influenced by an evolving, but distinctly indigenous, tradition.[10] With a detailed description of a single homicide case, I attempt here to explain that the Tiwi people have retained a distinctive identity and modes of behaviour (cf. Roth 1989). I do not imply that Tiwi culture is a coherent whole. It was not uncommon, I found, for various people to hold divergent views on so-called traditional matters. I witnessed arguments over, for instance, the proper pronunciation of words in the song language, the most suitable place to bury the dead, the application of taboos, the proper order of the dancers and the right way to dance in mortuary ritual. There did not really exist one commonly shared and coherent view (*the* native's point of view') to be automatically followed. Ritual praxis, for example, was something that had to be negotiated. This process reflected both social rivalries and a kaleidoscope of 'little traditions', and perhaps also uncertainty or ambiguity about what had been transmitted from the past (cf. Borofsky 1987). The Tiwi, as I understand it, creatively produced authority in their performances, in which people cooperated on the basis of mutual obligations. In other words, they were continuously shaping their culture with their own creations and reworking, alluding to, re-enacting, and selecting from the cumulative store of previous creations.

To answer the posed questions above in relation to the homicide case it is necessary to know more about the victim's life history, his social situation and relationships, the changing culture in which he was living, and significant events before and after the killing. Furthermore, what was at stake in conflict and violence has to be considered, especially in homicide, on the islands, people's shared and conflicting interests and divergent interpretations of events and other people's behaviour in relation to the case over time (cf. Ross 1993: 17), and the contextual constraints within which they had to operate.

In the next chapter, I place the research in its social and historical context. This chapter includes a discussion of the social transformation of Tiwi society in the twentieth century, the continuation of marriage politics despite a change from polygyny to monogamy, and the accommodation to the wider society. I relate the life histories of two individuals, the victim and his father in chapter 3. These biographies reflect how the lives of two (male) Tiwi persons were affected by the historical process sketched in the previous chapter. The victim was perceived as having much in common with his father, who played a prominent role, as a killer par excellence, in an ambush in the beginning of the century. I follow the representation of this history and its use against the later victim by his opponents at the end of the 1980s. This story offers a good example of how Tiwi sneak attackers operated before the imposition of the legal system of the Australian nation-state.

Chapter 4 discusses the trouble in which the victim was involved shortly before his death and continues the presentation of events directly following on the homicide, from the point at which it could no longer be denied that the victim had been killed up to the funeral. In chapter 5, the funeral and subsequent purification rituals are described.

Two seasonal yam rituals, one on Melville Island and one on Bathurst Island, dedicated to the victim are covered in chapter 6. How the Australian criminal justice system dealt with the case and Tiwi perceptions of these proceedings are the subject of chapter 7. (A discussion of who Tiwi people blamed for the homicide runs through the chapters.) Chapter 8 presents the post-funeral rituals for the homicide victim and the aftermath in the lifting of the last mourning taboos three years after the killing occurred. I draw my conclusions from the case in the final chapter.

CHAPTER 2

Tiwi Culture Amid Change

Melville and Bathurst Islands are located north of the Australian coast in the Timor Sea (map 1). Melville Island (5,700 sq. km) is separated from Bathurst Island (2,070 sq. km) to the west by the Apsley Strait. The nearest distances to the mainland are approximately 50 km from Melville Island to the south and about 50 km to the east. Directly south of the islands on the mainland is the city of Darwin, the Northern Territory's capital. The Clarence Strait separating the islands from the mainland, with the three little Vernon Islands strung between, is known for its strong currents (Mountford 1956).

The two tropical islands, eleven degrees south of the equator, are relatively flat except for a small ridge running over Melville Island from the west to the east, dunes in the northwestern point of the island and a few scattered hills in the southeast of Bathurst Island. Both islands are covered with open forest, savannah, swamp and pockets of rain forest. Saltwater creeks meander inland from the sea. There are also fresh water streams, ponds, a few falls, and swamps. Mangrove swamps interspersed with cliffs and white sandy beaches dominate the coastline. Sand banks, coral reefs, and islets are to be found off-shore.

By all accounts the Tiwi in the pre-contact era lived in a rich environment with an abundance of natural food sources (see Hart and Pilling 1960; Goodale 1971). Like other Aboriginal peoples, they were a foraging society. During the twentieth century the Tiwi gradually came to live in three major townships, designed in Western style. Before that they lived dispersed over the islands in semi-nomadic groups. Nowadays most of the food is bought in the local stores but foraged bush and sea foods still form a substantial part of the diet. People take pride in their foraging activities – although these outings might be limited due to other commitments and occasional lack of the funds necessary for motorised transport – and value highly natural foods.

Tiwi had (and have to a certain extent) an extended body of knowledge they applied in the management of their natural resources (see Stevenson 1985). The three major seasons recognised by the Tiwi almost coincide with those distinguished by white people in the monsoonal climate of northern Australia; the dry season (*kumurakini*), the build-up (*tiyara*), and the wet (*tamutakari*). Furthermore, Tiwi divide these major seasons into thirteen flexible (and at times overlapping) minor seasons (Stevenson n.d.). In exploiting environmental resources, detailed knowledge of seasonal changes and the corresponding availability and edibility of plants and animals were also important. Life in the dry season, when people could move out in small groups over the land and hunt unimpaired by the tall grass, was something quite different from life in the rainy season, when people lived in close quarters and conflicts and illness tended to increase.

In foraging activities there was and is a division of labour between the sexes but also an overlap (cf. Goodale 1971: 151–4, 1982; Harrison 1986: 160–3). Both men and women hunt and gather small marsupials, snakes, lizards, goannas, wild honey, crabs, mangrove worms, and turtle eggs. Mud mussels, oysters, cockles, and whelks are collected more often by women than by men. Men generally do not collect the various species of yams (with one significant exception, the *kulama* yams to be processed in a seasonal ritual) or cycad palm fruits. Almost exclusively, males hunt wallabies, buffaloes, pigs, turtles, dugongs, crocodiles, flying foxes, and magpie geese. Men fish off the reefs and in the creeks, although fishing is not an exclusively male affair any more. Women can fish with hand line and hook from the shore (cf. Harrison 1986: 160). Goodale asserts that in the past there was a more rigid sexual division of labour. She relates this to a gender division of space in the Tiwi language: items exclusively foraged by women were in the male domain and vice versa (1982: 202–3). In spite of this perhaps ideological division, women extracted the main part of the food from the mangrove swamps which, linguistically speaking, are feminine in gender. In terms of quantity and productivity, women were the main providers. As members of polygamous households they usually cooperated in extracting bush and sea foods. Of course, some individuals were more successful in the food quest than others. A person with good foraging skills, irrespective of sex, has prestige in Tiwi society.

When women and men alike came across smaller animals they killed them using sticks. The men, depending on their age and physical condition, had greater physical strength than most women. Little children could be left behind in camp in the care of elderly women and men.

Notwithstanding the fact that there were a large number of bachelors, they could always rely on the food brought together by female relatives, their mothers in particular (cf. Hart and Pilling 1960; Hart 1970). Men could engage in the less reliable endeavour of hunting larger game. The right to employ techniques for killing larger mobile animals was reserved for men. Unlike the women, they utilised carved throwing sticks and a variety of spears in hunting and fishing. Nowadays guns and harpoons, again used only by men, have replaced most types of spears and all throwing sticks in hunting. I was told that in the past when knives were scarce, these were kept by the men and only handed over to their wives temporarily when they needed to use a knife.

Exploitation of the environment was related to territorial affiliations, membership within the districts into which the islands are divided (see map 2). Those who belonged to a particular district, known as a 'country' or *murukupupuni*, had free access to its resources; others had to gain their permission (in the past there have been a few cases in which influential men tabooed an area for others). Membership in such a country could be obtained in numerous ways, in particular by birth or residence in the area, father's membership, or when an ancestral grave was situated there (cf. Hart 1970). Within a country a smaller group of people could have more specific rights in a sub-district (also regarded as a 'country'). The size and number of countries, as well as their boundaries, changed over time (cf. Pilling 1958) as a result of demographic and political processes (cf. Sutton and Rigsby 1982). Before Tiwi went to live in the townships there were large encampments headed by influential senior men with large polygynous households. When an area became too densely populated, such senior men could send their younger brothers away to an uninhabited or thinly populated area to found a new country. People also shifted to other countries to obtain or join marriage partners. Another reason given for people moving or being sent elsewhere was that this was a way of offering each other protection and it would prevent them being wiped out. Men could acquire membership in the country where they resided, while women still belonged to their father's country even when their residence was elsewhere.

Spiritual links with the land are important. Spiritual conception takes place when a father (sometimes his sister, father or father's sister) dreams of spirit children (*putaputuwi*) in his country. Patrilineal identifications, such as dances (choreographed by men in one's patrilineage), and the *irumwa* or 'dreamings' (emblems of the patrilineage inherited from one's father and mostly, not always, including the father's and father's sister matrilineal clan association, *imunga*), mark species and environmental features characteristic of a country. People face their countries in ritual, and ritual calls of burial place names and their mention in songs are further examples of people's expression of belonging to the land and to their countries. In Tiwi eschatology the spirits of the dead (*mopadruwi*) are supposed to go to where the spirits of their actual and classificatory fathers and father's fathers 'live'; that is, their burial places. Because of these burial places populated by patrilineal spirits, the descendants have rights in these areas. When the living come to these territories they identify themselves by calling out to the spirits of the dead and stressing the particular kin relationship. The spirits can be asked to assist in hunting and for many other favours. When an influential man who has many offspring dies, his patrilineal grandchildren can form a social grouping, a 'one-grandfather-group' (*aminiyarti*). Such a group has a special solidarity and is considered a 'company' or 'fight company' as its members join in fights. They hold rights in the area of burial of their common father's father, and in the past such a group could occupy a 'country' or a sub-district. Patrilineal descent is thus important in relation to spiritual conception, mortuary ritual and territorial rights.

In the past, as both Hart (1930) and Pilling (1958) have noted, the islanders did not identify themselves as Tiwi but rather as members of the various countries (and among themselves they have continued this practice until today). In 1930, Hart coined the term Tiwi ('human beings') as a 'tribal name' because it had come into use in contexts where they distinguished themselves from other Aborigines (1930: 170–1). Sustained contact with outsiders led to the creation of a new and communal identity of the islands' people. Hart's adoption of the term Tiwi (or as some would say, his 'invention' of the Tiwi) probably contributed to its general acceptance by non-Tiwi and Tiwi people alike.

When the passage of the *Aboriginal Land Rights (Northern Territory) Act 1976* granted the Tiwi the islands as their land, they decided that they did not want to be represented by the Northern Land Council, which operated from the mainland; they formed a separate land council to represent the islands, the Tiwi Land Council. As Goodale points out, it became necessary to determine where people had territorial rights in a country and how many of these countries had to be represented. After internal negotiations, twelve countries to which Tiwi people were assigned 'traditional ownership' were listed. In 1981 the number of countries was renegotiated, and two years later this resulted in a list of seven countries, as some countries merged. Each of these countries had its own delegates to the land council (Hart, Pilling and Goodale 1988: 130–4). The 'final' list of countries (ibid.: 132) still existed in 1988–90. The seven countries were Munupi, Malau, Rangku, Tikelaru, Wulurangku, Impinari, and Mandiupwi (see map 2). The countries seemed to have become fixed. In 1991, however, negotiations began for a rearrangement and division of some countries. When I left the islands in November 1991 no decisions had yet been made, but the following year the area known as Mirrakawuyanga was acknowledged as a new country. This area is located west of Shark Bay in the north of Melville Island, between Munupi and Wulurangku.

The flexibility required by local political processes is also apparent in Hart's analysis of 'the struggle for prestige and influence', particularly in marriage politics, among the Tiwi (Hart and Pilling 1960: 51–77). Although his analysis bears on the situation of Tiwi people still living in the bush in the northern part of Bathurst Island in the late 1920s, it is basic to an understanding of this society. Tiwi struggled for prestige and influence at the end of the 1980s as much as they had sixty years earlier. In between, concerning the situation in 1954, Goodale found that, 'Personal achievement appears to be the dominant value for which Tiwi males and females strive during their existence in the world of the living' (1971: 337). Hart presents a good picture of 'the prestige and influence system' as it operated among Tiwi in the country Malau, where Catholic missionaries and Japanese pearlers had had comparatively little impact on the marriage practices (Hart and Pilling 1960: 53), at about the time the homicide victim was born there.

Despite the change from polygyny to nominal monogamy in Tiwi society, brought about by the active involvement of the Bathurst Island Mission as we will see below, marriage politics have remained an ongoing concern. I will summarise Hart's argument and briefly discuss some of the aspects of what he called 'gerontocratic polygyny' in Tiwi society.

According to Hart, Tiwi were involved in a struggle for prestige and influence over others to which they devoted most of their lives:

> The 'game' was one of trying to win friends and increase prestige and influence over others. The 'assets', in a tribe with such minimal material possessions as the Tiwi, were mostly intangible ones such as friendship, 'help', goodwill, respect of others, control over others, importance, and influence. (ibid.: 52)

Success in one's efforts could be measured by the possession of surplus food. This not only enabled the possessor to make gifts and hence create dependencies, but also gave him time to devote to social, ceremonial, and political life. Apart from the food that was given by the men's wives to their close relatives, the distribution of food was controlled by men. A surplus of food could only be brought together by a female 'workforce'. So in the end it was on control over women on which a man's success in gaining prestige and influence depended heavily. As Hart puts it, 'Women were the main currency of the influence struggle, the main "trumps" in the endless bridge game' (ibid.). In order to become influential, ambitious Tiwi men strived to establish polygynous households; the acquisition of wives was a main objective of a man's political career. For this he needed other people who were in the right position to give him, directly or indirectly, or to promise him future wives. Hart distinguishes two general means by which men could obtain wives, by bestowal and widow remarriage.

Bestowal was the most prestigious and difficult way to get a wife. It meant the promise of a future daughter of a young woman when she had her first menses. If a man had a wife bestowed on him, it would still be a number of years before she could join him, if everything went right. Only fully initiated men could have wives. Hart states that men began competing for wives in their twenties, after the lengthy initiation procedures. He estimates that on average a man was between 35 and 40 years old before he could actually receive a first wife in this fashion. The practice of bestowal accounted for a considerable difference in age between marriage partners. It must be noted that the accomplishment and time of the actual delivery of bestowed wives involved a good deal of politicking. One way of improving a man's chances of obtaining a wife was for him to live in the encampment of the donors. In any case, this made the man in question dependent on the donors for a very long period, and they aspired to get all they could out of the deal too (Hart and Pilling 1960).

In principle, female babies were thus married off before they were born. Women always remarried whenever their husbands died; prolonged widowhood was extremely rare in Tiwi society. Young men had a better chance to acquire an old widow than a bestowed woman as their first wife. On the death of an old polygynist a substantial number of women could marry other men. Young initiated men were then sometimes able to obtain the eldest widows, who were less valued in the influence struggle by the senior men. These elderly women proved to be useful persons to set up a household with. A senior woman was a skilled food producer herself who could instruct and guard the younger wives eventually added to her new husband's household. By marrying a widow, the husband became the stepfather of her children from the previous marriage. He had the right to rename them, and in doing so replaced their father. Consequently, he was entitled to have a say in the arrangement of new marriages for the widow's daughters and the bestowal of her future daughter's daughters. At the same time, whenever he could he would try to use secondary rights in the marriages of his close female relatives – sisters, sisters' daughters, and mothers – as 'assets' in the influence struggle. The politically skilful young man, therefore, acted as an agent for others or on his own behalf in marriage politics to enhance his influence and prestige. Initial successes in this realm would likely attract more success, as senior influential men tended to favour young up-and-coming men rather than their contemporaries and main competitors. As a result of this, a man's later success would be decided on by his political achievements when he was in his thirties. For most of these men, marrying an elderly widow was a prerequisite to the start of a political career and to success in the formation of an extended polygynous household. They became even more influential when they fathered daughters of their own and could bestow their daughters' female offspring.

Tiwi men had varying degrees of success in this struggle for influence. Political achievements depended on age and ability, on networking and gaining maximal returns from one's 'assets', and also on cooperation with their womenfolk who became clever politicians in their own right as they grew older. Many men remained bachelors all their lives. Only a few succeeded in founding an establishment of their own. More often than not an establishment was dominated by senior brothers working together, 'a multi-adult cooperation' based on the pooling of their interests. In the vicinity of such an establishment, satellite camps could exist. These smaller camps relied in part on the surplus food produced by members of the main camp. Throughout the year, the camps in a country shifted in accordance with the food quest, partially determined by seasonal changes and exploitation of the various habitats. Most of the time life centred on these camps. Larger groups of people gathered together once in a while and these occasions could involve crossing country boundaries, for cooperative hunts (at grass-burning time), battles, seasonal rituals, and post-funeral rituals. Senior men in particular participated in these activities, which granted them opportunities to socialise with others, to settle disputes, and above all to enlarge their prestige and influence.

There were, as I have already noted, many bachelors in Tiwi society, which allowed for a number of senior men to have exceptionally large polygynous households. The initiation of males served, among other things, to discipline the young men. Their physical separation from the main camps and the taboo on sexual intercourse ideally kept these young men away from the women. Hart asserts that this 'compulsory celibacy did not, of course, mean chastity'. The environment of forest and mangrove swamps was favourable for them to have sexual relationships with married women, their female age-mates being married to much older men. When detected or under serious suspicion, a man had 'to stand for spear' or, to avoid this, move away from the area. In a formal 'duel' the husband threw a volley of spears at the man who allegedly had made him a cuckold; the matter ended when he was hit (ibid.: 80–3). According to Hart, these duels were 'their only formula for settling disputes, and these occasionally became sufficiently broadened to warrant being called warfare' (ibid.: 83).

In short, Hart argues that the isolation of the islands and the plentiful food supply of the area enabled the development of a social, economic, and political system controlled by a number of senior men, heads of large polygynous households, on the basis of their political achievements. Influential Tiwi men could obtain an exceptionally large number of wives, the successful ones counting between twenty and thirty women as their wives. It must be noted, however, that not all these wives lived with their husband at one time (and some never did). The number of wives, an index of prestige, included promised wives not even born or still in the care of their mothers, the wives actually living with their husband (which could amount to ten or twelve women), and deceased wives (ibid.: 17).

Older men could thus accumulate many wives because the sex ratio of married people was very uneven (cf. Maddock 1986: 68): while the number of married men was kept low by prolonged (and in many cases lifelong) bachelorhood and a very substantial delay of their marriages, the number of married women was carried to an absolute extreme, with no age restriction. These and other explanations have been given as to how some men could marry so many wives and keep the younger men from marrying (cf. Warner 1958; Maddock 1986; Keen 1982; Burbank 1988; and Keen 1988 for further references and discussion). Probably, as Keen makes clear, 'the complex interplay of a variety of factors has to be invoked', including the formal kinship system as one of these factors (1982: 621).

Frederick Rose argues that polygyny was in the interest of females, for as co-wives they could share in the burden of looking after children, the older wives could instruct the younger ones, and their marriage to a much older man had economic advantages because these men 'were the most experienced paterfamilias by virtue of being the most effective organisers of production and distribution' (1987: 204–5, passim).

Hart appears to give priority to the senior men's control of food production over their control of human reproduction. Hiatt, however, suggests that it 'might be that production is the servant of reproduction, not the reverse' (1985: 44). A factor relevant in the Tiwi context is the practice of male initiation in the pre-mission era. The annual yam rituals were major events in the promotion through seven grades of initiation for young women and men alike. Nevertheless, the lengthy initiation procedures only had an effect on the men's marriage age. The women were already married from the day they were born, so to speak. The young men were treated differently (and had other instructors); males and females went through only some elements of the initiation together.

The young men were not allowed to marry until their initiation was completed and they were 'free men', probably in their twenties.

Keen infers from Goodale (1971) that '[i]n Tiwi society there was no clear correlation between ritual induction and the age of marriage' (1988: 95; see also Maddock 1986: 125, 141). He is correct with regard to Goodale's data concerning the situation in 1954, but at that time the marriage politics of the Bathurst Island Catholic Mission had already undermined the Tiwi gerontocracy. Uninitiated and not fully initiated young men could obtain women of about their own age ('bought' from older men and raised at the mission) as wives from the missionaries, provided that they allowed their children to become Catholics and that they would have only one wife. The Catholic missionaries also introduced other values, supported monogamous couples, and were able to enforce their own laws and state law (they could rely on white police and the Australian criminal justice system). Hence, the young men could no longer be kept from marrying. At the Bathurst Island Mission there was a 'complete ecclesiastical ban' (Mountford 1958: 60) of the 'pagan' initiation and mortuary rituals at that time (cf. Fallon 1991; Gsell 1956). The former rule that men had to remain bachelors until they were fully initiated was dropped. Tiwi people accepted the marriages of younger men as a fact of life, and as they grew older some of them were initiated after all. Pragmatically, the initiation procedures were shortened and limited to the performances of the yam ritual wherein the participating men did not 'marry'; that is, they slept apart from their wives. Tiwi call this initiation 'short-cut' and it must be seen as very different from the situation in the pre-mission period when all men were kept from marrying until they had completed initiation. The high incidence of polygyny had ceased to exist. In the earlier period there was a direct connection between ritual induction and the delayed age of marriage of men.

I now turn to a further discussion of Tiwi social organisation, which permits considerable flexibility and leaves room for political manoeuvring.

A Tiwi person belongs (through his or her mother) to a 'skin group' or *imunga* which can be conceived of as an exogamous matrilineal clan (cf. Pilling 1958: 51). (Goodale calls it a matrilineal sib, 1971: 71.) Such a clan often bears several names designating its particular associations. Tiwi describe the clans as grouped together in several clusters that are ideally exogamous. Within these clusters, some clans tend to be seen as more closely related than others. The alignment of the clans depends on the history of exchange of marriage partners, in which patterns of co-operation between mutually exogamous clans and reciprocity with other (aligned) marriageable clans emerge. The grouping of clans therefore is in constant flux (cf. Pilling 1958: 52; Brandl 1971: 86, 92). The marriage politics of influential men in the past sometimes led to decisions by such men to merge two clans or to form a new clan out of a segment of an older clan. These men were powerful enough to bend the rules to justify unconventional marriages or to broaden their scope for the exchange of marriage partners. However, a 'law' made by such an influential man (*arulukani*) did not always take hold, nor was it necessarily acknowledged by all members of the merged clans (cf. Pilling 1958; Brandl 1971). Consequently, no general agreement on the precise alignment of the clans and their membership exists.

Spencer (1914), Hart (1930), and Harney and Elkin (1943) recorded a three-way division of the clans. Later researchers found a division of four or five groupings (Berndt and Berndt 1988: 66–8; Pilling 1958; Goodale 1971; Brandl 1971; Grau 1983). Pilling (1958: 60–1, 338–42) notes that a fourth grouping resulted from the segmentation of one of the major groups recorded by Hart. Tobias Arapi, the later homicide victim, described the latter (the Mullet people or *takaringuwi*) as 'one body, one group' (because his father belonged to this grouping it meant for him, he said, that these people 'call me son'). He explained the alignment of the clans to me by drawing lines in the sand with a little stick. Each line represented a matrilineal clan. He put the lines together in five groups, one of which consisted of a single line that stood for the Fresh Water clan (*antaluwi*); other people placed the Bloodwood Sap clan (*kurawi*) in this group too. Both clans were set apart because of their irregular marriage patterns. Jerome Pamantari considered these two clans as somewhat incestuous, he referred to a popular myth of the frill-necked lizard, who seduced his sister the black cockatoo (see Osborne 1974: 90–2) and said the people of these clans likewise 'humbug [court] one another', 'still doing it today'.

It is tempting to leave the exceptions aside and to speak of moieties in terms of the broad (although incomplete and time-bound) dual division of the clans, and of semi-moieties in terms of the four main groupings (even less stable and, within them, some clans considered more closely related than others), two on each side. Pilling (1958) and Goodale (1971) have done so, and therefore, not to add to the confusion and lacking more suitable terms, I will put these groupings of matrilineal clans, 'moieties' and 'semi-moieties', in inverted commas.

Tiwi call the members of mutually exogamous clans *aramipi* or 'relations', ranging from the members of one other clan to members of all those clans with whom one's own clan ideally does not exchange marriage partners (one's 'semi-moiety' and one's 'moiety'). Closely allied clans can and do fulfil obligations for each other ('helping out'). Ideally, 'relations' support each other physically (join in fights), materially (supply food, money, services and goods), and verbally ('speak up' for one another). The exchange of marriage partners between matrilineal clans is called *keramili* or 'change 'em over'.

For demographic and other reasons (for example, realignments of clans), people are unevenly distributed between the clans in terms of numbers, age and gender. Members of a single clan can have an exchange of marriage partners with more than one other clan. Clans cooperate in fulfilling obligations resulting from this exchange of marriage partners, but they also compete in trying to obtain partners from other clans with whom they can marry (and this appeared to be amendable). A realignment of clans can negate an exchange arranged in the past, for example, when a partner is expected to be given in return in the next generation.

The matriclan is exogamous. Preferably, one marries into one's father's matriclan, the clan where one 'comes out' (referring to the father's sister). Furthermore, one's own and the alternate generation levels (the second ascending generation from ego, the second descending generation from ego, and so forth) are conceived of as one generation and are ideally endogamous (cf. Pilling 1958: 73).

A Tiwi male ideally marries his *mawana* or 'mother's brother's daughter', whereas a female's first preference is to marry her *amini* or 'father's sister's son'. The second preference is for a female to marry her *mawanyini*, or 'mother's brother's son', and for a male to marry his *amoa*, or 'father's sister's daughter'.[11] Brandl found that the terminology used – *mawana* being a potential spouse of a male's own generation or the second descending generation; *amini* being a potential spouse of a female's own generation or the second ascending generation – points at a trend of men 'marrying down' (in the second descending generation rather than the second ascending generation from ego), which in the past privileged the older men and limited the number of women younger men could marry (1971: 188–93). Furthermore, senior men were owed the respect of their juniors, who were thus in a weaker position to press marriage claims.[12]

Goodale (1962, 1971) distinguishes several types of 'marriage contracts', but notes that 'in every type of contract one primary factor will influence the ultimate choice of a woman's husband: that of being assured or hopeful that a reciprocal contract can and will be made' (1971: 114). The type A contract, according to Goodale, encompassed every female's first marriage and was arranged by her mother's father and her future husband at the time of her mother's first menses, before she herself had been born.[13] The other types of marriage contracts could only follow on this ideal and most prestigious one (from a male point of view) and resulted in a woman's later marriages.

Derived from this contract is type A2, when a brother of the prospective husband gets the woman after the first husband's death. Type A3

leaves the original contract intact, but the husband passes the wife on to
another man. Type B is a father-arranged contract, and type B2 occurs
when the husband passes the wife on to a brother before he dies. Type
C is arranged by the woman's brothers. Type D is arranged by the sons
(de jure, but de facto possibly by the mother). Type E is elopement,
arranged by bride and groom (1971: 54–7). I recorded cases of all types
except type D (but see Hart and Pilling 1960: 19–21, 27, 55–6). When
asked, my informants denied this type of marriage arrangement occurred or could happen. Hart mentions an additional category of 'disputed', either 'stolen' or 'shared', wives. These women appeared in any
man's count of wives but their marital rights in them were not clearly
determined in terms of exclusiveness (ibid.: 28–9). To give just one contemporary example, a man tried to 'steal' a woman, his potential spouse,
from her actual husband. Then the husband's younger brother stirred
up a fight, enforcing the claimant's retreat. Thereafter, the younger
brother declared that from then on he came first and his brother second. Consequently, the brothers shared this one wife (although in the
case of the younger brother she was someone in between a sanctioned
lover and a wife).

At the end of the 1980s, the term 'promise' for a promised wife was
used in both strict and rather broad senses. It could mean a man
expected a wife to be given by another clan or 'semi-moiety' in return,
and therefore was his 'promise'. It could also refer to a classical marriage
deal. The idea of an exchange underlay these marriage deals. Jerome
Pamantari, for example, nearly sixty years old, had a mother-in-law of
twelve, a marriage deal following on the one her father had obtained for
his father's brother's sister's daughter. And Mike Kerimerini, a bachelor
approaching his thirties, had an affair with a widow in her late fifties,
regarded the six-year-old daughter of his mother-in-law as his wife,
expected to acquire a young widow of his classificatory brother, and in
the meantime hoped to get a sister of his brother-in-law (in which he succeeded). Men of considerable age still had female toddlers promised to
them as wives. In a number of cases wives resisted their husbands having
more than one wife (one woman argued that the 'mission blocked that')
and in other cases wives assisted their husbands in having their rights
acknowledged (but not to the extent that promised wives would become
co-wives). Only rarely did a man actually live with more than one wife.

Young women often resisted arranged marriages with partners they
did not like, including men they considered 'too old'. Some women married white men. Men and women also married other Aboriginal people
and Aboriginal people of mixed descent (and sometimes an exchange
of partners was extended to them). Besides this additional heterogeneity in the choice of marriage partners, there were 'unmarried' mothers

and women without children who remained single. What persisted from the era of extreme polygyny were marriage politics, the resultant webs of arrangements binding people, and lover relationships.

Men have to support their mothers-in-law (and their husbands in addition) in providing them with money, goods, services, and so forth. When a man who has invested in a mother-in-law does not obtain his promised wives because they have married other men or remained single, his 'promises' have to give him in turn. The relationship with a mother-in-law is an avoidance relationship out of respect. She is not directly addressed or openly spoken to by her son-in-law; she can, however, make demands when no one else is present as a go-between, and the son-in-law may give her things by putting a hand around the arm with which he gives. They can speak with each other, but only softly.

The same accounts for another important avoidance relationship, the relationship between brothers and sisters (with the exception of the very young and the old) who have a mother, mother's mother or mother's mother's mother in common. They use intermediaries or they turn away from each other and direct their speech elsewhere in talking to each other, pretending to speak to someone else (for example, when a sister is sitting alone, her brother calls out in the plural to attract her attention). The practice of sister–brother avoidance cannot always be adhered to nowadays. A health worker, for instance, expressed how she felt uncomfortable, due to a 'feeling inside', that she had to cooperate with her 'brother' within the context of health care, whereas in other contexts she avoided him. Brothers can draw on their sisters' resources and have secondary rights in their marriages. Sisters nowadays also act as chaperones of their brothers' wives and girlfriends (hence, the identity of the girlfriend is a public secret). The brothers' wives hold their sisters-in-law responsible for the fidelity of their – the brothers' wives' – husbands.

The relationship of men with the mother-in-law's mother and mother's brother is another one of respect; when they are spoken to it has to be sensible talk, no nonsense or 'gammon'. This is in contrast to brothers-in-law who in a kind of joking relationship exchange verbal abuse (the swear words have to be thrown back, as it were: 'What about you? You f—', etc.). As these men are expected to exchange sisters, their verbal exchanges appear to be an ongoing testing of their mutual relationship.

Men who have a love tryst with a woman give her beer and money. The lover relationships (cf. Berndt and Berndt 1988; Burbank 1988; Hiatt 1965) follow the rules of an exchange of partners or 'change 'em over'. These informal relationships are mostly affairs with potential spouses (or, exceptionally a 'father's sister', although this is frowned upon). A female informant told me that 'every woman got to have one husband

and one boyfriend'. The contradictions between this informal system and the formal one are expressed by Tiwi with humour (when one is not involved). Ideas about romantic love have been introduced to Tiwi society. (The English word 'love' cannot be directly translated in Tiwi.)

The frameworks of matrilineal and patrilineal descent are both important for Tiwi. 'You follow your mother', said Tobias Arapi, 'in other ways you follow your father.' The role of matrilineal clans has been discussed above. They also discipline their own members. As indicated, patrilineal descent, besides the transference of character traits, dreamings, and dances, among other things, is particularly important in mortuary ritual, in which the emphasis on particular kinship ties and identities can be negotiated and expressed.

Within the broad constraints of the kinship system, individuals stressed a network of kin relationships and downplayed other kin relationships. It was not always possible to stick to the rules in marriage politics, and then sometimes people manoeuvred others by tracing them via other people in a suitable kin relationship (see also Hiatt 1965). In a context wherein everyone had ties of kinship with all others, it came down to the specifics of choice. It thus depends on how ties are used, what people in practice in everyday life do with these, and if a mutual understanding is ignored a conflict can arise. With regard to the situation in 1928–29 Hart notes, 'It seemed that the primary purpose of a kinship system is to promote ease and prevent strain in everyday, face-to-face living, and the other aspects of kinship and clanship are secondary or subordinate to that primary purpose' (1979: 125). Williams, in her study of disputes in an Aboriginal community in northeast Arnhem Land, clearly states that the kinship terms there, to a certain extent, were also negotiable:

> The contractual nature of the obligations is indicated by the fact that each individual can specify through several equally accurate genealogical links kin-named relationships with any other individual except parents and full siblings. The agreement of two or more people to use a given set of kin reciprocals therefore signals the contract subject to the approval of others whose relationships with the principals are affected. Relations between people change, reflecting individual changes in ambitions, goals, loyalties, affection, and so on. Change[s] in kin terms are negotiated by individuals striving to achieve the best fit between the kinds of obligations that inhere in particular kin reciprocals, personal relations, and aspirations. As a consequence, a grievance arises not as a breach of *kinship* but from a breach of a contract whose terms are specified by kin referents. (1987: 68–9)

With limited means and resources Tiwi individuals are constantly forced to make choices, although it is impossible to make everyone happy. Time after time, social relationships have to be negotiated and given substance by sharing company, food, money or whatever. The significance of this mediated affectionate attachment became clear to me when a young Tiwi man told me, 'I always give my "grandfather" cigarettes so I have something to cry for when he dies'. What matters here is their personal relationship, not the cigarettes. Cherished relationships are characterised by warmth, affection, respect, and the utmost care for the other person. To be sustained, these relationships must be continuously fed.

In Tiwi society it is the person who makes the request who decides about a gift (for example, money, goods, services), not the donor (see also Peterson 1993). Blunt refusal makes the other ashamed (*aliranga*), which has to be prevented at all costs; and refusal can have other repercussions, such as being blamed for harm that befalls the person who made the request. A Tiwi man called this 'family pressure'. For example, in one Tiwi township the bank agency was closed after A$50,000 was discovered missing because the employees could not resist the demands of their relatives and friends to 'borrow' money.

The demands can be numerous and manifold, especially in the contemporary large-scale townships. One informant said she did not like to go to another township because there were 'too much relations there'. McKnight shows that the increase in violence and fighting in an Aboriginal 'supercamp' on Mornington Island was due to the large population and 'high relational density'; compared with the pre-settlement small camps (dwelling places) of about twenty closely related people, the more heterogeneous settlement of about 600 people, where one had to fulfil obligations to numerous actual and classificatory kin present, did give rise to conflicts and violence (1986). I frequently heard Tiwi say a township like Nguiu, with a population over 1200, was 'too big'. The population of Nguiu consists of far more clans (whose members have to support each other vis-à-vis those of other clans), and clans of greater numerical strength, than the population of Pularumpi (about 300 people). Tiwi considered Pularumpi relatively peaceful. The situation in Nguiu, where trouble easily snowballed, was seen as getting out of hand. At the end of 1991, some Tiwi leaders developed plans to establish a new but smaller-scale township in their country of origin on Bathurst Island.

The seamy side of life is recurring conflict and violence. Such conflict demarcates the social and emotional interests in individuals' involvement in networks with regard to infringements at a certain point of time. Identity claims can be lodged in this small-scale society, where everyone is either classificatory or actual kin, but from the perspective of an individual some relationships gain significance at the cost of others, and conflicts indicate an individual's stand in relation to shared identities acknowledged concerning issues in dispute. Over time one's identifications, the cherished networks of social relationships, shift like patterns in a kaleidoscope. This, of course, involves politicking. I follow Boissevain's description of politics as people competing with each other 'for valued scarce resources, for prizes which form the important goals of their lives' (1974: 232). Tiwi individuals pursue political goals and hence they have to defend interests. In these politics one's choices are context-dependent, decisions are made on the basis of what relationships are deemed important, and these determine whether conflict and violence are avoided or not (see Myers 1986a: 16–7). Articulation of what is contested in such a close-knit society implies social distancing between opponents.

Anger about a perceived wrong and drunkenness, according to Myers, probably both 'provide the same excuse for violence: ignorance of the identity of the other' (ibid.: 119). It is also evident in a historical case I describe in the next chapter in which the killers pretended 'not to know' their victim. Their father, however, recognised his close relationship with the victim. In his anger he asked his clan brothers from elsewhere to retaliate, and to execute capital punishment of his own sons. I was told these sons were already somewhat estranged from their father because of 'humbugging' or courting his younger wives. The case demonstrates that social bonds of whatever nature cannot be relied upon unconditionally. Uncertainty about the consequences of social actions is an important theme of this work.

The infliction of physical violence (for instance, 'a good hiding') by people who are certainly not intoxicated occurs, mostly following an acute moral wrong as perceived by the perpetrators of this violence. The majority of the population, especially children and most of the women, do not drink alcohol. (During my fieldwork an estimated 70 to 75 per cent of the population did not drink regularly in Pularumpi.) Nowadays the consumption of alcohol is restricted in all three communities. People who do drink (only beer is available) are seldom moderate drinkers. Alcohol not only affects people's health but is also frequently related to tragic accidents. In recent years the death toll in car and boating accidents as a result of intoxication has been extremely high: in 1987–91, it accounted for at least twelve violent deaths. More often than not the perpetrators of violence are inebriated: alcohol figures in nearly all homicides of the past two decades. What must be noted, however, is that in general the use of alcohol is perceived differently by Aboriginal people than by mainstream Australian society. Brady and Palmer write, 'An inebriated person, in Aboriginal understandings, becomes a member of a different order of reality than the one who is not intoxicated' (1984: 2). These authors assert that drunkenness gives the person in question licence to do things (for example, utter grievances, inflict physical violence, and engage in sexual relationships) that otherwise would have severe social consequences. Drinkers themselves are not held fully responsible for their actions. When things threaten to get out of hand, others have to intervene. This, in particular, tends to be the case when an intoxicated person is angry, for this 'may lead to violent assault and even homicide' (ibid.: 27). Brady and Palmer note, 'it appears that physical harm is deemed to be a consequence of lack of vigilance on the part of consociates rather than the drunken excesses of an assailant' (ibid.). Tiwi people realise that white authorities do not accept intoxication as an excuse. A Tiwi woman, for instance, scorned a man who had told the police that another Tiwi man, who had caused a fatal motor vehicle accident, had been drunk. She said that it was wrong to tell this to the police, for now it was the other man's 'own fault'. This woman was a drinker herself.

There is no doubt that many Tiwi people are opposed to the drinking and the violence often following it; men and women – but mainly women, who with their children suffer the consequences most repeatedly bring up the issue (see also d'Abbs 1987). In 1989, for example, the Nguiu Mothers' Club undertook action to have the beer outlet closed there. A man said it would force him to get his beer from Darwin by dinghy (importation of beer is banned) and if it cost his life he did not want his female relatives to dance at his funeral. The drinkers are always relatives, which makes it difficult to refuse them money for beer or not to let them have beer at all. Furthermore, as Tonkinson points out with regard to a community in the Western Desert, there exists no traditional way of dealing with the consequences of the introduced substance, diminished responsibility is attributed to drunken people, and only a minority of the drinkers tends to cause problems and this fluctuates over time (1988: 404–6). On Melville Island two nuns, based in Pularumpi, organised and supported Alcoholics Anonymous groups and on occasion gave people who wanted to the opportunity to follow the so-called family sobriety programme of the Catholic missions on the mainland. They considered alcoholism a disease. If it may be so termed, it must be noted that the disease has reached epidemic proportions in Australian society as a whole.

A number of Tiwi people said to me that they started heavy drinking after the loss of a significant other (e.g., a mother or a spouse). Drinkers and mourners alike are in danger of doing harm to themselves, if not directly then indirectly, by provoking others. Both categories of people can express themselves freely and usually get support and protection from their fellows. The licence given to these groups comes close to personal autonomy: in contrast to others, they do not have to worry about the possible consequences of their behaviour. Aboriginal drinking is an organised and meaningful social activity (see Collman 1979; Sansom

1977, 1980). Among Tiwi drinkers, beer is a currency that gives substance to social relationships. People are paid for their ritual services with cans of beer. Tiwi males give their female partners beer when they engage in extramarital affairs. The use of beer cuts both ways: it cements social relationships and it enables a temporal disregard of the restrictions and conventions that go with social ties in everyday experience.

A conventional way to avoid an escalation of a conflict or further trouble is to move away. There were residential shifts of people back and forth between the townships on the islands, but dependent relationships with others in the township, commitments to work, children in local schools, and difficulties in finding suitable housing elsewhere, among other factors limited people's mobility.

In the following section I will give a sketch of the contact history until the very recent past, how the wider society impinged on the Tiwi world that appears to have been isolated for several thousand years (cf. Kirk 1983).

*   *   *

In 1636 and 1705, the crews of ships of the Dutch East India Company explored the north coast of Melville Island and the west coast of Bathurst Island. The first expedition did not go ashore, but members of the second one had some interactions with the islanders. The Dutch discovered nothing that they considered valuable, such as metals, minerals or spices (Robert 1973; Swaardecroon and Chastelijn 1856). The Portuguese, based on Timor, possibly raided Melville Island for slaves until about 1800 (Hart and Pilling 1960: 97–8; Campbell 1834: 155–6). For centuries perhaps, but at least since the 1780s, an Indonesian prau fleet gathered annually at Macassar (the present Ujung Pandang) before the praus set off to the north Australian coast, and its crews worked from Melville Island eastwards. The monsoonal winds brought them to and from Australian waters. The so-called Macassans came to collect prized varieties of sea-slug or trepang during the wet season (Cense 1950; MacKnight 1976: 181–2). Long-lasting relationships were established with Aboriginal people on the coast of Arnhem Land (Warner 1958: 453–68; Berndt and Berndt 1988: 17–19). This seems not to have been the case on Melville, although remains of Macassan activities have been found in the north of the island (Searcy 1909: 46).

A British expedition led by Matthew Flinders explored the north coast of Australia and came across Melville and Bathurst Islands in 1803 (Flinders 1814). In 1818 another British expedition, led by Phillip King, had to complete the surveying work of Flinders. They established that Melville and Bathurst were two islands (and named them accordingly).

They did not land on the islands, except in the north of the Apsley Strait; they were driven away from there by the islanders (King 1827[2]: 318–22). The British wanted to take possession of the Australian north before other colonial powers could do so, and planned to establish a settlement south of the Indonesian archipelago. They expected to be able to trade with the Macassans, who frequented the north Australian coast, in order to penetrate the Indonesian market and to introduce it to European commodities. In 1824, Fort Dundas, the first colonial settlement in north Australia, was founded on Melville Island. The population (some 120 people) consisted of marines and soldiers, forty-five convicts, and a few farmers. The settlement had to be abandoned within five years, as the trading ships expected did not turn up, the inhabitants suffered from disease, and some of them were speared to death in sneak attacks by the Tiwi (Campbell 1834).[14] I was told in great detail about the experiences of a man named Tampu who had been taken prisoner by the British but managed to escape. Next, he went to a camp at Kulimbini, a waterhole. Tampu told the people there about the white people at Fort Dundas. Together they crept up through the mangroves and attacked a white man who was washing clothes in the creek, peppering his body with barbed spears.

In the 1860s Tiwi fought the Larrakia, both in the south of Melville Island and on the mainland. The main objective of the raids for both sides was to steal women (Pye 1985: 13–5). The South Australian government wanted to colonise the Northern Territory and acquired it in 1863. Six years later Palmerston (the present city of Darwin), the principal port in northern Australia, was founded (G. Reid 1990: 28, 35). The main shipping route westward went along Cape Fourcroy, the southwest point of Bathurst Island (Searcy 1905: 47). Navigating around the islands was difficult, given the strong currents and many rocks and shoals. Time after time, ships were wrecked on the islands' shores. The Tiwi obtained iron cutting tools from these ships (Hart and Pilling 1960: 98–9). Geologists sent by the South Australian government briefly explored Melville Island for mineral resources in 1877 and 1905 (Hingston 1938; Brown 1906; Gee 1907). Among the white people in Palmerston the islanders had a reputation for hostility (Foelsche 1882: 17; Sowden 1882: 21), probably as a result of their raiding the Larrakia in this area, the earlier failure to establish friendly relations with them at Fort Dundas, and their subsequent attacks on people who visited or were stranded on the islands.

The turn of the century marked a watershed in the relations of the Tiwi people with wider society. The islanders became acquainted with the crewmen of southeast Asian pearling luggers who worked near the islands, and they got on well (Pilling 1958: 17).[15] White timber traders and buffalo hunters (Timorese buffalo were introduced by the British between 1824 and 1829) came to Melville Island, being leased to a customs collector (Simpson 1954: 133). After an earlier failure, the buffalo hunter Joe Cooper based himself at Paru, in the southwest of the island, in 1905. He had a workforce of Aborigines from the vicinity of the Cobourg Peninsula, to which young Tiwi men were added. Cooper's Melville Island presence, backed up with guns, gave white men the opportunity to visit the island in safety, as Spencer noted (Mulvaney and Calaby 1985: 271).[16] His employees, however, began to use their rifles in raiding Tiwi camps in order to steal wives. Tiwi men responded with counter-raids. Finally, as a result of this trouble, the federal government (who had taken over the administration of the Northern Territory in 1911) ordered Cooper and the mainland Aborigines to leave the island in 1916 (Gsell 1956: 47–9; Pye 1985: 15, 31–2).[17]

In the meantime, in 1911, Father Gsell had founded a mission on the southeast point of Bathurst Island. The government had granted land to this Roman Catholic priest of the order of the Mission of the Sacred Heart and declared part of the island a native reserve (Gsell 1956: 40–3; G. Reid 1990: 140). In the early 1900s, Tiwi gained access to Darwin by working aboard ships, as labourers in town or as domestic servants for Europeans (Hart 1930: 168). At the time they gained an understanding of the powers of the state's law-enforcement agencies in Darwin as well as on the islands (cf. Pilling 1958; Gsell 1956). The legislation designed to 'protect' Aborigines enabled the responsible white authorities, among other things, to restrict their movements, to put them in custody, and to deport so-called offenders (Rowley 1986: 230ff.). White officers patrolled, killings were outlawed, and offenders were taken to court. With the enforcement of the national law, the pax Australiana on the islands, and spears being less effective than guns, the old-fashioned sneak attacks were no longer possible (albeit a few incidents occurred).

Father Gsell settled on Bathurst Island to pursue his programme to transform Tiwi society. This priest of French origin scorned 'the social system of the aborigines' which he considered 'an integral, absolute communism' (1956: 32). He aimed to break the power of the 'party' of gerontocratic polygynists, to turn this foraging people into agriculturalists, and above all to make them Catholics (ibid.: 38). To bring Tiwi people under his control, he wanted them to live at the mission. In this his missionary interests and the interests of the Australian government went hand in hand (ibid.: 111). Gsell started off his mission station with four Filipino employees and, within a year, another priest and also two nuns, and eight children of mixed descent to begin a school with, arrived (Pye 1985: 33–4). In succeeding years further personnel were added to the mission staff. Vegetables and fruit were cultivated in the area being cleared around the mission; Tiwi men occasionally worked there in exchange for food and tobacco. After some time, when sufficient trust had been established, families began to visit the mission. Some boys were allowed to attend the school, where they received some religious instruction. The missionaries directed their attention to the youngsters whom they hoped to convert eventually to Christianity. Now and then, girls stayed for a short while at the mission and made friends with the nuns (Gsell 1956).

In 1921, one little girl came to Father Gsell to escape an arranged marriage with an older man. The missionary decided to present two pounds' worth of goods to the old men who had followed the girl, in order to set her free. These men accepted the goods, and the missionary was, as it were, in business. From then on many young Tiwi 'wives' were offered to him so that by 1938 he had 'bought' 150 girls. These young women were raised at the mission convent by nuns. In their late teens they were allowed to marry to Tiwi men of about their own age, and of their own free choice, on condition that their young grooms promised to remain monogamous and that their future children would become Catholics (Gsell 1956). In this way, the Bathurst Island Mission undermined the polygyny and gerontocracy of former Tiwi society. The exchange of marriage partners between matrilineal clans, however, remained intact in these new marriages.[18]

The marriage politics of the mission, and later the suppression of 'pagan' rituals, must have had a strong impact on Tiwi initiations. Indoctrination and seclusion at the convent of a large number of young Tiwi woman eligible for initiation prevented their initiation at an appropriate age. A major factor must have been the unprecedented opportunity for young men to obtain a wife from the mission at an age at which they could not have completed initiation. With this option, Tiwi males did not have to undergo the harsh initiation procedures previously required before they could be married. Changes in the Tiwi way of life, in addition, made problematic the isolation of young male initiates in the bush for long periods of time. The missionaries gave the new and monogamous couples protection. They further provided rations (including tobacco), medical treatment, and provisional housing. Their marriage politics 'created a Tiwi population which regarded the Mission as its home' (Jones 1963: 21). The Bathurst Island Mission flourished and the number of Tiwi attached to the mission increased with the years.[19] The missionaries punished the local people who violated their rules; sometimes offenders were sent to Darwin and tried there (cf. Ritchie 1934; Pilling 1958; Priest 1986).

In the 1920s there was a large camp in the south of Melville Island. Tiwi there obtained goods from Japanese pearl divers in return for the sexual services of Tiwi women. This camp was broken up by white officers (Hart and Pilling 1960: 102–3). In the next decade the Japanese pearl divers moved to the north of the Apsley Strait near Garden Point (the present Pularumpi). Mission and government authorities resisted the Tiwi–Japanese relations, which they considered prostitution. In 1937, a government ration depot was founded at Garden Point in order to control the situation (Harney 1965: 74–5). In line with the government policy of those days, patrol officers took children of mixed descent away from their mothers (cf. Cummings 1990); they also deported lepers to Channel Island in Darwin harbour. Tiwi people still remembered how frightened they were of these men, who forcefully took people away from their midst. The children of mixed descent were brought to a so-called half-caste mission. From 1940 there was such a mission, established by the Bathurst Island missionaries, at Garden Point (cf. Brogan 1990).

During the Second World War, Tiwi people came in contact with military personnel. There were several naval bases in the Apsley Strait and another base at Cape Fourcroy in the southwest of Bathurst Island. Tiwi people worked for the armed forces and as guides aboard ships of the Australian navy (cf. Hall 1989). In 1941, the resident patrol officer shifted the government ration depot to the central north of Melville Island, where he founded a war settlement at Snake Bay. Four years later this would become a government settlement called Snake Bay (the present Milikapiti). After the war Tiwi people continued to work for the Australian army at the army barracks in Darwin, living with their families at Bagot Native Reserve there.

Since the Second World War the majority of Tiwi people on the islands have lived in the three settlements. Until the 1970s they were subjected to white superintendents. In the early fifties the government thought it necessary to accord them the status of 'wards' in order to prepare them for 'assimilation' into white Australian society (Rowley 1986: 238–42; Pilling 1965). So-called pagan rituals were forbidden at the mission settlements. Some people became devout Catholics. Other Tiwi people nevertheless kept performing these rituals, out of view of the missionaries. From Brandl's thesis (1971) it appears that the influence of the Bathurst Island Mission was particularly strong and had an effect on the way mortuary rituals were performed, if these were performed at all. In 1968, the 'half-caste mission' at Garden Point was abandoned; it was to become a government settlement as well. In the 1970s community advisers, replacing the superintendents, assisted the elected local councils. Later these councils obtained the right to make decisions of their own. From the 1960s onwards, Aboriginal people gradually acquired the same rights as other Australians, such as the right to vote, to drink alcoholic beverages and the right to social security benefits.

With major changes in government policy and the formation of the Tiwi Land Council, a cultural revival (referred to earlier, see p. 17) has been taking place on the islands since the seventies. The Catholic mission on Bathurst Island has changed its policy too and traditional rituals were no longer suppressed. The church nowadays supports Tiwi 'culture' – and wants to integrate it with Catholicism at the same time.

On their remote islands, the Tiwi are still economically dependent on the state. The community councils and the land council strive to develop further existing economic enterprises and to initiate new ones to lessen this dependency. Not all Tiwi aspire to a mainstream Australian lifestyle, nor do they all want the constraints of permanent jobs. Notwithstanding the remoteness of the islands, Tiwi people are in touch with the world at large. Western commodities and information about what goes on in the world are part of their lives. The members of one Aboriginal family with whom I was closely acquainted, for example, sponsored financially a child in the Third World. The mortuary poles erected in a Tiwi postfuneral ritual can afterwards be sold to an art gallery in Japan or the United States. The Tiwi living in Western-style townships have incorporated many elements of the wider society, but this has been done in a selective way. Of course, there exist ambiguities as a result of the need for some Tiwi people to operate in mutually exclusive fields of cultural action (for example, in adminstration, health and education). In general, however, it appears that the historical process of this people's encapsulation in the Australian nation-state has not necessarily compromised their distinctly Tiwi value and belief systems.

In the next chapter I present the life histories of two men, the later homicide victim and his father, that give a somewhat more personalised view of the changes that have taken place in Tiwi society in the twentieth century.

CHAPTER 3

The Victim and his Father

'His father was a killer', Nancy sang, 'now he is killed himself'. Walking back and forth from the place where Tobias' body was lying, she depicted a person making trouble. Nancy voiced an old grudge: at the beginning of this century Tobias' father, Kalikalini, had shown that he was a killer par excellence when four men were killed in an ambush and a fifth one speared in his side. The victims were brothers of Nancy's father.

   In the weeks and days before Tobias met with his death, the story of these killings had been told frequently in Pularumpi. My informants emphasised that Kalikalini could hardly wait to put his victims to death. Tobias was seen as the same kind of person as his father who was said to have been a 'real murderman' (*kwampini*): aggressive, fearless, and reckless. Tiwi sons ideally 'follow' their fathers (and classificatory fathers too): they are supposed, among other things, to adopt their father's character traits and other features of his behaviour (e.g., his way of walking, talking, and singing) and identity (cf. Grau 1983). Not all sons actually develop the same personality as their father (cf. Hart 1954), but it is an expectation that they will do so. In ritual performances fathers and sons can replace each other. On at least one occasion, when the ambush was re-enacted in a dance, Tobias enacted the role of his father. He approached the central dancer, a son's son of the earlier victim who had escaped with a spear in his side, from behind and put a spear alongside the dancer's chest (David MacDougall, personal communication).

   In the weeks before his death, some people had grievances and old grudges against Tobias. Hart notes that an accuser 'went into minute detail, not only about the actual offence, but the whole life career of the defendant' (Hart and Pilling 1960: 81). The connected life histories of Tobias and his father can help us to understand the grievances and old grudges. The biographies of these two Tiwi people give a historical dimension to the case, covering the changes that took place in Tiwi society and how these affected the lives of two (male) individuals in the twentieth century. These life histories further provide information about the victim's social background and the conflicts he was involved in before the killing. After the homicide, knowledge about the victim's social background, about who was on bad terms with him, and about his life history was relevant for Aboriginal people trying to discern the motivation for the killing and the identity of the possible killer or killers (cf. J. Reid 1983: 112). This knowledge could also provide justifications. Kalikalini's life can be contrasted with the life of his son as the circumstances under which they lived changed over time.

*   *   *

Kalikalini was born near Cape Fourcroy (along a main shipping route to and from the recently established town of Palmerston) in the southwest of Bathurst Island, some time in the 1870s. He grew up in this area, known as the country Tikelaru. Like his mother, he belonged to the Mosquito clan; his father was of the Red Woollybut Blossom clan. Kalikalini would gain a reputation as a sneak attacker (*kwampini*).

The actions of Tiwi sneak attackers (*kwampi*) had to do with competition over women or with retaliation for grievous bodily harm or death (which in turn were usually a result of 'woman-related' trouble). The *kwampi* used techniques of deception; they attacked to kill or injure in the night, just before dawn, or during the day when they pretended to come as friends (Pilling 1988: 94). I was told that, besides smoking tobacco, they would not eat much (only a little of the mash of prepared cycad nuts) because too much food would weaken them. The weapon used by the sneak attackers was the spear almost exclusively, especially a heavy multi-barbed spear (the one-sided *tungkwaliti*, and the two-sided *arawuringkiri*). 'The ideal pattern for *kwampi* was for the brother of the man unjustly murdered to sneak up and kill his murderer', Pilling writes; 'He cut the veins in his shin [indicating he was bereaved of a maternal brother – EV] and painted his [two-sided barbed spear] with blood so that it would find the murderer quickly' (1958: 140). In these ritualised proceedings they also had their bodies painted with natural ochres and adorned with ceremonial objects and, according to Pilling, in cases of retaliation for a death, their nails trimmed (ibid.: 139). As well as the heavy spears, they could also carry a bundle of thin, light spears, tied with a string, on their shoulders. They untied and picked up the spears with their toes. After a killing, sneak attackers painted their bodies with white clay (cf. Goodale 1971: 178) and pulled out their beards, which are both signs of mourning.

Signs of aggression by sneak attackers and fighters alike were spitting, putting their beards and goose-feather balls in their mouths, and yelling particular calls (e.g., the sound of a shark chasing its prey). My informants said that there had been no female sneak attackers. In the same way that the right to employ techniques and certain weapons for killing larger mobile animals was reserved for men, the killing of adult human beings was a male preserve.

The following account is a composite of the various versions of the story of the killings at Matalau as told before and after Tobias' death by people in his intimate social networks.[20] In the days preceding his violent death it was told to me time after time with the utmost vigour concerning Kalikalini's actions. In 1954, both Goodale (1971: 177–9) and Pilling (1958: 326–9) recorded a version of the story. In their accounts Kalikalini is not mentioned, perhaps because he had died a few years before and his name was still taboo (this could have been circumvented) or because their informants did not attribute such a prominent role to Kalikalini. Hart (1928/29), however, recorded a fragment of the narrative in his fieldnotes, noting that Kalikalini was the first one to attack and spear one victim (Takampunga) from behind. The 1988 raconteurs were almost all descendants of the major *dramatis personæ*, that is, the victims and a senior man who forewarned them. They were not disinterested narrators, for they mostly identified closely with their respective ancestors, whose interrelatedness became hypothetical for the current situation. In other words, their views on selected events from the past also tell a story about the social drama in current history.

Some time in the nineteenth century, Jurukuni, an influential man in the country Rangku (north of Tikelaru), sent two younger brothers away to Melville Island. There they settled in the area around Snake Bay, which at that time was uninhabited or thinly populated. One of the brothers was Tayuni. He founded a new country, called Wulurangku, on the western side of the bay; his brother somewhat later founded a country on the eastern side (cf. Goodale 1971: 179). In time Tayuni became an influential man with many wives and offspring.

His sons were able fighters. In the early 1890s, according to Pilling, Tayuni and his sons were involved in a series of sneak-attack raids and counter-raids in which eight people were killed (1958: 312–7). In 1905 or thereabouts, Tayuni's sons figured in another series of sneak attacks. Five of them had set out to avenge the death of a brother. They went to the country of the killer, where they encountered a group of travellers. A crippled man, named Yingkerlati, had trouble keeping up with these people. Tayuni's son, Aramukuwani, who had proven himself to be a reckless killer, wanted to put this man to death (Pilling 1958: 326–7). Yingkerlati's right leg had been destroyed when he had climbed a tree to cut the upper part, which fell down on him. He was a tall 'blind man, cripple with walking stick . . . didn't know people want him with spear'. Yingkerlati's 'blindness' might be interpreted as figurative speech: He was not able to see his enemies. There at Turupi (in the northeast of Melville Island), Tayuni's sons discussed what they would do with him. It was getting dark. The old man came closer. Aramukuwani said, 'Hey, see that man we got to hit him! We got to spear him properly'. Takampunga, another one of the sons, objected to his brother's proposal. 'Hey, we don't do that, that's our friend (*mantani*)!', he replied, 'We can't do that, we don't wanna be cruel, cruel down old man'.

'Ah, it's alright', said Aramukuwani, 'it's alright, we only spear him goal [like a target], from here to that . . . long way, you know, we throw spear. We don't go close, only spear.'

'What you can do that', Takampunga reckoned, 'I don't wanna do that.' 'Let us put a halt to this', he continued, 'that's our friend. We leave him! Our father will be angry with us.'

Aramukuwani now responded, 'No, we don't spear, don't kill him. We chuck him from here to there.'

Takampunga recognised the man's identity and their relatedness. Yingkerlati was one of their 'friends' or 'relations' (*aramipi*); that is, a man of a closely related mutually exogamous clan. Members of both clans supported each other in the accomplishment of marriage deals and in fights. What is more, the old man was their father's *mawanyini*, mother's brother's son. The relationship with one's *mawanyini* (or *mawana* for females) in Tiwi society is one of the utmost affection, mutual support, and generosity. If Tayuni's sons injured or killed the old man they would seriously violate the established rules. This man was simply too closely related. Myers reports of the Pintubi of the Western Desert that many revenge expeditions turned back after the attackers, realising their shared identity with the intended victim, became 'sorry' for him and gave up their plans (1986a: 118). In contrast to Takampunga, Aramukuwani in his aggressiveness and recklessness, and perhaps his anger in seeking revenge for his brother, denied his shared identity with the old man. He went ahead and threw his heavy multi-barbed spear. The injured man tried to run; he looked around and asked who the attackers were. Tayuni's sons told him:

'Oh, you know me?' Yingkerlati asked.

'Yeah, we know you . . . we thought another man, we didn't know', the attackers responded.

'Oh, come on, don't tell lies, no doubt', said the old man.

Tayuni's sons pretended they had not recognised Yingkerlati and had mistaken him for another man. They took the man from where he had fallen and carried him up to a higher place because the tide was coming in. The brothers made a fire for him, but Yingkerlati died. The killers went through the smoke by way of ritual cleansing. They wailed and pulled out their beards, a sign of grief. Yingkerlati's young wife (some said an 'old lady') had followed him. She had seen what had happened to her husband, and said: 'Oh, you mob [group of people] you gotta watch out, cause that your father find. They gotta do something to you mob when they hear that news, you know, your old man [Tayuni], gotta be trouble.' The woman went to the group of travellers some three and four miles ahead of them. She related to these people what she had witnessed: 'My husband there, getting kill [in the sense of being hit or injured]'. After revealing the identity of the killers, she reckoned, 'They been kill him. But he still [is a]live, must be dead now.' From there they all went to where Yingkerlati was.

The brothers had run away in the direction of their home camp in the Snake Bay area. That night they camped halfway, at a waterhole called Teracumbi. The following morning they walked further to their father's camp where they arrived at the beach (named Pantjo). People who saw them asked one another: 'Look, hey, what happened this mob? They have no whiskers [beards] there. They pulled them out, something wrong!' Thereupon their father Tayuni questioned them:

'Oh, I know you mob, you killed somebody. You tell me truth, which one man?' he asked.

'Yeah, we tell you truth', his sons agreed.

'Then what name?' Tayuni went on.

'Blind man, we couldn't know. It was dark', they lied.

'Who that man?' their father persisted.

'You know that blind man, Yingkerlati', the sons confessed.

'Oh, you shouldn't do that! You should let him go. Where he now?' said Tayuni.

'He is dead. We didn't know him. We thought somebody', they lied again.

Tayuni decided to punish his sons. He told their wives to sit with him and not to sleep with them because they had put his *mawanyini* to death. He thus enforced them to abide by a mourning taboo, they could not have sexual intercourse. In addition, he ordered the women to throw their food away so his sons had nothing to eat: 'All right, let them sleep. Hungry . . . for they didn't find any tucker.' The next morning they had to paint their bodies with white clay. One of the raconteurs commented: 'When they murder, they got paint white. And they know murderpeople . . . If they murdered somewhere from Tumalumpi, or Tikelaru, or Rangku, like that, painted white, they know straight away.' Tayuni's final and secret verdict was capital punishment: 'You mob gotta be finished!'

He might have had two other reasons to get rid of these men. Tayuni headed a very large encampment and was responsible for its people, and his five sons kept giving him trouble. In response to their frequent raids in other countries, counter-raids could be expected. Then people lived in constant fear; they hid in the mosquito-infested mangroves, unable to light fires without revealing their presence (cf. Pilling 1968: 158). Two of Tayuni's granddaughters said the brothers did 'humbug' (were amorous suitors of) his younger wives. The relationship between father and sons surely was considered too close for Tayuni to challenge his sons in the conventional spear-throwing duel (see Hart and Pilling 1960: 80–3).

Tayuni sent a message to his classificatory brothers, belonging to a cluster of four closely related clans known as the Mullet people (*takaringuwi*), in other countries. To authorise the message he made a 'letterstick' (*poruntiki*), a small carved piece of wood, that would be carried by a messenger.[21] With five v-shaped cuttings in his letterstick Tayuni indicated his sons (whose dreaming was the crocodile, the pattern of the cuttings derived from the shape of this animal's tail) had to be killed. He had set out an appropriate time for it to happen. After his death, when the dance ceremonies in the post-funeral rituals for him started, his sons had to be 'finished off'. He did not want them to dance for him. This message went to his 'brothers' Miputingkimi in the country Malau, Jurukuni in Rangku, Tumpuka in Munupi, and to Kalikalini in Tikelaru. Miputingkimi kept the letterstick in his possession; he would lead the expedition.

After some time Tayuni died. Aramukuwani and a few of his brothers went to Rangku to inform their relatives in this country of Tayuni's death and of the final rituals planned for their deceased father. A special type of song, 'when somebody arrives after long time',[22] was performed by Aramukuwani. In the metaphorical song language it told about his father's death. An old man from Snake Bay, who had turned it into a song of his own for a seasonal yam ritual, sang it for me:

Nanunga (the swordfish) was watching him.
She tried to watch him [the crocodile, that is, the deceased]:
'Why from the place where he lay down [Tayuni's grave at the beach] the water is splashing [the crocodile had dived down into the water, meaning Tayuni had died]?

After Aramukuwani's visit to Rangku, his deceased father's 'brothers' held a meeting. They each agreed to make a number of barbed spears of the type used in man-killing (*arawuningkiri*). When they made themselves up to go to Wulurangku for the final ceremony, the people of the countries on Bathurst Island would meet at a place called Tuwtu. A man who had worked for the army during the Second World War indicated how the roles were distributed between the sneak attackers: '"I'm in charge", said Miputingkimi, "I'm general. Kalikalini, captain of war. Jurukuni, capman." He didn't have spears, only Kalikalini!'

The Bathurst Island people (from Rangku, Malau, and Tikelaru) paddled across the Apsley Strait in dugout and bark canoes. They landed at Garden Point beach; from there they went inland to Kulimbini waterhole, walking further along a track to Mungaru (south of Shark Bay). After passing through this area, the attackers crossed Murikaujanga Creek to Matalau. One informant stated that these Mullet people had come close to the sacred seat of Kalikalini's clan (Wulintu or Nodlaw Island in Shark Bay). All mullet (*takaringa*), their united clan emblem, jumped out of the sea: 'Ooh, maybe today we got to hit those men!' The men were painted with ochres and carried spears when they arrived in Matalau. The people at Matalau heard them coming and were saying to one another: 'Oh, look that mob, that's from Rangku and Tikelaru. Oh, yeah, they come in for corroboree, that old man. Yes, yes.'

At night, Miputingkimi directly organised the first of a series of dance ceremonies leading up, in space and time, to the grand mortuary final ritual (*iloti*) for Tayuni. The bereaved sons had to dance in these small rituals but were a bit reluctant because they did not want Miputingkimi and Kalikalini, reputed sneak attackers from countries they had raided, to 'square' with their father in the final rituals. The mortuary poles to be erected at Tayuni's grave had been made, however, so things could progress. Miputingkimi selected male teenagers who he thought were ready for the initiation. These young men had to perform in the dance ceremony as well. Furthermore, 'anyone' was free to dance in this mortuary ritual. The rituals were directed towards the dead man's dreaming place and the sacred seat of his clan, Wulintu. The dances and accompanying songs had the dreaming of the dead man, the crocodile, as their main theme. The famous crocodile dance depicted the spearing of the mythological Crocodile Man, Irekopei, by Tiwi sneak attackers. On the cleared ceremonial ground, Miputingkimi performed the songs for the ritual:

> Plemarepe (name of a crocodile) dives into the water.
> We see that splashing water and look into the water
> where we see all bubbles underneath [the crocodile was on the bottom].

In other words, he sang that Tayuni had died and his spirit would have to follow his paternal ancestors (of the crocodile dreaming). Miputingkimi composed a second song for Tayuni's bereaved children (or *mamurapi*). He gave them a clue as to what their 'fathers' were up to with them. The second line refers to the accompanying dance (called *ampikatoa*), an extremely energetic dance in which the performer, his body held straight, moves forward in the ceremonial ring fiercely throwing up dirt from under his feet. This is an allusion to the tantrums of a little child to symbolise the separation between the children and their deceased father, as well as the anger the former felt at his death. (It seems even more appropriate here because the sons had stood up against their father.) Miputingkimi sang:

> All these crocodiles [Tayuni's sons] sink down
> and going round they make the water sloshy.
> These crocodiles are holding ground and looking up;
> People on the shore grab them by their tails
> [Tiwi used to fight crocodiles with their bare hands].

One of the men who performed these songs for me commented: 'And that mob couldn't understand what that mean. That meaning, you know, that trouble. They wouldn't know. They should know quickly, pick it up that word, you know, but can't do it.' Tayuni's sons failed to grasp the hidden meaning of the lyrics. Kitiruta, a brother-in-law of these men, appeared to have understood.[23] He tried to warn them with a physical sign. A grandson of Kitiruta, whose father had passed the story to him, recounted while mimicking their voices how they failed to grasp this warning too:

'Hey, that old man', Takampunga said to his brother, 'Kitiruta been scratch me hard.'

'What for?'

'I don't know, must be something wrong.'

'Oh, is nothing this mob', his brother Aramukuwani replied, 'this mob nothing. We start here. You must not worry about that, this nothing, he scratched you.'

'No, look! He been scratch me here three times . . . got blood running here [left upper arm]', Takampunga worried.

'Oh, it is nothing. Don't worry about that. This mob can't do nothing', Aramukuwani reckoned.

'All right.'

The next day Kalikalini saw Miputingkimi and Jurukuni leave the camp. He went after them:

'Hey, you mob go!'

Next Kalikalini said to Miputingkimi and Jurukuni, 'Hey, what time we go kill 'em this mob?'

'Wait, wait', said Miputingkimi, 'Wait. Don't worry about that, one day, you know. Only when we get ready. Yeah, we gotta meeting place, what day we gonna do that, kill these people.'

'What about now? We gonna kill 'em!', Kalikalini name him. He want to kill them straight away.

'No, no. We can't', his elder 'brothers' said, 'but when time come, we do that.'

('You know, that Aramukuwani smart, you know, he might finish 'em, people, you know', a raconteur added his comment.)

Kalikalini disagreed 'Maybe this mob turn around, and he kill 'em all . . . from Tikelaru, Rangku, Malau.'

'No, no, they can't', Jurukuni and Miputingkimi reassured him.

The following morning Miputingkimi went to look for a suitable place in Matalau to have the next dance ceremony (performed every second day). He found an open space near the mangroves bordering the salt water creek. Miputingkimi looked at the tide running out. When the water went out it would leave a plain dancing ground, an ideal spot to trap Tayuni's sons because it was a boggy place (note that this was the same kind of place as where Yingkerlati was killed). Miputingkimi went into the salt water and pushed three sticks in a line in the mud. Then, he returned to the camp. Miputingkimi told the people they had to prepare themselves for the next dance ceremony early in the afternoon. He informed his companions the tide would be out and instructed them on his strategy for the forthcoming ambush: 'We got to walk, keep going dance (*yoi yoi yoi*). When we see that number three stick there we hit them there.' They agreed, 'Yes, all right.' One of the tellers commented: 'From there everybody hungry, you know, hungry to kill these people, Aramukuwani-mob. They smart too, you know. They kill lot of people that mob, man, woman, kids . . .'

People painted up for the ceremony with yellow and red ochre, and added ceremonial ornaments such as goose-feather balls, false beards, armbands and rings. The painted geometrical and colourful designs on people's naked bodies had a striking effect; they were also decorated with cicatrices. The bodies of the men were covered with these scars in the shape of the two-sided barbed spears (cf. Basedow 1913). The sneak attackers used red ochre exclusively, as a granddaughter of Tayuni pointed out: 'But Kalikalini and Miputingkimi, they did use anything . . . and they get all in red, because they got spear them . . . make them die today. They didn't put yellow! And all in red, all in red . . . they got murder people today.'[24]

Miputingkimi and his companions walked them to the predetermined place. 'See that stick there', Miputingkimi said, 'We go there, dance there.' 'What about that on top there?' Aramukuwani suggested. 'No, no good there, bad place', Miputingkimi reckoned, 'That better place.' The same informant further explained these proceedings: 'If they should go on top there this mob would be finished, all that Miputingkimi-mob, but lucky Miputingkimi he been taking way muddy place.'

The people all went to 'that paddock' where they performed crocodile dances. Takampunga composed a song for this occasion [he might have done it at a later date, as it reflects his fate, but my informants insisted he sang it then]. When he had sung it for the first time, the group of men at the edge of the ceremonial ring took over the singing of his lyrics, beating time with their hands on their thighs, while Takampunga and his brothers danced:

Peiapuna (name of a bird, the heron,
considered the crocodile's mother) calls out.
[That is, the singer was warned.]
People are chasing him (the crocodile)
whereupon dives he down in creek
and comes out at other side.

Kitiruta's grandson implied that Takampunga had become suspicious, 'must have peeked here' (his orientation in telling us was as if he was his grandfather on the scene). Kitiruta turned around. He had a look: 'Oh shit, they got no balls left, only all skin.'

In their excitement, the prospective killers' scrotums had tightened so their testicles were no longer visible. Men in the chorus next to Kitiruta also looked and read the sign: 'Oh shit, they been ready to kill 'em those people.' Tayuni's sons went on dancing crocodile. Kitiruta tried to warn Takampunga by scratching him with his fingernails (a conventional way to warn someone of a danger; note that the sneak attackers trimmed their fingernails, as they did not recognise their social bonds with their victims).

Takampunga immediately told Aramukuwani: 'Hey, he has been scratching me again, hard one too.'

'Ooh, it is nothing this mob', Aramukuwani said.

'No! But about this one, look blood! Hmmm', Takampunga showed him.

'Nothing that mob, they can't do nothing', his brother repeated.

Kitiruta knew he had to do something to get the message through. He instantly composed the following song to accompany the next crocodile dance:

They have no balls left (*ninka*, nothing),
trouble is coming on soon for this one skin group (clan).

Kalikalini poked Miputingkimi with his foot (a sign of friendship, here employed to alert him). Tayuni's sons in the ceremonial ring now understood what was going on. Kalikalini quickly turned around because Kitiruta had 'been waking up that mob'. He untied his bundle of spears with his toes, picked up a spear and turned around.

Kalikalini's spear hit Takampunga (the teller's cracking his knuckles marked the sound of the spear contacting the victim's chest). Takampunga had moved as well, therefore the spear only grazed him on the right flank from behind. The sneak attackers had all now gone for their spears. All the other people were running away, trying to get to safety. In the meantime, Kalikalini speared two of Takampunga's brothers to death.

They all went for Aramukuwani. He had a bundle of spears too, but the suddenness of the attack forced him to leave them behind. He ran fast. 'They try, three, four spears, couldn't catch him. He run like hell, no matter boggy place.' The pursuers picked up their spears, carried them up, and chased after him. Aramukuwani nearly reached the mangroves. 'Oh, come on you mob, get him properly!' Miputingkimi, who had no spears, called out, 'Quick!' 'Oohh, give me that spear!' he ordered. A man pulled a spear out of a corpse and handed it to Miputingkimi. He broke it in half. Then, 'He chuck that spear . . . bang . . . [cracking of knuckles]'. It cut Aramukuwani's tendon from behind and went out through the knee, '. . . pum . . . that spear came out this way.'[25] Aramukuwani fell flat on the ground.

Miputingkimi turned around. He did not want to look. They pierced Aramukuwani's body all over with a dozen spears. Someone tried to hit Aramukuwani with a small axe, but Kitiruta intervened: 'Hey, stop, stop!' Kitiruta yelled, 'Don't do that. He is all right. Spear all right. You can't kill him with tomahawk, you know. He is not wood, that's spear enough. . . . You don't need one axe. They got to die soon.'

One of the brothers, Takampunga, had managed to escape with a spear in his side. Still performing the crocodile dance with zig-zag manoeuvres he dived into the creek and disappeared into the mangrove swamps. The tide was out. Takampunga walked over the air roots of the mangrove trees so he would not leave tracks behind in the mud. He broke off the spear in a forked branch of a tree. The attackers ran after him. They were looking for his tracks but could not find him, and let him go.

Aramukuwani, as it happened, was still alive. Miputingkimi showed him his father's letterstick. 'Look, you know what happened?' He said to Aramukuwani, 'You been killing that cripple man before, you, name Yingkerlati. Your father sent letter to us, Tikelaru, Rangku, and Malau, Munupi, like that. This what happened, you killed him off. Sorry, we don't wanna kill you, only you father make trouble, but you mob killed blind man. While that finished, no more trouble again, finished.'

Miputingkimi thus made clear to Aramukuwani the reason why he and his brothers had been attacked.

With the killings at Matalau a balance had been reached, and therewith the 'trouble' had been terminated as far as the leader of the punitive expedition was concerned. Kalikalini employed a visual sign to indicate the accomplishment of the counter-killings: he stuck his spears in the ground beside the bodies of his victims. [Jerome re-enacted this by pushing an iron bar, denoting a spear, in the earth next to Tobias' corpse.] The attackers went to the creek and painted their bodies with white pipeclay.

A raconteur, whose dreaming is the crocodile, gave the story of the fight mythical proportions in stating: 'Irekopei (crocodile) was there [in the creek], but they didn't fight that alligator.' In other words, Takampunga (Takampunga is the name of a crocodile) had got away alive. In the mangrove swamps he met up with an old woman. She helped to hide him from his pursuers and removed the remainder of the spear from his chest. Afterwards, Takampunga returned to the Snake Bay area in his country Wulurangku.

In due time, he replaced his father, Tayuni, as the 'big man' in Wulurangku. Like his father he had many wives and children, and his descendants still dominate local politics in Snake Bay. At the beginning of the 1930s, an Australian patrol officer arrested Takampunga at Woolawunga in the north of the Apsley Strait (see Ritchie 1934: 70–7).[26] He had leprosy and was deported to the leper colony on Channel Island in Darwin harbour and there he died. Tiwi perceive leprosy as a punishment for a wrong or the violation of a taboo effectuated by *amputji*, the Rainbow Snake. As one of the tellers pointed out, 'but he died at his turn, Channel Island'.

The four victims were buried together in one hole. After this, the attackers went south to the place where Yingkerlati had been buried to perform the final mortuary rituals for him.[27] Then they turned back and held a joint concluding mortuary ritual (*iloti*) for Tayuni and his killed sons. Kalikalini and Miputingkimi performed songs and dances that had the crocodile and the mullet fish, the dreamings of the deceased, as their main theme. Finally, they went back to their countries.

The story of the killings at Matalau is very popular among the Tiwi. The narrative might be seen as an inversion of the less-well-known myth of Irekopei.[28] It explains how Tiwi came to possess the barbed spears used by sneak attackers. According to this creation myth, Irekopei, the Crocodile Man, lived near Cape Fourcroy in the country Tikelaru. Irekopei was the first to make heavy multi-barbed spears, but he refused to teach his spear-making skills to Tiwi people from Melville Island.

These people decided to kill him. They sneaked up and threw their spears at the man's back. Irekopei, his bundle of barbed spears in his arms, dived into the sea. After a while they saw something come up to the surface. The man had turned into the first crocodile. Irekopei's large, wide-open mouth was the result of his screaming in pain. The bundle of spears had turned into his tail, with one barbed side of a spear upwards. The people who killed Irekopei and their descendants became known as the 'crocodile people'. From then on Tiwi people carved their own barbed spears in imitation of Irekopei.

In the narrative of the killings at Matalau, time, place, and the actors are reversed. Kalikalini came from Cape Fourcroy in Tikelaru to Melville Island in order to spear reputed killers of the 'crocodile people' (their dreaming was the crocodile, they all had crocodile names, and their dance depicted the myth mentioned above). The events in the myth of Irekopei initiated the era of sneak attacks with barbed spears, whereas the dramatic killings at Matalau were the last big event in which the old-style sneak attackers (*kwampi*) figured at the conclusion of this era. This Tiwi institution ceased to exist as a result of the enforcement of state law on the islands. The killings at Matalau thus became the last such episode.

The narrative contains several mythical dimensions; for instance, the mullets that jump over the water and the crocodile Irekopei in the creek. Real people, familiar and related to the raconteurs and the audience, take on the proportions of mythological ancestors. Only the main characters have a symbolic significance and their roles are elaborated on. The events take place in a familiar setting and adorn the tracks and locations with new meaning (not unlike the shaping of the landscape by mythological ancestors in creation myths). The narrative might also be seen as a foundation story for Snake Bay.[29] The graves of Tayuni and his sons, the presence of their spirits, legitimate their descendants' rights in the area. Some people still felt uncomfortable in the neighbourhood of the burial place. A forty-year-old woman told me: 'The spirits of those four men are still there at Banjo beach. They are completely painted up. They stay in the mangroves there. Some people have seen them all painted up, there at the beach. I have never seen them, but you can feel . . . feel someone staring at you. I don't know, you feel funny.'

The killings at Matalau is a story people can relate to, about people to whom they are closely related, and whose positions vis-à-vis each other are well-known. Seemingly trivial details suffice to bring the whole sequence of events to mind; these reveal a whole world to the audience. A swift movement with the shoulder in the crocodile dance, for instance, represents Takampunga being speared by Kalikalini. The ambush at Matalau was the subject matter of many songs I recorded. Often aspects of the story were used as metaphors in other contexts, such as the singers dealing with a conflict they were involved in, uttering grievances, expressing emotions in mourning; the dramatic fourfold killing was exemplary of killing as a prominent symbol of transition. In short, Tiwi actors selectively made use of events and characters of the past in their discourse about the current state of affairs.[30]

Following Macdonald, the Aboriginal fight story might be seen as 'a historical tale which concerns one's own people and which highlights the enduring dynamics of social relations and social processes' (1988: 180). The fight story not only 'highlights' but also serves a function, enabling Tiwi performers to work out unresolved situations in social action. Allusions, such as a single word or a minimal dance movement, sufficed not only to bring to mind a story well known to the audience, but also to recontextualise it, and by the selection of a particular emphasis marked the position taken by the performer on a current issue if that did not already follow from common knowledge of that person's background.

*   *   *

Kalikalini had gone on the punitive expedition from Tikelaru. Ideally, he would marry into the clan of his father (Red Woollybutt Blossom), but this clan did not give him women. First, the pull of the Bathurst Island Mission, taking increasing numbers of young Tiwi females into the convent, probably already had become too great. Second, fathers from the southwest of Melville Island who had promised their daughters to men from Tikelaru chose not to deliver them; they planned 'instead to hire them out as prostitutes to the Japanese pearling boats' (Hart and Pilling 1960: 44). This forced several men from Tikelaru, Kalikalini's relatives, to marry their own paternal half-sisters of a different clan. According to my informants, who gave a number of examples, it occurred because 'they were short of women'. The Tiwi kinship system allowed for these marriages but the mission disapproved (cf. Berndt and Berndt 1988: 84). Kalikalini seemed to be in a favourable position in that he appeared to have a say, or was able to enforce it, in the future (re)marriages of his sisters (also of the Mosquito clan). Men from Malau 'called out for Kalikalini'. They were interested in obtaining his sisters as wives, and also in having an able fighter as their ally.

Kalikalini 'swap 'em up all his sisters' and took them with him to Malau. There he married them off to a man of the Stone clan, named Wamiri, whose country of origin was Tikelaru (although his decendants claim it was Rangku) and whose father was of the Woollybutt clan, as was the case with Kalikalini. Wamiri turned out to be a clever marriage broker. He had acted as an agent for an influential man, one of his clan elders from Malau, who 'didn't shop out all his daughters' but passed them to Wamiri. In this exchange of marriage partners, Kalikalini received at least three other wives from Wamiri and his brother Pintawuni; two of their maternal half-sisters (Stone clan), one of them Tobias' future mother Daisy (Stone A, *pungalalula*), and a classificatory sister of a very closely related clan (Stone B, *aringkuwila*). Wamiri later would declare, after some trouble had occurred between them, that those two clans were one (Brandl 1971: 97–8, 114). Wamiri and Pintawuni were notorious fighters. Kalikalini assisted them in their fights. In a locally famous battle at Pignanappi beach (in the north of the Apsley Strait on Melville Island), Kalikalini was said to be 'the first who took his goose-feather ball (*tokwainga*) in his mouth', a sign of aggression, meaning he initiated the fight.

Kalikalini was characterised as a 'tough man' (*arini*), a 'real murderman' (*kwampini*). Such a trait helped to deter competitors and earned the man in question prestige. Tobias told me his father was a 'bad boy, he killed seven people'. Not all homicides, however, were justified (e.g., the killing of Yingkerlati). Like Aramukuwani, Kalikalini killed irrespective of proper justification. Young Tiwi men used to hang around in the mangroves 'hunting' for the younger wives of old men gathering food. The amorous suitor waved with his hand which was painted on the palm. If the woman consented, she sneaked away and they had sex. A young woman of the Stone clan, with no children yet, in Malau resisted Kalikalini's advances. He sneaked up and waited until she was isolated from the other women, gathering waterlily roots by herself. Kalikalini then speared her to death. The killing of women and children, if they were strong and healthy, was considered wrong. I was told Kalikalini's youngest wife Martha (she died in May 1989) never left his side, for he had threatened that if she had an affair with another man he would immediately spear her. It seems that he wanted to assign the status of an exclusive wife, or *ningika*, prestigious from a male point of view, to Martha (cf. Goodale 1971: 45–7).

The mortuary ritual for Kalikalini's young daughter Donna, who died of a sickness, is another indication of his rising prestige in his Malau years. She 'got a funeral like a Queen, princess' at Purkali'inga (on the other side of the Apsley Strait from Garden Point). Many people attended the rituals. Kalikalini's 'brother', Tampajani, invented a new dance about a sailing dinghy. It became a favourite dance of the actual and classificatory descendants of Kalikalini and his 'brothers' (also to be performed in the mortuary rituals for Tobias). The girl's mother was stolen from Kalikalini by his maternal half-brother, Tajamini. They had a fight over her. (Tobias would even the account by fighting over the wife of Tajamini's son Sam, his 'brother'.) I recorded a number of cases in which a younger brother stole one or two wives of an elder brother. The elder brother let them be because they were too closely related. The younger brother had some rights to his senior brother's wives as well, and often obtained these women after the latter's death; before that, a wife of his could be the younger brother's lover. Tajamini, for instance, stole two young wives from Pamulanpunini, who did nothing about it 'because Tajamini was his brother'.

Kalikalini's children were born in Malau. Tobias had been born there in about 1927. Tobias spent part of his childhood at the Bathurst Island Mission, where he also received some education.

In 1938, according to Tobias, Kalikalini attempted to return with a group of people to his country of origin, Tikelaru. 'It's my country', he had said, 'follow me!' When they arrived there by canoe, four blackened saplings stood on the beach, connected by a string. The message was clear: 'nobody pass'. Nevertheless, Kalikalini went ashore. In doing so, as a trespasser, he broke a 'law' made by his mother's brother. The uncle approached Kalikalini with a spear. Kalikalini grabbed the spear and 'got cranky' but he was not allowed to return to his country ever again. The 'Law' was very strong in those days, Tobias explained. He added that the 'Law' was still very strong, for he was not allowed there either. It is an extremely severe punishment for Tiwi people to be banned from their country, because they belong to that land and strongly identify with it.[31] The event, of course, diminished Kalikalini's prestige.

After the episode at Tikelaru, Kalikalini went with his wives and children to Garden Point on Melville Island. Kalikalini worked for the government at the depot, which was founded in 1937; he helped clear the area of trees. Kalikalini continued to be employed at Garden Point when the place was taken over by the Roman Catholic Mission as a site to raise children of mixed descent from the islands and elsewhere. A number of women said, 'Kalikalini killed [hit] his wife in front of the mission' (some said 'in front of Welfare', that is, the Native Welfare Branch of the Department of Native Affairs, responsible for the government depot). He had to put on the hair shirt, an old flour bag, and had to remain standing up (or so they insisted) in the vicinity of the mission buildings for one week, according to my informants.

A woman of mixed descent, who had been brought to the mission for half-castes as a young girl, recalled that Kalikalini was in the habit of severely beating his wife, Tobias' mother. Her son Jacob (here favourably contrasted to Tobias) frequently took her to the convent, she said, to have her wounds dressed by a nun. Two older Tiwi women said that they were always warned about Kalikalini, 'Watch out for that man, he spear, cunning, crook, killing'. A man of mixed descent, also raised at the mission, remembered Kalikalini as a tall man with a beard, who always carried a bundle of spears in one arm and 'fighting sticks' (clubs) in the other. He did so because he was 'one of those killermen'. He camped under the mango trees behind the mission buildings. When the mission boys teased him, he spat ('they spit when they really go for one'), chased them, and eventually threw a barbed spear. During the Second World War, Kalikalini made barbed spears for members of the Armed Forces stationed at several bases around the Apsley Strait in exchange for food and tobacco. Tobias once told me that during the 'Japanese War' military personnel asked his father, 'You did killing today?' whereupon he would answer in the negative. It was said, according to him, 'Old man is really a criminal'. Tobias stressed that his father had stopped killing people. In the tense situation in which he found himself at the time, it seemed so important to Tobias that he referred me to Simon Pamantari, an influential man, to have it confirmed.

In these years, Tobias' brother Jacob, who was slightly older, with their father's consent, was captured for initiation.[32] I was told that when he returned from the bush he had two infected scars across his chest. The application of these cicatrices by the (prospective) brother-in-law who had seized the initiate, and vice versa, denoted an agreement between the two men that they could marry each other's sisters. Jacob later obtained an old widow, Fanny Groves, with a son by a previous marriage, of his father's clan.

Unlike Jacob, Tobias was one of the many young Tiwi men who received an adolescent wife from the Bathurst Island Mission. In 1948, he married his eighteen-year-old bride, Gloria Palurati, in church. Nevertheless, this union was part of the exchange of partners between the clan of Tobias' mother (Stone) and the clan of his father (Mosquito). The couple stayed at the mission in the Aboriginal living quarters of Myilly Point by the Apsley Strait.

Their first child, Janice, was born thirteen months after the church wedding. Gloria gave birth to two more daughters, Laura and Claire. In March 1952, when the youngest baby was only a few days old, a tragic incident occurred. The eldest girl, Janice, nearly three years of age, disappeared. She had apparently followed her grandmother, who had left the camp to collect firewood. Tobias swam across the crocodile-infested sea strait but did not succeed in finding her. When the tide came in, someone saw her body floating in the strait. The little corpse was taken out of the water. 'She died in water', Tobias told me, 'but I think she been drowned'. One woman gave me an account in great detail of how she had been strangled by a certain man and how her dead body had been retrieved. Stressing that the little girl had been put to death, she further stated, 'But she wasn't full! Full of water, nothing! She been dead long time.' Tobias was grief-stricken. He covered his face and body with excrement, or as Laura expressed it, 'he painted himself with shit (*kineri*).' When little children are no longer breast-fed, in tantrums they throw dirt at their parents. This use of dirt as a symbol of parent–child separation is a convention of Tiwi mortuary behaviour. Tobias employed faeces as an expression of his deep grief and because it was a dreaming of his father's father (*amini*). Tiwi say they 'follow' their father's and father's father, and in Tiwi eschatology so do the spirits of the dead. Thus Tobias emphasised his patrilineal identity as his and his daughter's spiritual track, so to speak.

Following this traumatic experience, Tobias and Gloria had to face another loss. The new baby fell ill and died, two days after her little sister. 'Last one daughter', Tobias said, 'she died. My wife was crook. Later I was thinking I was too young, didn't care about babies.' His words draw attention to the fact that the role of a young Tiwi father first came into existence during the mission period and was without precedent in pre-mission Tiwi society (or even before the first church wedding in 1929). In retrospect, Tobias seems to have seen himself unprepared for that role. Gloria, for whom the death of her firstborn child no doubt was also a hard blow, had to observe a number of taboos, both because she had just given birth to a child and because she had lost another. According to some elderly Tiwi women, the death of the baby had to be attributed to the violation of a taboo. Mothers with newborns (as well as menstruating and pregnant women) are not allowed to go near water, salt water being even worse, because in that event the spiritual Rainbow Snake (*amputji*) will cause sickness. Gloria had gone too close to the Apsley Strait, and therefore her baby had contracted influenza. It must be noted, however, that although child mortality rapidly decreased in the 1950s and early 1960s as a result of hospital births and other medical care provided at the local mission, a number of babies and small children still died of diseases and bacterial infections. The Bathurst Island Mission had become overcrowded; people were living in close quarters and sanitary conditions were poor (cf. Pye 1985).

In the early 1950s, Kalikalini also died. According to Tobias, his father was between 70 and 80 years old then. The man of mixed descent cited above said Kalikalini had always been a strong man, but around 1950, Kalikalini went to Paru for one week and died there; the informant said he had never understood why. He was buried on Melville Island across the Apsley Strait, opposite the Bathurst Island Mission.

In contrast to Miputingkimi, who had become a Catholic and was buried in the Catholic graveyard of the Bathurst Island Mission, Kalikalini resisted the priest who wanted to baptise him. 'I want to go hell', he said. Their respective positions reflect a split in the Tiwi population of the 1950s between people who had become (nominal) Catholics and a shrinking group of 'pagans'. Kalikalini, who had named himself Mopaditi ('devil' or spirit of the dead), was buried out in the bush on Melville Island. The Catholic mission suppressed Tiwi rituals, and when, a few months later, the post-funeral rituals (*iloti*) for Kalikalini were in progress, the priest in charge came across the Apsley Strait to disturb the ceremony. He pushed against the mortuary poles at Kalikalini's grave, to his later regret, as in his words 'these symbols of paganism had to be destroyed' (Fallon 1991). When the priest left in a dinghy with outboard motor on his way back to the mission across the strait, according to my informants, the motor exploded, and was never to be found again: Tobias and Simon had warned the priest. Simon had a dream about Kalikalini's spirit, who told him that he had taken the motor.

In 1951, Tobias began to play Australian Rules football in Darwin. For seven years he played for the Wanderers, one of the Darwin clubs with Aboriginal players. During his life he performed all kind of jobs. Tobias went to work for the Air Force in Darwin in 1953, and continued there for four years. After that, he was employed as a diver on a Japanese pearl lugger (in 1953, for the first time since the war, the Japanese began to work again in Australian waters). Nine months later he returned to the Bathurst Island Mission but soon shifted to the so-called half-caste mission at Garden Point. His brother Jacob used to work there as a saw-miller. In July 1959, Gloria died suddenly. She was buried in the local Catholic graveyard.

Relatives took care of their daughter, Laura, while Tobias moved to the forestry station at Pickataramoor. He worked there until he met a woman of about his own age at Snake Bay. In December 1966, he married this woman, Kate Maruwaka, a widow with three daughters from two previous marriages. Unlike his first wife of the Mosquito clan, Tobias' new wife belonged to the Pandanus clan. This meant he somehow had to arrange for his own clan, the Stone clan, to return a woman to the Pandanus clan. With Kate and her daughters, Tobias lived at Nguiu, thereafter at Paru and Pawularitarra, and then again at Garden Point.

In 1968, the Catholic mission sold its land and nearly all its property at Garden Point to the Australian government. It was decided that Garden Point would become a Tiwi township. Tobias then worked with the local housing association, and later had jobs gardening and collecting garbage. Jacob stayed with his wife, Fanny, nearly thirty years his senior, at Garden Point as well. In 1971 or thereabouts, after heavy drinking, the two brothers came into conflict. It happened under a mango tree in the back of the Old Camp (that is, in the middle of Sam's camp at the time of my fieldwork). Tobias took a barbed spear and thrust it into his brother's back. One man remembered that the spear broke off, leaving its point in Jacob's spine; he drove the injured brother to Snake Bay, and from there Jacob was flown to Darwin Hospital. Tobias scolded himself.

He told me that they both were drunk. Jacob had had a bottle of liquor, 'hot stuff from town'. I was told by another man that Jacob had been 'going round' (had an affair) with his brother's wife. From the moment the point of the spear was removed from Jacob's back, he was paralysed and confined to a wheelchair. Each year around Christmas-time he was flown in from Darwin to visit his friends and relatives.

In the 1970s, the Welfare Department (of the Northern Territory) brought a group of Tiwi people who were living in a bush camp in the southwest of the island (Pawularitarra) to Garden Point to increase the indigenous population of the new township, which had been laid out in Western style. In April 1975, in line with the new developments, a police station was opened at Garden Point to police both islands. Kate by then had given birth to three daughters and a son; Heather, Ralph, Shirley and Evelyn. At the end of May 1976, Jacob died in Darwin Hospital, and was buried in a new graveyard near the remains of Fort Dundas, in Garden Point.

Three months later, Tobias' life took another dramatic turn. During the school holidays at the end of August, Tobias with his family and others were camping in the open air near a waterhole called Kulimbini, a two-hour walk from Garden Point. About midnight, Kate and her teenage daughter Judy went down to the waterhole to get water for the morning. Tobias and other men were playing cards a few hundred metres from the water. On her way back, Kate was bitten on the ankle by a snake. Judy raised the alarm. Tobias and the other cardplayers rushed to where Kate and Judy were to see what was wrong. The presence of the snake told its own tale. Tobias captured the reptile. He took an axe and cut it to pieces. Someone was sent to Garden Point to get help from there, but help arrived too late. Tobias put the snake, a death adder (*pwamika*), in an Esky (cool box). He was worried about his wife: Kate felt sleepy and went to sleep. Tobias looked at her frequently to see if she was all right. Within a few hours after the snake had bitten her, however, he found that she had passed away. In the afternoon Kate was buried in the graveyard near Garden Point; the Esky with the poisonous snake was placed on top of the grave mound.

Bruce Kerimerini, a 'brother' of Tobias who camped with him at the waterhole, alluded to a connection between the death of Tobias' brother and the death of his second wife. He stressed that Jacob's dreaming was the poisonous snake, '*taringini*, cheeky one'. A few other people who told me the story had not been there at the time. One man said that both Tobias and Kate had been drunk, and therefore they had not taken care to make a fire, which would keep snakes away. In this version of what happened, Tobias and his wife did not notice the death adder when they spread out a blanket to lie down on and as a result the woman had been bitten. Such an account, implying in Tiwi perceptions a serious accusation of neglect (a punishable offence), fits in with the animosity between Tobias and several other people around the time of his death. Tobias often mentioned that Kate had died of a snake bite at the waterhole, leaving him with their small children, the youngest daughter, Evelyn, only eighteen months old. At times when he told of these events he was overcome with grief, as his third and last wife, Marylou, had died an untimely death a few months before we became acquainted in September 1988. One of Tobias' sisters took care of the baby and children. 'She died last five years ago', Tobias said, 'All my brothers and sisters all died on the islands. I am only by myself, three wives died, only by myself.'

Tobias regretted he had speared his elder brother Jacob. When he told me about this tragic event in his life he performed a song in a mournful voice: (Jacob saying) 'Why you been hit me youngest brother?/You and me, fight!/You [and] I growing up together./Fight!' Following Jacob's death this song had been composed by Noah Jarangarni, a senior man and father's sister's son of the two brothers, for the seasonal yam ritual at Garden Point in 1977. Having grown up together for Tiwi people implies feelings of great affection. Furthermore, given the ideology of fraternal generosity, brothers who share one or two parents, or even a grandparent, ought not to fight with each other. Tobias was well aware he had committed a serious wrong. Whether he had been punished I was unable to find out. It seems unlikely, for the grievance was still aired and appeared to be unsettled in 1988. As far as the state's criminal justice system is concerned, some people said Tobias had been in jail for having inflicted grievous harm on Jacob but others denied it. Tobias never mentioned to me he had been in jail.[33]

Widowed twice and bereaved of his only actual brother, Tobias stayed in Garden Point, where he got the job of police tracker. Stories went around that when he was drunk and had arguments with other people he used to put on his uniform. Once, I was told, Tobias had a sharp exchange of words with a few women. He asserted that they couldn't touch him because he was a policeman. Thereupon he went away and came back in his complete uniform, hat and all. One of the women took his hat, threw it on the ground, and stamped on it. People who had known him for years told me, 'He was a good bloke when he was sober, but when he was drunk he was a mongrel'. Another anecdote dating from these years was that Tobias owned a yellow motorbike that made a terrible noise. He rode around on it in the Old Camp the whole night, disturbing everyone's peace. Although Tobias usually was a very charming man, I witnessed how at times he could be edgy when he was intoxicated. He was often compared with his late father, who also had a reputation for being aggressive.

At Paru, Tobias told me, he fell in love again with another woman named Marylou Kilimirika. She was a childless widow who had left her first husband Fred. Then Marylou joined her sister Dorothy as a co-wife. Both sisters were married to Sebastian. The latter died, leaving the two sisters widows. Marylou's third husband, Tobias, married her in church on Boxing Day, 1987. Tobias kept two photographs, one portraying the new married couple and the other portraying bride and groom with his family in front of the Catholic church, an old army hut dating from the Second World War, at Garden Point. Tobias and Marylou lived in the Old Camp.

With the start of the dry season they went to work at Putjamirra Safari Camp, about 20 km north of the township. There they demonstrated their hunting skills to small groups of wealthy tourists from all over the world. On a Sunday morning in early June they were to go to the tourist camp but had trouble in finding transport. Tobias borrowed Simon's 4WD car. The previous night, men with permits had been able to take away a lot of beer from the Social Club. As a result of this many people, including the couple, had been drinking throughout the night. Tobias and Marylou had to find someone not too drunk to drive the car. Finally, a neighbour in the Old Camp agreed, although he had little experience in driving on dirt roads and was inebriated as well. They went on their way, Tobias next to the driver and Marylou in the back of the vehicle. Most of the way, Kevin Wangiti, the driver, drove at considerable speed. Then they came to a bend in the road and as they rounded the bend, the two men saw a patch of loose sand. Kevin lost control of the steering, the car rolled over. Marylou was thrown out of the back and then crushed and trapped under the side of the car. Except for an injury to Tobias' back, both men escaped unharmed. They went to see what had happened to Marylou. 'He was looking for his wife but he only found a head', said one of her clan sisters when relating the accident to me. Kevin and Tobias were unable to lift the car off the body. Marylou was dead. Pamela Wurukwati, a 'mother' of Kevin (who happened to be in the mangroves looking for crabs nearby), told me that Tobias chased Kevin around the car with a pocket knife.

Initially, Tobias seemed to have given free rein to his anger towards Kevin. The white management of the tourist camp, a husband-and-wife team, told me that Tobias had been angry at Kevin in his grief but that they had talked him out of it. He acknowledged, they said, that he himself had been drunk too. In our conversations Tobias never uttered any resentment in relation to Kevin. He just pointed him out as the driver of the car and said this man would have to go to court for it in due time. Four months after the accident he expected the court case would have taken place. He did not know when it would be, he said, but it had to be soon. Kevin had written the date of 11 September, the date to go to court, on the wall in his hut. For reasons unknown to Kevin, it had been postponed. Marylou was buried next to Kate in the local graveyard. Kevin did not attend the funeral, according to Simon, because he felt ashamed.

Despite the relatively small number of cars, this type of fatal motor vehicle accident occurred frequently on the islands at the end of the 1980s. After such an accident the place where it had happened became taboo and the road was blocked off. A special ceremony (*ampurapra-punga* or *purumatrapangari*) had to be held to 'open up' the road again. Someone selected as a ritual worker made a mortuary pole. The spot was ritually cleansed with smoke and a few dances relating to the dreaming of the deceased were performed, accompanied by a song series about the cause of death. The mortuary pole was erected at the place where the victim died, and the close relatives of the deceased cried and wailed at the pole. At the end of this small ceremony for Marylou, Tobias placed the yellow bucket she used in foraging activities upside down on the pole.

When such a sudden and violent death occurred, people remained near the surviving spouse. A female friend stayed with a young widow whose husband had died in a car crash, she explained, because 'she might do something to herself'. Tobias' eldest daughter Laura came from Darwin to live in the Old Camp in order to keep an eye on him. Several times Tobias expressed deep grief when showing me his marriage certificate and wedding photos. He took my wife and me to the grave of his first wife, Gloria, in the 'old cemetery' which had become part of the township. Tobias weeded the grave mound quite rapidly, as Tiwi used to do when visiting graves of relatives. The graves of his two other wives, in the graveyard near Fort Dundas, he wanted to show us another time. He planned to have a concrete slab put on his wives' graves before he left Garden Point at the start of the wet season. Tobias told us that he did not want to marry again because he had lost three wives. It had been 'too much' for him, he said; he wanted to 'keep the bad luck away'.

CHAPTER 4

'The Message that it is Murder'

We have seen that Tobias suffered several strokes of bad luck in his life: he lived in exile from his country, lost two daughters, speared his brother, and his three wives met untimely deaths. Tobias expressed his feeling loneliness, as all his actual brothers and sisters had died. The violent death of his last wife, Marylou, seemed to have broken his spirit. Tobias told Jeanette and me he was very tired and thought he would not live long.

Then, a month before his death, he had an affair with Jasmine Pamantari, a woman of the Pandanus clan. Being with Jasmine comforted him. This affair got the widower in trouble, as Jasmine had been promised and married to someone of another clan (Stone B). She had been given to Andrew Munuluka in return for Andrew's clan sister, Sally Wangiti, the wife of Jasmine's brother Dick. For years Jasmine desperately wanted to have a child.[34] In the second half of 1987 she had become pregnant at last. On the day Tobias married Marylou in church, Jasmine had a miscarriage in the Old Camp after an exhausting day of hunting and drinking. She was grief-stricken.[35] A few months after Marylou's tragic death (in June 1988), Jasmine and Tobias became lovers. Tobias pointed out that he longed for her because she reminded him of his deceased wife. Andrew, Jasmine's husband, found out about the affair. The deceived husband had a right to punish Tobias (cf. Pilling 1958: 44; Goodale 1971: 132). Andrew fought with Tobias and injured him, a blow with a club to his head left a scar. An ordinary case of adultery would have ended here. Andrew, the husband, had punished the wrongdoer. Tobias, pointing to the scar on his forehead, told me that he did not care. Andrew also abused his wife. Jasmine's relatives gave her a baby of a 'sister' to take care of, hoping perhaps they could stop her from seeing Tobias. She and Andrew later on were to adopt the child.

Tobias demonstrated his defiance in continuing his adulterous relationship with Jasmine; things became even worse because he began to name her as his wife. He ran into conflict with his neighbour Isaac Pamantari. Nancy Kerimerini said she had to take away a small axe from Isaac several times when he was pursuing Tobias. 'He got wild', she explained, because Tobias 'called Jasmine his wife'. Isaac considered Jasmine his daughter. Jasmine's natural father was dead. He had decided that after his death, his 'brother' Isaac had to 'take over' his wife Maureen, Jasmine's mother. At that stage, Maureen and Isaac were already lovers. As a result of his marriage to Maureen, Isaac became Jasmine's stepfather. He had, as Pilling rightly points out, 'the right to act against whosoever may improperly try to secure his daughter' (1958: 44). Isaac was one of the most senior men of Tobias' clan (Stone), and a man who took such a matter very seriously. In previous years, Isaac had attempted to get Tobias' daughter Laura (of the Mosquito clan) as his wife, but she did not want him. Therefore Isaac strongly objected to Tobias having his stepdaughter. In Pularumpi people frequently referred me to Isaac as a store of knowledge about ritual, genealogies and trouble cases. Moreover, he could exert considerable influence in being the most senior man among the numerous members of the Pamantari patrilineage in this locality.

Jasmine's senior clan brother, Jerome Pamantari, was another man who did not like to see her with Tobias. Tobias' second wife, Kate, a woman of the Pandanus clan like Jasmine, had been Jerome's maternal half-sister. Jerome claimed Tobias had never given him a woman in return for his sister. Why should he allow Tobias to have a second 'sister' if he had not yet reciprocated for the first? Besides, Jerome was after a clan sister of Tobias. Jerome surely did not want to give up two of his clan sisters free. A violation of the rules of reciprocity in the exchange of marriage partners between clans is taken as a serious wrong. Brandl, for instance, reports a case from the end of the 1960s of a man who had been 'poisoned' because he 'had two wives from one clan and had done nothing about arranging that women from his own clan be exchanged for them' (1971: 476, 474–8).

Furthermore, Tobias' relationship with Sam Kerimerini, his elder 'brother', was one of tension. Sam's wife Nancy had been Tobias' lover for many years. Tobias even openly said that her second son was his. Their long affair had ended some time before when Tobias had maltreated her and broken her leg with a blow from a club. She said she no longer wanted him. Sam fought his 'brother' Tobias. He told me he used his fists (suggesting he gave him a fair go; boxing had been introduced by the missionaries as an alternative way of fighting) and as an experienced boxer came out of the fight the winner. The fight meant justice for the aggrieved husband and terminated the extramarital affair.

According to the local police constable, there had been no fist-fighting between Sam and Tobias, but they had fought each other with large clubs. When Nancy had her leg broken, 'Sam had given what he could' in the unequal fight. The policeman had locked them up in the cells of the local police station overnight.

Tobias often teased Sam. One night, for instance, he had come to the Social Club and told everybody he had given me the name of Sam's father, Tajamini. (Note that in the past Sam's father had fought Tobias' father over one of the latter's wives, a wife stolen from him by Sam's father.) Initially Nancy had adopted me as her 'son'. In being the first to name me, Tobias acted as my principal father (cf. Hart 1931). Indirectly he thus claimed Sam's wife by strategically giving Sam's father's name to me, overruling him. Sam response was to give me two other names. From then on he would always greet me saying, 'My son, my own son. Your daddy (*ringani*) here, [I made you] important, two names.' The friction between these 'brothers' was related to a contradiction in Tiwi social organisation: Ideally brothers had to cooperate, but there was also competition between them for the same category of potential spouses. Tobias could expect little support and protection from his elder 'brother' Sam because he had made him a cuckold and he was also held responsible for the death of their common clan brother, Jacob.

Friction also existed between Tobias and Karl Hansen, the white sailor who lived with Laura. Karl argued with Tobias in the club and was said to have accused his father-in-law, in Tiwi terms, of short-changing him. He was also annoyed about the financial consequences of Laura's supporting her father. It was Laura's responsibility to take care of her father, and to ensure he ate sufficiently well, because he was having a 'hard time' after the loss of his beloved wife. Tiwi perceived it as a real possibility that persons in deep grief would neglect themselves or do some harm to themselves, and in many cases this was true. Karl further raised strong doubts about Laura's fidelity. They repeatedly had ferocious fights. I witnessed Tobias warning him to stop maltreating his daughter, who according to Tobias, was pregnant. When a namesake of Karl died, Tobias turned up with a new name for him. From then on he was called Andy. This happened to be the name of a mentally disturbed man who had lived on Bathurst Island (see Pilling 1958: 62). Tobias told me that he thought Karl was 'no good in the head'; he did not trust him.

Another man distrusted by Tobias was Oscar Pamantari of the Fire clan. This younger 'brother' of Isaac (their fathers were brothers) was a potential spouse of Tobias' daughters too, and a former lover of his step-daughter Ruth (it was said Oscar had sired her first child). Oscar was obliged to assist Isaac in preventing any man from unjustly taking their 'daughter' Jasmine. What is more, like Tobias' clan, the Fire clan had long-established relations of exchange of marriage partners (and lovers) with the Mosquito clan and the Pandanus clan.

On the first of October 1988, Tobias' brother-in-law Jerome, the man who had given him his half-sister of the Pandanus clan and said he had not had a woman in return, became angry with him at the Social Club. Jeanette and I were sitting with Jerome and Nancy. Tobias joined us. When Tobias left for a moment to get beer, Jerome told us that Tobias could not be trusted. He said Tobias had killed his own brother by spearing him in the side (an extremely serious offence). He repeated this accusation several times and said Tobias' father was a killer. The previous night, according to Jerome, Tobias had been chasing after 'that old man', meaning Jerome's 'father' Isaac, with an axe (another wrong). Nancy in these circumstances had to speak up for her 'brother' Jerome (they had their mother's father in common): she added that she had tried to take the axe away from Tobias (without mentioning that earlier Isaac had run after him with an axe). She began yelling loudly at Tobias as he returned. Nancy said that Kalikalini had killed her 'fathers' (father's brothers). In other words, instead of directly voicing their disapproval of Tobias' affair with Jasmine (Nancy's rival), they brought up a number of grievances, suggesting Tobias was mischievous. Tobias did not respond to the allegations.

He continued his affair with Jasmine. Jeanette, my wife, acted as a go-between. Unfortunately, in time Tobias' girlfriend became more demanding. She started to ask for more and more money. Tobias hesitated to give in to her demands, because he knew it would cause more trouble. He reminded us of the scar on his forehead. The night of 8 October, after a renewed request for money, Tobias had Jasmine with him in his hut. The day after, he told us that he had had an unexpected visitor: 'That one lady came to me last night. She was with me. And then came her husband. They asked me for money.' Tobias refused to pay the money. Both Jasmine and Andrew went away angry. Tobias said it was difficult for him, particularly because she was 'a nice lady': 'It's a hard time for me. I don't want troubles. That lady, when she is with me she reminds me of my own lady [his deceased wife]. I'm having a hard time.'

Jasmine's husband, a man in his thirties, had to deal with an adulterer nearly twice his age. On the one hand, Tobias' seniority demanded that the deceived husband pay him due respect. On the other hand, the elder man had transgressed his rights as Jasmine's proper husband. The situation was an embarrassing one and one that did not occur under the gerontocratic system of the past when their roles vis-à-vis each other would have been reversed (Hart 1954: 257–8; Hart and Pilling 1960: 80). Andrew asked for compensation, a way of setting matters even and, thereby heading off a conflict. Tobias waved away the threats of the angry cuckold. He underlined his words with the performance of a few songs, composed by his ancestors, emphasising his fearlessness: 'You don't know how to fight anybody, you coward (*aldukuni*)!/You, nobody can hit me on the head with a club [making the sign of a hand on the head]./You only big nose (*untetukuni*)!' Tobias explained that it meant something like, 'You put yourself tough man but [in fact you are] nothing'. Another song about a fight between two men also elaborated on this theme: 'You really tough, you hit me on the head with big bar./I put a scar on myself [that is, I am the really tough man, *arini*], I can hit you, I can hit you, hit you a bar on the head./I kill you!' (Note that the iron bar at the scene of the killing was believed to be the weapon probably used against Tobias.) The following nights Tobias performed these provocative songs in the Social Club within hearing distance of his opponents. Within that week Jasmine's stepfather, Isaac, backed up by his relatives, returned a sung and performed warning directed at Tobias.

On 15 October, Tobias acted as a ritual worker in the final mortuary ritual for a man of the Pamantari family. At the instigation of Isaac, the killings at Matalau became the main theme of the post-funeral ritual. At the end of the rituals the workers, including Tobias, received their payment. They were symbolically paid with barbed spears (standing for money on this particular ritual occasion; another dreaming of the deceased, for instance flour, could likely have been chosen). The accompanying song series related how Kalikalini and Miputingkimi had speared the victims who had neglected Kitiruta's forewarning.[36] (They were also designated by their clan names; Kitiruta was a member of Andrew's clan.) Every time Isaac and his relatives gave out money, and made the dance movement of spearing the recipient, they called out: 'Matalaula!' (people from Matalau) and '*ninka!*' ('nothing', that is Kitiruta's warning that the visitors were ready to kill because their testicles were no longer visible, more freely translated as 'spears get in, get out!' or 'look out!'). The warning that people were prepared to kill fitted in with the ritual context but Tobias understood it also as a hidden message directed at himself.[37] He immediately fled to Milikapiti.

The next day, however, Tobias returned to Pularumpi. His worries in relation to the trouble, defined by him as 'woman problem', seemed to have increased and he appeared determined not to stay for long. We worked until late at night to get down on paper the translations of songs he had previously performed for me. Tobias insisted on this because, as he pointed out, there would be no other time since he would leave for Milikapiti any moment, possibly the following day. The songs dealt with – among other things – his father's banishment from Tikelaru and his sad longing for his country, fights over women and fights between brothers. He had also composed a song claiming Jasmine as his wife which he planned to perform in front of her husband in the next yam ritual at the end of the wet season: 'She loves me./You can do nothing about it!/If I want she can be my wife.'

For one reason or another Tobias prolonged his stay in Pularumpi. He dreamt a lot – always a sign for Tiwi that one is in trouble (cf. Pilling 1958: 111). He had one extraordinary dream about a mortuary ritual. Simon Pamantari was singing. Just before Tobias awoke they asked the question, 'What shall we do?' (Simon later would ask this question at the inquest following on a mortuary ritual after Tobias' violent death.) Tobias thought it had something to do with the Pamantari family. He went to tell Simon, Bill, Isaac and other men of this patrilineage, to which his girlfriend belonged, about it.

In the story of the killings at Matalau, recounted so many times in the weeks and days before Tobias' death, Kalikalini was characterised in negative terms. Whatever was brought up against Kalikalini filtered down to Tobias. The raconteurs favourably contrasted the remorseful character Miputingkimi to the unrepentant killer Kalikalini, aggressive and unscrupulous. In the current situation it reflected the tellers' moral disapproval of Kalikalini's son in contrast to Miputingkimi's 'son' (son's son's son), Andrew, the deceived husband.

In the days preceding his death, it was frequently put to Tobias that he had killed his own brother. In cases of a wrong committed within the clan, Tiwi matriclans, with the consent if not the participation of the senior representatives, ideally discipline their own members. The death of this elder brother of Tobias had posed a problem for his clan brothers in that they had been unable to retaliate without causing further loss of life in their own ranks. It meant, however, that Tobias (a clan brother) no longer could count on their support. On another level, he lacked support from the people from his country, Tikelaru, because his father had been expelled from this country (although the leader of this country later denied a total ban). Therefore, Tobias was 'nothing', according to Roger Imalu, his 'father' (Mosquito clan) and the leader of the sub-district or country in which the township was located.

Tobias' plans to leave Pularumpi were a theme of our conversations. On 18 October, in a mortuary ritual on Bathurst Island, he was a ritual worker again. Tobias sang: 'All the smoke comes in my eye and I dance.' Tobias had trouble with his eyes; he complained of problems he had had with his eyes in the past. During the next week Tobias wore sunglasses. His eyes hurt, he said, 'like needles' had penetrated them. Tobias' eye trouble might have had a deeper meaning. According to my informants it represented a feeling, *kumrupunari*, 'foggy, can't see properly' (from smoke, *kumuripini*). The song was performed by Tobias in *kulama* style. It seemed an allusion to the songs about the eyes in the yam ritual (*kulama*). Such a *pitjara* or eye-song was thought to be effective to 'see one's enemies better' in the future. Also, Yingkerlati was 'blind' and defenceless because he did not see his enemies. The next week Tobias went to see the doctor at the hospital in Nguiu on Bathurst Island. He went with a party from Pularumpi. Among them were his pregnant daughter and his girlfriend, who was accompanying her sister. His girlfriend's sister was flown to Darwin Hospital. Tobias' trip to Bathurst Island with Jasmine raised suspicions. This was usually the case when potential lovers were seen together (cf. Pilling 1958: 222). It convinced Tobias' already suspicious opponents that he did not intend to give up his affair with Jasmine. When they arrived at Nguiu, he should have said that he had gone to look for his son because he needed money. He came back too late to see the doctor. Tobias said that the doctor was too busy. Soon the story went around Pularumpi that he had been 'going around' again with Jasmine. The trip to Bathurst Island with Jasmine and others had aggravated his already precarious situation.

It is almost certain that Tobias felt the increasing tension in the community. He started to avoid Sam's camp, where before he often played cards. Gradually, he became more and more isolated. When we were sitting in the Social Club one night, Tobias invited me to Putjamirra Safari Camp. He worked there now and then as a guide. He said he wanted to show me the place before it closed down for the wet season on the last day of October. Immediately, Jerome and Nancy, who were sitting nearby, reacted furiously. Tobias was untrustworthy because he had killed his brother. They told me I was in Pularumpi to study Tiwi culture, not to go to that 'bloody tourist camp'. As he had done before, Tobias stood up and went somewhere else. Another day Jerome had found Tobias in our place when he paid us one of his daily visits. The two men did not exchange a word.

In the morning of 24 October, Tobias told me of a frightening experience. A cool breeze and noises at his window at the back of his hut had awoken him during the night. Then he had seen a *mopaditi* (spirit of the dead) that, as he said, 'was staring at me'. The spirit stood at his window. Tobias had never experienced this before. 'I feel funny', he told me, 'It makes me nerves [nervous]'. A vision of a *mopaditi*, painted up with white clay and holding a barbed spear, was a premonition of someone's death. It was usually a (grand)father or spouse of the dying person (Tobias' father called himself Mopaditi, or death devil). It impressed Tobias so much that he asked me to put in new bulbs on his verandah and in his one-room hut. Fires and electric lights (and mirrors, according to some) kept the spirits of the dead at bay.

On 28 October, Sam's elder brother Bruce came by dinghy from Nguiu to Pularumpi. I was told he wanted his share in the tax refund his son had received. First he visited Sam's camp. After a discussion with Sam he went to see Tobias at his hut. The two men had a talk. Bruce was carrying a gun. He said he wanted to shoot flying foxes in the mangroves on his way back to Bathurst Island and he left at two o'clock in the afternoon when the tide was right. When Bruce had gone, Tobias told me he wanted to tell me an 'old story' later on, but it was the last time I saw him alive. Tobias informed me that he had made a telephone call to Milikapiti. He planned to go there during the wet season that had just set in. His daughter Heather had spoken against this idea and protested. She resisted his coming. Tobias made the sign, moving his hand, that she was talking 'too much'. It was no good, he said, for a daughter to speak to her father that way.

In the afternoon, it was said that Andrew had to go to Bathurst Island because his father was very ill and was expected to die. The cattle truck that was being used to transport people and that would bring him to Paru, where he would cross the sea strait to Nguiu, left from Sam's place (the driver was a man of the Stone clan). Andrew would stay on Bathurst Island for the night.

At four o'clock that afternoon I did not go to the Social Club. I did not want to fuel the disagreements between Jerome, Sam and Nancy on the one hand, and Tobias on the other. Jeanette and I sensed an enormous tension. Tobias, however, went to the club. He drank beer and played cards. Nancy later told me that Tobias had given her, her sister Jessica, and Jasmine a jar of beer and kissed them to say goodbye. He would leave for Milikapiti, 'looking for another girlfriend', he had added jokingly.

The next morning Tobias' body was found in the Old Camp.

*   *   *

In sum, the information above shows a mounting crisis as a result of Tobias' continued infringements of what other people perceived as their rights. He did not terminate his affair with Jasmine, a woman promised and married to someone else, despite a fight with the deceived husband, physical threats by her stepfather, and cautions given in a ritual context. Grievances and smouldering old grudges against Tobias were aired in public. He neither accepted an offer to settle the matter by restitution nor did he move away to prevent further escalation of the conflict. We might safely assume that his opponents gradually began to consider him a stubborn wrongdoer.

Technically speaking, Tobias had a case, for his clan (Stone A) and the clan Jasmine had been promised to (Stone B) were one and the same. But this argument might have failed to find support because the amalgamation of the clans, declared by Wamiri who married off 'sisters' of both clans to Tobias' father, was not acknowledged by all. Besides, as a preferential rule of marriage, Jasmine ought to marry in her father's clan: this happened to be Tobias' clan. Jasmine was Tobias' *amoa*, that is, a potential spouse of second preference. She could be Tobias' wife in line with Tiwi rules of marriage if Andrew and Jasmine ended their marriage and the people with rights in an eventual future marriage of Jasmine (notably her stepfather and her senior clan and her actual brothers) agreed to it. When Isaac was fairly young, Tobias' father had given him a widowed maternal sister of the Mosquito clan as his first wife. Consequently, Tobias might have expected Isaac, his 'mother's brother' and 'full uncle', to give him a wife. The relationship of a man with his mother's brother could be one of tension because the mother's brother was supposed to help his sister's son to obtain a wife (Hart and Pilling 1960: 86). Such a marriage deal, however, seemed unlikely as long as Tobias' daughter was unwilling to take Isaac as her husband. Like Tobias, his daughters were strong and forceful personalities. It is doubtful if he could or even wanted to force them, within a very short span of time, to take partners they did not like (re-arrangements that of course created new problems).[38] Jasmine was still married to her promised husband. What is more, Andrew had an infant daughter who in theory (a not uncommon situation) could be bestowed on Isaac.

The stepfather had moral support from his 'son', Jerome Pamantari. As a senior man in Jasmine's clan, Jerome could exert influence on the future marriages of his clan sister Jasmine too. In trying to obtain Jasmine as his wife, Tobias violated the rules of reciprocity in the exchange of marriage partners between their respective clans. Jerome made clear he would not allow him to have another woman of his clan before he had met his old debt. Jerome argued that he should have a clan sister of Tobias' (whose actual sisters were all dead) also because he had organised post-funeral rituals for her father. This woman, a daughter of Anna Wangiti (of the Stone clan), was married to another man and had been promised to another man altogether, although Jerome disputed this for he had been told she was his 'promise'. Other informants (not of his clan but the Mosquito clan, the clan to whom the woman, according to them, had been promised) considered Jerome's aspirations to Anna's daughter too far-fetched. In between Tobias' death and the post-funeral rituals for him there was a long-lasting dispute, escalating into a series of serious fights, over this woman. Jerome had not been involved in this. During the final mortuary ritual at Tobias' grave he told me he had seen Tobias' spirit during the night taking this woman away from him, another way of saying he realised his chances of ever getting her had been lost.

Finally, Jasmine's brothers had the right to protect their sister as well. She had been given to Andrew in return for Sally, the wife of Jasmine's brother Dick. Dick, however, had sworn off drinking and violence. He was a devout Catholic (or a 'good boy', as Tiwi of other inclinations said with some pity). The night of the killing Jasmine's two living brothers and her adoptive brother, Roy Mornington, were in Pularumpi. Dick came back from a trip to Milikapiti about 9 pm. He had brought his younger brother Rodney with him from this other township on Melville Island.

In this clash of interests Tobias could not count on protection from his own clan (Stone clan) because he had had a hand in his own brother's death. We have seen that he was embroiled with his 'brother' Sam. The visit of Tobias' elder 'brother', Bruce Kerimerini, might have been a mere coincidence. Bruce, however, was the senior clan member who would ideally have to give his consent to an eventual punishment of his younger 'brother'. There had been precedents in the past that people who allegedly had committed a serious wrong were given up by their clan (see Pilling 1958). Three senior Tiwi men independently told me in relation to a concrete case that they would take the alleged offender aside and individually ask him point-blank what had happened. They described this as a procedure to establish the accuracy of the alle- gations.[39] Bruce might just as well have paid Tobias a social visit.

If we accept Nancy's statement that Tobias gave his (former) lovers a jar of beer then this must be seen as a serious provocation. Tiwi males hand beer, often 'take away' cans, to their lovers when they want to make an assignation. During the time of my fieldwork, giving beer openly to a potential and unsanctioned lover (or even to her mother, the prospec- tive mother-in-law) usually meant a fight in the end. More often than not these were ferocious fights and a wide range of weapons was used. In one case the gift of a single can of beer initiated trouble that went on for sev- eral months.

During the murder trial the forensic pathologist told the court he had found a card on Tobias' body, an ace of hearts folded into four. Assuming Tobias had the card on him before dropped to the ground under the mango tree, there might be two explanations. Tobias might have cheated in the card game or the card had been superfluous. Another explanation is that the card was a message. Incomplete sets of cards were mostly thrown away. Cards that could not be used in a particular game were usu- ally laid aside, and folding them would make the whole set useless for other card games. If he cheated, why would he take the trouble to fold the card into quarters and risk detection in doing so? Why was the folded card an ace of hearts? My hypothetical explanation is that this card was some kind of communication between lovers. In the past Tiwi people painted the palm of their hand when signalling, by waving and pointing, to a secret lover. At the end of the 1980s, they frequently used the expression 'number one' for things and persons that were desirable or important (for instance, 'number one boss', 'number one meat', or in the card play metaphor 'number one' for the winning card). The 'number one' in cards is, of course, the ace. In Pularumpi the symbol of the heart (probably the type of graffiti best represented) for a lover relationship is just as common as in the rest of Australia. An ace of hearts card folded into four, might be used by lovers (who already had a fixed meeting place) to pass a message secretly in a public place.

Jasmine's husband had gone to Bathurst Island in the afternoon. While her husband is away a woman's father may be assigned some of the husband's responsibility of protecting her (cf. Goodale 1971: 100). We will see that on the night of the killing, when Andrew was away, Tobias wanted to talk with Isaac about something but Isaac did not want to know about it.

The list above suggests that Tobias' prolonged affair with Jasmine, whom he claimed as his wife, had far-reaching consequences in relation to the interests of a large number of people. He was virtually surrounded by people whose interests in marriage politics were harmed by the prospect of letting Tobias claim Jasmine. Tobias was well aware of the trouble he was involved in. It seems he was prepared to take high risks. In the weeks preceding his death he was warned in various ways. Nevertheless, he continued to see Jasmine. The initial conflict, a case of adultery, had escalated.

A conventional Tiwi way of avoiding an escalation of a conflict or escaping punishment is to move away to somewhere else. Tobias often talked about leaving, adding that he did not want trouble, but he lingered in Pularumpi for the succeeding weeks. He persisted in his wrongdoing, as it was obviously perceived as such by his fellows. In such an extreme case, when all other means had failed to change the offender's behaviour, the ultimate punishment, killing, would likely occur without that person's close relatives intervening (Berndt and Berndt 1988: 344). Hart describes how before white intrusion Tiwi dealt with alleged adulterers in the majority of cases (Hart and Pilling 1960: 81–3, passim). If the accused had not run away, the (senior) man who has been cuckolded voiced his grievance against the offender at night in camp. Witnessed by a crowd of people, either in a large camp the next day or on another occasion, the deceived husband faced the man he accused of having seduced his wife in an open space. The accuser, his body painted with white clay and holding spears, performed an 'angry, loud harangue [that] went into minute detail, not only about the actual offence, but the whole life career of the defendant' (ibid.: 81). Following such a tirade he would throw spears at the accused man. When the latter, after much dodging of the spears, had finally been injured, the matter was settled. In exceptional cases where the accused refused to become a passive victim, a number of men would put him to death and his relatives withdrew their support or were restrained (ibid.: 80–3).

Sansom in his study of Aboriginal fringe dwellers in Darwin (1980) regards this Tiwi spear-throwing as a classic example of 'moral violence'. Features of the infliction of moral violence are a verbal proclamation of reasons, the presence of witnesses, complete surrender of the victim, and sanction by a group that takes responsibility as a whole. The execution of punitive acts of moral violence follows certain phases. First, the executioner works by repetitive shouting of charges, seeking consent from audience and victim. Then he or she may make several attacks, each again preceded by a proclamation of reasons. Finally this person restates the charges in order to have the consensus and commitment of those present reconfirmed. During the whole procedure there has to be general agreement about the defined nature of the staged punishment, and, therefore, the executioner monitors the audience for signs of disapproval. A failure to attune the performance to general acceptance may turn the punishment into an offence (Sansom 1980: chapter 4). As Sansom points out, 'What is guarded against is the allegation of individual culpability and, his representations accepted, the inflictor of moral violence is licensed by a collectivity which must then share wholly in the responsibility for his acts' (ibid.: 97). He distinguishes moral violence from interpersonal violence of varying degrees of seriousness, mainly indicated by the sort of weapons taken up. Fighting with the use of a lethal weapon such as a knife takes interpersonal violence to its utmost level of seriousness (ibid.: 105–6). In contrast to moral violence condoned by a group, interpersonal violence is considered a 'business' restricted to the antagonists directly involved.

A milder form of the physical expression of moral violence, recognised as another level by Sansom, is giving a beating (Tiwi say 'a good hiding'). It differs from the other level, the throwing of spears as described above, in that it is not effected with a lethal weapon (ibid.: 102–7). Sansom states, 'moral violence is violence that belongs not to the order of interpersonal struggle but is owned by a collectivity' (ibid.: 106).

The problem is that the distinction between interpersonal violence and moral violence is a mere typology that does not necessarily hold in all cases, let alone all Aboriginal societies. In the context of late twentieth-century Tiwi society, the execution of violence had increasingly been monopolised by the Australian nation state. Tiwi spear-throwing in cases of adultery with its possible fatalities could no longer be staged without the risk of intervention by white police (cf. Hart and Pilling 1960: 83). Even in the spear-throwing, termed a duel by Hart, the violence was interpersonal, although morally approved of by a group of people, in that personal grievances were acted upon (cf. Williams 1987: 94). The Tiwi institution of spear-throwing had ceased to exist, but not the right of the deceived husband to act with violence against the man who made him a cuckold. As we have seen, Jasmine's husband punished Tobias. This was not the end of the matter, however, because Tobias continued his affair with her and claimed her as his wife, which was a claim considered unjustified by her stepfather and others. Jasmine's stepfather was allowed to stop Tobias from taking her as his wife. Furthermore, Tobias' insistence on obtaining this woman of the Pandanus clan brought him into conflict with Jerome, who argued that Tobias violated the rules of reciprocity concerning the exchange of marriage partners between clans; a breach of a norm that sometimes led to a killing. Tiwi in addition could give licence to anyone, although with preference to the aggrieved persons, to kill a persistent wrongdoer. In other words, a culmination of wrongs might outlaw the wrongdoer.

In short, this is a case that contains elements of both interpersonal *and* moral violence. In a case where a larger group assents to a punishment beforehand, it may no longer be considered solely the 'business' of the antagonists proper, as in ordinary fights, but instead of a wider group who share responsibility for the punishment eventually executed. Several old grievances and grudges may be revitalised as an effective means to rally the support of a wider range of people to exert pressure on an alleged offender to adopt another attitude and, in case this does not have the desired effect, to create a basis for their consent with a subsequent punishment. Tobias must have realised the threat, judging from his worries. The initial reactions to the killing of some people from Pularumpi indicate that the homicide was regarded by them as justified. Many people knew about the trouble concerning the attempted wife-stealing and could read the signs (Tobias used to take Jasmine into his hut); it did not need to be spelt out at this stage. Instead, it was stated that Tobias' father was a killer and, consequently, Tobias had been killed himself, as well as that Tobias had 'killed' his elder brother (more or less in the same way). To put it slightly differently, a balance had been reached and, upon this, the trouble was finished as far as these people were concerned. The plunging of a 'spear' into the ground next to the corpse further indicated this. The proposal of a medical explanation of the cause of death might be seen as an accounting for the killing to achieve a similar effect. No one was to blame.

The response to Tobias' violent death differed considerably from the reaction to a killing that occurred in Milikapiti in November 1989. Then a planeload of police had to be flown in from Darwin to prevent an outraged crowd of the victim's relatives and clan members from lynching the man who had stabbed his wife to death. In the present case it seemed as if people were trying to cover up for the killer. Tiwi inferred that a fight had taken place. The man who closely inspected the area surrounding Tobias' hut later told me that he thought the victim had been caught up in a brawl.

The card players under a streetlight at a distance had recognised the raised voice of Isaac over the noise of barking and howling dogs. One card player, Alan Pamantari, had also identified the voice of Anna Wangiti, a woman of the Stone clan who lived in Sam's camp. Simon gave the following account to the local police constable who interrogated him the second night after the occurrence:

> I hear noise from that Old Camp just after I get to that card game; I heard men arguing and dogs barking. I think that because of the noise there was a fight there. I heard only one voice clear and that was Isaac. I just hear his voice; it was too far to understand what he say. The argument went for a long time. When I came home I look at the clock and it was 10 past 1; I could hear the argument until then. (Transcript of Proceedings, Supreme Court of the Northern Territory, SCC No. 186 of 1988, p. 340.)

Isaac made contradictory statements to the police. The morning Tobias' body had been found he told the constable: 'When I got back to the camp I went straight to sleep. . . . I didn't wake up in the night. I didn't hear any noises or fighting last night.' But the following Monday in a second statement, this time to a police detective, he said, 'We were arguing' (ibid.: 402–3). Several participants in the card game told me that they assumed a fight had been going on. The length and loudness of the argument are significant, pointing in the direction of the infliction of moral violence similar in style to the 'angry, loud harangue' cited above.

Suggestive of the violence being moral violence also are the apparent passivity of the victim, his partial undressing, and the consent of local people, demonstrated among other ways in their putting forward justifications and their reluctance to speak out. With regard to witnesses, besides the card players who overheard the voices, we can only say for sure there was one but there might have been more. Tobias had a reputation as a skilled fighter. Besides the little fractured knuckles of one hand, the post-mortem revealed no further evidence of any considerable physical fighting on Tobias' part. Sansom describes this feature of moral violence as follows: 'for the infliction to occur, the victim must first be totally awed into passivity. Not attempting to escape, not retaliating, not protesting with words, not assuming a posture that protects the body, the victim by comportment answers the demand that he consents to the infliction' (1980: 92). Earlier on I mentioned that Tobias' shirt was lying to one side and the upper part of his body was uncovered. The contexts

wherein he might have pulled off his shirt at night were subjection to ritualised punishment or a tryst. In two cases of ritual punishments I witnessed, men had to peel off their shirts before taking club beatings. In
ordinary fights I observed, the opponents did not necessarily undo their
shirts. As we will see, Nancy, Tobias' former lover, would turn the
removal of a shirt into a meaningful symbol in her performance as a
'widow' or *ambaru*, a ritual role depicting aggressiveness in a fight
and sexual jealousy, in the mortuary rituals for Tobias. This innovative
dance movement was adopted by Oscar Pamantari, a man who some
people claimed to have seen coming from the Old Camp on the night
of the killing, and his 'brother' Isaac Pamantari, who was Jasmine's
stepfather.

What at first sight seemed to have been an ordinary fight that got out of
hand or a drunken brawl might in fact have been an execution. In this
society where spear-throwing as a means of dealing publicly with a wrongdoer had been suppressed, there remained only interpersonal violence.

The people living in the Old Camp, except for Simon who did not
drink and who participated in the card game, all claimed they had been
drunk during the night of the killing. We have seen that sneak attackers
pretended not to 'know' their victim in their anger to seek revenge for
grievous bodily harm or a death.[40] Acknowledgement of the bonds of
kinship and friendship would make them feel 'sorry' for the intended
victim, which would make the execution of violence impossible. As
Myers points out for the Pintubi Aborigines of the Western Desert,
'drunkenness may provide the same excuse for violence: ignorance of
the identity of the other. Given this view of accountability, one can
understand the threats to get revenge "any time, when I am drunk"'
(1986a: 119). Tobias had been fatally stabbed in the chest, a clue that
with regard to Tiwi body symbolism indicates a possible identity for the
killer (cf. Brady and Palmer 1984). The painful chest or breast points
towards a relationship with the deceased of a 'mother' and 'mother's
brother' or, the other way round, of a 'child' [female speaking] or
'sister's child' (and the people heard yelling had these relationships with
Tobias). But I hasten to say that it is also one of the most effective places
to stab someone to death. When a death has occurred, Tiwi people move
away from the place because that location becomes taboo (*pukamani*). It
might have been a mere coincidence that on the night of the killing
Isaac shifted from his hut, three steps from where Tobias' dead body was
lying, to a building further away.

Although the people from Pularumpi at this stage seemed to consider
Tobias' violent death a justified homicide, it was perceived as unjustified,
and, therefore an offence by the deceased's children from the other Tiwi
townships. Simon, following in his grandfather Kitiruta's footsteps,

became the elder who enacted the conventional role of a peace-maker (*pongkini*). He attempted to organise an inquest. The question of who was guilty of the killing was a complicated one, for the answer was not necessarily limited to the actual killers (see also Elkin 1964: 119–21; Maddock 1988). The aggrieved (the dead man's children) found little support the first two days following the killing, but this could change in time. The intervention of police, homicide being an offence against the state, meant that the matter would be taken out of the hands of the Tiwi. Some Tiwi people, Simon Pamantari, for instance, opted to 'let police have it'. Simon, a man with conflicting loyalties, told me he feared a series of killings and counter-killings in raids (each retaliation had to be supported by about ten adults, he said) between the townships if the police did not intervene; the cost in lives would be too high. It was better to have white police take one person away. The people the Tiwi told me they suspected of having killed Tobias were all more or less closely related to the majority of people in Pularumpi. This web of interrelationships made them in a certain sense untouchable in this locality for, as Berndt points out, 'any accusation against or by one person inevitably involves others' (1965: 202–3). Those who were held responsible for the killing had wide kin support in the township, dominated by one patrilineal descent group and the three matriclans involved (Stone, Pandanus and Mosquito clans, and perhaps the Fire clan in addition). Direct accusations in such a situation of interdependencies equalled social suicide. Tobias' relatives in the other townships took his violent death as an offence. Adjustments had to be made so the offender could eventually be punished.

The police here can be viewed as an external agency that could pick out the killer(s), taking fingerprints and using a computer, Tiwi assumed. This would obviate Tiwi people having to discredit themselves in making accusations that would possibly affront many other people related to the accused (people who considered the homicide justified). The police in late twentieth-century Tiwi society have the function of punishing an offender from outside which may be compared with the former sneak attackers. For sneak attackers and white police alike the same term, *mantatawi* or 'dangerous persons', is used.

Over the weekend it had been uncertain if Tobias had indeed been killed, but from now it could no longer be denied.

*   *   *

On the Monday morning a number of people were sitting under a tree near the place where the mail could be collected. Someone called out. Nancy Kerimerini ran off and signed to me to come with her. 'It's Mike', she said, 'He has gone crank. Maybe he got the message, that it is murder.' This meant Tobias' death would become police business that had to be dealt with by the local people concerned. 'The message' that Tobias had been killed erased the possibility of a medical explanation.

Mike walked fast but stumbled along. Nancy's son seemed to be in a daze. After a while he started talking. He had a quick private conversation with his mother. Tobias had died at eleven o'clock on Friday night. The police had received the news from Darwin. Mike was on his way to the Old Camp. He had two large bandages stuck on his bare chest; on his head he wore a black cap on which R.I.P. had been written in white letters.

In Sam's camp he walked back and forth. Then he filled his cup with water at the tap and went on to the verandah where Tobias' daughter Laura and her white sailor friend Karl were sitting. He told them something. Karl's face flushed red, and he blinked his eyes repeatedly. Laura moved away. The sailor went to get his stainless steel skinning knife from of his hut and started sharpening it.

In the meantime, Sam and Nancy took turns at card playing. Maud had also come to the camp. She took over the cards while Nancy went to inform Sam, who had walked away, of what their son had learned at the police station. Nancy returned. We both noticed that Isaac had gone looking around in the bushes behind the Old Camp. When I asked her what he was doing she was silent at first and then she said, 'Maybe he is collecting wood'. Such a thing appeared rather odd to me, that he should be doing that in the green bushes at that time of the day.

Nancy decided we would go back to the shop. She said to her husband that she wanted to tell Pamela, her 'sister', something. As we walked under the mango trees we saw Isaac reappearing beside Tobias' hut looking hurriedly in all directions. The police van drove into the Old Camp. Nancy whispered that Isaac's hand was swollen, and I replied he should go to the clinic to have the health workers have a look at it.

Tobias' daughters had gone wild in Milikapiti, according to Simon when I visited him in his hut. 'They went mad there', he said, 'They won't have the funeral here but in Milikapiti. If the funeral would be here in Pularumpi they from Milikapiti won't come to the funeral. They will not be at the funeral.' The location of Tobias' grave would be an issue in several meetings of his close relatives.

Tobias' children and their close relatives had a meeting on the verandah of Maud's house. The local police had declared that no one was allowed in the Old Camp. In the meeting Tobias' daughter Heather was the most vocal. She argued that the coffin had to be followed by another coffin. Heather wanted to avenge her father's death. 'That fucking police can't do fucking anything', she said. 'We must kill that person who killed him, not let him go.' Then she seemed to have changed her mind, 'or let him in jail forever'. They kept guessing who could have been the 'murderer'. They wondered whose voice or voices the card players had heard and why they did not speak out. Two daughters were especially annoyed that the people of Pularumpi would not tell a thing. They decided they had to do it themselves, 'kill that fucking murderer'.

Their anger was directed towards the local police, the local people's lack of interest in other people's business, and the liberal policy of local authorities towards fights. Heather voiced it as follows,

> That fucking police here, can't do fucking anything. In big cities, Melbourne, Sydney, if there is someone killed they have the murderer the next day. Here in this little community they can't find him. [She continued] That bloody card players! If there is a fight in Milikapiti everyone is going to look there, kids and everyone. Here is somebody killed and they didn't even take a look. On that club there should be restriction of six can [cans of beer]. When there is a fight on the club no beer for two sessions or so. They should close that club.

'We must do it our own way', the vocal daughters kept saying, 'Do it the same way!'

Walter Kerimerini summarised what was at issue: it would have to be decided if the matter was to be given to 'whitefella law' or 'the Law'. Elderly people, relatives from Nguiu, would come to help them with that decision. He said that maybe Tobias' 'full uncle', Isaac Pamantari, had killed him. Tobias' children agreed that the funeral would take place at Milikapiti.

The two police detectives from the Darwin Criminal Investigation Branch (CIB) and the coroner arrived by special plane. They went into the Old Camp with the two local policemen. The heavy rain and lightning forced them to leave the scene, leaving one police officer behind to keep an eye on the site, which was cordoned off again.

When shortly afterwards a truck with elderly people from Nguiu drove into the township, police intervention was already an accomplished fact. The men – including Tobias' 'brothers', Steven Tampajani and Bruce Kerimerini, and his 'father', Jack Munuluka – came for a meeting with the bereaved children. They overruled the earlier decision of the latter that the funeral would be in Milikapiti. It was now decided that Tobias would be buried next to his father Kalikalini at a location near Paru, opposite Nguiu, on the Melville Island side of the Apsley Strait. In subsequent meetings the burial place that was decided on was changed under pressure from the respective localised groupings: from Pularumpi to Milikapiti, and from Milikapiti to a place not far from Nguiu.

Around 4.15 pm the police had organised a line search in the Old Camp in order to find 'the murder weapon'. Local people participated in this search. A crowd watched the search from the other side of the road. One of the detectives walked around in the Old Camp with Isaac, who was pointing at Tobias' hut. He was sent off to the police station. Then the detective came to the people who were watching. Before he could ask his question as to whether they had been playing cards, Roger and Bill said they did know anything about it. Other people did not respond either. Tobias' daughters became angry. 'Tell him, fucking cowards, tell him!', they yelled. The lingering tension increased. The daughters kept screaming at the other people. They blamed the people from Pularumpi for refusing to talk and urged them 'to give him [the killer] a hiding'. The search for the weapon in the Old Camp was without the desired result. Tobias had been stabbed to death, according to the police. Mike had already learned this early in the morning. The iron bar could no longer be considered the possible weapon. Those who participated in the search were told to look for a large knife. The type of knife described was in day-to-day use by the local people, mainly for eating and hunting, but at this point all the large knives seemed to have disappeared from the Old Camp. Only a very small knife with a broken blade had been found near Karl's hut.

As the local people were reluctant to speak, the detectives ordered the police tracker to bring the Tiwi people one by one to the police station, where they would be interrogated. The detectives, who did not keep a record of this, estimated that they saw between forty and fifty people in the course of two days. Some people who were held as 'possible suspects' were interrogated more than once. On Tuesday afternoon there was only one man left on the list of possible suspects. The detectives were under the impression that this man, Kevin Wangiti, was telling them lies. After he had located a knife at the beach and 'confessed' he had killed Tobias, he was charged with the murder. Kevin told me about the repetitive and lengthy interrogations: 'They didn't believe me. Kept telling, telling . . . pushing . . . "tell truth". You can't win.' For the detectives, the reliability of Kevin's 'confession' rested on the assumption that the locations of the stab wounds on Tobias' body, pointed out by him with a pen, could only be known to the murderer. These 'facts', however, were already common knowledge in the community, but the police did not know this.[41]

The Aboriginal police tracker had told people the details the day before in the Social Club, after the line search in the Old Camp. Although Tobias' daughters from Milikapiti and Nguiu at first were angry that the beer canteen had been opened, they nevertheless followed their elder sister Laura to the Social Club. There they were drinking beer with Karl, Sam, Nancy, Jeanette and me. Jasmine sat within earshot with her back turned to the family group; Jerome was also sitting nearby.

Nancy's son Mike entered the club and came to where we were sitting; he told us in great detail about the wounds that had been revealed by the post-mortem report. He showed how Tobias had been fatally stabbed in his chest. A knife had pierced his windpipe, said Mike; that was where the blood he had vomited came from. With his hands he pointed out the size of the 'Rambo-knife', the assumed 'murder weapon', the police were looking for. A salient detail was that Mike also spoke about a stab wound in Tobias' back. Kevin confessed to this 'fact' that had been made public knowledge. The results of the autopsy, however, showed no such wound.

*   *   *

Just after sunset, the wailing resumed. About 7.15 pm, Nancy performed a mourning song, walking back and forward, in front of Maud's house: 'When me, I did not care before when I was young and Kalikalini came. I did not care when one man said "nothing" (*ninka*) but Kalikalini got his spears and killed us.' She took the side of her father's brothers and referred to the killings at Matalau by Tobias' father. Jerome, who came from the Social Club, called out to Jeanette and me, signalling that he had seen and heard something. 'It wasn't the old man. It wasn't Isaac who killed the old man.' Nancy confirmed what Jerome said. It had been a young man who lived in the Old Camp. 'Tomorrow we do it!' he told us. 'We kill that man, the person who killed the old man.' He wanted me to return his present, a weapon, a sharp fighting stick (club) he had made himself. 'Tomorrow we'll do it', he added.

Tobias' bereaved family stayed in Maud's house, as people were not allowed in the Old Camp. Inside the house, Sam was in deep grief. Heather had her hand in his; she was quiet, her head hung down. Sam cried. Laura, sitting bare-breasted, wailed loudly while covering her eyes with a piece of cloth. Jerome said he knew someone had been put in police custody. The next day he would kill that man. He said he would dress himself as a woman and wear a petticoat because he was the dead man's brother-in-law. In other words, he would replace his late sister Kate and retaliate for her husband's death. At the time (the morning Tobias' body had been found) we did not do it, he said, but now we will do it.

In grief and anger, this group from Pularumpi stressed the ties that bound them to Tobias' bereaved children, the aggrieved party. Maud's husband Lester, for instance, bent over Sam and Tobias' daughters. He hit himself on the head with a large knife. Heather then took the knife away and put it behind her; with this she accepted his sorrow and their mutual relationship. Nancy sang once again. She said she was singing for the children, that they would take care of Sam when they did it that night: 'They did it once, they might do it again.' Then she wailed. 'He was my lover', Nancy said. Sam straightened up. He made the sign of a baby with his hands in front of him. 'My little brother, why he?' he said to me. Sam sat down and wailed.

This mourning session shows the 'juggling of identities' (D. Rose 1992: 153–64) that took place in adjustment to the altered situation. (Jerome had first assured his 'father' Isaac 'didn't do it'.) In their grief they recognised their shared identities with the deceased and his children. Heather from Milikapiti, who had talked back to her father when just before his death he wanted to flee to her, acted as the spokesperson for the bereaved children. She could do so because she had less strong ties in the local community than her elder sister Laura. She also was a more vocal person, like her late father (her nickname was The Noise). Her anger was directed outward, to other people, and perhaps distracted people's attention from her own refusal to help her father earlier when he was in serious trouble. The deceased children's close relatives in Pularumpi now stressed their identification with them. Jerome proposed retaliation, replacing his sister, the bereaved children's mother. The attention of the bereaved children was directed to Sam, Tobias' 'brother' and therefore the children's 'father'. Nancy presented him as their surviving father who was in danger of being killed as well. This senior 'father' had to be protected by them. She herself stressed she had been Tobias' lover and thus was the children's 'mother' in more than one sense. In other words, Jerome, Sam and Nancy, who had been in conflict with Tobias, now stressed how closely they identified with him. Instead of being Tobias' disgruntled brother-in-law, a husband deceived by him, and an ex-lover who had been jealous and maltreated, these people emphasised their shared bereavement. They placed themselves in the position of Tobias' children's parents to be protected and followed instead of being suspect and prosecuted. In unison with these children they proposed retaliation, lending them moral support. The bereaved children readily accepted the strengthening of their ranks, and deep grief temporarily replaced their anger.

The next day the community was still in a state of tension. The people who belonged to Sam's camp negotiated the story they would tell the police. To put it briefly, they had come home drunk from the beer canteen and that was all they knew. After a person had been interrogated at the police station, the person discussed with the others what had been said.

After sunset the wailing resumed. Heather went around in the township screaming continuously, 'We do it the same way!' Her threats illustrated that her anger had not diminished; the fact that the case was in the hands of the police did not satisfy her.

At 10 pm Kevin Wangiti was officially arrested. The police came to Maud Calley, the health worker, to get the medication for his high blood pressure. From then on, Tiwi people from Pularumpi expressed opinions that they did not believe he actually had committed the crime he had been charged with. That night Martha Arapi, Kalikalini's only surviving wife, dreamt that Kevin had not killed Tobias. When Tobias' corpse was released the next day he was to be buried next to his father.

CHAPTER 5

The Funeral Rituals

Ordinary life in Pularumpi came to a standstill on 3 November 1988. The shop, the school, and the council offices were closed. The people from Pularumpi and Milikapiti went to Pawularitarra by truck (see map 1). To get to Pawularitarra the people from Nguiu just had to cross the Apsley Strait in their dinghies. They would, together with most of Tobias' children, accompany the coffin that had been flown into Nguiu on Bathurst Island.

Tobias would be buried at Pawularitarra on Melville Island next to Kalikalini. Pawularitarra was an abandoned bush camp where Tiwi people lived until the early 1970s. Tin shacks and an empty well were all that remained of the site. Kalikalini's grave was located at the far end of an open space behind the former camp. Kalikalini had refused a Roman Catholic funeral and, therefore, he had been buried out in the bush. In the late twentieth century Catholic funerals were taken for granted, but the 'pagan' mortuary rituals were no longer suppressed. Tiwi burial ceremonies were interspersed with Catholic liturgy conducted by a priest. For Tobias, a funeral mass would be said in the open air at Nguiu and then the coffin would be brought to Pawularitarra, where Tiwi would proceed with their funeral rituals. Tobias' burial drew hundreds of people; this was not only because of his seniority and his wide-spread social networks in all three townships, but also because of the manner of his death.

The mortuary rituals, or *pukamani*, are at the core of Tiwi cultural life, as death is, according to Hart, 'the natural phenomenon around which the Tiwi had woven their most elaborate web of ritual' (Hart and Pilling 1960: 90).[42] In the late twentieth century the mortuary rituals and the seasonal yam ritual, or *kulama*, are the two major rites of passage (cf. Van Gennep 1960) still performed. Whereas involvement in the latter has

89

become a concern of a limited group of people, almost everyone partici-
pates in the mortuary rituals at one time or another.

For analytical purposes I will make a distinction between the funeral
rituals (including the cleansing rituals around the time of the burial)
and the post-funeral rituals. The post-funeral rituals consist of a series of
smaller rituals and conclude with an elaborate ritual called *iloti*. (These
rituals will be further discussed in chapter 8.)

The concept of *pukamani* not only refers to the mortuary rituals in
general but also to all which or who are subjected to behavioural restrictions or taboos.[43] Anyone closely related to and anything closely associated with a recently deceased person (objects, persons, dogs, places, and
names) become *pukamani*. To put it another way, whatever might be subject to the attention of the new spirit of the dead will be *pukamani*.

I first present a general account of the funeral rituals mainly based on
my observations of two dozen Tiwi burials over a period of fourteen
months in 1988–89, as well as comments of Tiwi people on those rituals.[44]
Then I describe Tobias' funeral and a number of cleansing rituals held
not long after the burial. The rituals for Tobias were more elaborated
than those in other cases: following his violent death his spirit had to be
neutralised, and relationships disrupted by the killing had to be renegotiated or restored. Police were present at the burial in order to
prevent any outbreak of violence. Plans for eventual punishment of the
killer(s) were postponed. There was too much uncertainty.

*   *   *

Deaths were often anticipated, both by the dying and their close relatives. Premonitions of death included unsuccessful hunting trips in the
country of the dying, remarkable sights or the sounds of birds and animals often representing a dreaming of the dying, a feeling in the appropriate parts of the body (for example, leg, shoulder, breast) indicating
the relationship with the person who will die, visions of spirits of the
dead just after sunset or at dawn in the neighbourhood of the very ill,
visions of spirits of the dead and the sound of a whistle in the vicinity of
(almost) fatal motor vehicle accidents, and other liminal occurrences
such as a black bitumen road-like band against a clear sky and rain
falling while the sun was shining.

People gave light, digestible bush and sea foods – such as mangrove
worms, stingray meat, and a mash of prepared cycad fruits – to very ill
persons to help them to regain their strength. When this failed, the sick
often indicated they no longer wished to eat and demanded close relatives come. People did all they could to put the very sick or dying at ease,
giving their attention and holding, massaging and refreshing the body

of the person in question. Devout Catholics would join together at the deathbed and say their rosaries. Moreover, many people came to visit the dying, and they would wail and hit themselves. An elderly woman who was about to die commented, 'They all came to say lovely sorry for me'. Sometimes relatives from the other townships would camp in the vicinity to await a death.

The very ill made it clear to the people present when their time had come and gave directions with regard to the mortuary rituals (e.g., the place of burial) if they had not already had done so. At the deathbed of an old man I was told the spirits of his dead father and spouses had come to take him with them. People monitored the weakening of his pulse going up along his arm. He had not completely ceased breathing when people began wailing and hitting themselves. I then was told that his spirit had gone. A friend of the deceased performed a mourning song telling the new spirit to move away and to follow his father to the latter's burial place.

The emotions of the bystanders at death were very intense. The bereaved called out things like, 'Why did you leave me alone?', 'I want my baby back!' and 'How beautiful you were!'; or used the kinship term of address in their wailing. People would hit themselves but were restrained by others from doing themselves harm; they tried to injure those parts of the body which identified their relationship with the deceased. During this loud wailing the immediate family of the deceased faced the dead person, others 'said sorry', wailing and hitting themselves, in front of the immediate family of the deceased (cf. Goodale 1971: 249). The wailers sometimes also interwove onomatopoeic sounds of a dreaming they shared with the deceased (e.g., the sound of a dingo, pelican, pig or jungle fowl) in their expressions of grief. The focused emotional expressions had a strong relational quality, identifying the mourners.

A special mortuary kinship terminology was used for different categories of relatives of the deceased. These terms indicated their relationship to the deceased and specific roles in the ritual drama. Appendix 1 lists the mortuary kinship terms used by my key informants. These terms are more or less in accordance with those recorded by Brandl (1971) and Grau (1983). Goodale (1971) first noted the existence of this special terminology. Brandl, following Needham in part, calls the mortuary kinship terms 'bereavement status-terms' (1971: 233). Bereavement status might be accepted as an appropriate expression indeed, for every mortuary kinship term denotes a specific position of being bereaved of a relative (comparable with 'widow', 'widower' and 'orphan' in English) that in addition guides these people's behaviour. With regard to bereavement status, it was the symbolic relationship to the deceased (and vice versa) that mattered and therefore it could encompass a gender relationship irrespective of the sex of the persons involved, both dead and alive. Furthermore, a number of bereavement statuses were connected with a specific body symbolism. The Tiwi, in addition, had adopted the English terms 'boss' for the person who directed a ritual and 'workers' for the people who provided services in relation to the mortuary rituals.

The close relatives of the deceased were dependent on the workers, (potential) spouses of actual and classificatory siblings of the deceased, because they themselves were subjected to a number of taboos (cf. Hart and Pilling 1960: 91–3). As Goodale points out, maintaining rigid behavioural restrictions after a death and for how long depended on: '(1) the degree of relationship to the deceased modified by the amount of actual contact; (2) relative age among those whose relationship to the deceased is otherwise equal; and (3) absolute age' (1971: 262). Close kin who had daily contacts with the deceased became *pukamani* immediately. The eldest in every category of person (mortuary kinship, see below) related to the deceased also directly became *pukamani*, while this status first applied to younger people at the start of the post-funeral rituals. The very young and very old did not have to follow the behavioural restrictions (ibid.).

A strict observance of *pukamani* rules related to death, according to my informants, demanded of the person in question: remaining undressed except for a skirt or loincloth but applying bodily paint and wearing ritual ornaments; not washing; abstaining from sexual intercourse; refraining from the consumption of food foraged by oneself; not coming near the shop; not playing cards; not using one's own hands in eating, drinking, and smoking; not carrying one's own food and drink; not leaving one's camp at night; restricting one's movements to an area not previously frequented by the deceased, with the exemption of mortuary ritual occasions (and then special precautions had to be taken).

In the late twentieth century strict observance of all these rules and taboos in relation to being *pukamani* was rather exceptional and appeared to be incompatible with the contemporary way of life of most Tiwi people. People who were fed and given drink by others, had their bodies elaborately painted with ochre, and who wore a number of ritual ornaments were said to be 'really *pukamani*'. Cleansing rituals with smoke and water partially released people from the state of *pukamani*, only to be adopted during the mortuary rituals. The degree and length of time people actually followed the ideal rules seemed to have become a measure of their expression of grief.

I found no evidence that Tiwi mortuary rituals varied depending on the sex of the deceased. Variation did, however, depend on such factors as age (or better, seniority) and the social position of the deceased (cf. Van Gennep 1960: 141). Another relevant factor was the type of death (Hertz 1960: 80); untimely and violent deaths were followed by relatively more elaborate rituals which drew a larger attendance. Furthermore, the intentions of the bereaved kin, their numerical strength and ability to pay, support of others and outstanding obligations, and the personalities, skills and creativity of personnel and the like were important.

Some people had to be asked as workers to perform a number of burial tasks. These people preferably belonged to the category of *ambaruwi* (see appendix 1), with the exemption of the deceased's actual spouse. They were asked by close relatives of the deceased fairly soon after the death. Only the workers were allowed to handle and dispose of the corpse. After the burial they would be paid in cash by the people who asked them to carry out the tasks. Close relatives of the deceased gave them cans of beer at the Social Club.

The loud wailing of the people present at the death alerted other people in the township. These people came to the place of death to view the deceased for the last time and they wailed as well. Soon after the death the dead body was moved, laid out, and wrapped in a sheet (sometimes the limbs were tied together) by the workers.[45] With this a first step was taken in physically separating the deceased from the world of the living. The death was announced in the other townships by a telephone call. The message was then brought to the bereaved relatives. People embraced each other and cried loudly. Very close relatives of the deceased came directly and with considerable speed. On arrival they hit themselves, wailed, and performed mourning songs. The others would come for the funeral. The rule of thumb was that when people died before 11 am, they would be buried the same day; otherwise, if outside agencies did not intervene, they would be buried the next day.

The ritual workers measured the corpse and started to make a coffin (in Nguiu and Milikapiti the local council provided the coffin). When the deceased had to be buried the next day close relatives stayed with the corpse. They performed mourning songs. A fire was kept burning or electric light left on to keep the spirits of the dead away. Some people also put a mirror beside them. Several close relatives threw white clay over their bodies.

Early in the morning the workers placed the corpse on a bed frame in an open space in camp. This space would become a dancing ground and was cleared by the workers. The close relatives, painted up and wearing ritual ornaments, sat near the corpse waiting for people to come for the funeral. A few male ritual workers went to the graveyard and dug the grave.

New arrivals went up to the dead body. They faced it, wailed and hit themselves (frequently on those parts of the body denoting their relationship to the deceased person). Those people who were more closely related to the newly bereaved directly approached them and did the same. Thus the wailing, 'saying sorry', was directed either to the dead person or the bereaved. If necessary the 'boss' of the ceremony, preferably a male of the *unantawi* (*pulanga*) bereavement status, gave directions and told those present where the person in question would be buried. He was assisted by *mutuni*. (A male *mutuni* could take the lead when no *unantawi* (*pulanga*) was available.) The deceased's will, if known, was usually respected. Most of the people were buried in the Catholic graveyards but some were buried at ancestral burial places in the bush or at the beach. The place where someone was to be buried was significant, for the patrilineal descendants could more likely claim the area as their country and for them it would later on be a focal point in mortuary ritual.[46] Two types of mourning songs could be performed throughout and outside the ceremonies, not connected with their structure in particular. These were *ambaru*-songs by the *ambaruwi* (including the actual widow or widower) and *mamanakuni*-songs by other (matrilineal and patrilineal) relatives such as *unantawi*, *mutuni*, and *mamurapi* (see appendix 1). When sufficient numbers of people were present, a dance and song ceremony (*yoi*) could start. I was told that it was not a proper ceremony because there was still a 'dead body around'.

Appendix 2 lists the various roles involved in the ritual drama (see also Grau 1983). The order of presentation is consistent with the Pularumpi-biased sequence in a full-scale dance and song ceremony (*yoi*). The people from Pularumpi said only the patrilineal relatives and *ambaruwi* were allowed to dance in the burial ceremonies. Matrilineal relatives such as the *paputawi* were considered 'too close'. This often led to conflicts with people from the other townships who were of a different opinion (cf. Grau 1983: 116–7). They did not, however, in all cases practise what they preached. Sometimes an elder from Pularumpi 'went crook' (got annoyed) when the dancing in other townships commenced in what the Pularumpians conceived of as the wrong order. According to them the *mamurapi* (*turah*) had to start with the dancing and not the *unantawi* (*pulanga*). The 'right' order then was: *mamurapi* (*turah*), eventually *kerimerika* and *kiakiei*, *unantawi* (*pulanga*), *mutuni*, and *ambaruwi* (see appendix 1 and 2). The actual widow or widower always came last.

Unantawi (male *unantawi*, female *unantaka*) is a generic term for the *unantawi* (*pulanga*), *mamurapi*, *kerimirika*, and *kiakiei*, to be distinguished from the more specific mortuary kinship terms *unantawi* (*pulanga*) and *unantawi* (*pularti*). The patrilineal *unantawi* consisted of the categories of bereaved people mentioned who could perform separately, jointly or as one body. Brandl states that when acting together they dance with (imaginary) spears and are designated as 'the *turaghawila*, or war-making, revenge party' (1971: 443). My informants said they represented not only sneak attackers (*kwampi*) but also spirit children (*pupaputuwi*), little spirits who were supposed to spear their prospective father (or his father, sister or father's sister) in his dreams, indicating a spiritual conception. What we have here is a double symbolism of death and rebirth, a transition mediated by a metaphorical killing. The performers, sometimes using real spears, concluded their dance with a stylised movement denoting the spearing while they exclaimed '*turah*'. One informant described this as 'their second birth in dancing'. The dance may consist of a few stylised movements but at times it may also be elaborated in a kind of narrative dance. The dance might depict historical events in which sneak attackers figured.[47]

The re-enactment of historical events as perceived by the performers, events they could relate to, would be employed to give meaning to a current situation. It might be that their representation of sneak attackers helped the bereaved relatives in their appropriate positions to avenge a death, to express their anger following the death of a patrilineal relative. The symbolic killing in the dances of the patrilineal *unantawi*, as an image of an abrupt and radical breaking of ties, enabled on the symbolic level the ritual separation of the deceased from the living. It is interesting to see how Tiwi in Tobias' case dealt with an actual killing ('reality') merged with the conventional theme of killing ('fiction') in the rituals. In this way possibilities could be explored. The mortuary rituals following his death enabled reflections on his life, his social and cosmological identities, and the killing.

In the ritual drama, given its purpose to direct the spirit of the dead from the world of the living to the world of the dead, the people of different bereavement status all play a role in the remembrance and dissolution of a particular metaphorical relationship with the deceased. 'Sibling' units – which are more elemental in Aboriginal kinship systems than the wife–husband relationship (cf. Williams 1981) – men and women alike, can be seen to enact male *and* female gender roles. It all depends on the symbolic relationship of a certain category of bereaved people, people of the same bereavement status to the deceased.[48] The point I wish to make is that relationships between categories of people and the deceased are emphasised. Tobias Arapi gave explanatory expressions for his actual and classificatory relationships to different clans, such as 'call me mother' and 'call me father'. Spiritual and physical conception, child care, pregnancy and childbirth, nurturing and being nurtured, and sexuality as well as body symbolism focus on a particular relationship with the deceased. In this way the deceased and the bereaved are symbolically reconstituted.

Besides the bereavement status, the performers stress cosmological relationships in ritual calls of personal and place names, a focus on ancestral burial and dreaming places. They denote their identities or put forward identity claims in patrilineal ancestor-choreographed dances or dreaming dances, or both. These dances might be performed apart from the mortuary kinship dances or in combination, one after the other or merged.

In late twentieth-century Tiwi society only a limited group of (mainly elderly) people were able to compose the ceremonial songs. Consequently, these people often had to perform songs for other categories of bereaved as well. The procedure in most mortuary ritual dancing events was as follows: after the men had indicated the beginning of the ceremony with a long call, a man at the edge of the ceremonial ring (*milimika*) would perform a song. The other men picked up the words of the song and repeated these, beating time with a hand against the buttocks, with sticks, or on a piece of corrugated iron.[49] Then the singer or the category of people he had composed the song for would dance. The dance ended with a particular dance movement and all the men called '*weya*' ('finished'). Men and women danced separately in the dance groups of a bereavement status. The dancers might be supported by befriended or related *ambaruwi* dancing at the edge of the ceremonial ground. The dances of the central performers were their dreaming dances passed down along patrilines, patrilineal ancestor-choreographed dances, and (more rarely) their own creations or innovations. These dances also included mortuary kinship dances to which people also could give their own individual twists and employ particular styles, choreographies and dance movements belonging to their patrilineage in a broad sense. As I have said, dances of both types were often performed one after the other or combined. At the conclusion of their dancing, these performers often wailed near the deceased (falling down next to the corpse or at the grave mound) or a substitute (e.g., the mortuary poles in the final ritual). How many dancers and dance groups there were of a particular bereavement status depended on the personnel available and willing to dance.[50] Sometimes a category of bereaved was not represented as a result of a shortage of people. The end of the ritual dance event would be marked with a long (mosquito or honey bee) call again.

A Catholic mass would be said either before the ceremony around the corpse or following it. Some ritual workers would bring the coffin. The climax in the wailing came when they put the dead body in the coffin and nailed the lid on it. The bereaved had to be torn away from the coffin. Before it was closed, the surviving spouse had physical contact with the deceased for the last time. A widower would lie on top of the body of his wife. I also witnessed a widow stepping into the coffin of her deceased husband. She bent her knees, lifted her skirt above his head and brushed it over his face.[51] I was told that in the past one of the wives used to do that. People all gathered close together around the coffin and wailed loudly as mourning songs were performed.

Then the coffin was put in the back of a truck and, accompanied by the close family and a few ritual workers, driven to the graveyard. The arrival of the deceased at the burial place would be announced to spirits of the dead. A bereaved daughter, for instance, called out, 'Daddy, mummy is coming!' The other people followed the truck bearing the coffin to the graveyard. People who had missed an earlier funeral went to other grave mounds, cried for the previously deceased and eventually performed a mourning song. Others sat down at the graves of close relatives, cleared them, and cried. A priest would bless the newly made open grave. While the ritual workers scraped and dug out a last bit of sand from the hole, the immediate family often embraced the coffin. Again, they had to be torn away. From the moment the coffin was lowered into the grave until the grave mound had been made there was more intense wailing. In the interim, people bent over into the grave frequently had to be taken away. Several times I saw family members drop into the grave, sometimes trying to dig out the deceased. A widower jumped into the grave and burned his pubic hair with a lighter.[52] People facing the grave wailed, and wailed, and, of course, mourning songs were performed. Kinship terms of address (e.g., *ilimaneiii!* for *ilimani*, 'mother's brother') were called out in wailing and sometimes the sounds of a dreaming (e.g., a pig's grunt) were reproduced. Personal belongings could be buried with the deceased. When the grave mound had been made, a sapling was placed at each end of the grave. At one end also a wooden cross was placed, painted white, with the name of the deceased written on it; the name in writing was not taboo.

Saying the Tiwi names and the English first name of the deceased and all Aboriginal names given by the deceased became taboo, not directly after death, as one might assume, but after the grave mound had been made. Namesakes of the deceased adopted another name. I observed in a number of cases that a close relative of the deceased called out the Aboriginal names of the dead person at the freshly made grave, and after that no one was allowed to use them, 'not even when drunken', until the name taboo had been released. Sometimes these names were already distributed beforehand to patrilineal (actual and classificatory) descendants of the deceased. When someone accidentally mentioned a tabooed name that person would strike themselves, whereafter it would be accepted it had not been done deliberately. Such a name should certainly not be used within hearing of close relatives of the deceased, this with regard to their feelings.

It depended on the close relatives of the deceased how long it would take to have the taboo on a name lifted. The lifting of a name taboo often coincided with the transmission of the name to a patrilineal (actual and classificatory) descendant of the deceased, but this could not happen before all the mortuary rituals had been accomplished. Then the consent of consanguines would be needed either to use the name again, to be mentioned in songs after the death of a paternal half-sibling of a different clan instead of that person's name, or to donate the name to a child or newborn baby, often but not always during the *kulama* ceremony. The right to name persons is vested in the mother's husband (cf. Hart 1931; Hart and Pilling 1960) and might be extended to patri-lineal relatives of ascending generations of the person to be named, both actual and classificatory. These persons might donate their own (often poetic) Tiwi names during their lifetime, give new names or names of the dead.

I found that besides the names of the deceased, also their voices on tape and photographs and videotapes depicting them would become *pukamani*. Cassette tapes would be erased or put away, and videotapes and photographs of the deceased would not be shown for some consid-erable time. People reacted to the voices on tape and images in the photos as if they were dealing with a living person (greeting, talking, touching, and so forth). Photos of the deceased were sometimes used in the mortuary rituals; this appeared to be a recent innovation. Another innovation was the occasional wearing of plain fabrics by the bereaved to distinguish dancing groups (like yellow, white, red, and blue) and black skirts for 'widows'. This innovation originated in Nguiu, where fab-rics were available from a silk-screen printing workshop. Clothing and fabric materials with multicoloured prints designed by Tiwi people were very popular all over the islands and frequently were used in mortuary rituals for loincloths, skirts, and ritual payments. One group of female dancers even had red skirts with a buffalo print, representing their patri-lineal group performing the buffalo dance. Goodale writes that in 1954 the use of a coffin and flowers in one burial were introduced (1971: 250). When there were (artificial) flowers in Tiwi burials at the end of the 1980s, these had more often than not been given by outsiders. But things that in one way or another commemorated the deceased, a foot-ball shirt for instance, could be placed on top of the grave mound.

When the grave mound had been made, both the mound and a dan-cing ground surrounding it were cleared of all hard objects and raked over by the ritual workers. A dance and song ceremony (*yoi*) similar to the one around the corpse was then performed. At the conclusion of their particular dance performance the bereaved fell onto the mound and wailed. Some people covered their faces with dirt from the grave. Young men ended their last dance by doing a somersault over the grave mound and bouncing on their backs. People would also hit themselves with any object available and had to be restrained by other, or closer, bereaved.[53] Within the framework of the mortuary rituals the mourners, with other people at hand to prevent them from doing serious harm to themselves, could safely express their grief.

The surviving spouse danced last. This person had had the most intimate contact with the deceased and, therefore, could be expected to be haunted by the spirit of the dead. The focus on the performer's genitalia and on intercourse as experienced and enjoyed when both were alive seemed to be designed in this role to give satisfaction to the deceased's spirit, to bemoan the loss of the couple's physical intimacy, and the breaking of ties.

A widow sat with her legs pulled up on the grave mound – a position described to me as a common one for intercourse – while she performed a mourning song. The surrounding people wailed. Two elderly female informants complained to me that some, mainly younger people were crying too early; they ought, as always happened in the past, to listen 'what they talk together when husband and wife'. A male elder formulated it in a similar way: one should 'first listen then cry', he said. Tiwi rituals were also times of 'ceremonial truce' (Goodale 1971: 188) or, as Turner would have it, times for redress (1974: 41). The widower who let his dead wife tell him to save some of his pubic hair for his second wife commemorated the fact that his wife was always jealous when he had other wives or lovers and frequently fought them until these women left him. Although the ritual performances fit in with established conventions there was room for the performers' personal experiences to become ritualised (cf. Kapferer 1986). The distancing in the mourning songs in the form of a dialogue with the deceased enabled a reflection on personal experiences. I will cite one other example to illustrate this point. A woman had been raped while her husband, a heavy drinker, was said to be 'going around' with other women. When he was drunk he accused her of having provoked the rape herself. After this, she committed suicide. During the burial ceremony the husband, among others, was accused by his wife's close relatives of being responsible for her death. His mother defended him, singing: 'When my son drank beer he didn't give her a hard time!' The widower's mourning song, however, consisted of an admission of guilt: (Dead woman saying) 'Why you went to see all those women?/You mucked [up] your own wife./Just go, and show your cock to every woman!'

On two occasions I saw a widower drop his loincloth (naga) at his wife's grave, a gesture associated with having sex. One widower and ceremonial leader had worn his loincloth, later left behind on his wife's grave, in every ritual he attended for more than a decade. It might seem a trivial gesture but I do not believe the widower, who I came to know well, saw it in that way: the loincloth reminded him and others of all those previous occasions and was charged with emotions. The loincloth left on the grave in addition might be seen as a symbol of death, implying the breaking up of a relationship, like the deceased's clothes that would be buried or destroyed. I recorded a number of cases of men burning the clothes of wives or lovers who either had left them or were considered unfaithful, and I was told it meant they were 'finished' with the person concerned.[54] According to local belief, the destruction of someone's clothes equalled killing that person (cf. Johnson 1980), hence the exchange of clothes was taken as a sign of friendship and trust. In pre-contact times Tiwi went naked, and bereaved spouses had to be satisfied with burning pubic hair. Goodale reports a case of a widower burning 'his wife's pubic hair as well as his own' while she was told 'that in the old days, the *ambaru* [widower or widow] used to copulate with the deceased in the grave' (1971: 268). Depilation, the cutting or burning off of body hair, marks a transition in many cultures. As with other ritual actions, its meaning depends on the context (cf. Morphy 1984). In Tiwi mortuary ritual the singed pubic hair symbolised the termination of the relationship between spouses. I was told that the 'new hair' would be 'for a new wife' or husband.[55] In 1990, a man sang in the yam ritual that he wanted to see the long pubic hair of a widow and to take her in the long grass (a euphemism for having sex with her). In the next chapter I will come back to the subject of Tiwi hair symbolism.

The subject matter of songs and dances identified a particular relationship or relationships with the deceased. A man, for instance, while making dance movements depicting him bereaved of his loincloth, sang an *ambaru*-song employing the voice of his deceased longtime lover saying that when she tore off his loincloth his erect penis slapped against her face. Herewith, he not only pointed out that the dead woman had been his lover and potential spouse but also that she was his paternal half-'sister'. In other words, the man had a double bereavement status, *ambaru* and *mutuni*, the latter status indicated by him being hit on one side of the face or cheek (see appendix 2) and in his using the lyrics of a 'father' he and the dead woman had in common.

People were often moved by the performances of widows and widowers, whether the sight of a young, beautiful widow dancing or an elderly widower who, biting on a piece of cloth in grief and anger, created a new dance at the grave of the third wife he had lost. He composed a song mimicking his wife's voice stating that they could no longer join together, from then on he would have to go in the bushes alone and have sex with himself. Encircling the grave he staged a new dance depicting masturbation.

Following the last dance the widow or widower was given a ritual bath by one of the *paputawi* and had her or his whole body rubbed with white clay. This partially released the bereaved spouse from the *pukamani* taboos. Female informants told me that in the past the maternal 'brother' of the deceased (*putani*) who washed the widow could take her as his wife. They said that men 'straight away' after the burial took the widows with them without waiting until the post-funeral rituals and a final ritual bath lifting the taboos had been accomplished.

People wailed together at the grave mound. Friends and relatives of the bereaved went to them and 'said sorry' in Tiwi fashion. Some were shaking hands. The newly bereaved and those recently bereaved by other deaths often gave each other support. Finally, but not always, the survivors stepped or jumped over the grave mound. I was told it was done so the spirit of the dead would not follow them (cf. Mountford 1958: 67). Some people said 'good-bye' (*nimpangi*) to the deceased. After the burial the family members often temporarily moved away from the township where they had lived with the deceased.

The day of burial could hardly be planned. If it was not at the weekend, bereaved kin employed or at school in the townships had a day off for a funeral.

Months later, a series of small post-funeral rituals were held during a break at noon, after working hours, or on a Saturday. The final mortuary rituals were mostly scheduled on weekends, following a pay day, on a Saturday or Sunday, or both.

Cleansing rituals with water and smoke, and ritual whipping served to drive out *pukamani* and chase the spirits of the dead away. The personal belongings of the deceased were taboo and, therefore, these would be destroyed, buried or thrown in the sea. I was told nobody wanted these things because it hurt the survivors to be reminded too much of the deceased. When not directly put away after death, things like clothes, mattresses and sheets would later sometimes be deliberately used as a focus in ritual when an emotionally compelling remembrance of the dead person was desirable. The house formerly occupied by the deceased and items hard to replace (such as cars, dinghies, VCRs, football trophies) would, however, be ritually cleansed with smoke. After cleansing had taken place, people might move into the house again or it might not be reoccupied for a considerable time, if ever. It would all very much depend on the emotions and needs of the people concerned.

Before the cleansing ritual, houses and yards would be taboo (only accessible to the ritual workers who gather the personal belongings of the deceased) and often marked as such. In case of a fatal motor vehicle accident, the spot where the accident had occurred would become taboo and the road would be blocked off. A special 'open 'em up' ceremony (*ampuraprapununga*) or cleansing rite with the erection of a mortuary pole would have to be performed before the road could be used again by traffic. Sometimes after the death of a senior person the road or pathway to that person's 'country', an area with an ancestral grave, would be temporarily closed. After the death of the most senior (important) person of a country, a relatively rare occurrence, the country may be ritually cleansed.[56]

Whether places other than the house occupied by the deceased and the place of death would have to be ritually cleansed varied depending on the social position of the deceased, the type of death, and, of course, people's sentiments and needs.[57] The need to ritually cleanse a number of places would be especially important after unexpected and sudden deaths, the most shocking of all. It was after these unforeseen deaths, I was frequently told, that the spirits of the newly dead bothered the living. The places frequented by these persons when alive would then be cleansed either in Tiwi fashion or by the Catholic deacon or priest by blessings with holy water.

After this description of Tiwi mortuary practices and their burial ceremonies at the end of the 1980s, let me now turn to the funeral of the homicide victim.

*   *   *

A new road was made to Pawularitarra in the bush, and the area was cleared because it was said to be infested with poisonous snakes. The stress on snakes had to do with the fact that these snakes were the deceased's dreaming and associated with his country (his country because his father was buried there). On the side of the strait, abandoned corrugated iron shacks marked the former bush camp. The well had dried up. Simon told me that when he lived at Pawularitarra he had met Kalikalini's spirit sitting at the well one night. Further out in the bush a few remaining mortuary poles of Kalikalini's grave were visible, as was an enamel dish left atop the grave mound. In the past Tiwi left food and water at the grave for the spirit of the dead (cf. Goodale 1971: 237, 252; Mountford 1958: 67).

People gathered in small groups at a distance from the old grave. Some of the ritual workers were digging a new grave next to the old one using a loader. The ritual workers also cleared a circular ceremonial ground (*milimika*) where the dancing would take place. Fires had been lit here at four points to chase away the spirits of the dead (cf. Goodale 1971: 250). This was only done at mortuary rituals out in the bush; no such fires were lit in the local Catholic cemeteries.

Tobias' close relatives painted themselves, mainly with the red ochres associated with the deceased's country of origin, Tikelaru. They were wearing ornaments such as bangles and cockatoo-feather head-dresses. The body paintings and ceremonial decorations disguised the bereaved from the spirit of the dead and set them apart from others (Goodale 1971, Mountford 1958).

One of the *ambaruwi* present at Pawularitarra, waiting for the arrival of the coffin, was Jessica Nemangerau. She walked back and forth between her temporary 'camp' and the new hole. In her *ambaru*-song she told how the deceased would come her (his *amoa* or 'father's sister's daughter') way: (Dead man saying) 'You should find my *amoa* (singing) for me.' When she walked back Jessica monitored her audience, faced them, and sang: 'They are all looking at me, and I have no teeth in my mouth.' This was greeted with laughter. Jessica sat down.

The corpse had been flown into Nguiu, where a Roman Catholic mass was said in the open air. At 11.30 am little boats approached Melville Island. Some people rushed towards the sea. The coffin was placed on the back of a truck. The people at Pawularitarra began wailing.

Jessica's sister, Nancy Kerimerini, stood up. She walked backward and forward from her 'camp' in the direction of the sea, from where the coffin was coming. She sang a dialogue between her husband Sam and his deceased 'brother': 'I am thinking very hard for you, my brother' (Dead man saying) 'Me too, my brother, because somebody been murder me.' Some people in the audience called out in appreciation of the song. Nancy explained to me she had made this song for Sam at his request. 'He could not understand, he did not understand why that (the killing of his brother) happened to him', she said. When the coffin arrived Nancy sang the first part again, but she cut the last part of the song. She said she did so because her husband was 'deaf', meaning he was unable to understand in both senses.

The truck with the coffin arrived at the burial place. At various places men and women wailed loudly. Nancy kept singing her *ambaru*-song. Tobias' children came with their dead father in the rear of the truck. They were painted with red ochre and, grief-stricken, had to be pulled away from the coffin. Jerome Pamantari, the principal ritual worker, stood in the back of the truck. He wore a black petticoat like a widow, because he replaced his late half-sister Kate who had been married to Tobias. In the past days he had often said he would kill the 'murderer' wearing a petticoat. The truck was pulled backwards and the coffin taken off by the ritual workers. It was placed on a tarpaulin next to the open grave. Tobias' children flung themselves on the coffin and embraced it. Other people were standing in circles around it, the loud wailing continued. Nancy repeated her song. When she was finished Jessica took over the singing: (Dead man saying to her) 'When we met together, you did not scream for me!' The song text not only referred to her screaming in wailing but also to the fact that she and the deceased had been sweethearts previously. Tiwi lovers used to meet each other in the bush or the mangrove swamps. Often young men went 'hunting around' for young women. When the girl resisted she would start screaming to alarm others. But in this song Jessica made clear she had not been frightened of Tobias in the past.

Jerome sang an *ambaru* song, walking back and forward, while lifting one hand in the air: (Dead man saying) 'You and I, we gotta have a good talk at Pularumpi.' The 'talk' in this type of song had a sexual connotation. The opposition of 'you and I', according to Nancy, showed Jerome had been sexually jealous of Tobias.

Jessica sang anew: (Dead man saying) 'Why are you singing short word?/You are my *amoa*.' Jessica had her own reasons for not performing an extensive widow song. Several years before, Tobias had asked her to become his wife but she had refused. Because her eldest son had died some time before she felt a relationship with a man was still taboo to her.

Jack Munuluka, a clan brother of Tobias' father, performed a *mamanakuni*-song: (Dead man saying) 'I have my father the same.' Jack replaced the deceased's father as the 'boss' in the funeral rituals. He used Tobias' voice as a rhetorical device.

Tobias' daughters continued their wailing. Jerome tried to get people ready to perform on the dancing ground next to the coffin. Some older men called out for the *mamurapi*. Several women and men went in separate groups up to the coffin. They hit themselves with their fists, wailed loudly, and fell down beside the coffin. Tobias' daughters picked them up. Care was taken to give the bereaved children plenty of water to drink.

Beside the dancing ground stood Harold Tampajani, a 'son' of the deceased, with a bundle of spears that were painted red. This man of the Pandanus clan was said to have 'nearly' used the spears to avenge Tobias' death. The local police expected trouble at the burial and were present in the crowd. This, the uncertainty about who had killed Tobias, and the absence of at least two men (besides the man charged with murder) on whom suspicion had fallen, made a proper punishment impossible on this occasion. Harold represented his father, Steven Tampajani, the principal *mutuni*, who had fallen ill. The bundle of spears expressed the intentions of their patrilineage and might be seen as a mere threat, because during the burial the bundle remained tied up with a string. In addition, the bundle stood for Kalikalini, Tobias' father and sneak attacker of renown, and the spears for his 'grandchildren' or *mawampi*, now united as a 'one-grandfather-group' or *aminiyarti*. The members of such a group, *aminiatuwi*, formed – among other things – a 'fight company', supporting each other in fights.

A long (mosquito) call was given to start the dance and song ceremony near the coffin. Tobias' 'brother' Bruce Kerimerini composed the songs for the bereaved patrilineal 'children' or *mamurapi* (*turah*): (Dead man saying) 'I put my kids on my lap.' The dead man s classificatory sons (including me) were the first to dance the *turagha*, depicting both sneak attackers and spirit children (cf. appendix 2). A group of female *mamu-rapi*, with Bruce and Sam's daughters amongst them, danced next. They danced at a slower pace, but otherwise the same as the men. Then the first group performed their dance for the second time. After the conclusion of this dance these men went towards the coffin, avoiding their 'sisters', embraced each other and wailed and cried. The women also danced twice. Jessica supported her 'daughters' by dancing in the background. Her sister Nancy sang a mourning song outside the ceremonial ground: (Dead man saying) 'Big mob people came from everywhere, came for me and my father.' In her *ambaru*-song she emphasised that the burial next to Kalikalini's grave was a prestigious matter because it had drawn a very large attendance, and therefore her actual and classificatory children appeared to be considered important. The dancing of *mamurapi* proceeded.

Next came the grandchildren of some of Tobias' paternal 'brothers' (*mutuni*), the *kerimerika*, who acted as one body with the *mamurapi*. Again, Bruce composed the songs: 'I made the *milimika* (clear place) for you fellow, so you got to dance, and playing around here'; and 'I made a clear place for these *mawampi* (the deceased's 'grandchildren').' The texts alluded to the playing around of spirit children. Some *mawampi* were descendants of Kalikalini's 'brother' Miputingkimi and ended their dance with a movement from the pig dance, turning their bottoms towards the coffin.

Jerome Pamantari directed Tobias' daughters, his nieces, to the dancing ground. They left the coffin. Theodore Wakipata, the husband of the eldest stepdaughter, Ruth, composed the song for Tobias' daughters and son: 'He was here, he had all those children because he married his (second) wife/We are all together now, all one family.' Tobias' daughters danced the *turagha*. The song text refers to the dead man's second marriage. I was told that the dead man had taken his wife's spirit (Marylou was buried at Pularumpi) to Pawularitarra: 'he brought his wife and he stay with all his family now.' Theodore stressed that the dead man's family, the living as well as the dead, was reunited at Pawularitarra. The female and after them the male *mamurapi* danced for a second time. During their dancing the audience showed strong emotions of grief.

Bruce repeated the song he had composed earlier. Several men performed the pig dance, marking their dreaming. They concluded by hitting themselves with their fists or falling onto their backs. Tobias' daughters had to stop them. The wailers focused on the deceased. Several men danced, looked at the coffin, jumped backwards high in the air and let themselves fall down onto their backs. A mother told her daughters to dance. These and a succeeding group of men belonged to the Munuluka family. Their wailing was very intense, suggesting that they distanced themselves from the trouble between Tobias Arapi and Andrew Munuluka. A lover of Carol, one of Tobias' daughters, went to her, embraced her, leaned with his head on her shoulder and cried loudly. When grieving like this, partners showed affection more openly than in their daily lives.

The next category of bereaved relatives were the *unantawi* (*pulanga*), led by the two most senior men of the Mosquito clan, Roger Imalu and Jack Munuluka. Kalikalini had been the second in line for the leadership of this clan. After the death of all influential clansmen of Kalikalini's generation, men of the second descending generation became the top generation and had to take over. Given the Tiwi system of alternating generations, Jack and Roger were clan brothers of Kalikalini and therefore 'fathers' of the deceased. They were the living people most eligible to head the mortuary rituals for Tobias. Roger sang: 'My *angimani* got a big penis.' Nancy explained to me he was 'swearing at himself' but that he mentioned his 'mother's mother's brother' or *angimani* Kalikalini instead of himself. He alluded, in addition, to Kalikalini's many actual and classificatory descendants. Roger danced with his hands in front of his genitals. He finished his dance by symbolically cutting off his penis with one hand.

Jack danced next. Then his sister Mavis Pamantari and two other women performed their dance in female style, moving their hands away from and towards their lap. Two of the ritual workers supported them a little while. Mavis (*unantaka pulunga*) embraced her husband, who tried to comfort her. In the next round she combined the previous dance with arm movements of the mullet dance (the mullet was Tobias' dreaming). The women wailed loudly at the end of their performance. Roger composed a second song verse for further dance groups of his bereavement status: 'Oh, my "granny", he got a big penis.' The younger men jumped up backwards into the air and let themselves fall back down onto their shoulder blades. Others hit themselves on their bellies with their fists. Bruce tried to hold them and helped them to their feet. Jessica sang outside the dancing ground: (Dead man saying) 'Why you give me (your) back?' Obviously a metaphorical way of saying death had divorced them. Nancy said her sister Jessica in her song pretended she and the deceased were lovers again, and the dead man asked her why she did not face him but turned away from him. She had indeed refused to marry him.

The time for the actual interment of the coffin drew near and people moved towards the open grave. Tobias' daughters had to be pulled off the coffin. The ritual workers took the coffin to the grave while the deceased's children wailed and cried loudly. The people flocked around the grave. The ritual workers dug out the last bit of the hole and cleared the sides. The coffin was lowered into the grave. Tobias' children tried to follow their father into the grave; people had to hold them and restrain them forcibly. There was an enormous eruption of emotional expression, especially on the part of the bereaved children.

While the ritual workers shovelled the earth into the grave, Tobias' lover Jasmine performed an *ambaru*-song: (Dead man saying to her) 'Why don't you come and talk to me now?/What about the other times I used to take you in my house?' She referred to her sexual liaison with Tobias. The 'talk' in this song is a Tiwi euphemism for sexual intercourse. She used to come to his hut after drinking hours late at night. In the present context it was not Tobias' hut where she was expected but in the seclusion of his grave (in the past a bereaved spouse went down into the grave).

The collective wailing, yelling, screaming and crying continued. People grouped in circles around the grave. In the inner circles the wailing was louder; on the outer, people went on with normal conversations. The loader assisted in closing over the grave. Four men pushed Heather to the ground as she again and again had tried to throw herself into the grave.

Isaac Pamantari, I was told, feared being given a 'hiding', a ritualised punishment, beating with a club. In his *mamanakuni*-song, using Tobias' voice as a rhetorical device, he directed himself towards the spirit of Kalikalini: (Dead man saying) 'Mind my *ilimani* ('mother's brother'), don't hit him (with a stick).' Isaac might have expected Kalikalini, his brother-in-law, to retaliate for Tobias' death. He sang at the appropriate time for a punishment by the living to be carried out.

A plastic bag with some of the dead man's clothes was buried in the grave mound which had been made. Plastic flowers that had been lying on the coffin were placed on top of the mound. The people flocked around the newly made dance ground. The grave was now included in the ceremonial ring.

The men started a second dance and song ceremony with a long (honey bee) call. Harold leaned on his bundle of spears. Bruce, again composed a song for his 'children', the *mamurapi*: 'Stretch your arms and dance *kutungura* and throw dirt with your feet.' The *kutungura* was an energetic dance in which the dancers used their feet to throw up dirt. More often this dance was called *ampakitao*, but Tobias had given it as a name to a 'son', so after his death the name and the noun *ampakitao* became taboo. As a result of this, Bruce had to use another word. He made it clear in the song that he was instructing them. As mentioned before, in throwing up the dirt, this dance expresses the anger of the children towards their parents. This cultural experience is played upon in the rituals as a strong symbol of the separation from the deceased parent.

Next, a group of young men, *mamurapi*, including Harold, danced the *turagha*. After this came a group of dancers who danced their dreaming, the sailing boat. My 'brothers' and I went round in the *milimika* on our knees, 'raising the sails' on the mast with our arms. Then we straightened our bodies, one arm up and one down showing how the wind filled the sails, and then stretched our arms backwards, 'the wind blowing in the sails', as we went around the ceremonial ring faster. After the burial there was a stronger emphasis on the dreamings shared with the deceased, identifying the latter with the spiritual world. The dance of the sailing boat had been choreographed by Tampajani in the mortuary rituals for Tobias' deceased sister Donna in the early 1930s (cf. chapter 3). These dances too had separation from the deceased as their theme.

While the first group of *mamurapi* danced, Nancy sang an *ambaru*-song, which she repeated several times. She had been Tobias' lover. Now she let him tell her in the song to go back to her husband and leave him alone. The focus of attention was redirected in the song. The sickness of Tobias' 'brother' Sam, Nancy's husband, legitimated her separation from him. She then had to take care of her husband, because the dead man wanted it. When still alive, he used to bring his sick 'brother' bush food: (Dead man saying) 'Look, you have to look after my brother well.'

In the ceremonial ring the dancing and singing of Bruce's song continued. The next group, people from the Wangiti patrilineage, performed the buffalo dance. Their dreaming, the buffalo, was associated with the deceased. With their feet and outstretched arms they marked the galloping buffalo. Then they held their arms like the buffalo's horns. Once again, these dances indicate an anger and aggression that induces a separation. In the end the buffalo was running away; the performers were distancing themselves from the deceased. They threw themselves on top of the grave and wailed. Their 'relations' called out to the close relatives of the deceased when they were not stopped from injuring themselves quickly enough or picked up from the grave mould.

Finally, while he was crying at the grave, Jack Munuluka composed a *mamanukuni* song. He could sing this because he was Tobias' 'father'. Jack's clan brother Kevin Wangiti was charged with the murder. In his song he was disclaiming any share of the guilt: 'Good job, police took him who did it quickly./If he was here, I would put a two-sided barbed spear through his chest!' Nancy said, 'It is like he put that man, he spear him with the knife and left him on the ground.' In other words, a retaliation for Tobias' violent death.

The next group to dance were the *mutuni*. Steven Tampajani, a thin old man, his body painted with yellow ochre, was sick and did not dance. He was the most important *mutuni* (later he would be buried next to Tobias).

William Palurati, another paternal 'brother' of the deceased, composed a song. He sang about his dreaming, a kind of mullet, that was shared with the dead man: 'He is here, big waves!' In his song William noticed the mullet (*takaringa*) in the water. He shared this dreaming with Tobias because both their fathers belonged to the Mullet people, a 'semi-moiety' (they were *takaringuwi*). In their dance the *mutuni* held their cheeks with one hand, marking their bereavement status of losing 'one side of their face.' The other arm was stretched out and held away from the body, moving up and down. This imitated the mullet moving its tail in the water. So the two aspects of their relationship to the deceased were here combined in one dance. William made up a second song: 'He is working his tail in the water!' The *mutuni* had their cheeks painted and finished their dance by bashing their cheeks with one hand. A woman of the *mutuni* bereavement status started her dance by hitting Steven in the face.

Men of the Palurati patrilineage sat on the ground with crossed legs and moved forwards. This was the turtle dance (*tarakalani*), once choreographed by their patrilineal ancestor. This dreaming dance identified a patrilineal group related to the dead man. Roger Imalu composed a song for his son, one of the *mutuni*: (He is saying to his son) 'Everybody will talk about you and scratch (one side of) your face.' The scratching is an allusion to the way Tobias met with his death. Roger stressed that his son's performance would make him 'important'; everybody would talk about him. Both his sons performed the next dance, beginning and concluding with hitting each other on the cheek.

After a short break, the last category of bereaved, the *ambaruwi*, performed. The first to sing was Cecil Jatukwani, who had been married to Tobias' deceased half-sister Patty: (Dead man saying) 'You dance for me, you Larrakian, because you had my sister.' Brothers-in-law jokingly exchanged insults in daily life. In the song Tobias called his brother-in-law a 'Larrakian', meaning Cecil ought not to have married Tobias' sister without returning a 'sister' to Tobias, hence the insult.[58] At this point Cecil was at least obliged to dance for him.

Simon was encouraging people to clap. Cecil went around the grave. He moved his knees apart and closed them, dancing *impula*, 'see the knees'. Normally Tiwi wives did not show their knees but kept them carefully covered. Moving the legs like this, showing the knees, is a Tiwi female strategy for seduction. Consequently, an adulterous partner (man or woman) was always hit with a stick on the knees. Actually, Cecil in his dance was pretending to have sexual intercourse with the imaginary spirit of the deceased. The last movements of the dance were as if he had finished copulating. Cecil composed a second song: (Dead man saying) 'That's the last time you gotta see me (what I am doing).' Other people danced as if engaged in sexual intercourse, facing the grave mound. Cecil, carried away by his ritual role, told one man, who was reputed to have a small penis, 'You big one, big enough to dance'.

Besides the dances mentioned here and the dances with fighting movements, another characteristic dance of the *ambaruwi* was that of the shark chasing the stingray. At Tobias' funeral there was one family group (Kitiruta) who enacted this dance. They pronounced the name of the shark twice ('*kutuntua, kutuntua*'). The grandfather of the dancers did this dance. They made the sounds of the shark ('brrruuhh, brruuhhh') and went around the grave mound, singing '*kutuntua, kutuntua*'. Finally they also wailed, hit themselves with their fists, and had to be stopped by the close relatives of the deceased.

The *ambaruwi* who acted as ritual workers were the partners of the paternal and maternal half-'siblings' of the dead person; in other words, the partners of the *mutuni* and the *paputawi* respectively. Alan Pamantari, the health worker who had discovered that Tobias was dead, sang next: (Dead man saying) 'Hello, my brother-in-law!' Tobias used to greet him in this way. He and his 'brothers' danced with fighting movements. Then Jasmine's sisters danced. Simon Pamantari told his daughters to dance. They were promised but not married to Steven Tampajani, the *mutuni*, and started by hitting him in his face. The wife of a maternal 'brother' of the deceased (*putani*) danced next. She kicked her husband on his leg. He followed her in her dance with the movements of waves on the beach. Other people in this category danced in the same way. Jessica danced *ambaru*. At the end of her dance she threw kisses to Steven, her previous lover (a gesture she adopted from her mother). She also threw kisses at the grave and in doing so expressed a lover relationship with the deceased. Alan sang again: (Dead man saying) 'If you go back to Pularumpi today don't talk to any man.' This was a communication between lovers. Nancy, however, told me that she thought the song was directed at her husband, Sam, on whom suspicion had fallen.

Simon's eldest son Rolf Pamantari danced. Afterwards he leaned on his wife and cried. Jerome suggested something to the group of older men of the Pandanus clan. He wanted the dead man's lover, his clan sister Jasmine, to dance. They agreed and passed on the message. 'His girlfriend before gonna dance now', Simon said, 'two girlfriends'.

Jerome Pamantari composed the following song: (Dead man saying) 'Oh, you get smelly skirts.' Jasmine danced, opening and closing her legs, around the grave. She lifted up the front of her skirt. Her husband Andrew Munuluka stood near the grave. He supported her, moving his hands, pushing backwards and forwards, like waves breaking on the beach. 'He didn't know dead man took his wife', Simon said to me, probably referring to the night of the killing. Jasmine danced a second time and threw her skirt off. She ended her dance on the grave mound as if she were engaged in intercourse.

Nancy Kerimerini was the second girlfriend who had to dance. She instructed her 'brother' Jerome about what she was planning to do. Jerome sang: 'You take my top off.' Nancy did a new dance. She entered the ring and took her top off. She did it a second time and danced bare-breasted. The undressing was part of the ritual role of the widow. Nancy made an innovation taken from her personal experience with the deceased. It would be followed by other people enacting this role in the future. When she had finished her dance, she joined Tobias' daughters who were sitting at the grave. Jerome was the last man to dance, 'the bencher' in the words of Simon (referring to the Australian Rules term for a reserve player). He repeated his former songs. Wearing a petticoat, he walked backward and forward on the dancing ground around the grave with one hand raised.

A long, loud and collective wailing around the grave mound was the final act of the funeral ceremony. Jack Munuluka sang a *mamanukuni* while he was crying: (Dead man saying to him) 'All right daddy, you may go home now.' Jack rhetorically established his importance in this song. He was the one who had directed the funeral ceremony. The dead man was happy with him. The grave was covered with a blue tarpaulin. The mourners stepped over the grave mound so the spirit of the dead would not follow them. After ten months the people would come back for the final ceremony. Until then the burial place and its surroundings would remain taboo and be a private hunting ground for the spirit of the dead.

*   *   *

After the funeral there were cleansing rituals to chase the spirit of the dead away from the places closely associated with Tobias while he was alive. He and his late wife Marylou had been guides at Putjamirra Safari Camp, some 20 km north of Pularumpi. In the Safari Camp the tents were already packed up, and two days after the funeral the camp would be formally closed until the next dry season. The bereaved daughters from Milikapiti – Ruth, Judy and Heather – gathered at Sam's place in the Old Camp, where their sister Laura also lived. This time they had brought wild geese to be shared with Nancy's and Jerome's group. Relationships were strengthened in this way because the daughters had become dependent on them as ritual workers. Later the trucks left for the purification rituals at Putjamirra. En route we passed a mortuary pole. This marked the spot where Marylou had died in the car crash; Tobias had placed her hunting bucket upside-down on top of the pole. At Pularumpi beach people spotted a crocodile. Nancy reminded me that Irekopei (the mythological Crocodile Man from Kalikalini's and Tobias' country at Cape Fourcroy) had been in the creek at Matalau, but that Kalikalini did not fight him (Irekopei was the dreaming of his victims who were dancing the crocodile dance). Oscar Pamantari tried to shoot him, 'the cheeky one', but missed. Jerome, the principal ritual worker, sang about Tobias' longing for his own country, from where his father, and consequently he himself, had been banned forever. The red cliffs and white beach at Putjamirra were very similar to those of his own country at Cape Fourcroy: (Dead man saying) 'I gave sorry that place Cape Fourcroy (Tupupruluppi).' Nancy explained that Tobias had always been talking about going back. He had been thinking about that while he had been sitting there.

Jerome and other ritual workers cleared the firepits at the camp. The place was surrounded with mortuary poles, a display of Tiwi 'culture' for tourists. Many of the poles had been sold to the European manager of the business after they had figured in mortuary rituals. One pole, made by Tobias, was covered with a towel; this showed that the poles even then were not completely decontextualised. This particular pole was much too charged with emotion for it to be left uncovered.

Nancy walked back and forth in the direction of the fireplace. She performed an *ambaru*-song telling the bereaved children that their father used to work there: 'Your father used to work here at this sorrowful place!/He used to make clear place, good place, Putjamirra.' She was making here an allusion to the aspect of ritual cleansing. Tobias cleaned the place and cooked bush and sea foods at that location. At this point he had the place cleaned for his children to dance (a conventional theme in mortuary ritual). Jerome, assisted by other male ritual workers, lit a fire to produce smoke.

Roger Imalu, a 'father' of Tobias, wailed. He was the boss in this ceremony. The men started with a honey bee call around the fire. Roger called out the significant place names from Pularumpi to Putjamirra (Irumokulumi (Pularumpi), Tuwanapula, Wotjitopi, and Tuoleipi). The other men responded with calling *weya* or 'finished' after each place name. Nancy, holding the mortuary pole with the towel, called out names of Tobias' *mutuni* to attract the attention of his spirit. She had to call out these names instead of Tobias' names, which had become taboo.

The ritual workers carried burning green boughs around the firepits to chase the spirit of the dead away with smoke and to beat the *pukamani* (taboos) out. The other people followed them. The campfires and Tobias' mortuary pole were given special treatment. Jerome gave Roger a harpoon-like spear (his dreaming was the turtle, which was hunted with a harpoon). Roger sang while he symbolically 'speared' a campfire that had been used by Tobias: 'Kalikalini used to carry the one-sided barbed spear (*tungkwaliti*) and stuck it in the ground.' Roger performed the dance because he was Kalikalini's clan brother.

Tobias' children and granddaughter, Laura's daughter who had come over from Darwin for the funeral, danced with imaginary spears. It was the dance of the *mamurapi*. They pretended to spear the same place. Mavis Pamantari, who was a clan sister of Kalikalini (Mosquito clan) and hence a bereaved paternal 'mother' (*unantaka pulanga*), danced with an umbrella. She too speared the place in her dance. She wailed and was supported by her husband. Then the dancers performed together; they constituted one group of patrilineal *unantawi*.

After this followed the concluding performances of the ritual workers and widows (*ambaruwi*). Jerome composed the following song: 'I am widow but I made the place clean first for my husband to lie down.' Jerome here criticised Tobias, who had in his opinion not cleaned their sleeping place well enough so that Kate, Jerome's half-sister, was bitten by a poisonous snake. The text further had sexual overtones in the widow preparing a place for her husband to lie down and at the same time referred to Jerome's ritual activities to put the spirit of the dead husband to rest.

The dance performances of the ritual workers had the termination of sexual intercourse as their common theme although it was acted out in their personal styles, directed at the focal campfire. A sudden kick or backward movement concluded the dances. Jasmine, for instance, lifted her skirts and the men pulled back the pelvis from an imaginary coital position.

The Landrover from the Safari Camp was treated with smoke in a ritual cleansing as well. The ritual workers were paid for their services. Jasmine initially refused to accept the money, suggesting she was an actual widow. Somewhat later, however, she took it. Because of this costly business, the cleansing of Tobias' hut was scheduled for the next weekend, when the children had had another pay day.

Late at night, Jasmine came to our place to compose a mourning song for Tobias: (Dead man saying) 'My *mawana* (potential wife) was doing lovely dance for me.' Jasmine noted that she had danced, both at the funeral and the 'smoking', as a widow. By lifting her skirts she showed him her pubic area for the last time, a conventional theme in Tiwi mortuary ritual. Jasmine cried. She told us how fond she had been of Tobias.

*   *   *

Tiwi people held that Tobias' spirit was still roaming around the village. Within a week after the purification rituals at Putjamirra, a sister of Oscar Pamantari died in Pularumpi. Isaac, her father's brother's son, was in deep grief and led the funeral as a *mutuni*. 'Go', he sang to her corpse, 'I will follow you soon'. Bruce and Sam Kerimerini were maternal 'fathers' of the deceased woman (*unantawi pularti*). Bruce had a bandage wrapped around his chest. He had fractured his ribs when he fell on the bed with the corpse while 'saying sorry'. Sam said he felt pain in his chest as well and would go to hospital for an x-ray. Their breasts marked the relationship with the dead woman. Tobias' stepdaughter Ruth was given the opportunity to earn money as an *ambaru*. The next day Tobias' little house would be ritually cleansed.

Early in the morning the ritual workers cleaned Tobias' hut and the surrounding area. They scrubbed the house with water, brought fresh sand for the dancing ground, and raked the area. The people gathered at Sam's place in the Old Camp. A mass would be said at Tobias' hut by the town clerk, a devout Catholic of mixed descent, and a non-resident priest.

The priest blessed the house and verandah as well as the spot where the corpse had been. During the mass more people came to the scene. At the end of mass the batteries of the cassette player playing religious music ran out. The priest spoke of 'magic'. He concluded, 'That is the end of mass. I invite you now to do your ceremony'. In this way the missionaries from Bathurst Island propagated an integration of Tiwi and Catholic ceremonies. This policy was usually met by Tiwi people on Melville Island with less enthusiasm than by those on Bathurst Island.

The participants, painted with white ochre, separated into groups. A fire was lit by the ritual workers using boughs from the mango tree to produce smoke. The ritual started with a long honey bee call. Jack Munuluka, the boss, began by singing: 'We got them burn him Kalikalini house.' In other words, this man (*unantani pulanga*, a 'father' of Tobias) had gathered the people for a ritual smoke cleansing of Tobias' house.

Tobias' close relatives walked in the smoke around the fire. Following this, the ritual workers went ahead with the green boughs bringing smoke to the taboo locations and so chasing the spirit of the dead away. The others followed. They went over the verandah and into the house. There the ritual workers opened the louvres of the two small windows. The singing and dancing continued. Nancy's elder half-brother, Alec Adranango, a man of the Pandanus clan, was one of the ritual workers. He sang: (house saying) 'Hey, you got to find cheek to burning this house.' In other words, one had to be tough to chase away the spirits of Kalikalini and his son. The bereaved children wailed inside the house, facing the place where Tobias used to sleep. Then the louvres were closed and the people left the house. Jerome, the principal ritual worker, sang: 'My friend put that spear up the house and somebody has been taken the spear away.' The gist of Jerome's song was that Tobias had been killed there; Kalikalini was his friend (*mantani*) or 'relation' because their fathers belonged to the same matriclan, the spear stood for Kalikalini's son. He continued: 'My friend Kalikalini's bundle of spears has been taken away.' In other words, Kalikalini's last surviving son had now also been killed. It was an allusion to Kalikalini's actions as a killer at Matalau, where he carried a bundle of spears. Kalikalini killed one man's sons, now his own sons (the bundle of spears) both had died as well, their lives taken away. The discourse in the lyrics was here on the level of the first ascending generation from deceased (whose spirit had to follow his father). Hence, on this occasion Jerome emphasised his identity as Tobias' father's 'friend'. Remember Jerome had put up a 'spear' next to the victim (like Kalikalini used to do after a killing).

The dancing ground was where the body had been found. This place was ritually cleansed with smoke. Martha Arapi, Kalikalini's only surviving wife, sat down at the place where the corpse had been lying next to the bin with smoke. The *ambaruwi* danced. Mike Kerimerini fell down, wailing 'Daddy, Daddy, Daddy'. The bereaved daughters wailed again. Jack and Roger, Tobias' 'fathers', composed a new song about the dreaming (mullet) they had in common with their clan brother, Kalikalini: 'In this place a big mullet was lying down and there was dancing around.' The big mullet (*tikupali*) that was lying down in the song was Tobias, a senior man. This meant that his body had been found at that location. The bereaved fathers and children performed the mullet dance.

A bucket of water was placed on the spot. Jack sang: 'I am Patuapura, big waves washed my head and my arms.' Patuapura was another name for Rocky Point, the petrified clan ancestress Pungalo holding her two children in her arms, on the west coast of Bathurst Island. This was one of the most sacred places on the islands. It belonged to the Stone clan (*pungaluwila*) of which Tobias and his elder 'brothers', Sam and Bruce, were members. Jack could identify with Pungalo through his father's sister (it was his father's dreaming). It was an appropriate song because the water in the bucket was used to wash head and arms by people thus identified. This cleansing ritual with water (*moluki*) released them of some mourning taboos until the final rituals, especially the taboo on playing cards. Tobias' bereaved 'parents', 'brothers' and (actual and classificatory) children, performing the dance movement of a diving mullet, washed their lower arms and heads with the water. The ritual workers danced in fighting poses, fighting off the spirits of the dead, in the background.

The dance and song ceremony recommenced. Jerome now sang: 'The women (Tobias' deceased wives) asked, "Why did you come and dance for our husband?"', denoting these spirits were jealous. The *ambaruwi* danced in their personal (inherited) styles. Jessica, for instance, threw kisses at the focal point of the ceremony, the place where the corpse had been found, representing her ex-lover Tobias, just like her mother used to do. Jasmine lifted her skirts, denoting the termination of her sexual relationship with the deceased. Some of the ritual workers were supported in their dances by bereaved affines, who in their dance made pushing movements with their hands like waves coming on the shore; as mentioned before, this dance had a sexual connotation for Tiwi. For instance, a maternal 'brother' of the deceased (*putani*) 'helped' his wife's sisters in their dances. At the beginning and the end of the dance the latter kicked his leg (denoting his relationship to the deceased; paternal 'siblings' or *mutuni* were slapped in the face). The number of ritual workers, seven males and seven females, indicated that it was a prestigious ceremony.

The bereaved relatives together laid out money for one ritual worker after the other. Jack composed a new song accompanying the payment dances: 'Miputingkimi, he followed Kalikalini.' Jack's grandfather Miputingkimi followed Tobias' father Kalikalini in killing people. In this song Jack put the senior man Miputingkimi last and made Kalikalini more important than his actual grandfather. To put it slightly differently, Jack acknowledged Kalikalini had acquired more prestige by his prowess as a fighter and killer. It was through organising the post-funeral rituals for Tobias that Jack hoped to obtain prestige for himself. He thus identified himself as related more closely to Tobias than the other 'father', Roger from Pularumpi. It was his grandfather who had been Kalikalini's companion, not Roger's grandfather. The money was brought to the ritual workers by Tobias' children, one by one, in their *mamurapi* dance with imaginary spears. When they were giving out the money they pretended to spear. The payments ranged from 40 to 100 dollars per ritual worker. At the end of the ceremony, an elaboration of a house 'smoking' that was usually a small affair, Tobias' son, Ralph, and daughter, Carol, from Nguiu arrived. They had come too late to participate in the ritual. They were led into Tobias' house, where they wailed.

*   *   *

Laura had had a fight with Karl; she went off with her sisters to Milikapiti. Karl took the plane to Darwin on the following day. He left in a hurry and told the members of Sam's camp to send him his belongings by barge. When not long afterwards two boxes with groceries arrived, Sam and Nancy said they were sad that Karl had gone. He did not return to the islands as far as I know.

Soon after the homicide suspicion had fallen on Isaac Pamantari in Pularumpi. I was told that Mary Adranango had declared in a meeting at Milikapiti that Sam had killed his 'brother' Tobias. Sam in turn accused Oscar Pamantari. Mary happened to be a cousin of Isaac and Oscar

Pamantari, they belonged to a 'one-grandfather-group' or 'fight company'. Isaac's 'brother' Oscar, a man of the Fire clan, was a clan brother of Mary (whereas both Isaac and Sam belonged to the Stone clan). In other words, Sam redirected the blame to Mary's clan. Sam's ill-feelings towards Oscar related to another trouble (about women). Sam's 'relations', people with whom Oscar was in dispute, were said to have seen Oscar coming from the Old Camp the night of the killing. Sam told me that Oscar had not gone to Bathurst Island with Sam's brother Bruce, as Oscar claimed, but that he had walked to Paru (on Melville Island, opposite Nguiu on Bathurst Island at the other side of the strait) during the night. There he had been picked up by the cattle truck bringing Nguiu football players from Paru to Pularumpi the next morning.

'I won't embarrass you but that old man is still accusing me', said Oscar when he came to visit me late at night, three weeks after Tobias' death. Oscar called me *mawanyini* (mother's brother's son) and on the basis of this relationship he could expect my support. Obviously, he wanted to get the record straight. He went on:

> But I was at Bathurst that night. I went away at two o'clock in the afternoon with Joshua and Bruce. When I came back the next morning and they told me I couldn't believe it. Oh . . . I have been police tracker for many years. I could follow the tracks and see who did it. (. . .) When I came all the tracks were covered. I was there too late, the tracks were covered, all covered. I will find out. I just don't say much when I go to the club and listen. They will tell once when they are drunk, 'I killed that bloke So-and-such'. The Law is still continuing, you know, from old days, still going on. Continuing.

Oscar further told me that the killing was 'about a woman'. 'It's not difficult to know', he said, but first he needed certainty – and then, snapping his fingers, 'same way'. The police had charged the wrong person with murder, according to him: 'He didn't do it, he might have turned himself in.' He said again that he would find out who the killer was even if it took a year. It was only a small community, according to Oscar, and 'I don't talk much on the club and I listen.' In addition, Oscar said he ran the risk of being 'poisoned'. A Tiwi man on the mainland, married to Sam's sister, was 'in business' (a sorcerer). The man might 'poison' him because he was 'going around with another woman' (Oscar was married to Sam's 'daughter' and former foster child). During the night of the killing, Oscar said, he had been with his girlfriend, his 'second wife' Emmy Jones, on Bathurst Island.

At the beginning of December, Sam was severely bitten by stray dogs. It occurred when he came from the club late at night. 'I kicked', he said, 'but they didn't go away'. Nancy commented that he had been attacked by the dogs 'because he didn't paint himself when it [his 'brother'

Tobias' death] happened'. He had been bitten by dogs, his dreaming, and had to wear bandages where he should have painted his legs as a bereaved 'brother' (*putani*) of Tobias. At Tobias' funeral, in contrast to his brother Bruce, who had wrapped bandages around his leg as a sign that he was symbolically injured by the loss of his 'brother', Sam had neither identified himself as such nor had he performed songs and dances.

By the end of the wet season, Sam could make up for this and perform in the yam ritual or *kulama*, which also had mortuary aspects, especially on the so-called 'night of sorrow'. In 1989, the two major yam rituals on the islands were dedicated to Tobias. In the next chapter I discuss the 1989 seasonal yam rituals. The rituals provided an opportunity for the participants to express their grievances and grief; there was an expectation that the person or persons who had killed Tobias would be named and eventually the killer(s) themselves would 'come out'.

CHAPTER 6

The Yam Rituals

At the monthly meetings of the Tiwi Land Council, Jack Munuluka and Simon Pamantari sat down together and exchanged old stories and *kulama* songs. Simon and Jack appeared to have a good time. Both senior men acted as 'boss' of a seasonal yam ritual or *kulama*, Jack in Nguiu and Simon in Pularumpi. Between them they developed a plan to organise a joint *kulama* on a large scale. Simon wanted his elder brother, Theodore, from Milikapiti to take part as well. According to their plans the 1989 yam ritual, dedicated to Tobias, would be held in the Old Camp at Pularumpi. The ceremonial ground would be under the mango tree where Tobias' body had been found. In this *kulama*, they said, it would be revealed who had killed him.

*   *   *

Nothing came of the initial plans. Jack dropped the idea. He told me he had hoped people at Pularumpi, and his 'relations' in particular, would tell him who had killed his 'son' Tobias. From then on he avoided visits to Pularumpi as much as he could. Jack said he could not make a telephone call to the health clinic or council office in Pularumpi because of the 'trouble there' but that he would find some way to let me know when his *kulama* at Nguiu would take place.

In the wet season of 1988–89 five yam rituals were held. Steven Tampajani had carried out the ritual on his own at Nguiu shortly before Tobias' death in October 1988. The other *kulama* men considered this 'too early'. Jack told Steven it was 'a shame' for it was extremely dangerous to perform the *kulama* alone; it would provoke sickness and death.

In February 1989, Theodore Pamantari and Dimitri Papuruluwi had their *kulama* in Milikapiti. Theodore composed the following song of revenge (*karinimawatumingumi*) concerning the killing of Tobias (I cite his translation): 'Why that man?/Where is that killer, where that murderman?/Where is the man who killed the old man?/We want to see him, and belt him, and topple-back him/He was lucky white police went there/We wanted to have a fight there and flog him.' Theodore expressed his anger about Tobias' violent death. He suggested police intervention prevented Tobias' family from laying their hands on 'the man who killed the old man'.

For a long time it seemed Isaac Pamantari would take part in the *kulama* at Pularumpi. He was well aware that people suspected him. Isaac had prepared a number of songs already. One of these, a 'talk about' song (*purakutukuntinga*), he revealed when in a state of drunkenness in the Social Club. It was a song full of swear words, stating he had been wrongly blamed. Simon was determined to have his *kulama* in the Old Camp when the time came. Several times he checked whether the grass would burn but found it was 'too wet'. Then, finally, he scheduled the *kulama* for the last weekend of March.

On the Friday they were to start, Kevin Wangiti suddenly turned up in Pularumpi; after five months in Darwin's Berrimah jail he had been released on bail. We were playing cards at Dick Pamantari's house when, unexpectedly, Kevin appeared there. Nancy Kerimerini told me to keep an eye on Mike; she was afraid he 'might get cranky'. The event appeared significant enough to postpone the yam ritual. Kevin's release brought into focus the problem of who had killed Tobias.

The police tracker left his job and went to stay temporarily on the mainland with relatives of his sister's husband. He could not remain in Pularumpi, he said, because of 'family trouble': 'underneath mango tree', that is, the homicide. When he was intoxicated, Sam Kerimerini, like Isaac before him, made a song of his public in the Social Club. Sam stated he had been falsely accused of having killed his 'brother'.

Simon definitely decided on having his *kulama* a fortnight after Kevin's return. Alec Adranango and Isaac Pamantari said they perhaps would perform another *kulama* later on. The latter was teased at the club because he had changed his mind. Throughout the ceremony in the Old Camp he did not come into the *kulama* camp but remained sitting within hearing distance. Jack Munuluka was to have his yam ritual in Nguiu five weeks later.

In mid-May, Edgar Tapalinga and Trevor Kiringarra held a *kulama* in Nguiu. Trevor was the present leader of the people from (the country) Tikelaru. Kalikalini had been banned from this country. Tobias' children held Trevor responsible in part for their father's death because, as a consequence of Kalikalini's fate, he had also been expelled from Tikelaru and had not been able to seek refuge there. In one of his songs Trevor complained he had been falsely accused. People had been talking behind his back. Trevor growled that it had been Tobias' own fault. He wanted to go to Pularumpi. The very fact that he had been killed there proved it was a dangerous place for him, a place where he did not belong. Tikelaru consisted of a number of smaller countries; Kalikalini had been banned from Tangio and Arapi. In his 'talk about' song Trevor stated he had never said Tobias was not allowed to stay in his country Tuwalakri: 'You fellow father [Tobias], he run away from here/I didn't say anything about our country Tuwalakri. You wanted that place [Pularumpi] and you died there/That's a wrong place!' Tobias told me, however, it hurt him and his father that they could not go back to their country.

*   *   *

The *kulama* may be best understood as a ritual complex encompassing a number of 'ritual genres', to use Turner's term (1973: 1100). At the end of the 1980s the ritual lasted three complete nights and the days in between. It was structured by the ritual procedures of processing a certain type of round tuber with hairy roots, called *kulama*. These yams were poisonous in a raw state but become edible when carefully prepared, roasted and soaked during the ritual. Whereas other kinds of yams were mainly dug out and prepared by women, the *kulama* yams had to be treated, solely in the course of the ritual, by men only. The annual *kulama* rituals were major events in the gradual initiation of men and women. The performance of the rituals when the *kulama* yams had ripened marked the transition of the wet season to the dry season. The rituals were concerned not only with the change of season and initiation but also with interpersonal conflicts, the dead, increase in the natural environment and food production, human reproduction, prosperity, health, and people's well-being in general. The rituals might be seen as psychotherapeutic in enabling the participants to deal with all sorts of 'trouble', such as fears, bad luck, complaints, grievances, and grief. These could be freely expressed in a forum in this ritual context without provoking counteraction (cf. Goodale 1971: 188). The poisonous *kulama* yam appeared to be a potent symbol of sickness and danger; when processed in the ritual, however, rubbing the body with a mixture of yam mash and red ochre was considered an effective prophylactic and healing act. As in rites of passage in general, a symbolic death or killing and rebirth were important to mark transitions in the *kulama* ritual (cf. Hertz 1960: 81). In sum, the *kulama* might be considered a complex ritual in which the participants, through purification procedures and subsequent symbolic actions to counter 'bad luck' and 'trouble', worked towards a renewal and regeneration of their world.

I will not dwell on the extensive and elaborate initiation procedures here, for in late twentieth-century Tiwi society these had become less relevant.[59] It appears that during this century the age of the initiates increased dramatically, the condition that male initiates must be bachelors was dropped, and in the latter half of the century the formal initiation procedures for women were no longer carried out. Whereas at the beginning of the century everyone was initiated, the number of people being initiated and performing the *kulama* has become fewer and fewer. My own findings confirmed Goodale's suggestion that initiation became limited to those 'able and willing to play responsible and leading roles in the ceremonial life' (1971: 206). At the end of the 1980s the mortuary rituals were indeed led almost exclusively by '*kulama* men'. Men in their thirties and forties who excelled in performing in the mortuary rituals were pointed out as being ready to be taken into the *kulama*. In the second half of the century the initiation procedures had become shorter and less elaborate (cf. Brandl 1970: 474; Grau 1983: 156). The eight men who participated in the two yam rituals I witnessed had all undergone a 'short-cut' initiation. The women had learned the song techniques by singing after the men. Two men in their fifties, who had entered initiation but failed in composing the intricate and complex *kulama* songs, told me that they had to give up on this account. They hoped the seven grades of initiation would be restored so they and others would be able to learn in small steps and at a slower pace.

Elderly people often spoke to me about the *kulama*, their previous songs and new ones, and what would happen in the ritual.[60] It is hard to put into words people's pleasure in performing well-composed songs. Skilled singers had virtually hundreds of songs committed to memory (cf. C. Berndt 1950). They had only to hear a song once to be able to perform it, even after lengthy periods of time. Certain words reflected the type of song, the stage in a particular ritual, and an emotion. Messages and grievances voiced in the *kulama* songs would reach the persons for whom they were intended (Pilling 1958). In recent decades these significant songs have also been transmitted via cassette tapes, for relatively few people were able to 'copy' (re-enact) these themselves and pass them on. Simon had bought a brand-new cassette recorder to tape the *kulama* songs. Jack recorded songs too. The songs they were taping were those of the first night, 'the night of sorrow', and the phase in the ritual called *ajipa*. These were the songs they had studied for a long time. Afterwards, they copied the cassette tapes and passed them on to people who liked to hear the new songs. Jerome's son Reuben frequently listened to his father's songs on tape. He told me he did so because he wanted to learn to sing in his father's style. (Some other men, including Kevin, had the same aspirations.) Following Tobias' death, Simon erased the tape he had of his 1988 *kulama* because the voices of Tobias and Marylou were on it and these had become taboo.

According to Tiwi myth, a number of mythological birds and animals participated in the first *kulama* rituals, led by an owl named Purikikini. The ritual was copied by the *ningawi*, small spirits living in the mangroves. Thereafter, a Tiwi man adopted it from these spirits and introduced its annual performance into Tiwi society (cf. Mountford 1958: 123–4; Brandl 1970: 467; Osborne 1974: 87–9; Grau 1983: 141–2; Venbrux 1993c: 146–7). In the *kulama* some references were made to the mythological beings who carried out the first performances of the ritual and laid down its outline. Jerome Pamantari stated, 'This *kulama* business grew out. One month no shower. They grab one young boy, grab him. Then paint him with turtle or stingray's fat, red paint. One month no *moluki* (bath), only paint. We try to do it again but nobody interested.' Previously, according to my informants, the men went about three miles into the bush and stayed there for a week, 'no more women there, only men'.[61] During the *kulama*, also at the end of the 1980s, the men were not allowed to 'sleep with missus on one blanket': they were *pukamani* and had to refrain from intercourse. 'Fire in the middle, cannot touch her, that's the Law', said Simon, 'we are single men for three nights and three days.' They painted themselves up and wore only a loincloth, even when it was cold at night or raining.

Every *kulama* had a 'boss' who made the decisions concerning the time and place of the ritual. Months in advance, men who planned to participate in the yam ritual were composing and practising their songs. The songs, especially composed for the occasion, were not to be communicated to others. Most of the singers were considered 'big-headed'; these people made sharp observations and were able to express themselves in striking and highly complex metaphors. It was not only the language and style of singing but also the contents that posed problems for newcomers to the *kulama*. The composition of *kulama* songs challenged people's artistic and intellectual powers, and at the same time they had to have the courage to bring out all kinds of 'trouble'. 'That's why it's a little bit hard, you know, for those young people', Simon Pamantari said, 'but we try to have two this year'. The two men he pointed out did not participate. Not even all the initiated men performed in the *kulama* annually. Tobias said he had to have 'a reason' to do the *kulama*. In Pularumpi four men 'missed out' in 1988. The next year two of them took part and the two others did not. Isaac, who performed the ritual neither in 1988 nor in 1989, did so in 1990 because his 'brother' Bill Pamantari had died. Simon said, 'old people [senior people in the past] didn't rubbish *kulama*'. Sam was said to have never missed one.

Ideally, the yam ritual was performed at the close of the wet season. The 'boss' decided when the ritual would be held but there were various indicators of the appropriate time (e.g., when the sky began to colour red in the evenings, the call of the frogmouth (*kukuwini*) or when the grass would burn). When possible the ritual would be performed by bright moonlight. Another concern was that there had to be enough bush and sea foods for the people taking part in the *kulama*.

Simon used to harpoon a turtle a few days before his *kulama* to secure sufficient meat. Children, grandchildren and other relatives provided the people in the *kulama* camp with food (steaks, mangrove worms, fish, and so forth). The ritual was frequently scheduled on the weekend following a pay day. The 'boss' made his decision known in the Social Club a few days before the ritual would take place.

There was only a minimal difference in structure between the yam ritual in Pularumpi and the one in Nguiu (cf. Goodale 1971: 213). To avoid unnecessary repetition I trace here the sequence of ritual events and deal with both rituals at once, although they took place in different locations and at different times in fact. As mentioned before, both rituals were dedicated to Tobias. Within the context of this account of the homicide case, I will have to confine myself to citing mainly those songs in which the participants had something to say in relation to the case; other songs I will discuss briefly to indicate their themes and the subjects that were treated in the course of the ritual.

*   *   *

Just before the 1989 *kulama* in Pularumpi, Jerome and Reuben went out to get mangrove worms. The *kulama* men had to rub these worms on their bodies, and should, so I was told, have used the sap of the milkwood tree in a similar way (cf. Spencer 1914: 94). Nancy and Jeanette gathered *muranga* yams, wrapped these in paperbark, and hid the yams behind a tree at some distance from the *kulama* camp. In Nguiu, these long, thin yams, white when peeled, were substituted by slices of white bread. On Friday afternoon, 14 April, preparations had been made for the *kulama* to be held in Pularumpi. The camp had been organised with firewood collected, shades erected, and mattresses and blankets brought to the camp. The site chosen for the ritual was not the place where Tobias' body had been found but an old ceremonial ground where Tobias and Marylou had participated in the *kulama* the previous year. Simon, a non-drinker, remained in camp while the others went off to drink. It was dark when they returned from the Social Club. Sam told me to make more light. He whispered there was a spirit of the dead around. Edmund Pamantari and his 'brother-in-law' Jerome were lying down on either side of a campfire.

Roger Imalu had been followed by his wife Vanessa and his girlfriend Melanie Wangiti. The five men would perform the *kulama*. Simon spoke to them about the last yam ritual when they had had seven men. One man (Tobias) was 'finished', he said, another one (his elder brother, Bill) was in hospital. Simon expressed his concern about the lack of interest in the ceremony. He stated that only five men, not mentioning the yam ritual of his brother Theodore in Milikapiti, still carried out the *kulama* on Melville Island. Present in the *kulama* camp were, among others, Nancy, Simon's sisters Mary (from Milikapiti) and Mabel, Jeanette and I, and the people already mentioned. Somewhat later came Tobias' stepdaughter Ruth, his daughter Heather, and Jerome's son Reuben. During the first night not only Tobias' daughters stayed in the camp to listen to the mourning songs for their father but also Oscar Pamantari (a man accused by Sam of having killed Tobias) and his second wife Emmy, who visited the camp to listen to the mourning songs for Oscar's deceased sister. Other visitors came and left during the ritual. Edmund was instructed by Jerome and would reach the fourth grade of initiation (*mikinatringa*), for which he had to perform his first song in the *ajipa* (cf. Goodale 1971: 207). With that, however, Edmund was considered almost fully initiated; he would only have to compose three songs for the *ajipa* in the next *kulama*. From time to time my 'brother-in-law' Simon told me to participate in ritual actions such as the dancing, fire-throwing and 'spearing' of the yams. He had Ruth sing after him.

Jack Munuluka was the 'boss' of the yam ritual held at Myilly Point in Nguiu from 18 May onwards. He had committed himself not to drink beer during the ritual. In the early 1950s Tobias had lived on the spot where it would be carried out. Two 'brothers' of Jack, Basil and Ryan Munuluka, took part with him in the ritual; they were all son's sons of Miputingkimi, Kalikalini's companion in the killings at Matalau, and 'fathers' of Tobias (his father's clan brothers). At the last minute Bruce Kerimerini decided not to take part in the *kulama*. He said he had to withdraw because his wife was very ill. Nevertheless, as it happened, he was present most of the time to listen to the songs.

Jack's sister Mavis had come with her husband from Pularumpi to support her brother in singing after him. Nancy, accompanied by Sam, Jeanette and me, had also come to 'help' with the singing. Mona Munuluka, the mother of Ryan, a bachelor, and four other women, including Marylou's sister Dorothy Kilimirika, participated as well. These women had lived at Paru outstation, on the Melville Island side of the strait, not far from the place where Tobias had been buried. They told me they had moved across to Nguiu on Bathurst Island because they were afraid of the spirit of the dead man. The women would not return before the final mortuary rituals for Tobias had been carried out. During the first night of the *kulama* several people came to listen to the mourning songs for their deceased relatives. Steven Tampajani, Tobias' paternal 'brother', and Tobias' children were present throughout the ritual.

The first night (*purimikuwalumili*) or 'night of sorrow' was conceived of as particularly dangerous. Children (but see Goodale 1971: 187) and pregnant women or women with babies had to be kept away from the *kulama* camp. The men painted their bodies with red ochre, the colour associated with danger, blood, revenge, and mourning. The threat came from a spiritual entity associated with the seeds of the tall spear grass, called *merakati*, and from the life-threatening presence of the spirits of the dead and the eventual approach of sneak attackers.[62] At dusk, the ritual could begin with a dialogue between the women and the men, as recorded by Grau: 'They are coming!' 'Who?' 'Murderers (*kwampi*)!' 'We will fight them!' (1983: 195). The two rituals I describe here were occasions in remembrance of an actual killing.

In Pularumpi, therefore, Simon wanted Tobias' former lover Nancy, to begin the singing. She faced Tobias' hut, uttering expressions of sorrow, '*agai-agai-agai*'. Then she proceeded with a song of mourning: (Dead man telling his deceased wives) 'Come along and make the *kulama* like my brother [Sam] and son [Simon]./Go and hear the *kulama*!/It's the first night they sing./I can't let my son and my brother sing by themselves.' Jerome was the next person to sing, because Tobias had been married to his half-sister. He walked backwards and forwards performing an *ambaru*-song too: (Dead man saying) 'How you gotta sing my son [Simon]?/I don't know how you sing my son./Maybe you will name those people who murdered me.' Jerome and the audience wailed. Sam and Nancy called out in appreciation of the song. Nancy commented, 'That's mean he good singer, giving him sorry, because he got good voice and he sing very well, he pronounce properly words.'

At dusk on 18 May 1989, Jack Munuluka stamped his feet on the shores of Bathurst Island. He faced Tobias' grave behind the moonlit mangroves on the other side of the Apsley Strait. Jack was said to be 'awakening' the spirit of the dead man, telling him he was going to carry out the seasonal yam ritual or *kulama*: 'My son, my own son listen to me!/I'm doing *kulama* tonight.'

Dorothy responded with a widow or *ambaru*-song. This woman, a sister and former co-wife of Tobias' last wife, Marylou, mentioned the names of her deceased husbands instead of those of Tobias: (Dead men saying) 'We are sitting in the mangroves at the boat-landing (near Tobias' burial place) listening to our father [Jack].' Jack called out again to Tobias' spirit at Pawularitarra.

The men lined up in the open space in the middle of the camp. The living and the dead were perceived as being very close at this time. In the Old Camp at Pularumpi the men turned to face the scene of the killing; at Myilly Point in Nguiu they faced Tobias' grave on the other side of the strait. The men lifted their arms, spat, and threw burning twigs in that direction. They repeated this at all points of the compass, while calling out '*kwai-kwai-kwai-hoo-hoo*'. When asked, they said it was about 'fighting business' and 'chasing devils [spirits of the dead] away'; this fire-throwing was intended to stop the fighting. The men and, after them, the women called out, 'Where they are fighting!' (*kapiurukwupari*). One of the participants explained to me: 'They are pushing all the people in the war and make them die. This *kulama* tries to stop them from making fights.'

After this ritual episode the men went back to their campfires but sat down apart from the women. They took turns in singing in the middle of the ceremonial ground. The singer first hummed at his campfire, putting the words of his song in the right order and metre ('line 'em up'). Then he stood up, sang aloud while walking around the ceremonial ground and beating time with two clubs. The song was repeated at their campfires by women married or closely related to the performer. Mourning songs ended in wailing. Songs of various types were performed in a particular style, in which the use of special words and the clubs were characteristic features. The rest of the night was designated as 'the time we are lying down' (cf. Goodale 1971: 185; Brandl 1971: 250). This lying down seemed to be associated with sleeping, dreaming, and death (in contrast to standing up). The men performed songs about grief or sorrow, grievances, worries, and complaints they had, and songs about gossip and false accusations or 'talk about rubbish'. Most prominent were the mourning songs about the deceased of the past year. Thus my informants also spoke about 'the night of sorrow'. In this context people used the appropriate mortuary kinship terms (cf. appendix 1). A number of other bereaved people came to the camp to listen to these songs. The performer concluded his song with wailing and hitting himself with a club. The women sang and the audience cried and wailed in unison with the performer. The song performances went on until after midnight, with intervals, as more and more people fell asleep and the songs, so to speak, ran out.

In Pularumpi, Roger sang about his 'son' Tobias: 'Those people from Pularumpi, they are bad soldiers (*kwampi*)/They cut in half my penis with a knife.' Roger indicated his bereavement status (*unantani pulanga*) and made an allusion to the killing. He continued: 'Those shit-people (*kulingumpi*), maybe they ate faeces and they been murder that man.' Eating excrement was a sign of madness; at the same time it alluded to excrement (*kineri*), a dreaming of Tobias' father's father. Destroying someone's faeces happened to be a technique for killing that particular person. Furthermore, Roger verbally abused the people who had killed Tobias. In ordinary life such an insult could not be left unchallenged. People would say, 'I am not a piece of excrement, I have a lot of names'. In other words, the singer urged the killers to make themselves known. He wailed, repeated his song, and wailed again, 'giving sorry man underneath mango tree'. Nancy inserted a mourning song of her own in her wailing: (Dead man saying) 'How would my father think about me?/I am a dead man.' The song seems to express wonder about how it could have happened, as both Tobias and Kalikalini were reputed fighters. As mentioned before, a son was supposed to inherit his father's character traits, and Kalikalini was a killer of renown.

Sam performed a song about the morning Tobias' body had been discovered under the mango tree. He knew he had been accused, by Mary among others, of having killed his younger 'brother'. As an elder 'brother', however, he was supposed to protect him. Sam pointed out in his song that he could hardly be blamed, as he had been asleep and was 'deaf' (could not understand, in both senses of the term): 'My own granddaughter Claudia came and she woke me up, "Why are you sleeping? Your brother is dead, you stupid!"'

Jerome also sang about Tobias. He alluded to twofold trouble, according to Nancy. First, Jerome made more or less an admission of guilt: he had been arguing with Tobias in the Social Club, claiming he was mischievous. Second, after a number of discussions the bereaved children decided he would not be buried in Pularumpi but somewhere else. Jerome sang: 'He [Tobias] did not do that/He would not do that, go away from this place/Maybe somebody here was talking about him/He [Tobias] is saying he heard people talking about him/That's why he run away from this place.'

Earlier I described Tobias' plans and attempts to leave Pularumpi. He stated he did not want the troubles he had become involved in. The only way to avoid an escalation of the conflict was to move away and Tobias was well aware of that. Then Jerome took the stance of his deceased half-sister Kate, Tobias' second wife: 'All my kids [female speaking, implying himself as their mother's brother] are crying for their father/They are all crying just like a frog.' After their mother's death, a paternal 'sister' of Tobias of the Alitaraka family had raised the children, the youngest being only eigtheen months old. (Jerome himself had become an orphan when he was a little child; a senior man of this family taught him things he would like to have learned from his father.) Therefore, they were crying like a frog or *alitaraka*; this reflected their personal experience of having been separated from their father before. At the same time the 'crying like a frog' was an allusion to their decision-making about their father's burial place, about which they kept changing their minds. Jerome was of the opinion that Tobias wanted to be buried in Pularumpi near his three wives and brother. He commented to me that it was 'silly' to split up the family. In his wailing he called out, 'Oh, my husband!', 'Oh, my children [female speaking]!' This denoted, according to Nancy, 'he got a big mob of family'. Next he addressed his 'father' Simon and his 'father's sisters', Mabel and Mary, in a mourning song woven into his crying: 'Maybe there was talking about him/That's why he ran away from Pularumpi/He lives by himself [made his home] at Pawularitarra.' This song ended with an expression of grief identifying Kitiruta's (actual and classificatory) descendants: 'ninka-ninka-ninka'. As we have seen, Kitiruta forewarned the victims of Tobias' father in this way. After his performance Jerome said to the audience, 'He [Tobias] left his brother [buried] here'.

Simon composed a mourning song about Tobias' last wife Marylou, who had died when Simon's car, driven by Kevin, rolled over. Simon's children were maternal 'siblings' (paputawi) of the dead woman. They were entitled to ask their father to organise the post-funeral rituals for her. Simon's clan related to the women's clan in terms of 'mother's brother'. Simon sang: (His children saying) 'Hey, what about you?/You did not make a ceremony!' (Somebody else talking to him) 'Well, you shouldn't make big fuss of this, because your daughter's accident.' It was a convention that the singer in a position of possible blame express an intention to destroy the cause of death; Simon's car had been the agent of the woman's death. He continued, 'Yeah, I will bust that car!' Nancy explained to me that people had asked Simon, 'Why do you not go to kill [hit] him [Kevin]?' But Simon held that it was 'his own fault', for he had consented to their using his car. Hence his next song line might be seen as an admission of guilt in answering the question: 'I won't do that!' Simon wailed and performed a mourning song in mamanukuni-style: 'I nearly bust 'em up that car!'; 'I nearly burned my car!' Nancy exclaimed, 'Tom is coming!' Simon sang fast like his 'father', the late Tom Palurati, a brother of Tobias' first wife, Gloria, and clan brother of Marylou. In 'following' this 'father', alluding at the same time to the high speed at which the car had been driven, the singer closely identified with his dead 'daughter'.

Jerome sang about a grievance. He claimed he would have been given a clan sister of Tobias' for organising a mortuary ritual for her deceased father, because he was a 'good songwriter'. During the time of my fieldwork he kept rebuking her relatives for not handing her over to him whenever he performed in mortuary rituals for these people. Once he even refused to dance at a funeral because he 'did not get a girl' from them.

Edmund performed a mourning song for Tobias: 'I am sorry for my [sister's] son, I lost him./I still think about him, he used to say *ilimani* [mother's brother].'[63] Sam sang about Nancy's performance at Tobias' funeral: (Saying to his 'children') 'There was a big mob of people who saw our mother dancing./There at Pawularitarra she did her top off.' He had not been amused at his wife's showing off in front of all those people.

Simon in his song for Tobias stressed his bereavement status (*marauni pularti*): 'To where is my mother's milk gone?/I didn't drink really milk!/Who did it, busting my mother's milk?' In other words, he sang, who killed Tobias? While wailing he called out, 'I am really sorry for you my mother's brother!'

Sam emphasised his bereavement status (*putani*) too in singing about Tobias' death. He had to sing about his injured leg: 'I am lying down here at Pularumpi/I got something, I got pain in my leg.' Sam forgot his lyrics. Nancy corrected him and added a last line: 'Something, maybe you got big boil on your leg.' Then, outside the ceremonial ground, she performed herself: (Dead man saying) 'My elder 'brother' is still thinking about me!' (She herself) 'We are having *kulama* with our 'son' [female speaking, Simon].' Jerome repeated his earlier song about Tobias.

In Nguiu, Jack then staged a song of complaint: 'My friends sent a letterstick [message] from Pularumpi to here/When I was reading that letterstick I couldn't understand it/That letterstick came from my 'mother's brother's daughters' but I couldn't understand/Only one telephone call I received.' Nancy explained to me his grievance was that he, being Tobias' 'father', had not properly been informed about Tobias' death by his relatives from Pularumpi. Mary's daughter Karen had made the phone call from Darwin. Nancy had no doubts about its contents. She shouted in defence of her husband, 'He wouldn't do that, one *amoa*!' In other words, Sam and Tobias had the same father's mother (*amoa*), and therefore it was out of the question that he would have killed his own 'brother'. They were related too closely, she argued. No one in the audience responded directly to her yelling.

Later that night Jack performed a mourning song for Tobias' last wife Marylou, as she was of his clan. He called her 'mother': 'Where about is my mother gone?/She won't come alive again/I was looking for her everywhere/I tried to call out for her but she couldn't answer me.'

The next morning each man made a sharpened digging stick (*arlukuni*) similar to a child's toy spear out of mangrove wood. The digging sticks were painted with red ochre.

The men ate the roasted *muranga* yams, which had been hidden by the women the previous day, or white bread instead. They lined up again in the middle of the ceremonial ground and put pieces of these yams in their mouths. As in the ritual of the previous night, they spat out the yam in four directions. This ritual action was repeated with water as well. The water was said to clear the voice (*muraka*, also throat) in the same way as the presentation of water to the close relatives of the deceased after a death. This ritual of spitting the yams and water seemed to be an inversion of the ritual of throwing fire: both were said to drive evil spirits away and to stop the fighting. It terminated the period of exceptional danger. After this, children were allowed to come into the camp.

The men sat down and employed two little sticks to clean their ears. Then they put these twigs upright into the earth (cf. Mountford 1958: 133); with this, one man said, the 'trouble' they had dealt with was 'finished' (the action seems analogous to the placing of a sapling at each end of the grave mound). In Hart's notes on a yam ritual the men said, 'Leave 'em there' (1928/29). I was told the ritual cleansing of the ears enabled them to hear sneak attackers (*kwampi*) approaching (cf. Grau 1983: 164). Hart states, 'The idea is that if you do this you plenty savvy [understand] you see nighttime, you will detect anybody sneaken along you, you no more forget anything etc.' (ibid.).

Next the male participants painted themselves with white pipeclay to resemble Purikikini, the mythological owl who carried out the first *kulama*. Having daubed their fingers in the paint, they again lifted their arms. With the right hand they put the clay on their right eye, with the left hand on the left eye. So they went on to paint the hair on their heads, shoulders, upper arms and chest; Hart (1928/29) observed them also painting their pubic hair. Goodale writes that paint would protect them against sickness and gave bodily strength and good eyesight (1971: 189–90).

One by one, the men took a bucket, substituting for the bark basket of earlier times, and lifted it above their shoulders. Each man faced towards his dreaming places and ancestral graves, directed the bucket, and tapped the bottom, calling out '*pooh*'. This ritual, as an element of the seasonal marking of the beginning of the dry season, was said to ensure the return of rain and thunder (cf. Grau 1983: 164, but see also Brandl 1971: 263).

The men left the camp, walking single-file to the jungle nearby in order to collect the *kulama* yams. There they dug out the yams with their sticks, taking the utmost care not to break any of the hairy roots, as damage to the *kulama* yams would produce sickness. The diggers spoke quietly to the personalised yams to 'awaken' them (cf. Brandl 1971: 263; Goodale 1971: 190–1). One 'boss' told me the removal of the rather large quantity of *kulama* yams would cause rains in his country, the sub-district where his father's father had been buried. The men walked back toward the camp as they had come, taking turns carrying the bucket of yams on their shoulders.

In the neighbourhood of the *kulama* camp, the men hid the bucket of yams behind a tree and covered it with tall grass stalks. Then there was a break until late afternoon.

At that time the *kulama* men renewed the white paint on their bodies. They took their digging sticks and hit the ground in the centre of the camp, calling out '*hoi-hoi-hoi*'. In Pularumpi the men encircled the ceremonial ground and went on their hands and knees to the middle while making the sounds of a dingo and scratching the earth. They did so, I was told, because the dingo was the dreaming of the eldest man in the *kulama*, Tobias' 'brother' Sam Kerimerini.

Then they cleared the ground of grass (at this stage all kinds of grass were called *merakati*, according to Pilling 1958: 161), stones, leaves, and so forth. With their digging sticks – the men in Nguiu used a shovel as a substitute – they made a large circular pile of sand, scraped away from the inside. In the middle of this ceremonial ring (*milimika*) they shaped a small circle by putting saplings half a person's height upright in the ground. This '*kulama* oven' was then filled more than halfway up with pieces of firewood. When this was finished they walked in each other's footsteps, counter-clockwise around the oven, beating time with two sticks, and performed songs that had cleansing as their theme. In Pularumpi, for example, Jerome stated that there was death and rubbish in the ceremonial ring; he used a loader to clean it up. Simon sang about another cleansing, a confession of the people who had killed Tobias: 'I am a cheeky bugger, I can kill everybody/And you only call yourself cheeky but you do not go and hit people like this/Well, you should come up and talk to us in front of these people sitting here.' In his song, in the Nguiu ritual, Jack stated he cleared the ceremonial ground to have a fight with the man who killed Tobias. He depicted this man as a coward: 'I am cleaning the place for this murderman/I will get two large clubs and crush his face/When he sees these large clubs he will run away.'

After dark the men painted in red silently sneaked up to the tree outside the camp where the yams had been buried under grass. The spirits of the dead were said to be near. The men symbolically killed or 'speared' the yams with stalks of spear grass. Then they put a bucket of water next to the one with the yams; the yams were uncovered and put in water. Next they ritually cleansed themselves, splashing their faces and bodies with this water, to remove the pollution resulting from the 'killing'. The yams were covered up again, and the men went back to the ceremonial ground.

Following the ritual bath the second night (*apurigianaga*) the men could sing about anything, 'whatever you think'. Back in the ceremonial ground Basil Munuluka sang: 'I myself wash away *pukamani* [referring to the red paint, associated with Tobias' country]/I am giving myself sorry because I am washing away *pukamani*.' He expressed his regret that he could not go on with an actual killing, avenging Tobias' death.

Ryan Munuluka had composed a song about the myth of Purukupali and Tapara, or the moon: 'Tapara and Purukupali had a fight, and Purukupali was wounded, got shot, at his leg by Tapara/He put blood [running] on the ceremonial ring (*milimika*).' As mentioned before, Purukupali killed his younger maternal 'brother' Tapara, the moon, who had seduced Purukapali's wife. According to Nancy, Ryan had inferred suspicion of her husband Sam. The allegory presented in the song text was suggestive. Sam and his younger maternal 'brother' Tobias, who had an affair with Sam's wife, had had a fight too. Sam had suffered a leg injury; literally, because he had been bitten on the legs by dogs (his dreaming) for, so I was told, he had not painted them following Tobias' death. Symbolically, because in an allegorical representation of Purukupali he became a bereaved maternal 'brother' (*putani*) of Tobias. Then, taking the analogy a bit further, the elder 'brother' had put blood on the younger one. Tobias, the younger 'brother', had been found dead covered with blood. In the purification rituals this location, where this yam ritual had been initially planned, became a ceremonial ground. The younger 'brother', Tapara or the moon, was represented here by the ceremonial ring. Red ochre, with the connotation of blood, had just been sprinkled on the circular ceremonial ground.

Jack took up this theme and stressed his bereavement status when he sang: 'Leeches have bitten me and a lot of blood comes running from my penis/I am bleeding [a lot of blood running] on where I walk in the ceremonial ring.' Jack's words were also suggestive of an allegation. As I said, the *kulama* men had splashed themselves with water (*moluki*) after they had symbolically attacked the yams. In the past the men and the yams went into a pond or billabong in a swamp (cf. Spencer 1914; Goodale 1971). One of Sam's dreamings was *iliti*. Sam's brother Bruce explained it to me as follows, '*iliti* when you go *moluki* in a swamp, round one like billabong, in that swamp you go *moluki* you feel itchy from that *iliti*, swamp at Bathurst Island, there *iliti*'. Jack did not mention *iliti* directly but stated that leeches had bitten him. These were the cause of him becoming bereaved of his 'son' Tobias, represented by his bleeding penis and the ceremonial ring. I believe the lyrics were left deliberately ambiguous (cf. Keen 1977; Pilling 1958: 97). It should be noted that Sam in the *kulama* in Pularumpi himself had sung that people in Nguiu and Milikapiti had gathered around and said he maybe had killed his 'brother' Tobias.

Another conventional subject to sing about was a boat. In the metaphorical songs about boats all sorts of relationships (to countries, dreamings, particular people or clans) could be emphasised. Then the men, one at a time performing in the ring, sang about their mothers-in-law. As mentioned before, this was an avoidance relationship, so the men referred to her by touching their own shoulder with a club and of course used metaphors (such as jumping over a rope, climbing up the branches of a tree or putting one's shadow on her shoulder), instead of speaking directly. The male performer stressed he was the one who had or had to have her daughter as his wife (even when the promised wife had married another man). Finally they sang about their children, sons in the Pularumpi case, mentioning their names. Although these children were adults, the performers described them as children competing (e.g., swimming, dancing, or running on the beach). After all this singing the people went to sleep. Around the camp, flying foxes gathered in the mango and cashew trees in the moonlight.

The following morning the men put pieces of red ant-bed on top of the firewood in the *kulama* oven. While they were doing this they sang about (male) wild honey bees: 'They are going in' (*talingei*). Tiwi used to make this observation of the bees moving in their nests high up in the trees by lifting their hand facing the sun and looking through their fingers. Where the bees were going in, one could find sugar bag (wild honey) in abundance. Wild honey could also be found in ant-beds, pieces of which were put between the surrounding branches high up in the oven. One man in Pularumpi sang about himself as a sugar bag fly going into the tree and making a lot of honey there. Goodale reports that the men in a 1954 *kulama* said, 'We are here, mother-in-law' (1971: 195). The branches holding together the pile of firewood were referred to as mother-in-law (*amprinua*, cf. Brandl 1971: 263). A common metaphor in singing about the mother-in-law was climbing up the branches of a tree (which in turn stood for the shoulder). When put in the earth oven later, the yams, treated as people, would be transformed. As Goodale points out, 'The yam has many fine rootlets resembling whiskers, and is referred to by the men in masculine terms as "the big boss of the country." As the ritual preparations proceed however, the yam becomes feminine. The men refer to it as daughter as they place it in the ceremonial oven, called its mother, for cooking' (1982: 207).

The fire in the oven was lit. The male performers, following this ritual action, could sing about setting on fire sleeping places (windbreaks, paperbark blankets) of their 'mother's brothers'; they did this pretending to be spirit children, because the 'mother's brothers' would not give them women (note this recurrent problem, also a source of conflict between Tobias and Isaac, could here be dealt with), and could sing about setting on fire the blankets and clothes of unfaithful women. In other words, they sang about 'woman trouble', about not getting the wives they claimed to be entitled to. In this context they could also sing about a spirit called *jamparipari*, said to punish wife-robbers.

With twigs from the fire the men burned the hairs on their arms and legs as well as their pubic hair. They shaved their beards off or pulled them out. Then the men painted their bodies with red ochre to resemble Tiringini, the mythological red-backed sea eagle who with Purikikini took part in the first *kulama*. One after the other, they sang again, this time about the irresistible attractiveness of their female cousins (*aminiatuwi*), pretending they themselves were these women. They pretended they were these 'sisters' with whom they had a grandparent in common, dead or alive, mentioned the women's names as theirs, employed high-pitched voices (in a female style of singing), postured and moved like them. The men stressed their attractiveness towards men, for instance, in depicting and singing about the way they walked, 'showing off'. Sometimes men combed their hair and made ponytails. (One man who had died, I was told, used to perform with a handbag and high heels.) These performances were taken to be humorous by the audience; the women portrayed would especially roar with laughter.

After this the men left the camp and returned with the bucket of yams. Each man walked around the oven with the bucket on his shoulder and then passed it on to the next man. They sang about a successful hunt and collecting tasty foods (stingrays, barramundi, mussels, cycad fruits) in abundance in their countries, stating how they shared these with people who could not go foraging. The bucket with the yams was placed next to the fire. Paperbark, and in Nguiu cardboard as a substitute, was laid on top of the bucket. One man had made a ring of the long, green stalks of spear grass that previously covered the yams. This ring of grass was called *tapara*, the moon. In the popular Tiwi myth, mentioned above, Tapara offered to bring Purukupali's son back to life within three days, but Purukupali declared that because his son had died all people would have to die. Tapara or the moon might be seen as a symbol of regeneration, as with the waning and waxing of the moon. The ring was put against the bucket with yams. Two digging sticks had been thrust into the ground in the ceremonial ring, one on each side just in front of the bucket. (At this point a handful of powdered red ochre was strewn on the floor of the ceremonial ground in Pularumpi.)

While the fire was burning down, mourning songs – again about the deceased of the past year – were performed. Most of the songs concerned Tobias' violent death. Before the yam ritual in Pularumpi, Nancy told me that at this stage the names of the persons who had killed him would be mentioned. Afterwards, she volunteered that to her disgust no names had been mentioned. Roger sang: 'That is the man [who killed Tobias], he should own up/But I have a one-sided barbed spear (*tungkwaliti*) here standing up beside me to shoot him back too/Maybe I got to forgive him after I have found out from the police.' Edmund proceeded: 'Oh well, people should find out that killer, because he killed my "son" [female speaking, Tobias].' Simon performed another song telling the killer(s) to confess the homicide: 'Those people, they murdered my "mother's brother" [Tobias]/Their fathers are rubbish [excrement] but his father was a murderman/Maybe that trouble was here with him, they bring it out because they been murder him.' Jerome, however, sang about Purukupali who said all people had to die because his son had died. He should not have said that, according to the singer; he was 'talking wrong thing'. Sam had left the *kulama* camp. Jerome told me that Sam was frightened. Roger and Simon had performed a so-called *karinimawatumingumi*, a song telling a 'murderer' to confess. He was urged to say, 'I am, I did it'. This was also a song of revenge. According to Nancy, this type of song, *purakutukintinga*, had to be performed when the fire was burning. Pilling notes such a song (for which he recorded the terms *parumukutjinga* and *watumukutjinga*) might be sung on the third day of the yam ritual. He writes, 'These songs were sung by a principal in a revenge killing. The singer of a *parumukutjinga* composes words about a person whose murder he had already avenged or whose murder he still intends to avenge' (1958: 101). The three men of the Munuluka patrilineage in the yam ritual at Nguiu were entitled to avenge the killing of their 'son' Tobias.

Jack was dressed up as the leader of a revenge expedition. He had painted himself all in red, wore a head-dress of cockatoo feathers and a goose-feather ball around his neck. Jack held up a bundle of red coloured spears, as formerly used by sneak attackers or *kwampi*, and sang: 'That murderman he should say, "I am the one who killed that man, I made you *unantani* (bereaved 'father')"/You should come here and say, "I am the one who killed your son"/If you don't come here I will kill you with a spear in the side of your body.' While wailing he performed a *mamanukuni* song: (Dead man saying) 'Just like that my "father"!/You get a spear and shoot him in his side.' Instead of himself the singer mentioned the name of his grandfather Miputingkimi and he referred to Kalikalini, who speared a victim in his side at Matalau, to which the song alluded.

Basil proceeded with the following song: 'Somebody whispered in my ears, "Maybe someone at Pularumpi has killed your 'son'"/But I was not told about the murderer/If they tell me who did it I will go and spear him!/I want to see him in front but they all sneak away/I want to spit him in his face.' In other words, Basil said the killers were cowards. By his intention 'to spit him in the face' he indicated he wanted to initiate a fight. Nancy echoed Jack's words in an *ambaru* song: (Dead man saying) 'Just like that my dad!/Hold up the spear and spear him in the side of his body.'

Ryan stressed a feature of Miputingkimi's fighting. Once, when his grandfather had no spears left, he went on to fight with his bare hands and knocked his opponents down. In the ambush meant as a counter-killing, Miputingkimi's victim had called out, 'Don't do that, don't kill me!' Ryan recalled this in his song: 'That murderman here, I want to grab him with both hands and knock him down/If he stays here with me I will get a spear and spear him/He will call out, that [supposedly] cheeky man now, "Don't do that, don't kill me!".'

When the fire had completely burned down, Tobias' children had to perform a *turagha* or man-killing dance depicting spirit children and sneak attackers. They had their bodies painted with red ochre and held spears, previously held by Jack but now untied, in their left hands. Their 'father', Bruce Kerimerini, who was fiercely beating time with two fighting clubs, sang the accompanying song: 'The shark went into Pupatu creek./Big waves made him invisible./At Wangaru there were big waves but the shark was underneath the water.' The song had been composed by Bruce's father Tajamini in the early 1930s for the mortuary rituals for Tobias' sister, Donna, who died as a little girl. The shark might be seen here as a sneak attacker who, under cover of darkness, invaded another country to kill. Tiwi depict the shark in shallow water as chasing its prey, the mullet (Tobias' dreaming) for instance. Tobias' children, instructed by Bruce, merged their dance with movements of the shark dance. The dancers symbolically speared the ashes in the middle of the ring. While they were dancing Jack called out to the audience, 'Their grandfather is a real murderman (*kwampini*)! He is not afraid of anybody!' Dorothy, their 'mother', composed an *ambaru*-song for them: (Dead man saying) 'You give them sorry, my son and daughters dancing.'

When the fire had burnt down the men threw the leftover firewood away in the direction of their countries, that is the locations of their ancestral burial sites, where they were supposed to go later on to burn the tall grass. The ashes were cleared with small green boughs. Spencer notes 'the idea of this being to cleanse it of all evil influence – if this were not done they believe the evil would go inside them and they would break out all over with sores' (1914: 101). Water from the bucket with yams was splashed on the hot embers, leaving a base of hot pieces of antnest. The men called out '*brr brr*', which, according to Spencer, 'is a cry indicating both defiance and the fact that, in any contest, the men making it are winning' (ibid.: 95). This call belonged to the shark dance and represented the shark chasing its prey. The ring of grass, the 'full moon', was placed on the embers. The yams were put within the ring and covered with paperbark. With their digging sticks the men dug sand away from around the oven and put it on top of the paperbark. The resulting mound functioned as an earth oven. The men sat on their heels, patted the mound, and shook their bodies in imitation of Alipiura, the mythological pelican, shaking its feathers when coming out of the water.[64] Again they made a call similar to the one mentioned above. I was told it was the sound of the pelican, and this call in a somewhat higher voice and repeated faster is also a feature of the pelican dance.

After about an hour, when the yams were nearly ready, they resumed the singing. The songs, related to the preparation of the yams, were about the roasting of bush foods, a bell ringing for dinner (an allusion to the meals they used to have in a canteen near the mission dormitories a few decades earlier), a table being laid for a dinner in a restaurant, and intentions of eating all the large amount of food oneself. The yams were dug out. After they had cooled, covered in the paperbark, they were laid on the bark, peeled, and sliced. The men mashed the soft yam with red ochre into a mix and rubbed it onto their bodies (head, eyes, chest, and joints of the limbs in particular). Special attention was given to rubbing the paste into the joints and the eyes. This treatment was supposed to give strength, I was told, so the men would not break their limbs while hunting and would retain good eyesight. Also women rubbed the paste on their heads, eyes, chest, arms and legs. The men gave their little children and grandchildren a similar treatment. Children who had trouble walking were brought to the camp to have their knees rubbed with the processed yams.

Then the men started to prepare themselves for the *ajipa*, the highlight of the *kulama*. Until then the body paintings had been monochrome, either in red or white. For this phase of the *ajipa* they used all four colours: yellow, red, white and black. Faces were painted in striking designs. The initiate in the 1989 *kulama* at Pularumpi, Edmund, had his face painted in yellow and black by his instructor Jerome. This time he was allowed only to sing a single song during the *ajipa*, while the others performed at least three songs. During the *ajipa* the men could show they were 'big-headed' (skilled composers, or as Tiwi say, 'songwriters') for the singing at this stage was considered extremely difficult. They could make use of a wide range of subjects but often their compositions, which were of unusual length, stressed remarkable and memorable events of the past year. Brandl notes that 'subjects external to the indigenous culture were incorporated in the subject matter' (1970: 476). This was also evident in Spencer's and later detailed accounts of the yam ritual. The *ajipa* song texts in Hart's fieldnotes show that the people he stayed with in bush camps in the northern part of Bathurst Island were very familiar with town life in Darwin at the end of the 1920s. Among the subjects were aeroplanes, the railway station, a gramophone, bicycles, an

architect's plans, a film show; all these things were fitted in with strik-
ingly keen observations (Hart 1928/29). Isaac performed for me his first
ajipa song, dating from about 1942. The song text told of a battle
between submarines and bombers north of Melville Island from the perspective of the crews inside them.[65] In the 1989 yam rituals the participants performed songs about modern means of communication on the
islands (satellites, telephones, VCRs and television sets), among other
things, and about an international yacht race from Bali to Melville Island
(that occurred months earlier), how these people despite the rough sea
had arrived safely. Like 'the night of sorrow', the *ajipa* drew a larger audience than other parts of the ritual. The 'bosses' recorded these songs,
popular for a long time after the *kulama*, on tape too.

Next, in the Pularumpi ritual, Sam sang that he had been falsely
accused of having killed his 'brother' Tobias: 'Those people at Nguiu
and at Milikapiti gathered around and were talking about me/They were
saying maybe I did kill my "brother", I am *putani* [bereaved of a maternal "brother"]/I would not do that, kill my "brother" like this.' When he
stumbled over his words the other men encouraged him to go on with
his song. Roger and Jerome in a song referred to the people in the other
townships who had been gossiping about people in Pularumpi concerning Tobias' violent death. They said the latter were not rubbish but had
a lot of names. In his last song line Roger alluded to one backbiter, a
bachelor in Nguiu: 'I didn't stay with my mother!' They had, further, to
sing about their 'fathers' and their relationship to them.

The *kulama* yams were put in the bucket of water again. The yams were
brought back to the tree away from the camp, and were left to soak. In
Pularumpi, the *kulama* men (and I) performed the mullet dance at the
ceremonial ground, making the movements of mullet jumping out of
the water. This dance of a dreaming of the eldest man in the *kulama*,
Sam, alluded to the yams soaking in the water. It identified Sam, and by
implication his 'brother', Tobias, with their respective fathers who had
the same mother; the mullet jumped out of the water near the seat of
their clan (*imunga*), Wulintu or Nodlaw Island. In a rather complex song
Roger linked his ancestral burial sites in his country, moving from the
north towards Pularumpi (from the grave of his father's brother at
Tupulurupi to the one of his father at Tuloriati), water being the theme
of his song, and his relationship to Tobias: 'At Tupulurupi I started to be
pukamani./I nearly washed myself at Punguwamiritigi./At Pungolumpi I
still have *pukamani* [cannot touch food]/I sit down at Tuloriati/My
father said, "Why are you *pukamani?*"/And I said, "I am *unantani*"
[bereaved of a 'son', Tobias].' Jerome sang about a shark, his dreaming,
in rough sea near his ancestral country. Coming through big waves the
shark had stronger fins than a shovelnosed stingray.

Then the men in Pularumpi performed songs about their daughters; for example, how an elder daughter taught the others to dance on the mudflat at the beach, or how the singer's daughters were playing and fighting at the beach, and the eldest one gave the younger ones a smack when they swore, after which they had to dance for her. At this stage, the male performers at Nguiu sang about their sons. Earlier on Dorothy composed the following song: (Kalikalini telling his son) 'That lady she is singing with a different voice.' Nancy explained to me she meant she had been drunk, as her sister had been when she died in the car accident. At this point, when the men came to the stage of singing for their sons, Dorothy added another *ambaru* song: (Tobias saying to his father) 'Maybe your niece [Marylou] is coming close to me.'

In Pularumpi, Simon proceeded with singing about his clan members: 'When they drink it's not very good/I am a bottle of liquor and my whole clan is drinking away/When they drink they have a wobbling gait/When they have finished all that beer they are telling all those stories.' Simon, who had given up drinking more than twenty years earlier, described himself as a bottle of liquor instead of in the conventional way by using the name of his clan ('I am Fire'). It was a severe criticism not only of his clanspeople's drinking but also of their talking about other people behind their backs: members of Simon's clan had accused Sam of having killed Tobias. The story had been spread from Milikapiti to Nguiu. No one had had the courage to speak out at the meetings organised by Simon after Tobias' death. Besides Simon probably thought the allegation to be an unsubstantiated rumour. Hence their drunken talk.

Finally the *kulama* men performed an eye (*pitjara*) song, so they would have good eyes, I was told, to detect sneak attackers or other enemies in the following year. Eyes or vision being the subject matter of this type of song, they could proceed to perform as if they were one of their dreamings, such as a bird. Edmund, for instance, sang that he was a jungle fowl, when he saw people he shook his wings and his feathers stood up (that is, 'he got fright'). And Simon sang that people tried to shoot him with a slingshot. The bird was a dreaming of his too. He, the bird, moved his shoulders, calling out, 'Nobody can shoot me because I am a good dancer'.

First thing the next and last morning, the men took the remaining pieces of ant-bed from the oven and threw these at a tree. This ritual action seemed to function as a kind of oracle. If they hit the tree, so they explained, it ensured that they would have game for the coming year. If not, they would just have 'bad luck' (cf. Goodale 1971: 204). Pieces of ant-bed were also placed against the large ring of sand encircling the ceremonial ground. This practice was said to guarantee the collection of abundant food in one's country, from the land and the swamps, until the next *kulama.*

After this the men could sing about the spirit (*imanka*). In Pularumpi the people left the camp because of heavy rains. Simon later performed the *imanka* song he had planned to sing for me. In Nguiu the 'boss' broke off the ritual early in the morning, saying he had given up because his own children had refused to dance on the previous day. To my knowledge no one, neither in Pularumpi nor in Nguiu, ate then any of the yams that had been left in the water, although several people told me they would do so later on. And so the *kulama* ritual was finished.

*   *   *

As in the mortuary rituals, a 'script' (Goodale 1971) or 'central narrative' (LeVine 1982) appears to be followed. In the rituals the performers or narrators fit their own stories within the overall framing story (cf. Venbrux 1993b). Before commencing a ritual, a performer can say, 'I have a lot of stories to tell' (*ngirramini-ingati-nuruwani*, literally, 'story-big mob-I got it'). The concept of *neramini*, also meaning 'talk, word, meeting, argument and trouble', appears frequently in the context of Tiwi rituals. My informants stated that people were 'arguing with one another'; Tobias Arapi spoke of certain *kulama* songs as 'fighting with words'. The rituals were not discrete rituals: elements of the *kulama* could be used in the mortuary rituals and vice versa (and many other rituals as well). The stories 'told' by the performers happened to be related to current happenings in their social life. As these stories run through the lives of the narrators, they help them shape their culture and adjust to new situations. Therefore, in this respect I do not perceive Tiwi rituals as events with clear-cut beginnings and ends (cf. Seremetakis 1991).

Often the performances, songs in particular, had layers of meaning. Many messages were difficult to grasp unless interpreted. This seemed to be part of the intellectual game. Sometimes other participants told a singer that they understood, sometimes they asked for an explanation and were given a clue, then they applauded the performer when they realised it made sense. A person who employed complex metaphors was considered 'big-headed' or a 'good songwriter' (*jerengapuranti* for a male, and *jintingapuranti* for a female). Much could be understood from the context; the intimate knowledge of the lives, social relationships and cosmological connections of others, and the part of the ritual in which a song was performed would often be enough to infer its hidden meanings. This understanding, however, was restricted to the insiders who had acquired the knowledge and special skills needed to compose or interpret the

songs, or both. They shared a common discourse that was not only difficult to master because this form of the language differed lexically from
the spoken one (cf. Osborne 1974: 3) but also because it required knowledge of its conventional application in different types of songs and at different points in the rituals, and the symbolism or the meanings given to
the literal wording that said little to others; besides this there was the necessary creativity of the participants in linking the conventional themes
with their own stories and personal experiences put in metaphorical language and action. Turner states, 'since a ritual symbol may represent disparate, even contradictory themes, the gain in economy may be offset by
a loss in clarity of communication. This would be inevitable if such symbols existed in a vacuum, but they exist in cultural and operational contexts that to some extent overcome the loss in intelligibility and to some
extent capitalize on it' (1973: 1101). The *kulama* ritual provided an arena
in which people could express themselves without hesitation; when frightened or insecure the singer was encouraged by the audience (cf. Goodale
1971: 188). Rhetorical devices such as the use of other people's voices,
dead or alive, and the ambiguity resulting from the multilayered meanings, of course added to the protection of the performer. In their performances the participants were able to generate new meanings. Their
contributions often contained messages that might be seen as embedded
in an ongoing social discourse. As Turner suggests, 'the more complex
the ritual (many symbols, complex vehicles), the more particularistic,
localized, and socially structured its message' (1973: 1102).

Perhaps the narrative character of Tiwi rituals and these people's capac-
ity to interpret clues is related to or has evolved from their skills as hunters
in deciphering animal tracks. Ginzburg writes, 'The hunter could have
been the first "to tell a story" because only hunters knew how to read a
coherent sequence of events from the silent (even imperceptible) signs
left by their prey' (1988: 88–9). The lyrics were highly metaphorical, only
intelligible to outsiders through expert interpretation. Writing about
Ilongot hunting stories, Rosaldo makes a similar point: 'In non-literate
small-scale societies, story-tellers speak to people who share enormous
knowledge about their cultural practices, their landscape, and their past
experiences.' As a result of this, details that say little to outsiders provide
clues that reveal worlds to the audience for whom they are intended
(1986: 108–9). Narratives might, in addition, help the performers to
capture their experiences which may be otherwise difficult to grasp and to
work out indeterminate situations (exploring possibilities), evaluate
these, and make these explicable to themselves and others (not unlike an
ethnographic narrative, cf. Roth 1989).

Ritual knowledge enabled the skilled performers to obtain prestige and
influence over others. They acted as the 'bosses' in the mortuary rituals

and in this way many people who wanted to have memorable and prestigious rituals were dependent on them. The ritual performances and songs had even more 'powers' (cf. Von Sturmer 1987) in their cosmological and social implications: to maintain and to regenerate the Tiwi world, to promote health, to mark transitions in people's lives and seasonal change, to (re)define identities and relationships, to argue a case, and so forth. As we have seen, all kinds of matters could be dealt with.

The symbols or signs in Aboriginal ritual, as Stanner points out, are not only indicative but also considered effacious: 'Power over the signs is productive of their objects', hence what we see is 'the deepening and the refining of the analogical perception' (1989: 121). In the *kulama* ritual the *kulama* yams are the main symbolic vehicle for quite a number of transformations. We see revealed a mediation between the following (among other) binary oppositions:

dangerous nature	salutary culture
toxic, inedible yam	strength-giving, edible yam
death, killing	life, rebirth
sickness	health
uninitiated children	initiated adults
conflicts/grievances	peaceful relationships
bad luck	good luck/success
reliance on staple food	food in abundance
wet season	dry season

The linkages of parallel transformations are equally important. For instance, the clearing and burning of hairy roots, body hair, and tall, dry grass (roots-hair-grass) connects yams, people, and country. The regenerative power from the ritual transformation of the yams induces similar powers in people and their countries or ancestral lands, and vice versa. We have here interrelations of the nurturing properties of food in general, human reproductive and productive capacities, and environmental regeneration.

A significant attribute of the *kulama* yam as a ritual symbol is its condensation, as Turner points out, as 'many ideas, relations between things, actions, interactions, and transactions are represented simultaneously by the symbol vehicle (the ritual use of such a vehicle abridges what would verbally be a lengthy statement or argument)' (1973: 1100).[66] Spencer notes, 'The island natives evidently regard the *kolamma*, probably because it has to be specially treated before being safe to eat, as a superior kind of yam, endowed with properties such as ordinary yams do not possess' (1914: 103). Goodale (1982), following Ortner, regards the *kulama* yam as a key symbol which links the resources of food and people. We have seen above how the ritual treatment of the *kulama* yam structures and ties together many things, not only laid down in the more or less fixed ritual procedure but also to be extended by the contributions of the participants, which generate new meanings. I see the symbolic role of the *kulama* yam mainly as a vehicle bringing forth transformations (the fact that people sometimes substituted potatoes for these yams shows that the symbolic properties are not inherent in the *kulama* yams).

From Spencer's account (1914: 92–110) follows a close association between the yams and the initiates. Both were treated in a similar way: 'captured', 'buried' under bark, symbolically speared, depilated, soaked in water, 'dug out', and so on. A symbolic killing and rebirth was undergone by both yams and initiates (cf. Goodale 1971: 222), and is characteristic of rites of passage in which symbolic death and rebirth mark transitions (Hertz 1960; Van Gennep 1960). Death was an important theme in the yam ritual during the first night, until the clearing of the ceremonial ground on the second day, when the yams were hidden at the base of a tree overnight and the fire was allowed to burn down on the third day. Initiates started performing in post-funeral rituals, corresponding with the initiation of the spirits of the deceased into the world of the dead. Recent spirits of the dead were supposed to come to the *kulama* ritual. The mourning songs and expressions of grief during the first night, 'the night of sorrow', duly emphasised the theme of death. Previous *kulama* songs could be used in these mortuary rituals intended to direct the spirits away to the world of the dead. The earth oven, a mound in which the yams were 'buried', was associated with the grave mound (indeed in one case I observed, the patting of the mound as in the yam ritual replaced a funeral ceremony). My informants claimed they were cured of illnesses at their ancestral graves, those of 'father's fathers' in particular. They asked their ancestors' assistance in hunting in their countries, which the descendants could claim on the basis of the existence of those graves. The participants in the yam ritual paid attention to their countries (including the patrilineal ancestors and dreamings), where after the *kulama* the grass would be burned. In a number of ways the mortuary rituals and the yam ritual might be seen as complementary in relating the spiritual world and the world of the embodied living.

There were many references to symbolic death or killing and destruction in the yam ritual. The dance with (imaginary) spears of the patrilineal *unantawi*, representing spirit children and sneak attackers, represent an example encompassing a symbolic killing. Death by means of homicide is so sudden and abrupt that it is a powerful image of separation in the *kulama* and the death rituals alike (cf. Burke 1974: 19–20).

Hertz, in his seminal work, notes the importance of a symbolic killing as a rite of separation in death rituals:

> It is [al]so true that natural death is not sufficient to sever the ties binding the deceased to this world, that in order to become a legitimate and authentic inhabitant of the land of the dead he must first be killed. [He sees this as an initiation, as the deceased] cannot be promoted to the ranks of the true spirits, until he has been ritually killed and has been born anew. (1960: 73)

Deaths in Aboriginal societies were often treated as if the persons in question had been killed (cf. Elkin 1964: 319; Spencer and Gillen 1968: 476; Maddock 1986: 156; Meggitt 1986: 246). Tiwi acknowledge sickness as a cause of death, but at the same time they represent deaths as if some human agency were involved, whether through the violation of a taboo by the deceased acted upon by a spirit of the dead, a 'poisoning', neglect or action by the living, or armed spirits of the dead coming to take the spirit of the dying with them.

In the ritual context, as we have seen, a symbolic killing frequently occurs. Rooted in the people's experience, killings of humans by sneak attackers (as well as in spear duels and fights) might be seen as an institutionalised way of dealing with conflicts (especially those related to 'woman trouble'). Of course, from their experiences as hunters these Aboriginal people are very familiar with the act of killing.[67] The most prestigious mode of killing is by spear, either in the hunt, sneak attacks, fights or the symbolic spearing of the deceased (by spirits of the dead, and in the dances with spears of the patrilineal *unantawi*, in the past the grave mound was literally speared), initiates, yams, and in spiritual conception. 'Killing' for Tiwi includes also hitting or injuring. Conflicts and fights are often terminated with a 'good hiding' or beating with clubs, ritual punishments encompass a flogging, the bereaved hit themselves, the spirits of the dead are chased away by hitting them with sticks or branches; the same happens in mock fights during mortuary rituals, the ritual whipping of initiates and young women during first menses, or the father hitting the hand of his daughter's first newborn child.

A third mode of killing or destruction entails burning, drowning, and burial. This happens to the belongings of the deceased and of living persons with whom one wants to break all ties. Analogous to the seasonal grass-burning is the burning of body, pubic and facial hair, and a cleansing fire is employed in ritual (in smoke rituals and fires to chase away the spirits of the dead, in fire-throwing and fire-jumping, and the *kulama* oven). Drowning in water is the acknowledged remedy against possession by certain spirits, and ritual baths punctuate cleansings and lift taboos.

Burials are used in relation to the deceased, their belongings, the yams, and initiates as physical separations denoting a change of status.

Killing in the senses mentioned above (actual or symbolic) appears to be a precondition for any transition in Tiwi society. Actual or symbolic death (of animals, humans, and human conditions) appears in Tiwi cosmology not to belong to nature but to the realm of culture.

The cult of killing happens to be exemplified by the ritually important barbed spears that stand not only for the kill (the main attribute of spirits of the dead and sneak attackers) but also for new life, people of the next generation (in spiritual conception, showing of a spear to the father of the newborn child, representing the future wife, and so on). The spearing links symbolic death and rebirth. This is clear in the *turagha* dance of the bereaved children. On the one hand, they act as sneak attackers killing the deceased, symbolising the transition of the deceased from the world of the living to the world of the dead. On the other hand, re-enacting their spiritual conception symbolises their becoming bereaved and a transition from the first descending generation to the top generation. One informant called it their 'second birth in dancing'. Killing in the hunt may be seen not only in the light of death but also as it provides people with food and nourishment. Thus on this basic level, killing in this society is necessary for the continuity of human life. In sum, on a symbolic level the act of killing – characterised by suddenness, and irreversibility – represents the radical breaking of ties and separation, employed to mark clear-cut transitions.[68]

Bloch took up the theme of symbolic killing in an essay entitled 'Prey into Hunter' (1992).[69] In part he echoes Hertz but he also adds a new element, emphasising what he has termed 'rebounding violence'. He looks at the nature of ritual processes following a set pattern the world over. According to Bloch,

> These irreducible structures of religious phenomena are ritual representations of the existence of human beings in time. In fact this ritual representation is a simple transformation of the material processes of life in plants and animals as well as humans. The transformation takes place in an idiom which has two distinguishing features: first, it is accomplished through a classic three-stage dialectical process, and secondly it involves a marked element of violence or . . . of conquest (ibid.: 4).

Bloch refers to the second process as the idiom of 'rebounding violence' (ibid.). In short, he argues that something is gained by the symbolism of violence which is part of many religious phenomena; the persons undergoing it are changed, for the violence acted upon them is rebounding, enabling them to enter a world beyond process, and appropriating and conquering an external vitality. In other words, the symbolic killing is a precondition for the participants to obtain the forces and vitality of transcendental entities, whether they be animals, plants, other human beings (and, I think, one might add the spiritual world). In this way, for instance, initiates are transformed from prey into hunters, from victims into killers (Bloch 1992). One need not agree with Bloch (and accept it as a universal phenomenon) to see that in the Tiwi *kulama* ritual and the mortuary rituals the symbolism is considered efficacious. The ritual transformations of the deceased, yams, initiates and bereaved undergoing the symbolic processes of death and rebirth have in indigenous exegesis an outcome indicating a supernatural vitality. I have mentioned these renewed forces, so satisfactorily represented by the moon – killed and regenerated – in the yam ritual above. Ritually processed yams and people (dead or alive) bring and incorporate good luck, well-being, nourishment, peaceful relationships, protection, health, and so forth. I referred to the nurturing, health- and luck-giving properties of yams and ancestral graves.

Tiwi people connect and interweave personal experiences with the central narrative of the ritual process. This intermingling of stories has a common plot, transition and consummation or conquest of external vitality. These processes are neither devoid of politics nor of emotion, ensuring the participants' engagement and promotion of their interests. The related dead, having been symbolically killed (not unlike the detoxified *kulama* yams), may be seen as extremely important sources of external vitality. The supposed closeness of the living and the dead (including other spiritual entities) enables the transmission to the living of forces beyond their world. Internalisation of these forces, for instance, is exemplified by the living when they speak with the voices of the dead, the re-enactments of vitality-promoting deeds of ancestors and spiritual beings, and the perceived favourable results from contacts with spirits of the dead (assisting in hunting and gathering, giving protection, taking the newly deceased to the world of the dead) and ancestral graves (healing, good luck, and so on).

In all this, Tobias' violent death had a special quality. His abrupt death in Tiwi conceptions did not rob his spirit of vitality or his prowess as a fighter. Tobias' spirit was frequently reported to have attempted to kill certain people. For example, Tobias' next-door neighbour, Geoffrey Adranango, who had been evacuated to Darwin Hospital at the time of Tobias' death, told me that there was something 'strange' going on at Tobias' place. At night, he said, he heard the door banging. He looked out but saw nothing. 'There are two', Geoffrey said, 'the dead man and his wife, two spirits'. Early in the morning he heard her chopping firewood. Geoffrey pointed to two pieces of burnt wood. 'They make fire there', he added. Geoffrey expressed his fear of those spirits but said he was safe because of his many dogs. At the beginning of May, shortly before his death, he said to me that Tobias' spirit had tried to strangle him. Mike, earlier, had also feared strangulation by the dead man's spirit. He was staying in the hut in the Old Camp that Laura had previously shared with the white sailor. Mike told me he heard someone at his door late at night. He opened the door and saw the spirit of his father painted all in white. The spirit had attempted to get his hands on Mike's neck; Mike quickly locked the door.

A vision of Tobias' spirit preceded a more serious occurrence. On the morning of 22 May, my wife Jeanette was minding toddlers with a few Tiwi women. One of the women became upset. She said she saw Tobias' spirit entering a building under construction nearby. She predicted something terrible would happen. Instead of Tobias' spirit, Jeanette observed Isaac going into the building. In the afternoon, a female health worker (a sister of the woman who had seen the spirit) went by car to Dick's house. She wanted to pick up Martha, Tobias' 'mother', who was very sick and could not walk, to give her a bath at the health clinic. When she backed up the ambulance, Dick's baby, who had crawled under the vehicle unnoticed, was crushed under the wheels of the car and died shortly after. The little child was Isaac's 'grandson' of whom he was very fond. At the funeral, Jasmine, her sisters and younger brother, who had been sitting in Dick's yard when the accident happened, were (at Jerome's instigation) punished for their neglect, by being struck on the back with a stick.

In the ritual processes Tobias' spirit had to be neutralised; hence the elaborate mortuary rituals and the dedication of the two major yam rituals to Tobias. I see the extraordinary ritual attention to Tobias' spirit as a symbolic process not only in terms of redress but also as a cosmological procedure for rechanneling and incorporating the dead man's vitality into the survivors. The dance of his children in the Nguiu yam ritual, for instance, expressed their anger and intention to avenge their father's death; and at the same time it transmitted the powers and character traits, such as aggressiveness and fierceness, of their deceased father and grandfather (a killer par excellence) to them. The yam and mortuary rituals play on the theme of killing. The actual killing of Tobias, as perceived and experienced, emphasised and reflected upon in ritual, enforced with its strong emotional appeal and sense of reality the ordinary ritual process, strengthening its perceived efficacy.

The narrative aspects of Tiwi ritual allowed the participants to deal with their grievances and grief in a personal manner, while at the same time integrating these ritualised personal experiences into the grand ritual scheme. As I said before, the participants can deal with troublesome matters, of utmost importance in their personal lives, in the ritual context without having to fear reprisal. The excitement and vitality of sex, destruction, arguments, fights, and killings are played upon in a symbolic way too. The negative aspects of life, both actual and imaginary, become transformed in the ritual process through a psychotherapeutic cleansing into positive forces strengthening the living. Here, I think, lies the preoccupation of Tiwi with sex and death, in their marking related-ness between all living and non-living entities. Sexuality and death, as Ariès has pointed out, are the two weak points in human society where nature penetrates culture (1983: 604).

Kalikalini's role in the killings at Matalau was worked out and selec-tively integrated in Tiwi ritual performances. Relevant experiences of the living were taken up continuously and carried on, even by following generations of performers, in ritual. The ongoing existential input into ritual, instead of being fixed on one and the same ritual content, shaped an emotionally compelling link between the participants and the chain of lived experiences of their forebears as well their surrounding world, including the spirits of the dead and other spiritual entities. Each ritual event of importance infused new things into the process, while their rit-ualisation (e.g., the relationship with a newly deceased) entailed the reliving of numerous emotion-charged past events. Analogous represen-tations, although stressed through seemingly trivial subject matters, revealed for the participants a spectrum of identifications and emotions. Tobias' violent death generated new meanings and, ritually processed, would become the source of signs to capture a multitude of new experi-ences. The point is that Tiwi did not simply deal with his death in a straightforward manner, but linked it with their cosmological existence, reshaping the event into cultural artefacts. To put it slightly differently, as a result of ritual elaboration the event of Tobias' killing was merged with the general theme of a symbolic killing and acquired multilayered meanings which could be extended in the encapsulation of future events (e.g., deaths of his relatives, other killings) and experiences (emotional reactions to death). Dealing with the killing of Tobias played upon the central ritual theme, albeit, as has been demonstrated above, with spe-cific identifications.

This chapter has presented a number of Tiwi views and comments on the homicide as these were given in a ritual context. The expectations of some Tiwi people that the 'trouble' would be brought out, and that the killers would be named or that these person(s) would make themselves known, did not come about. Kevin Wangiti, the man charged with mur-der by the police, had been released on the eve of the Pularumpi yam ritual, which was therefore postponed a fortnight. In July he was put on trial and this time the final mortuary ritual for Tobias was postponed. What happened to Kevin and how the Australian criminal justice system dealt with the homicide we will see in the next chapter.

CHAPTER 7

'Nothing but the Truth'

Thus far I have discussed how the case unfolded over time in the local arena. In the course of this century, however, the Tiwi have become increasingly subjected to the enforcement of Australian national law. Tobias' violent death was considered an offence against the state (the Crown) and, therefore, the involvement of the national criminal justice system was inevitable. In this chapter I shift attention to the police investigation and the case in the Australian criminal courts. The focus is on the interplay between the state's criminal justice system and local Tiwi dealings with the homicide.

The victim's children decided to await the results of the murder trial before having the final mortuary ritual, so the alleged killers could eventually be flogged on the latter occasion. According to Nancy, Kevin knew who had committed the homicide but had declared to Sam he could not tell until after the trial. Kevin then would enlighten Sam and his own patrilineal relatives of Tobias' clan, who would retaliate, do it 'the same way' and 'don't let it to police', she added. Who actually killed Tobias is not at issue here, but rather the different points of view within Tiwi society and, in this chapter especially, in the wider context of the Australian judicial system.

The intervention of white police, two detectives investigating the homicide, was an accomplished fact when the victim's close relatives had still not decided how they would deal with the matter. The police investigation heightened the tension but was also welcomed by people with conflicting loyalties. The actions of the detectives did not meet the expectations of a number of Tiwi people, who believed they would follow up decisive clues, such as fingerprints (the equivalent of the Tiwi way of deciphering foot tracks). Kevin, the man who was charged with murder by the police, would not have done the deed, according to many Tiwi

people in the township; he 'did tell a lie' to the police. This view was cor-
roborated by a dream of Martha Arapi, the victim's 'mother' (his father's
only surviving wife) and a senior woman of the Stone clan.

Kevin had confessed to the crime and signed the so-called record of
interview with police as being true. First, I will focus on the process of
police interrogation to show how Kevin's confession came into being
then I will discuss the case in the criminal courts.[70]

*   *   *

In chapter 4, I related how the police became involved soon after Tobias'
body had been found in the Old Camp on 29 October 1988. The local
police constable took statements from Tobias' neighbour, Isaac, and
from Kevin, who had found the corpse. The Tiwi police tracker told him
he had heard a conversation between Tobias and Kevin when coming
from the Social Club the previous night. A forensic pathologist and a
coroner were flown in from Darwin. The pathologist examined the
corpse on the spot but did not detect the stab wounds at that stage. Then
Tobias' body was taken to Darwin for an autopsy. The next day, the local
police constable interviewed Simon, who had come home from a post-
funeral ritual in Milikapiti.

On Monday morning, 31 October, the constable received a phone call
from Darwin in which he was told the results of the post-mortem. This
information came to the ears of the tracker, who immediately went to tell
the people of his camp. In the white section of the community the story
went that the police had a 'red-hot' suspect (said to be an elderly man
who, according to the white adult educator, 'When he has had a couple
of beers gets very emotional. He seems to have been yelling a lot that
night'). The local police cordoned off the scene of the crime again. No
one was allowed into the Old Camp.

In the afternoon, two detectives from Darwin's Criminal Investigations
Branch (CIB) and a coroner arrived to investigate the killing. They were
briefed by the local constable. A search for 'the murder weapon' was conducted around the Old Camp. Local people were called on for help. The
search was unsuccessful. Isaac had to demonstrate in the Old Camp what
his movements had been on the night of the killing. He was sent to the
police station for interrogation. The onlookers were reluctant to talk to
the detectives. Afterwards in the Social Club, Mike told his relatives,
including Tobias' children from other places, in great detail about the
stab wounds that had caused Tobias' death (including an alleged but non-
existent wound in the back to which Kevin would refer in his confession
the next day). During a search of the houses in the Old Camp, the local

police constable located a sharp skinning knife in the hut of Karl and Laura. The knife was seized as evidence but never examined.

Isaac was interrogated by the detectives for ninety minutes. A younger clan brother, Phillip Wangiti, acted as interpreter. The lengthy interrogation was summarised in a short statement. Contradicting his previous statement to the local police constable, that he had been asleep, his statement now was that Tobias had come to him:

> Last Friday night I went to the club. I was drunk when the club closed and I went straight home. I didn't have supper, I just laid down in the kitchen behind my house. It was late when that dead man [Tobias] sang out to me. I went outside and talk to him. It was just drunk talk. He was drunk too. We were arguing but we did not have a fight. We were arguing. I can't remember what we were talking about I kept telling him to go home. I went back inside to sleep and that dead man was talking to himself. I do not know who stabbed that dead man. I went back to sleep and did not hear anything until Kevin came and got me in the morning.[71]

The detectives appeared to find this statement satisfactory.

They started a series of interrogations of local people at the police station. Over two days the detectives interviewed an estimated fifty people who were brought to them by the tracker. Their aim was to eliminate possible suspects one by one. Statements of the card players revealed that voices had been heard, including Tobias' voice, in the Old Camp on the night of the killing. The raised voices of two other persons had been recognised too: these were the voices of Isaac Pamantari and Anna Wangiti. Anna was brought in from Milikapiti, where she had gone because of the 'trouble'. Nancy coordinated the statements the members of Sam's camp would make to the police. She and her husband Sam would state they had been drunk and had gone home from the Social Club. Anna would say that she had been drunk too. Mike had walked her home from the club to Sam's camp.

Following a reconstruction of his movements on the night of the killing with the detectives on Tuesday morning, Mike declared he had come from the club. He found his parents at his sister Maud's house having supper. After that he went back to the club. Tobias, Anna and three other people were still sitting there. Mike left, taking Anna with him. They walked along the path behind the health clinic, where they stopped for a little while. When they were behind Kevin's hut, so Mike told the police, he heard a conversation that sounded normal between Kevin and Tobias, and he assumed the latter had come along in front of the health clinic. Anna left Mike and went in the direction of Kevin's voice, singing to herself. Mike walked past the hut where his parents lived and saw they were not yet at home. Then, to get to his own house, he had to cross the main road to the barge landing. Mike could see some people standing under the street light near Alan's house, waiting for a card game to start. It is important to note that Mike said he had *heard* Kevin and Tobias talking. Under cross-examination during the murder trial he admitted he could only tell for sure he had heard Tobias and was much less certain about the other voice. Having been on the other side of the buildings, he clearly did *not see* them, and he could not recall whether the lights were on or off.[72]

The detectives learned from a bar keeper of mixed descent that Tobias had been on bad terms with a number of people. The main ones Tobias had argued with were Karl Hansen, Andrew Munuluka and Sam Kerimerini (in relation to 'some family trouble').[73] Simon Pamantari had stated to the local police constable that, before the local police station was established, Tobias had speared his brother in the back when both were drunk. He said that killings with spears had ceased but in the past, according to Simon, tribal killings were carried out with spears only. It was a matter of 'the old men and the family'. Laura told the detective in charge that her father had had fights, 'only fist fights', with Isaac. These fights occurred in the Social Club about a month before Tobias' death.[74] The police obtained a wet pair of shorts from Isaac. He claimed he had worn these on the night of the killing. The pair of shorts, with a stain on them, had just been washed. The coroner or crime scene examiner took the shorts with him (the shorts were not examined either). During the murder trial the coroner claimed he had also taken a swab of blood from Tobias' verandah.

The police interrogations brought a number of conflicts between Tobias and other people to light, although most people were reluctant to speak to the police. The detectives had a short list of suspects. As the investigation went on, one after another was eliminated from this list until by Tuesday afternoon only one person was left. The remaining suspect happened to be Kevin, a bachelor who lived in the Old Camp not far from Tobias. He had found Tobias lying under the mango tree on Saturday morning. The police knew that Kevin had driven the car that had rolled over and killed Tobias' last wife in the previous June. They inferred that there was animosity between Tobias and Kevin regarding Tobias' wife's death. From hearsay the detectives believed that Tobias had said to Kevin, 'I kill you with an axe'.

After repeated interrogations, Kevin went with the police to the beach and produced a knife from the sand. He finally confessed to having killed Tobias. He was charged with the murder and put in prison on Tuesday, 1 November, at 10 pm. The detectives brought their investigation to a halt.[75]

No attempt was made to satisfactorily relate the knife to the stab wounds other than by its size. A police forensic biologist examined the knife but only found traces of sand and grit, no blood. It must be noted that numerous knives of this type could be found in the local community, as they are used in hunting and eating. Even toddlers used to play with them. The detectives thus relied heavily on Kevin's confessional record of interview with the police. In the case of Aboriginal suspects a reliance on a confessional record of interview with the police is very problematic.

As a result of experiences in the past, Australian judges have become more cautious concerning confessions made by Aborigines. A number of rules have been formulated to serve as safeguards and to determine whether such confessions will be admissible as evidence in the criminal courts. Investigating police have to apply these so-called Anunga Rules (see below) or run the risk that the confession they have obtained may be rejected as evidence by the judge.

A general principle of Australian law is that people do not have to incriminate themselves; therefore, the rules of evidence say a confession or relevant statement has to be voluntarily given. The police first have to caution the persons in question that they have the right to remain silent, and that anything they say might be used against them as evidence in court. As Chrisholm and Nettheim note: 'The police sometimes complain that these strict requirements hamstring investigation of crime, that innocent persons have nothing to fear in speaking up, and that the rules protect only the guilty by warning them to say nothing' (1974: 66). This being the case, the application of the Anunga Rules concerning Aboriginal suspects complicates matters for the investigating police even more. Despite the best intentions of the investigating police, a great deal can go wrong in their communications with Aborigines.[76]

The same applies to Aborigines in court (cf. Liberman 1981, 1985). The present case points to difficulties due to language problems, cultural miscommunication, the stress of the situation (experienced differently by Aborigines, including the strain of loyalties to other people which are little understood by non-Aboriginal people), unfamiliarity on the part of white officials with the local way of life, unfamiliarity with the court rituals on the part of the Aborigines, and fears – as experienced and perceived – of the powers of the police. Tiwi people regard white police officers as 'dangerous persons' (*mantatawi*). Even when the Anunga Rules are applied, the decision as to whether the caution is understood by the Aboriginal suspect is still left to the discretion of the interrogating police officer. I will cite three examples that place the reliability of confessional records of interview with Aboriginal suspects into question, then I will discuss how Kevin's confession to the murder came about.

At the end of 1988, during the trial of a Tiwi man, who was eventually acquitted of sexual assault, Justice Maurice of the Northern Territory

Supreme Court warned the jury to be wary of statements made by the accused in a record of interview with police. 'The level of miscommunication in the record of interview produced quite comical results', he said. 'It would be a joke if this man's liberty did not depend on it' (*Northern Territory News*, 8 March 1989). When Justice Maurice was speaking, another Tiwi man in Darwin's Berrimah jail was awaiting the committal hearing after which he could face a murder trial, concerning Tobias' violent death, in the NT Supreme Court. The case of the Crown against Kevin Wangiti also rested mainly on a confession, one made in a record of interview with police.

The justices of the NT Supreme Court are aware of the problems Aborigines face in the national criminal justice system. Chief Justice Foster set down guidelines for police officers in the interrogation of Aboriginal suspects in a case known as *Regina versus Anunga* in 1976. Three years later, the NT Police Commissioner issued the so-called Anunga Rules as instructions to all police officers in the Northern Territory (Foley 1988: 174–8). These rules require that Aboriginal suspects be accompanied by 'a prisoner's friend' chosen by the suspect, and that the interrogating police's caution of the right of the accused to remain silent and not to incriminate him or herself must be understood. These preconditions, however, are not enough. The rules further say: 'Even when an apparently frank and free confession has been obtained relating to the commission of an offence, police should continue to investigate the matter in an endeavour to obtain proof of the commission of the offence from other sources' (ibid.: 175). Failure to apply the Anunga Rules may lead to the rejection of confessional records of interview as evidence in court. This happened to the Tiwi man who was acquitted of the sexual assault charge, mentioned above. In general, according to Loorham, the rules have not been met enthusiastically by the NT police force. To them 'the rules are a nuisance and there is much pressure from the Force to have them watered down' (1982: 4).

A lack of enthusiasm on the part of the police is understandable because the Anunga Rules make it more difficult to take action against Aboriginal suspects. Following Tobias' death, probably caused by a stab wound to his chest, the detectives and the crime scene examiner (the coroner) were sent to Melville Island to solve the case. It is likely they were working under strong institutional pressures, short of time and resources. Nevertheless, with regard to instructions to the police and also to the judicial principle of fairness, to mention at least some of the basic considerations the detectives were supposed to show in their dealings with Aboriginal suspects, I find it hard to grasp why these experienced detectives placed so much confidence in a confessional record of interview. Their reliance on a confession to the murder is clearly demonstrated by the failure of the detectives 'to obtain proof of the commission of the offence from other sources', as would have been in line with the Anunga Rules. It is well known, especially in legal circles, that Aboriginal suspects tend to give in to pressures exerted on them by investigating police.

Loorham reports on Kumajay's case, in which a young Aboriginal man confessed to a rape in a 'long, detailed and apparently credible record of interview'. At his committal hearing, however, the plaintiff, 'under cross-examination by the counsel for the accused, admitted she had made the story up' (ibid.: 3–4). Another case in point is Kevin Condren, an Aboriginal man from Queensland jailed for life in 1984 for the murder of a woman, 'mainly on the basis of a confession to police he claims was fabricated'. Fresh evidence revealed that at the time the murder occurred Condren was in police custody, arrested for drunkenness (*Australian*, 22 December 1989). Indeed, one might wonder with Loorham (1982: 4) how reliable the record of interview is.[77]

With regard to the record of interview with police, the underlying assumption is that *no one* will confess to a crime she or he has not committed. In Western common sense the consequences of such a confession will prevent an innocent person from admitting the crime.[78] Signing a confession as being true means incriminating oneself, especially since a suspect must have been cautioned beforehand by the investigating police. The record of interview is supposed to be an accurate or true representation. However, during police interrogation Aboriginal suspects appear to make confessions regardless of whether they did or *did not* commit the crime. The verbal warnings and the presence of a friend, as instructions to the police now require, *do not* prevent innocent Aboriginal suspects from confessing to the police.

As Geertz (1983) points out, common sense might be seen as a cultural system. The 'facts' do not speak for themselves but have to be interpreted. Reasoning from common sense means that a whole body of cultural assumptions is taken for granted. When the logic and truths of Western common sense may be seen as culturally biased, can these, with the principle of fairness in mind, be extended to judge on the 'facts' situated in a radically different cultural setting? Lakoff and Johnson state: 'It is because we understand *situations* in terms of our conceptual system that we can understand *statements* using that system of concepts as being *true*, that is, as fitting or not fitting the situation as we understand it' (1980: 179). Aboriginal people with different conceptual systems from those of mainstream Australian society understand the world in a different way from white Australians. They have 'a very different body of truths' (ibid.: 181). Undoubtedly, it is the police intention that justice will be done as they see it. In the case of Aboriginal suspects (and for other cultural minority groups, and perhaps any suspect, too) the utmost care is needed, for, as Lakoff and Johnson write, 'the idea that there is absolute objective truth is not only mistaken but socially and politically dangerous' (ibid.: 159).[79] Although the Australian criminal courts may take so-called customary law into consideration, this is mostly done at the end of the court proceedings and mainly in connection with sentencing (Bell 1988).[80]

Aboriginal people are overrepresented among those prosecuted by the criminal justice system (Fisher and Hennessy 1988: 91). The imprisonment rate of Aboriginal people is extremely high (Langton 1988: 201). In 1990, this rate was more than 14 times the imprisonment rate of the Australian population as a whole (Horton 1994: 1284). Both Eggleston (1976) and the (Australian) Law Reform Commission (1986) stress that Aborigines are the most vulnerable when involved in police interrogation. In a study of Aboriginal youth and the criminal justice system in South Australia, Gale, Bailey-Harris and Wundersitz state there is no proof that Aboriginal youths commit more crimes than white youths, but as a result of social (class), cultural and racial bias the former receive harsher treatment by law-enforcement agencies, especially in the initial stages of criminal prosecution (1990: 6, 8). Mickler reports how, despite strong protests by Aboriginal people themselves, misrepresentations of Aboriginal youth as criminals in Western Australian newspapers turn out to be powerful as a political instrument counteracting Aboriginal interests because these journalistic practices 'create or reproduce public knowledges about race relations, common senses about Aboriginality' and 'public opinion' thus shaped has a direct impact on government policies concerning Aborigines (1992: 322–3, passim).

In the context of the Australian criminal justice system, wherein judgements are mainly made by non-Aboriginal people on the basis of 'common sense', mainstream Australian representations of Aborigines seriously affect the lives of persecuted Aboriginal people. Interrogations by the police form the key to their further involvement with the state's criminal justice system. Unlike the public hearings and communications in court, these interrogations take place in private. During police interrogation the Aboriginal suspect answers questions formulated by the interrogators. The resulting account is a construct that may reflect the situation of inequality.

Kevin had made a statement to the local police constable on Saturday, 29 October. He told how he had found Tobias early in the morning and had warned the health worker. He had gone to the Social Club to drink beer the night before. There he had seen Tobias alive for the last time. 'Then I went to Dick's for supper and then I came home', he said. 'I went to sleep as soon as I got home.'[81]

The detective sergeant in charge of the investigation went through this statement with Kevin on Monday, 31 October. Kevin confirmed it. In a declaration (dated 5 and 8 December 1988) this detective presented his interviews with Kevin in the form of questions and answers. After going over the statement, he asked Kevin if he had seen Tobias after he had left the club on Friday night. Kevin replied, 'No, I went to Dick's for supper and then went home to bed, I didn't see him.'

The next morning the detective spoke to Kevin again at the police station (I cite once again the detective's declaration, which was later read out in court):

> 'Kevin I have been told by someone that on Friday night after the club closed you were seen talking to that dead man at your house.'
> 'Who told you that.'
> 'That doesn't matter, were you talking to him.'
> 'No I had supper at Dick's and went home and went to bed.'
> 'Did you see the dead man.'
> 'No.'

He had now told the police his story three times and he kept to it. Kevin was told he was *seen* talking to Tobias. This was false information on part of the police, as Mike had told the local constable he had *heard* a conversation between Kevin and Tobias (referred to as 'the dead man'). Voice identification, as the defence would point out, is much more problematic than visual identification. My informants, for instance, could not distinguish the voices on tape of two men, Isaac and his 'son' Jerome Pamantari, let alone the voices of Tiwi people skilled in mimicking other people's voices.

The allegation must have been an unsettling experience for Kevin. He could infer someone in the community held a grudge against him, and that the police apparently did not believe him. At this stage he was not allowed to know who was speaking against him.[82] This, however, is extremely important because Tiwi, ideally, have 'to speak up' for their 'relations' (*aramipi*, people belonging to their exogamous cluster of matriclans), no matter what their personal opinion is.

We might safely assume Kevin did not know what he was up against. On Saturday morning he had found a knife in a box in his hut. It was not his knife, he was sure. He took it with him to the house of a friend elsewhere in the township. Kevin went to another house because the area where Tobias died had become taboo (*pukamani*), and, therefore, he could not stay in his own hut. There is a cultural imperative to move away from the place where a death has recently occurred, a taboo related to the possible destructive actions of the new spirit of the dead, or *mopaditi*. In contrast to another neighbour of Tobias, Kevin had slept in his own hut during the night of the killing. This suggests he had been unaware of Tobias' death. Had he known about it, he presumably would have moved away to somewhere else, like he did for the following nights.[83] The police, unfamiliar with Tiwi mortuary practices, overlooked this point. Kevin knew the police had been looking in the Old Camp for knives. The detective had made it plain that there were suspicions about him. Kevin took the knife he had in his possession to the beach and buried it on his favourite place for fishing. The township of 300 was in a state of tension. Tobias' children were pressing people to speak out and threatening a counter-killing. The interrogations at the police station, for which anybody could be picked up at any time, disrupted people's daily routines. My friends feared a confrontation in private with the unknown white policemen; some people hid when the police van was coming their way. Kevin was a man who suffered from high blood pressure.

At 1.15 pm Kevin was called into the police station for the second time that day. This time the other CIB detective interrogated him. The detective reported the interview in a declaration (dated 19 December 1988), again in a question and answer fashion. The detective in charge was said to be present during the interrogation and would take over later on. Below I will cite the detective's declaration (also read in court). Once again Kevin was asked to confirm his statement. Then he was questioned about his movements on the Friday night. The detective asked him what he did after he finished at the club:

'Then what did you do.'
'I walked down to my friends and had some supper.'
'What were the friends name.'
'Dick's.'
'From there where did you go.'
'After I had supper I went straight home. Camped at my place. Shut the door and went to sleep.'[84]

After this the detective started all over again, questioning Kevin in more detail. Kevin said he had supper at Dick's house. When asked who was at the house, he mentioned Dick, and Dick's wife and children in addition. From a statement by Dick's wife, Sally, to the local constable it had become clear that Dick was not at home when Kevin visited. The answer would be in accordance with local understanding if he meant 'Dick' or 'Dick mob', since a camp (house and yard) is referred to by using the name of the most significant person in the group that lives there, whether this person is present or not (it is also more convenient in view of recurring fluctuations in group membership). Indeed, Kevin's answers to the next questions indicate there was some miscommunication between

Kevin and the detective: 'Who else.' 'His wife.' 'What is her name.' 'Sally and the kids.' Obviously, 'Sally and the kids' was not the woman's name, but she and her children belonged to Dick's household. Once they thought the interviewee had told them Dick was at home, the police assumed Kevin 'began to tell lies' (the local police constable, personal communication). Still, Kevin did not confess to the murder. On the question of where he went afterwards, he repeated what he had already told the police six times: 'Went straight home, shut the door and went to sleep.' Asked if he then had talked with Tobias, Kevin again responded in the negative and said he had not seen him. Next, the interrogator put questions to him indicating his statements were false. Kevin did not reply to these questions.

First, the detective said, 'Kevin, other people have told me that Dick wasn't home, he was on Bathurst Island that night. Do you want to say anything about that.' The detective had it wrong. Dick had not been on Bathurst Island that Friday. He went to Milikapiti on Melville Island, and he came home around 9 pm.[85]

Second, he told Kevin that Sally Pamantari had told him (as a matter of fact, she made her statement to the local police constable) she had given Kevin some meat but he did not stay at her home. Kevin had never said that he did. Sally had said Kevin went home after he stayed at her place for a little while. Apparently, the detective assumed that when Kevin had supper at Dick's house he ate it there. Kevin, however, took his supper with him to eat at his own place. The detective, unfamiliar with the local way of life, apparently inferred Kevin had told him a lie, because to have supper at Dick's house he would have to have stayed there longer than he admitted.

Third, the detective told Kevin that Mavis Pamantari had said that after he left Sally he called at her house. According to Mavis (his clan sister), Kevin had come to her house, carrying a plastic bag, and received some food from her at his request. This was such an everyday thing for Kevin that he took it for granted. From a Tiwi point of view, it was commonplace that he ask his relatives, his 'daughter' Sally and his 'sister' Mavis, for food.[86] What he had explained earlier to the police were his *directional* movements on Friday night. From the club, he walked down with his 'daughter' to her place (to the west), instead of to his hut in the Old Camp (to the south). There he played with his 'grandchildren', did 'stop there' as Tiwi say, and obtained some meat as his supper from Sally. Then walking past Mavis' place (somewhat further back to the west) he demanded in passing some food from her as well. Following the rule of brother-sister avoidance they hardly spoke to each other. After this triviality he 'went straight home' (that is, in a straight line to the east). In his statements Kevin had been true to his sense of movements but the detective was under the impression he had held something back deliberately. It was not the first instance of their talking past each other.

Finally, this detective said to Kevin: 'Mike has told me that he saw you speaking with that dead man [Tobias] late that night. Do you want to say anything about that'.[87] As I noted earlier, Mike had said he had *heard* them talking. The detective did not specify what time was 'late that night'. Kevin chose to remain silent to these questions. In Tiwi ways, he could not contradict the supposed statements of his relatives. The Tiwi people referred to by the detective were his 'daughter' Sally (father's brother's son's daughter), his clan sister Mavis, and his clan brother Mike. With a positive response to the misleading propositions Kevin would also unjustly compromise himself and his earlier statements to the police.

At his trial Kevin testified that the detective hit him three times on the back of his head and pressed him to 'tell the truth'. Given the powers of the police, both as perceived and as experienced, it takes a lot of courage for an Aboriginal person in Kevin's position to deliver such testimony. The police denied the alleged violence. It was the word of the accused against that of the police officers (see also Eggleston 1976: 30, 57–8). Anyway, Justice Fisher rejected Kevin's evidence and accepted the version of the police on this topic.

The pressure on Kevin, and this was beyond police's ken, was that he was isolated from other Tiwi people. In this face-to-face society social reality is defined in a collective process; what one says in public is consented to by other people, especially one's 'relations'. People who go their own way, alone and by themselves, are out of touch with reality. They are perceived as mad, 'no good in the head' (with the exemption of a 'magic man'). In ordinary Tiwi individuals, loneliness inspires fear. As Sansom puts it in connection with Aboriginal fringe-dwellers in Darwin, 'It is a short trip from company into fright' (1980: 209). Loneliness here implies being without the other people on whom one depends in defining a situation. Sansom quotes the African Chagga, who have an expression for this that can be translated as 'to talk out of fear'. Paraphrasing Steiner, he writes: 'For them, loneliness is when the familiar man-worked material things of one's immediate surroundings become an animated reproach and live for one because one's fellows no longer do. And their animation is no comfort. Left on his own, the Chagga householder finds that "the posts of my house are hitting me"' (1980: 208–9). For Tiwi this is also the case, for instance, in unfamiliar rooms, especially small rooms with the doors closed.[88] The Tiwi have a term for a policeman, and it is likely it reflects the dreadful experience of being on one's own; *jimanipirni* or 'he hit me'. This reasoning suggests Kevin might have perceived the allegations that his relatives contradicted him as so many blows at the back of his head. Therewith, the versions of both the white police and their

Aboriginal suspect were true. In other words, the detective may not have physically assaulted Kevin but Kevin experienced the reality of an assault.[89] (Likewise, Tiwi experience the loss of a significant other as a physical attack on their body.) One can imagine what a Tiwi person must feel when alone, without the comfort of his or her own, under police interrogation. An Aboriginal suspect, if the pressure is kept up long enough, is likely to say anything to escape this stressful situation. Sansom, on the basis of his research among Aboriginal fringe-dwellers, found, 'What policemen may in such circumstances do is inculpate a man, bind him in the tangled sayings of his loneliness. The structure of the situation dictates that in order to escape "You gotta talk fast" and "You gotta gib themfella lotta bloody humbug"; and the purpose of fast talking and humbug is to get away – escape' (1980: 209). In this context, the right of an Aboriginal suspect to remain silent is a misnomer.

The detective sergeant in charge took over the interrogation of Kevin from his colleague. He reiterated, 'Mike told me that when he was walking home from the club you were talking to that dead man [Tobias].' Kevin did not reply. Next, the detective asked him if he had got any knives he had not seen. Kevin did not reply. The detective repeated the last question. Now Kevin said, 'That one that killed the dead man'. It is impossible to tell from the written declaration whether this utterance by the suspect was meant as an addition to what the detective stated, a question as to which knife he wanted to see, or as an affirmative answer. Obviously, the officer was after the murder weapon.

It has often been argued that Aborigines are unassertive when confronted with authorities (this is one of the reasons underlying the Anunga Rules, cf. Foley 1988: 175). To put it slightly differently, Aborigines tend to say what they think, from gesture and intonation, a person in authority wants to hear. Explanations given in the literature for this phenomenon are:

- politeness on their part (Petri 1954: 12; Coldrey 1987: 87);
- lack of personal confidence in the questioner (Strehlow 1936: 334; Elkin 1947: 179–80);
- their powerlessness and lack of comprehension of what they are agreeing with (Elkin 1947: 179; Liberman 1981: 249; Coldrey ibid.);
- disadvantages due to language problems, cultural differences, ill health (for instance, many Aborigines suffer from hearing loss), and illiteracy in varying degrees (Petri ibid.; Foley 1988: 164–71; Law Reform Commission 1986: 56);
- the strain of the situation (Sansom 1980: 208–10, see above);
- a strategy of accommodation, playing on Anglo-Australian aspirations to be superior (Elkin 1947: 176–7; Liberman 1981: 248–9), and also to avoid trouble (Strehlow 1936: 334);

- a feature of the way Aborigines communicate, preferably not contradicting others (Liberman 1981; cf. Von Sturmer 1981).

These explanations do not exclude each other. Liberman, focusing on the problem of communication and discourse, in relation to Western Desert Aborigines states,

> Individuals do not assert themselves or their points of view too vigorously, but maintain a self-deprecatory manner which emphasizes the importance of group cohesiveness over individual aims. Competitive arguments are discouraged, and Aborigines avoid directly contradicting others in order to prevent their embarrassment. . . . Question and answer sentences are rarely as intensive as similar discourse among Anglo-Australians. Generally, it may be said that interaction among Aboriginal people is unassertive. The round-the-rally production of consensual decisions does not proceed according to a variety of alternatives; rather, one possible solution is formulated at a given time and elaborated or amended over the ensuing course of talk. Unpopular formulations die a death of silence (1981: 248).

We have seen that Kevin did not contradict the alleged statements of his relatives but remained silent. When the other detective took over the interrogation and asked if he had other knives, Kevin complied with the intention of that question, namely supplying the murder weapon being sought. The detectives, already suspicious gave much weight to Kevin's assertion. Kevin pointed out he had a knife that was buried at the beach. He was not cautioned when the next question, incriminating when affirmed, was put to him: 'Do you know anything about how that old man was killed.' Kevin did not reply. After that, he said he had buried the knife. It must have looked to Kevin as if he had compromised himself, for the detective asked, 'How did you know it was the one that killed the dead man?' I take this as an invention on part of the police, albeit not one deliberately made. The accuracy of the detective's statement can be disputed on the grounds that until then there was no evidence Kevin's knife had in fact been the lethal weapon. The reading of Kevin's previous answer, 'That one that killed the dead man', is all-important here. Following the detective's apparent understanding, Kevin admitted he had a knife that could be identified as the lethal weapon. But this is anything but clear.

As I said earlier, it was obvious the detective was after the lethal knife, the so-called murder weapon. The previous day, the police with the involvement of Tiwi people had conducted a line search of the Old Camp for this purpose. The detectives had been asking about a knife of certain dimensions. What Kevin was doing, in my opinion, was helping the police: he did not feign ignorance about the detective's interest in the knife 'that killed the dead man' (which would render him suspect) but asserted this knowledge by giving a specification of the proposition ('any knives I haven't seen') put to him by the detective, and inviting him to guess. Finally, after repeated silences he could say something harmless. As Von Sturmer points out, 'Aborigines are very aware of personal dignity and suffer its loss badly' (1981: 17). One might assume Kevin did not want to appear inadequate (cf. Coldrey 1987: 87).[90] Furthermore, Liberman makes it clear that 'Aborigines are engaged in a continual process of sense-assembly in court' (1981: 247), and the situation for Aborigines under police interrogation may even be worse (ibid.: 255). Unfamiliar with the structure of the proceedings, they tend to be confused and do not know what they are up against. Therefore, they are constantly on the lookout for clues about what is going on. In conjunction with the strategy of accommodation mentioned above, Aborigines frequently comply with what is put to them, either in verbal or non-verbal communication, as well as from their understanding. What was the purpose of this question, 'Any knives I haven't seen'? Kevin responded, 'That one that killed the dead man.' (Again, question marks were omitted in the written account.) The trap, set by the detectives unwittingly, snapped.

Kevin's silence prompted the detective to ask for the second time: 'How did you know it was the one that killed the dead man.' It is possible, and I believe this was the case, that hitherto Kevin had not linked the hypothetical 'murder weapon' with the knife he had. First he made clear that he understood, or wanted to know if he understood, that the detective meant the knife with which Tobias had been killed. Second was 'other knives', plural. It is likely that this amounted to confusion, forcing Kevin to search for the significance of this rather complicated proposition. Kevin admitted he had an *other* knife. Ready to assist the police, he was prepared to point out where it was. By silence he disapproved of the question, 'Do you know anything about how that old man was killed.'[91] The next question was, 'Kevin who buried the knife.' Whereupon he said, 'I did'. Then the detective asked what is, in my reading, the leading question: 'How did you know it was the one that killed the dead man.' All of a sudden, the buried knife was the one that killed. What was worse, the first or the second part, 'know' or 'killed'? Impaired by his lack of fluency in standard Australian English and by a total disregard of non-verbal behaviour, Kevin was caught in a web. How did this make sense? Kevin said, 'I know'.[92]

Kevin was first asked to consent to showing the detective the knife and then was told by the detective that he would 'tell the judge about that'. Accompanied by four policemen, Kevin was taken to the beach, where he dug up the knife. Kevin declared, 'I use it for fishing sometimes'.[93] His burying the knife at the base of a tree might seem an awkward thing to do, but for the Tiwi people putting away an object where it could be found again, so it was at hand for use, was a standard procedure to prevent such a tool from being lost. On Sunday, Kevin had been fishing at the beach. He favoured the spot for his hand-line fishing and he needed a knife to cut up the bait.

Kevin was on the hook, so to speak, and the policemen returned with him to the police station. From there the interrogators shifted to the courtroom.

Let me interpose a comment on this new setting. The setting closely matched the fortnightly sessions of the Court of Summary Jurisdiction held in the room. In this court there were a magistrate and a prosecutor (usually a police sergeant) in plain clothes, and the local police officers in uniform who served as the staff of the court. The detective sergeant (the one who had said to Kevin he would 'tell the judge about that') and the other detective were in plain clothes too. The detective in charge of the investigation, the highest in rank, gave orders to the local uniformed police officers. Dick would be Kevin's 'prisoner's friend' (an awkward term suggesting the suspect was a prisoner, which he was not). Dick had been brought to the police station with his wife by the local police. He was called into the courtroom. The detective constable asked Kevin why Dick was present. Kevin said, 'Because he is a witness'. The detective, 'What is a witness?' Kevin, 'For the murder'. The detective, 'I mean why is Dick Pamantari sitting here?' Kevin, 'To help me'.[94] Given the close resemblance of the whole setting to a session of the local court, Kevin might easily have had the false impression that a court procedure was taking place (the only person lacking was a solicitor for his defence), if not an actual session of the court.

In trying to make sure the caution would be understood by Kevin, the detective said to him: 'Mr. Wangiti, I am now going to explain some things to you, and after I explain things to you I am going to ask you to tell me what I have said.' Kevin phrased his understanding as follows, 'You're going to ask me things, then I can say them back to you.'[95] It might have not been clear to him that this was intended to caution him, and it might have opened him up even more to say what he thought the detective wanted to hear. The detective told him he would type everything on a piece of paper and take it to the court. (Months later, Kevin asked me to explain to him the court proceedings, of which he understood little.) What did the detective mean? How confusing. Were they not in the court? Asked by the detective what the court was, he replied, 'Going to jail. For the murder.'[96] After the interrogation, in which Kevin confessed to killing Tobias, the typed version of the record of interview was read back. I assume the interrogators shifted to the courtroom because there was tape-recording equipment there, but they did not record the actual confessional interview on tape. Only afterwards, a so-called 'read back' was recorded on tape. Kevin and Dick signed the record of interview as being true.

I want to represent the suspect's side of the story, as to what in his perception had occurred during the procedure of police interrogation. This representation is based on my frequent conversations with Dick and Kevin, as well as on their statements in the Darwin courts. Dick, as the 'prisoner's friend', was allowed to have a chat with Kevin in Tiwi before the local courtroom interrogation commenced. Kevin said to Dick, 'I turned myself in' and 'I blamed myself'. He used the expression *jima-nipirni*, 'he hit me', for the police detective. Dick later asserted this in court. Kevin further told him he did not kill the old man. According to Kevin, Dick said to him he 'shouldn't do it', that is, have turned himself in. In a spontaneous conversation in which Kevin brought up the topic, he said to me, 'They kept telling me to tell the truth'. After some further deliberations by Kevin I asked him why he had made the confession to the police. He said, 'They didn't believe me. Kept telling, telling . . . [making the sign of ongoing repetition] . . . pushing [accompanied by a sign of pushing, and then inserting with altered voice:] "Tell truth!".' Kevin added, 'You can't win'.

Unfortunately, Kevin's experiences are not unusual. Andrew Ligertwood, a lawyer who worked for Aboriginal people in South Australia, reports he 'had little success in preventing suspects confessing to the police, despite my most strenuous assertion . . . of their right to remain silent' (1988: 197). He states that 'Aboriginal suspects will usually agree submissively to propositions put to them. The police do little to avoid this tendency and *virtually all* defendants confess to the crimes alleged against them' (ibid.: 196, my emphasis). And John Coldrey, a Queen's Counsel with a wide experience of criminal cases involving Aborigines and the Director of Public Prosecutions for Victoria, writes, 'Even when the Aboriginal suspect comprehends the questions being put to him there remains the tendency to give an answer that reflects what he thinks the questioner desires to hear. Later when confronted with answers that are clearly erroneous the suspect will say in explanation: "He forced me to say those things" or "He made me talk too fast"' (1987: 87). The provision of a 'prisoner's friend' will be of little help to the suspect when this person is subjected to the same pressures, and therefore is also unassertive in dealing with the interrogating police.

I will be brief in my further discussion of the confessional interview because the main point has been made. When the subject of the knife was raised, the record of interview began to take the form of a confession:

* What else can you tell me about that knife?
  That knife was still there at my camp.
* When? [Earlier on the interrogating detective had spoken about 'the night that that dead fella finished up'.]
  On that night.
* Which night was that?
  Friday night.
* Did anything happen on Friday night?
  Yes.
* What?
  I had an argument with that dead fellow?[97]

The admission of the events leading up to the killing came out step-by-step in short answers to questions of the what-happened-then type. The crucial question, of course, was where Kevin eventually stabbed the victim:

* Where did you stab him?
  (No answer.)
* I am giving you this pen, can you show me where you stabbed that dead fellow?
  ([Kevin] Indicates top left hand side of chest, Left hand side of back, top of left shoulder and top of left leg. Holds pen in the right hand.)[98]

That was it. The police were convinced only 'the murderer' could know the location of the stab wounds (the local senior constable, personal communication). However, this information was common knowledge in the local Tiwi community by then. Kevin repeated the supposed knowledge of the wound in the back in his confession.

The situation looked grim for Kevin. He was arrested and charged with the murder. If he was convicted for murder he could get a life sentence. The law of the Northern Territory takes this very literally (Bell 1988: 368). The CIB detectives had arrived in Pularumpi on Monday at 2.15 pm. The next day at 10.00 pm, Kevin was lodged in the local cells and the detectives went off-duty. They got on the first plane back to Darwin, taking their prisoner with them. Three months later, Kevin was brought back to Pularumpi for a day to attend the Court of Summary Jurisdiction for the first part of his committal hearings in the room where he had made his confession to the police.

*   *   *

On 2 February 1989, the first session of the committal hearings was held at the local court. The previous day I had met Anna Wangiti in Milikapiti. She was terrified, for she had to be one of the witnesses. It troubled her. Back in Pularumpi I was told Isaac and Sally, two other witnesses, were 'chasing'. They had been ordered to the police station to sign a piece of paper stating that they would not leave the township. Sally and Mavis, also scared to death, said to Jeanette and me that this was the first time in their lives they had 'to go court'.

In the main office of the police station the prosecutor, Richard Simpson, described the committal hearings to me as a 'jigsaw puzzle'. The first part, involving the Tiwi witnesses, would be heard in Pularumpi. He warned me not to think this was the whole case. The second part of the matter, the other pieces of his puzzle, would be heard from the police officers in Darwin. The police theory, he explained to me, was that the victim had threatened the accused because he had caused his wife's death. The accused feared a 'payback'. To prevent this happening he killed Tobias. Upon my expressions of doubt, he said, 'Kevin is not the kind of person who deserves any mercy'.

Kevin was brought into the police station unshaven and wearing a crumpled shirt and a threadbare pair of shorts. (Kevin was always clean-shaven and spotless in his dress.) His lawyer arrived later and met him there for the first time. The solicitor, a non-Aboriginal man, appeared not fluent in the English language. He spoke softly (quite a number of Aborigines are somewhat hard of hearing as a result of ear infections).

The court case greatly interested Tiwi people. Tobias' daughters had come from Milikapiti to learn more about the circumstances of their father's death. Other people had come to be supportive of the witnesses. Kevin's relatives, although they also expressed that they felt uncomfortable, had turned up to see him. Most of the people remained outside the courtroom on the verandah. First, there were a few other cases in the court. One of the witnesses became annoyed because he had to be present at the police station at 9.30 am. The court case did not begin, however, before 1.30 pm. The police presented the first half of its case against Kevin. The Tiwi witnesses, one after the other, were called in.

The first two witnesses were the barmen in the Social Club on the night of the killing. The first one gave a deep sigh when it was over, the second was bathed in sweat. They had to say how drunk the victim and Kevin were.

Sally, the next witness, had to say a few things about when Kevin paid a visit to her place that night.

Then Mavis was questioned. The prosecutor seemed to want to put her at ease by asking her Aboriginal name. The name was taboo and, therefore, she replied 'Too hard'. Her attempts to make clear she could not talk with Kevin because of a brother-sister avoidance rule were wasted on the court, despite her testimony that 'he is my brother. I cannot speak to him . . . culture, you know . . .'

The police tracker came next. Under cross-examination he said that when he brought Kevin to the police station in the car, Kevin had said: 'I didn't do it.'[99]

Anna stated that she had been drunk. The tracker had walked her home from the club and left her there.

The court rituals were certainly confusing to Isaac. When he was sworn in, a bible was put in his hands; moving the book from one side to the other, he was at a loss what to do with it. The magistrate could not understand a word of what he said to the prosecutor, and told the latter he needed an interpreter. A younger clan brother of the witness (who had also been present when he made a statement to the police) volunteered. He said that on the night of the killing Tobias kept bothering him while he wanted to sleep.

Another witness was the health worker who was relatively fluent in English. He said: 'On that night I had been watching a movie on television before I came out on the street lights just outside my house where a game of cards was in progress and I stayed there for a while during which time I heard voices of two people which I identified.' These were the voices of the two previous witnesses. He remarked, 'I don't recall hearing the conversation that was carried'. He further said Kevin had asked him the next morning 'to come to go and have a look at the body of the deceased to see what was wrong and because he thought he may be dead'.[100]

Simon Pamantari was the last witness. After a number of questions had been put to him, the prosecutor turned to the magistrate: he suggested an interpreter would be of assistance. The magistrate adjourned for a little while to give him the opportunity to get one. Nothing was said to the witness. People were leaving the courtroom. For Simon the situation was baffling. 'It's finished now?', he asked a few times, but there was no answer. After the break and the second part of Simon's testimony, the local part of these committal proceedings came to an end.

Before he adjourned the matter until the next hearing, the magistrate made a comment on the proceedings: 'I'm totally unimpressed with what's happened here today.' He told the prosecutor he ought to have provided 'proper interpreters' for 'a good number' of the witnesses.[101]

In Pularumpi Kevin's solicitor happily agreed with the police theory of a 'payback'. He said this on the verandah of the police station to Simon and other Tiwi people who were there. When we were working together on a set of mortuary poles for a ceremony, Simon made fun about it with his elder brother, Theodore. 'Payback, payback', he loudly mimicked the solicitor. They roared with laughter. Kevin was supposed to have acted to prevent a 'payback': for them it stretched the concept beyond recognition. The hearings provide a good example of how communication can go awry in cases involving Aborigines. Some of the Tiwi people who visited the public benches in Pularumpi saw this ordeal as humiliating. When he failed to comprehend the English spoken by Simon, a senior and very influential man, the magistrate 'talked to Simon as if he was a little boy'.

On 13 February 1989, the second session of hearings was convened at the Darwin Court of Summary Jurisdiction. Tobias' daughter Heather had come to the capital of the Northern Territory. She, belonging to the group of people who would have to seek redress, hoped to find out more about the killing. Heather became convinced Kevin had not killed her father. Kevin's elder 'brother', Arthur, was present in the building of the Magistrates Court too. Arthur Wangiti had staked out a career in administration. Now he was there to help Kevin. It had been unwise of Kevin, he said, to speak to the police. He personally knew of an Aboriginal man who got away with a serious assault because he only let a lawyer talk with the police. It would have been better, he said, if Kevin had contacted him, but at the time he was overseas. Dick, the 'prisoner's friend', was to be the only Tiwi witness. Outside the courtroom a CIB detective showed the knife, an exhibit, with much confidence to the prosecutor. Dick fixed his eyes on the knife. Back home he asked me if I had realised the blade was wrong, the deed could not have been done with that knife. Through Kevin's solicitor, Arthur talked with Kevin beforehand. Kevin told him he did not do it ('*karlu, karlu*': an assertive 'no'). On behalf of his younger 'brother', Arthur instructed the solicitor to plead 'not guilty'.

The (former) local senior constable appeared as the first witness in court. He gave detailed and lengthy answers to the questions of the prosecutor. Next came a detective who had interrogated Kevin. He put forward further police evidence against Kevin (the detective in charge was on holidays, the forensic pathologist was ill). The solicitor did not object to the admission of the confessional record of interview, the knife, and photographs of the crime scene taken from a distorted angle as evidence. There was just one question in cross-examination, namely if a 'prisoner's friend' had been present when Kevin had made his first statement to the police about how he had found Tobias' dead body under the mango tree.[102] Photos taken of the corpse during the post-mortem were also shown to the public benches. I saw Heather, the daughter of the deceased, shrink back. Photographs of a dead person are taboo (*pukamani*), and very distressing when shown to Tiwi people, especially a bereaved person. The photos must have been really shocking. Later, nearly moved to tears, Heather told my wife and me:

> I keep picturing him, how we found him in Pularumpi at the Old Camp . . . Everytime . . . it comes before my eyes. At that court I was so upset. I was sitting in front and that man showed those photos. It was so upsetting . . . I was shaking . . . It upset me. I didn't know what to do [whether] to go out or burst out in tears. Later I was sitting in the car . . . burst out in tears day and night.

The third and last witness was Dick Pamantari. This time there was an interpreter. It seemed of little help. There were lengthy silences in response to the questions of the prosecutor. No answer as to what had happened at the police station. The magistrate suggested more leading questions be asked. 'I only sit there', Dick said. There was eye-contact between the two police officers, who had taken a seat in the public benches, and the witness when he was asked how Kevin had been treated: 'Policemen friendly?' – 'Yes.' 'No trouble?' – 'No trouble.'[103] Under cross-examination Dick said Kevin had told him he was 'going to give himself up'.[104] At the conclusion of the committal hearings the magistrate was satisfied the evidence was sufficient to commit Kevin to trial. Kevin would have to stay in jail.

After the committal hearings in Darwin, the solicitor of the defendant said he feared nothing could be done for Kevin any more because of all 'the evidence in writing' against him. Arthur Wangiti, in discussing the matter with the interpreter, Karen Adranango, and me, said it was 'too late'. Kevin had told him not only that he had not done the deed but also that 'someone from the police had punched him three times'. He would have told Dick that too. Karen asked why she had not been told about that, for she would certainly have brought it to Dick's mind. Arthur named a policeman he suspected of hitting Kevin: 'He is a cheeky one.' 'Kevin did tell lies' (to the police), said Karen, he made it worse for himself. He (being innocent) should not have said he had done it, according to her. The strange thing was, she added, that we still did not know what had been going on that night: 'No history of fight.'

The next day in Pularumpi, Jeanette and I had to tell people about the hearings time after time. Kevin's relatives readily accepted his denial of having killed Tobias as it confirmed what he had told them earlier on in the local courtroom (and it was not expected he would lie to his elder 'brother' Albert either). Pamela Wurukwati, a 'mother' of Kevin, had told him he would have been better to follow her advice to go to the mainland after the car accident in which Marylou died had occurred. According to her, Kevin responded, 'Yeah, I fool that I didn't do that mammy'.

Several people told me that it had been unwise of Kevin not to have spoken to his relatives first before he took the blame upon himself and 'did tell lies' to the police. Phillip Wangiti, who had acted as an interpreter in the Pularumpi part of the committal hearings, gave the following comment: 'Those judges only want to keep on going, going. It looks like the Chamberlains' court.'[105] Many Tiwi people said to me that in their opinion Kevin had not done the deed. They backed this with what sounded like character references: Kevin was said to be a 'good bloke', not 'the worried person' to have been a killer, and so forth. Dick, who had seen the knife taken from Kevin during the committal hearings in Darwin, asked me afterwards, 'Did you see that knife? It was not sharp, hey? It was not sharp!' He made a drawing of the blade in the sand.

Nancy still voiced suspicions about Isaac. 'He [Isaac] should hurry up with the *iloti* [final mortuary ritual] for Oscar's sister. They might come and pick him up. Maybe he did it', she said. Maud and Nancy further stated that Oscar had been in the Old Camp on the night of the killing and not gone to Bathurst Island with Bruce and Joshua as he claimed: both men would have said it was only the two of them who went there in a dinghy. It must be noted that Sam was on bad terms with Oscar at that time. (By the end of 1991, the trouble had been settled and Oscar was no longer blamed by Sam and his close relatives.) Possibly Isaac was still held responsible for the death of his first wife, Kalikalini's sister and Kevin's mother's mother, who had rolled into a campfire when Isaac was with his lover, Jasmine's mother. People of the Mosquito clan, including Nancy, who made the allegations that Isaac had perhaps killed Tobias might have taken the fate of the senior woman of their clan into account.

Kevin, who was released on bail, turned up unexpectedly in Pularumpi on the last day of March. At the club Jerome told me spontaneously, 'Somebody here did it. He didn't do it.' From a Tiwi viewpoint, Kevin's coming back to the township did indeed suggest he had not committed the homicide. As mentioned earlier, the yam ritual was postponed. Despite his former intentions, Isaac did not take part in the ritual. Mike went away to the mainland because of the trouble in relation to the homicide. Kevin, Dick and I frequently went out fishing; during one of those trips right up a creek in the jungle on Bathurst Island, a spot favoured by Kevin, he said to us we had to go there when he was in jail again. Kevin told me about his life, his time in Berrimah jail, how he remembered the night before and the morning after the homicide and his experience of the police interrogations. He lived at the house of his 'daughter' Sally, for whom he had bought a washing machine, and Dick. After some time, a widow named Felicia Munuluka and her two daughters moved in with Kevin. (Felicia and Kevin had been secret lovers when they were teenagers and Felicia boarded at the mission.) They planned to marry some time in the future.

In July, Mike had returned from the mainland, saying he was 'in business' (meaning sorcery). He worked in the bakery so he could save money for the final mortuary ritual. This ritual would be after the murder trial, 'when Kevin is back'. During this ritual, so I was told, the senior members of Tobias' clan were entitled to say who had killed Tobias. 'Maybe they gonna give them good hiding or do it the same way', said Maud. 'That mob makes that decision.' Sally stated it could be said after the ritual (*iloti*), 'They might do it the same way.' 'Straight away or at night, that's the Law', her husband Dick added. 'I think we do it black-fella way', said Simon. Heather and Bruce both told me it was two men from Pularumpi. In Pularumpi the names of Isaac and Oscar were the most frequently mentioned. Once Oscar would have silenced Isaac and Mike when they were yelling at the club. Jerome came to me, upset, because my 'brother' Mike had mentioned Tobias' name; he threatened to spear him. In July there was another rumour, which was that Chuck Wangiti, a clan brother of Tobias, in Milikapiti had been told it was two other men, namely Jasmine's adoptive brother, Roy Mornington, and her youngest brother, Rodney Pamantari. Mike and Maud were shocked by this. Mike said, 'I don't want to live here any more'. The two men had been in Pularumpi on the night of the killing; as well as her 'fathers', Jasmine's brothers had a right to protect her as well. The new allegations created uncertainty.

*   *   *

In Darwin the North Australian Aboriginal Legal Aid Service (NAALAS), according to its president quoted in the paper, was wrestling to clear a backlog of cases – 'the result of a huge demand on the service'. Legal associations had offered to help, and 'a prominent Melbourne QC had also offered his services for free for four weeks' (*Northern Territory News*, 16 March 1989). On 31 March, Kevin was released on bail. It had taken the barrister from Melbourne three days to get Kevin out of jail. Arthur Wangiti paid the necessary A\$3,000 (Kevin earned A\$100 a week on Melville Island); his elder classificatory brother would support him throughout the murder trial. The accused stayed in Arthur's apartment in Darwin.

The murder trial, held at the Northern Territory Supreme Court in Darwin, lasted three weeks, from 24 July until 11 August 1989. On the Friday before the trial was to start, I met the barrister in the NAALAS offices. He would take up Kevin's defence, assisted by the solicitor in charge of the Aboriginal legal aid service. The senior barrister consulted me on a number of cultural matters that could be relevant to the case and he explained some legal matters to me. In a criminal case like this the defence had the advantage of having notice of the prosecution's evidence beforehand, and this had already become clear with the committal hearings. The prosecution, on the other hand, had no right to know about the accused's defence (cf. Chrisholm and Nettheim 1974: 64). On Sunday, the Tiwi witnesses were flown to Darwin; they were all lodged in an Aboriginal hostel. During the day the witnesses were 'proofed' by the Crown prosecution; that is, they had to tell their stories so that the prosecutor knew what kinds of questions he could ask. 'Practising what to say', was how one of the Tiwi witnesses described it.

It is not possible to describe the trial in great detail here; the transcripts consist of nearly 1,000 pages. I will select only a few relevant issues and events. The court proceedings might be described as a ritual. Justice Fisher, in wig and red gown, had not only judicially but also literally a high position at the back of the courtroom: distanced, 'His Honour' overlooked the whole thing. At the bar table were the deputy permanent Crown prosecutor, Peter Smith; the counsel for the defence, Patrick Norman; and the solicitor, Curt Jameson. Jameson gave the Queen's Counsel, Norman, instructions on behalf of his client. The lawyers behind the bar table were in wigs and black gowns. Their resemblance one to the other was at times confusing for the Aboriginal witnesses: one man asking one thing, the other man another thing or the same thing over again. Although they fought a judicial battle, Norman referred to Smith as 'my friend', and Smith spoke of Norman as 'my learned friend'. The Aboriginal witnesses – also unfamiliar with court rituals such as the oath-taking, standing up, and bowing – were likely to be confused by the phrasing of questions (putting at least two alternatives in one sentence), in addition to the other language problems they had to face (cf. Liberman 1981).

The questions were framed by the people in wigs. This was not always understood by the Tiwi witnesses. Isaac, for instance, returned questions of his own. 'Why?' (to what purpose), he wondered, was a particular question put to him. For Simon a number of questions were so obvious that he could not see why these were asked at all. When asked what a certain police officer had said, for instance, he pointed out where this policeman sat in the public benches. He told the lawyer to go and ask the man for himself.[106] Sometimes, such misunderstandings were met with laughter in court (as also had happened to Dick in the committal hearings). At the beginning of the trial Kevin entered a plea of not guilty. The judge and the jury of twelve were all non-Aboriginal people.

The first week of the trial was spent on a so-called *voir dire*, in the absence of the jury.[107] The aim of this procedure, on the instigation of the counsel for the defence, was to find out whether Kevin's confession had been obtained by 'violence and trickery'. If this could be proven, then the admission to the crime could not be held as evidence against him. By subpoena the counsel for the defence received from the Chief Commissioner of Police, among other things, some fifteen statements to the police that had neither been presented to the Crown prosecutor nor to the defence. These revealed statements on conflicts between the victim and a number of people other than the accused, of witnesses who alleged they had heard a fight that had taken place in the Old Camp during the night of the killing, on a man who had been arguing with the victim that night, and about another knife having been found. Were these thrown out because they did not fit the police theory? At any rate, they were unfavourable for the Crown's case.

Norman went in hard on the detectives. Arthur Wangiti, who sat beside me in the public benches, thought the case had been won when the police started contradicting each other. Norman elicited answers that made it clear that the investigation had not been conducted with great care, to say the least. The policemen denied the allegation of violence. Asked why he had thrown out a statement about a man who had been arguing with the victim late that night, the detective in charge said, 'If I can explain, they were two elderly gentlemen who, when they had a few drinks, got cranky, and this had been going on for some time and it was – I think it's normal in Darwin, you know, you have those sorts of people, and it was nothing more than that.' The statement of the witness Simon as to what he had heard, also thrown out, he dismissed as 'very unreliable', adding that the man in question was 'an elderly gentleman'. He seemed unaware that in Aboriginal societies the senior men in particular, more than other people, are entitled to speak on delicate matters. He preferred to go on what was 'normal in Darwin'. Unreliable and inaccurate also were the notes in the day journal of the local senior constable taken at the time (the only – and contradictory – record of the movements of the police), in contrast to a statement of a crucial interrogation of Kevin, put down on paper from memory more than a month after it had been conducted. A fortnight later the statement was produced again by the other detective, who signed it as a statement of his own. The 'prisoner's friend', Dick, told the prosecutor that Kevin had been forced to answer the questions of the detective. When asked how, Dick said, 'Just asked'. It did not come across. The accused, in a sworn testimony, however, specified the threat. He said he had to answer, or else they would 'keep on asking', and 'probably lock me up'. He testified that before Dick was there, he had been hit by the detective. The prosecutor got him hopelessly confused.[108] At this point Arthur was of the opinion that Kevin had ruined it for himself, the case was lost.

The Crown prosecutor presented what the policemen had been telling the judge 'as a classic detective mystery of the country house variety, lacking only a butler', meaning everyone in Pularumpi was a suspect: the police had 'no clues at all', and had followed 'the classic procedure of the detective in that situation . . . with a view to discovering motive, means and opportunity'. About the trickery aspect, the false information given Kevin, the detective had said he thought he was talking about the

wrong night. Justice Fisher would not accept that. He said: 'He mightn't
have the prescience of Sherlock Holmes, but still he's a bumbler like
Dr Watson if that's what he says is the case.' After lengthy judicial argument, the judge's ruling on the preliminary matters was that in accordance with the Anunga Rules, the evidence was inadmissible up until the
point of the discovery of the knife. He rejected the allegation of violence
on part of the police, and ruled the record of interview to be in line with
the Anunga Rules, and, therefore, admissible as evidence to be led against
the accused.

After some further argument, the actual trial began.[109] The prosecutor
presented the Crown's case in addressing the jury. The same Tiwi
witnesses were called as during the committal hearings. For them,
like Aboriginal suspects under police interrogation, it was an ordeal.
They frequently told Jeanette and me they wanted to go home, home as
soon as possible. One man who had given up drinking beer 'hit the
booze' again. At the hostel the Aboriginal witnesses tried to assess the situation with the bits and pieces of what one or the other had been asked.
The counsel for the defence, who now also had the hidden statements
to go on, gave Isaac a hard time.[110] In all fairness, it must be admitted
that the defence lawyers also could take advantage of the vulnerability
of Aboriginal suspects and witnesses (cf. Ligertwood 1988: 203). An
Aboriginal person can pretend to be ignorant as a means of obstruction,
and so not have to incriminate her or himself or to contradict others
(Liberman 1981: 250–1). A Tiwi man, commenting on this case, said
to me: 'When a guy is smart and he did it, he will find a way to get away
with it.'

During the overnight adjournments and at noon we went with Tiwi
people to sample the diversions of Darwin life, ranging from a bingo
game to a striptease show. Kevin beat a white man in a snooker game,
which we both interpreted as a sign that good luck was going to come
his way. For his elder 'brother' Arthur, who sat out the whole trial and
whose remarks I came to regard as a kind of barometer of Tiwi views on
its progress, the adversarial court procedure appeared to be a strange
thing. He was rather radical in the views he expressed. Arthur went
along with positive and negative developments, alternately predicting
victory or doom. The Tiwi witnesses, outside the court, showed the same
tendencies.

I will note one more question that has to do with the standards of
proof and the rules of evidence. As I said earlier, it is impossible within
the scope of this chapter to discuss all the issues on which there was
argument in court. Elkin writes that Aboriginal evidence – due to political, social, and economic inequities, language problems, and court pro-

cedures – is unreliable in court (1947: 183, 179–88). Sansom regards Elkin's article as 'an essay of apology' to account for unreliability, for from a non-Aboriginal point of view it is unreliability that Elkin is talking about (1980: 208). Sansom argues that 'the Aboriginal witness transports rule-governed speech behaviour into court'. Aborigines dodging the issue, 'entering the disclaiming referral' in his jargon, mean they are not allowed to speak about it, although they might know (ibid.: 41n2, 25–6). Aborigines under police interrogation or in court, according to Sansom, leave the 'jurisdiction' of their own group and are subjected to the jurisdiction of the national law. As a result of this situation of isolation, which is a frightful one, they may say anything. The interesting point is that when afterwards Aboriginal people return to their own group, social amends will have to be made, and in an adjustment to the situation, on the basis of the persons' declarations to the outsiders and the effects of the latter acting on these, the group assessment of reality will be redefined. Hence, later statements and testimonies by the same persons tend to reflect the shifts that have occurred (1980: ch. 9).

To the outsider the different outcomes of this interplay in time, the new testimony in comparison with former statements, appear contradictory and therefore unreliable. Justice Kriewaldt, for instance, writes, 'the difficulty of being able to distinguish between truth and falsity when an aborigine is telling the story is . . . formidable, and in my opinion, insurmountable' (1960: 29–30). Strehlow would not endorse the reliability of Aboriginal evidence in court, but he points out that they can and do make the difference between truth and untruth. Telling the truth or a lie is socially embedded: there is no reason, with regard to important matters, to tell the truth to people not entitled to know nor to lie to those who have to be told (1936: 331, 323, passim).

Tiwi people do surely recognise the distinction between truth and falsity, but the crucial topic is what is considered 'truth'. The 'truth', at a certain point in time, must be socially acceptable and accepted. Consequently, I believe, when the detective 'forced' Kevin to 'tell the truth' he got what Kevin thought he wanted to hear. In the altered context, separated from his community, the nonsense (or 'lies' in the Tiwi context) he produced was truthful for him in terms of his dealings with the detective. Dick (Jasmine's elder brother) was his 'witness'; he was forced to be such, and would have 'to help' him in making social amends later, as well as being his agent in a forthcoming Tiwi definition of the situation: Kevin did tell lies to the police. By 'giving himself up' he had probably done other Tiwi people a service too (leading the detectives away from the real or other trouble, and getting rid of the policemen with their prying questions), and some time in the future these people would have to even the score. (When he was released on bail, Kevin was provided with a wife, a former widow with two daughters, which meant an enormous status elevation for him.) I have already mentioned that Tiwi people, in and outside the court re-assessed the situation every time new and relevant information came to them, and this in turn led to a consensual redefinition of what was going on. Tiwi people had believed that the police would find out who had killed Tobias by taking fingerprints and using a computer. We have seen that Tiwi people from Pularumpi were reluctant to speak out. These factors suggest, among other things, that reliance on people's testimony was not considered by most of the local Tiwi the best way to proceed (and the inquests failed accordingly). In the local arena, blaming one person involved others as well and thus could have important social consequences, whereas the police tracking down the killer(s) through fingerprints or such a mysterious device as a computer would not produce such consequences. Let us return to the court case.

Three witnesses from the forensic section of the police were called by the Crown: the crime scene examiner, the forensic pathologist, and a forensic biologist. Under cross-examination it was revealed that the officer who carried out the examination at the scene of the crime had forgotten to take fingerprints, had not examined the sharp stainless steel knife belonging to the white sailor, and had not noticed that there were initials carved in the handle of the blunt knife produced by Kevin (that were not his). He claimed he had taken a swab of blood from the victim's verandah and sent it to the forensic biologist; the biologist gave evidence that she had never received it. She had, however, examined the clothes that had been fetched from Kevin after he indicated in the confessional record of interview that he had worn these on the night of the killing. No blood was found on these clothes. The forensic pathologist, who had done the post-mortem, told the open court there was definitely no wound in the victim's back (as the police tracker had told other Tiwi people and Kevin had mentioned in his admission to the crime). He estimated the time of death, as the victim was alive and mobile after the stabbing for some time (thirty to ninety minutes), as between 1 and 3 am. This was consistent with the time the card players, as noted in the unproduced statements, had heard the noises mentioned earlier coming from the direction of the victim's house, between 10.30 pm and 1.10 am. The pathologist – to whom the two knives taken by the police were presented – said that, without excluding one or the other, it was more likely that the white sailor's sharp knife had caused the fatal wound than the blunt one unearthed by the accused.

Another *voir dire* took place. Norman wanted to get evidence as to whether an Aboriginal man thought the supposed lethal weapon could cause the fatal wound. He argued against the objection of Smith that the witness, Alan Pamantari, was 'unqualified'. Norman said that this man had used such knives all his life, that he was 'still engaged in the essences of a hunting-gathering society' which involved knives, and that as a health worker he had experience with knife cuts and wounds. Alan was handed the blunt knife and a close-up photograph of the fatal stab wound, taken during the post-mortem. He said, 'From my experience I would say that a knife like this wouldn't – I can see that that's a clean cut and it would be very difficult for this knife to cause that clean cut.'[111]

The Aboriginal health worker then affirmed that he had experience with steel-blade knives of European origin and of those dimensions. He further said he was an expert hunter and declared that he knew the difference in cuts, on animals as well as on humans, made by a blunt knife and a sharp one. He conceded he had not compared the wounds on the humans he treated with the knives that caused them. His expertise was not acknowledged in the Australian court. Justice Fisher ruled against it and upheld the objection of the Crown prosecutor. He said:

> Well the fatal point here . . . is that this witness says that in the treating of wounds, knife wounds . . . : 'I have not looked at knives causing cuts I have treated.' But quite apart from that, your avenue of expertise would be in the realm of a pathologist, or we'll admit surgeons [Norman argued surgeons used scalpels, not large skinning knives]; but if need be I'm sure that a surgeon would have more to say about it with the vast number of examinations that he has made. I mean, I can't get over the fact that if I were to admit this evidence of opinion, you might equally call a slaughterman [not saying what was against the evidence of a butcher].[112]

The pathologist who had taken measurements, however, was not able to give this kind of evidence about the wound.

What we have here, basically, is a difference in method: in the words of the historian Ginzburg, between the scientific, experimental method involving the repetition of phenomena and measurements in contrast to the individualising 'interpretative method based on taking marginal and irrelevant details as revealing clues' (1988: 92, 86). He points out that the qualitative approach, in which 'tiny details provide the key to a deeper reality, inaccessible by other methods', was followed by the art connoisseur Morelli, the psychoanalyst Freud, and Conan Doyle's Sherlock Holmes. This is not suprising, according to Ginzburg, because all three authors had medical training; they were familiar with 'medical semiotics', 'the discipline which permits diagnosis, though the disease cannot be directly observed, on the basis of superficial symptoms or signs, often irrelevant to the eye of a layman'. He traces the origin of this conjectural method back to the deciphering of animals' tracks in hunter societies (ibid.: 87, passim). Presented to the judge in the present case was an Aboriginal hunter, thoroughly familiar with the second method, who could read the signs of a knife cut in flesh. He told how he made his inference on the basis of a concrete, seemingly trivial, detail – which had escaped the attention of a forensic scientist – from his experience. (Likewise, he could retrospectively decipher animal tracks, identify individuals by their footprints, and at first sight tell the homicide victim was dead because his body did not respond to the flies crawling from the mouth.) A Sherlock Holmes-like detective could hardly have done better. Underlying the whole issue was not only a discrepancy in method but also a biased assumption as to who was 'qualified' as an expert witness. If it was a matter of method solely, the expert evidence of psychiatrists probably would be inadmissible as evidence in Australian criminal courts.[113]

After the first two weeks of the trial the Tiwi witnesses had given their evidence in court and gone back home to Pularumpi. When the matter was adjourned till Tuesday the following week I decided to go back at the weekend as well. I wanted to pay my respects to Simon's wife Ella who was about to die. It was believed the trial would only last for one or two more days.

In his summing up, towards the end of Kevin's trial, the Crown prosecutor suggested to the jury that the accused, in contrast to his representations in the confessional record of interview, had told lies in his earlier statement to the police. This was his explanation of why Kevin would have done so:

> [T]he accused was well aware when he made that statement [that 'he had been to Dick's for supper and then he went home to sleep'], that that time – the time soon after he left the club, was the time that mattered in relation to the deceased. That was when the deceased met his death. I would suggest to you that those falsehoods indicate preknowledge on the accused's part, knowledge that he needed to cover up, lies that he needed to tell.[114]

After Smith had put the Crown's case to the jury, the counsel for the defence summed up all the opposing evidence. Norman stated, among other things, that there was no evidence for the time suggested by the Crown, but that there was evidence the victim was still alive after midnight. He also wondered how the accused could come out of a mortal wrestle on a concrete verandah and stab the victim, as the Crown would have it, without any bruises or a drop of blood on him. Besides, there were other people with motive and opportunity, and another knife (means) had been found. The main issue, of course, was the reliability of the confessional record of interview with the police. The defence and the prosecution held diametrically opposed views on this. Then it was up to the jury 'to decide facts in the light of the law as put to them by the judge' (Chrisholm and Nettheim 1974: 69). After a little more than two hours, the jury returned a verdict of 'not guilty' of murder, and a verdict of 'not guilty' of manslaughter. Kevin was released and could go back to the islands.

I was informed about the final stage of the trial by telephone calls to the Aboriginal Legal Aid Service. On Friday evening, 11 August, I learned from his counsel that Kevin had been acquitted. Kevin told me to bring Felicia the good news; he would return the next day. Unfortunately, I did not obtain an account of the judge's summing up to the jury. When I asked Kevin about it, he said, 'I didn't listen'.

A year after he charged Kevin with the murder, the detective in charge of the homicide investigation told me at the Darwin Magistrates Court (where another Tiwi man charged with another murder had been brought before the magistrate) that the case was 'over and done with'. The solicitor in charge of the Aboriginal Legal Aid Service said to me that Kevin had been 'extremely lucky' to be defended by the senior barrister from Melbourne; this was not the way these cases were usually run. His counsel had succeeded in casting 'reasonable doubt' on the charge by the Crown that Kevin had killed Tobias. Under the law the accused is presumed innocent until proven otherwise; but, as Norman put it, how could he prove he was innocent?

Kevin had been in jail for five months. That was just his 'bad luck', said the solicitor. When he was put in jail he lost his relatively well-paid job with the council in Pularumpi. During the murder trial he was not entitled to social security benefits, we were told when we visited the offices in Darwin, because he was on the Community Development and Employment Program in Pularumpi (and he was not paid if he did not show up for work). It has been argued that the focus on sentencing disguises 'the real punishment' for the accused person, as many harrowing and traumatic experiences are endured in the pre-adjudication process (see Gale et al. 1990: 7).

I have tried to make clear how partially illiterate Aboriginal people can become captured in the imaginations of mainstream Anglo-Australian culture, in which the written word and the imposition of 'common sense' on these people, who do not subscribe to the underlying cultural assumptions, is a basis of power over them.

The ongoing impact of the national criminal justice system on Aboriginal societies reflects the reproduction of political inequities. In my discussion of the present case I elaborated on the cultural miscommunication involved. The shifting Tiwi perceptions of the processes of criminal prosecution were also considered. The case shows the extra-local and the local political arena as inseparably intertwined. The outcome of the murder trial, the accused being 'not guilty' of the alleged crime, was one upheld by quite a number of Tiwi people from the outset. The statements held back by the police but elicited by the counsel for the defence put the circumstantial evidence in another light. The detectives, on the basis of *their* logic and concepts (e.g., what was 'normal in Darwin'), selected the information to fit their appraisal of the situation and what they considered 'true' (see Lakoff and Johnson 1980: 179). They relied so much on the one confessional record of interview, which was considered truthful by them but which merely reflected the unequal situation of police interrogation, that no further steps were taken to investigate the homicide.

Tiwi people were of another opinion. The close relatives of the homicide victim had decided to wait to perform the final mortuary ritual until after the murder trial, as that served as another occasion to 'find out' who had killed Tobias. Smaller post-funeral rituals had been performed in Pularumpi before Kevin went on trial. Afterwards, extremely elaborate final mortuary rituals of the Bathurst Islanders and Melville Islanders were held simultaneously at Pawularitarra, the place where Tobias had been buried. The post-funeral rituals and an aftermath on the third anniversary of Tobias' death, the lifting of the name and photo taboo, will be discussed in the next chapter. These rituals in themselves were achievements, not customs to be automatically followed. It took a tremendous effort to organise the grand final mortuary ritual (*iloti*).

CHAPTER 8

The Post-funeral Rituals

'I have some ideas . . . two men. With the *iloti* it will come out . . . flog them', said Heather Arapi to Jeanette and me. We were sitting in the shade of the mangroves at the beach in Paru, waiting for a dinghy to take us across the strait to Nguiu in order to attend a funeral there. On our way in the back of a truck from Milikapiti to Paru we had passed Tobias' grave, a few kilometres out in the bush. At that point, Heather and Ruth started wailing. They wiped their eyes with a piece of cloth. Ruth's husband Theodore gently touched my arm. 'Pawularitarra', he said softly, 'Pawularitarra', while pointing out into the bush.

Tobias' children attended virtually all mortuary rituals on the islands during the time between their father's burial and his final mortuary ritual, rallying support and creating debts. Time after time, they reminded people what had happened to their father. Mortuary rituals for other people were also occasions for them to express their grief concerning the loss of their father. Frequently they acted as ritual workers, expecting this to be reciprocated in the forthcoming ritual. Such a ritual did not automatically result from factors such as the social position of the deceased and the type of death, but required hard work. People had to be mobilised, funds raised, and the ritual performances negotiated. Commitment by the performers rested on exchange relations with the organising group on various levels. Tobias' children and his 'father' Jack Munuluka were determined to hold a prestigious *iloti*, involving memorable performances, much money, many mortuary poles, and the attendance of a large number of people.

*　　　*　　　*

183

The ideal types of Tiwi mortuary ritual may be divided for analytical purposes into funeral and post-funeral rituals. Much of Tiwi mortuary behaviour directly preceding or following a death was ritualised, such as wailing and the performance of mourning songs for the dying or newly deceased, the announcement of a death, the eventual wake, the disposal of clothes and personal belongings of the deceased, purification with smoke and water, and the 'opening up' of roads after fatal motor vehicle accidents. The actual burial was bracketed by two elaborate dance and song ceremonies (called *yoi*), one around the corpse in camp (not considered a 'proper ceremony'), and another around the new grave mound.

If, where, and when post-funeral rituals were to be held was a matter to be decided on. Every *unantani* (*pulanga*) or *mutuni* could organise his own post-funeral rituals for the deceased. Thus for one deceased more than one complete series of post-funeral rituals could be held, and grand final rituals (called *iloti*) for one person at different locations. When there was no 'bush' grave available, another grave containing the clothes and personal belongings of the deceased could be made, or there would be no grave at all. (The disconnection in place of the funeral and post-funeral rituals probably dates back to the time when the performance of the latter had to be hidden from the missionaries.) Sometimes there was a joint final ritual for two or three dead people. The number of poles erected at a final ritual ranged from a single sapling, painted white, or a borrowed old pole, to twenty or so elaborately carved poles in striking polychrome, painted in geometrical designs especially for the one occasion.

A number of months after the burial, therefore, a series of post-funeral rituals could be held. These rituals began with the handing of an axe, fire and ochres to selected ritual workers, either in three separate small rituals or in one go. Thereafter, a series of small dance and other rituals could be organised on different days and be continued until the beginning of the final mortuary ritual, the *iloti*. The *iloti* (literally 'for good' or 'forever') was an elaborate dance and song ceremony (*yoi*) of the same type as those performed with the burial but involving all categories of personnel available (cf. appendix 2 below). The chosen ritual workers prepared the mortuary poles to be erected for this ritual. At the conclusion, the poles would be relocated around the grave mound (a grave with either the deceased or the deceased's clothes and personal belongings) when there was one (made) close by.

The axe-giving was a minor ritual, which also could be headed by male or female matrilineal bereaved kin (cf. Brandl 1971: 482), in which an axe (*walemani*), its handle painted white, was given by representatives of the organising group to selected ritual workers. The dance movements depicted the cutting of a tree. The ritual workers who received the axe could then start to chop down the trees needed to make the mortuary poles. Formerly these trees were cut in the area surrounding the grave, an area that was taboo. Only the ritual workers were allowed to go there. For fear of the destructive actions of the spirit of the dead they worked together. Other trespassers in the tabooed area would be speared, and it was still believed serious harm or death would come to any people, except the ritual workers, who went there. The ritual workers stripped the tree trunks of their bark 'skin' and carved these in the particular shape they had in mind. Every pole had to be unique, although there were some conventional forms of which individual ritual workers produced variations.

The presentation of fire (*ikwoni*, e.g., a box of matches or a lighter) to the ritual workers, in a dance depicting the pre-contact mode of making fire with sticks, was the sign that the carved poles could be 'smoked'. The practical purpose of this procedure was to dry out the poles above a fire so they would not crack, and to give the poles a blackened surface as a background for the painting. The expressive aspect entailed a purification of the tree trunks with smoke. At the end of the 1980s, Tiwi used the black contents of dry-cell batteries, mixed with PVC glue as a fixative, to give the poles a deep black surface. The mortuary poles would be mainly judged on the brightness of the painted colours, and therefore a deep black was desirable.

In the next small ritual the workers got the paints (*tilamara*), red and yellow ochres and white pipeclay, to put on the poles. In their dance movements the donors depicted the painting of their faces and arms. My informants stated that the painting of the poles was similar to the most prestigious painting of human faces and bodies, when lying down, in elaborate designs. The geometrical designs closely resembling those of the facial and body paintings were applied rhythmically to the mortuary poles. A number of people had developed a distinctive style, intertwining conventional motifs with motifs that identified the makers with other people (e.g., their 'fathers'). There was a strong emphasis on individual originality and creativity. The number, size and quality of the poles were a source of prestige both for the makers and the organisers of the post-funeral rituals (see Goodale and Koss 1971).

After these initial rituals followed a series that focused on the dreaming of the deceased. Mountford (1958: 68) calls these 'preliminary ceremonies' and Goodale (1971: 282) 'preliminary rituals', a term adopted by later authors (Brandl 1971; Grau 1983) because these rituals preceded the final mortuary ritual, the *iloti*. Strictly speaking, I believe this to be incorrect. Ideally, the rituals started in the localities of the living and went on in space and time until the beginning of the *iloti* at the burial place, an area reserved for the spirits of the dead. There was no restriction on the number of these rituals to be carried out to direct the spirit of the deceased from the world of the living to the world of the dead. When the close relatives were satisfied with the performances of these rituals, known by the general term *ilanigha*, one of the relatives called out for the *iloti*. Then people 'broke' the *ilanigha*; or else, in theory, these type of rituals would go on infinitely. One or more (depending on the number of residential groups) *ilanigha*, previously performed in the area of residence of the participants, would be carried over to the *iloti*, and re-enacted in the ceremonial grounds of the final mortuary ritual. With the *iloti* the transitory rituals came to a halt. From then on the person in question belonged to the spirits of the dead (*mopadruwi*) 'forever' (*iloti*). As I understand it, the series of small rituals were liminal rather than preliminary. Each *ilanigha* might be small compared to the *iloti* but nevertheless its ritual goal was to chase away the spirit of the deceased from the living and to direct this spirit to its destination.

The first *ilanigha* began with a dance in which the performers stamped their feet hard on the ground, 'really hard, punch 'em ground properly' (*amprenuwunga*). This resembled the 'awakening' of the spirit at the beginning of the 'night of sorrow' in the yam ritual. In this way the performers gained the attention of the spirit of the deceased. Stamping hard on the ground was for Tiwi a feature of a good performance. The dance performances were accompanied by song and percussion (besides the stamping of the dancers, the others clapped with bare hands on their buttocks or used two wooden clubs or a stick on corrugated iron). All over the world, as Needham (1967) points out, transition and percussion go hand in hand. The Tiwi are no exception to this phenomenon. The people who attended an *ilanigha* faced in the direction of the burial place of the deceased. A goose-feather ball (*tokwainga*) on a cord could be softly thrown in a little arc in the direction of the spirit's destination, 'where we go', three times, while people called out, 'hooo . . . ayeh'. An important element of the next *ilanigha*, 'the *ilanigha* right through' until its finish with the *iloti*, was an energetic dance called *ampikatoa* or *kutungura* in which dirt was thrown up with the feet. As I said earlier, this dance represented the tantrums of a little child when loosening the ties to its parents, a life-cycle event applied in the ritual context as a symbol of separation. Young men thought to be ready to undergo the initiation (that is, being an *ilanighi*) were told to perform this dance, but other people could do it as well. What we have here is a double shift: the beginning of the initiation of the spirit of the deceased into the world of the dead, and the beginning of the initiation of young men into the world of initiated adult men with ceremonial responsibilities. It might be seen as a succession of the generations in subsequent ritually marked phases; the two types of initiation coincided, restoring the social fabric after a death.

Other rituals in these series included dance ceremonies that had a dreaming of the deceased, in song and dance, as their theme. Established dreaming dances could be performed and entirely new dances created. Part of an *ilanigha* could be another of the following rituals: a mock fight with the ritual workers, tree-climbing and fire-jumping by initiates, or tossing the initiates or a goose-feather ball in the air instead, and a mock fight between (potential) spouses (cf. Spencer 1914: 110–11; Mountford 1958: 71–4; Goodale 1971: 284–8). When the ritual workers had been working on the poles in the area surrounding the grave, they returned to camp at night. There, in a ceremonial ground, they could have a fight with the organising group. The two groups of people threw sticks, clubs, and spears at each other which had to be dodged; after that, they wrestled. The ritual workers were considered polluted by having been in touch with the spirits of the dead. The mock fight could be staged to 'chase *pukamani* [taboos as well as the spirits] away'. The performance of this ritual had become rare because most workers tended to make the poles in the townships and transported these by truck to the place where the final ritual would be held.

There was considerable variation in the performances of the second ritual that may be distinguished as two separate rituals. A fire was lit at the base of a bloodwood tree, and either initiates climbed the tree or people held the tree and shouted ritual calls. Next, the participants jumped over the fire. The tossing of novices in the air could be replaced by the tossing of a goose-feather ball. The third ritual, the mock fight between actual and potential spouses (*paumati*), usually took place shortly before the *iloti* commenced. These people hit each other with green boughs, a procedure accompanied with much laughter because there was licence to touch people in (potential) lover relationships. The *paputawi* were hit on the legs, the *mutuni* on the cheeks, places marking their relationship with the deceased. Other people could be hit anywhere, 'because we in *ilanigha* we *pukamani* so we gotta kill each other with leaves', as Nancy explained to me; the spirit of the deceased was still there and, when he or she was a potential spouse, the dead person used the same kinship term and had the feelings corresponding with that relationship as those people who attacked with green boughs had to those being attacked. In other words, the hitting with leaves by (potential) spouses released from taboo the ordinary kinship term for a potential spouse, which was equally applied by the deceased to the persons attacked; 'that *pukamani* will go away after that'.

Before the *iloti* four categories of bereaved people had to go around a fire and burn the hair from their legs. Each category of these bereaved sang about a conventional subject matter (see appendix 1 for the mortuary kinship terms): the *unantawi* (*pularti*) sang a song about a boat, the *mamurapi* (*turah*) a song about the cause of death (e.g., sickness), the *ker-imerika* a song about 'devil' or spirits, and the *ambaruwi* a song about pos-sible amorous suitors of the deceased. This 'smoking', accompanied by a dance, was regarded as a protective measure. In October 1989, a group of people arrived too late at a ritual of two days for a deceased woman. The widower was so angry that he told them to go straight for *iloti* and that they were not allowed to 'go in fire'. These people, frightened lest harm befall them, nevertheless went somewhat further into the bush and carried out the 'smoking' ritual. My informants stated that in addi-tion to purification of death-related pollution, people might 'go in fire' to warm themselves (for the ceremony) and to 'throw away all the bad luck [for instance] no number in the cards, got throw away all those in the smoke'. On the one hand, being in touch with the spirits of the dead was considered dangerous and life-threatening. On the other hand, it was considered to promote people's well-being, health, and luck. These ambiguous collective representations reflected ambiguous emotions towards the deceased (cf. Freud 1983).

Preceding the *iloti* people could paint their bodies or had them painted, and adorned themselves with ceremonial ornaments (various bangles, head-dresses of cockatoo feathers or woven pandanus leaves, and on a cord around the neck, goose-feather balls). Not all people attending the rituals did this, but ornamentation expressed people's engagement, a sort of index of being 'really *pukamani* [bereaved]'. Of course, there were people who were more and others who were less dog-matic. But there was also a tendency for those who had been in close contact with the deceased, those very closely related to the deceased, and those in ritual leadership roles to apply facial and body paintings and wear some ornaments. Mountford (1958: 92) regards the body paint as a disguise for the spirit of the dead; its application, among other things, depended on the emotions and personality of the people con-cerned, and context (healing properties were also attributed to the paints).

When coming to the ceremonial grounds where the *iloti* would be held, the ritual workers went first. With clubs and sticks the workers hit the earth in the ceremonial ring (*milimika*) and the mortuary poles, erected in a line. They shouted '*hoi hoi hoi*' (like people did in the *pau-mati*), driving away the spirits of the dead. Then the other bereaved rushed forward and wailed collectively, holding the poles (some people hit their bodies against the poles, especially those parts of the body denoting their relationship to the deceased). Next, a fire was lit in the ceremonial ground and circled by the participants. A previous *ilanigha* ritual, or such a ritual accompanied by a song from the last yam ritual, would be performed. After the call for *iloti* this series of rituals was ended, and people proceeded with the dance and song ceremony (*yoi*) that formed the main part of the *iloti*. This time, in contrast to the funeral rituals, a full-scale ritual involving all categories of bereaved would be staged. A description of the full sequence of personnel, dances, and songs is provided in the two appendices. In the funeral rituals the matrilineal relatives of the deceased were considered 'too close' but after the lapse of time they did perform in the post-funeral rituals.

As in other rituals, mourning songs could be performed apart from the centre stage. There was a difference in nuances and wording of these songs at the time of the final ritual, in contrast to the type of songs sung at the burial and the yam rituals. When 'crying for a dead body' people used 'straight words', but with the final ritual the song language employed was more metaphorical and interspersed with words that did not have a literal meaning but had strong emotional connotations and were, therefore, 'hard words' (so emotionally charged that people found it hard to pronounce them). For instance, when a widow after some months arrived at her husband's grave, in connection with the final ritual, she performed a special type of widow song in that different way.

They had 'pay day', as Tiwi said, with money collected on a blanket (from the *unantawi, mamurapi turah, mutuni*, and sometimes *paputawi* as well) and laid out to be distributed to the ritual workers by the actual spouse of the deceased, the bereaved children or parents. Care was taken to show exactly what amount of money was given by a particular person to whom. Disagreements were likely to arise at this stage about debts or the quality and size of the mortuary poles. The monetary payments, sometimes also fabrics, were carried around in a dance and handed to the ritual workers. When the ritual workers were satisfied with their payment, they lifted their poles from the ceremonial ring and in a small ritual relocated these in a formation around the grave; if there was none the poles were left in the line where they had been put before the beginning of the final ritual.

The actual widow or widower was ritually washed, and released from the mourning taboos, by a sibling of the deceased. The survivors rushed to the grave, wailed and hit themselves, dropped on the grave mound, and cried collectively for the last time. They said farewell to the spirit of the deceased and left. Their ornaments could be left behind on the grave mound.

*   *   *

Unless obliged by a very close relationship to the deceased, Tiwi perceived of their sorrow, ritual performances and services as gifts. These 'gifts', including dances and songs, were not free. Such gifts and the ritual payments, once made, always had to be reciprocated in a balanced manner on future occasions. The web of mutual ritual obligations pulling people in after a death was an important phenomenon on which the whole 'ceremony business' thrived.

Following a death the close patrilineal relatives faced the hardship, perhaps helping them in coping with their grief, of finding sufficient money and support to fulfil their obligations to the deceased and at the same time to the people to whom they had outstanding debts. Other people, of course, had also contracted debts to them or were close kin unable to refuse, and preferably these people would be mobilised to give their support or would be commissioned as ritual workers. With regard to the burial, the need for help from ritual workers was acute (see Hart and Pilling 1960: 89–95) but the number of ritual workers and the amount of money to be paid them might be limited. The time between the burial and the final ritual was used to raise and save funds, ensuring people's attendance by attracting debts from them, creating new debts from other people, and rallying kin and, when necessary, ritual leadership support. Tiwi reckoned the time to a forthcoming ritual in the number of 'payweeks' (the weeks with a fortnightly pay day following on 'nothing' or *moyla* weeks). Recently bereaved relatives of different deceased frequently supported each other in their sorrow and (if permitted by their respective kin relationships) in mutually fulfilling ritual tasks and obligations. In closely following the practices of several skilled Tiwi politicians I learned how they developed master schemes in manipulating with identities, credits and debits. (This could be, for example, arranging a short-cut deal such as allowing an old mortuary pole to be used and thereby lowering the debt that would be created, selectively attending mortuary rituals, following their own interests in making identity claims or suppressing identity, masking a lack of money by pumping it around a few times on a single occasion, pressing people in crying poor and so 'taking' the winnings in card games.)

A person's ritual exchange networks could be expanded or relatively limited. The 'bookkeeping mentality' described by Hart (Hart and Pilling 1960: 92) for the 1920s prevailed (and not only between mourners and 'nonmourners' as he suggests). I found that people were often careful to make sure that their contributions were returned, restricting their outgoing payments to people in their own township on whom they easily could exert pressure to repay them as soon as the occasion arose. The same accounts for helping out bereaved relatives in making their ceremonial payments. To have prestigious and memorable rituals, skilled performers were desired. Only a very small percentage of the population was able to compose the ritual songs. These persons tended to be involved more in the ritual exchange networks than others. These people, when not directly obliged themselves, had their price and often sold, so to speak, their ceremonial leadership and performing skills dearly. People commissioned as ritual workers would be directly paid, but the closely-related bereaved would also become indebted to more distantly-related people who had to be asked to enact ritual roles, the bosses in particular. In an extreme case a female relative of the deceased might even be given as a wife to the boss of the mortuary rituals.

Kinship relations were not always clear-cut because people could be related to each other in more than one way. These circumstances gave ample room for political manoeuvring. An emphasis on the relationship and shared identities with the deceased was expected. The point I wish to stress, however, is that in Tiwi rituals skilled performers often had more or less hidden agendas.

Clever politicians, with sufficient knowledge and ability, could rhetorically enforce 'identity claims' (Burke 1974) that seemed to be far-fetched at first sight. In other words, they were able to exploit choice in a kaleidoscope of multiple identities in order to promote their own interests and those of their allies. The intellectually challenging tracing of relationships in ritual took place in, among other things, metaphorical song language, the selection of dance movements, ritual calls, and wailing. Bloch states that in much of political anthropology there is a shared presupposition that politics is the conscious exercise of power. In this view it is inevitable that authority will be questioned, and, therefore, power that is not normally challenged is not the focus of attention (1973: 3). The rhetoric in ritual is mostly taken for granted and remains unchallenged in a direct way. According to Kertzer this is precisely what explains the success of ritual: it 'creates an emotional state that makes the message uncontestable because it is framed in such a way as to be seen inherent in the way things are. It presents a picture of the world that is so emotionally compelling that it is beyond debate' (1988: 101). In the mourning songs the voice of the deceased was frequently used as a rhetorical device legitimating the performer's point of view. Influential Tiwi people could, as they said, 'make a law' not to be broken by others. Such a person even stated, 'I am the Law'.

In mortuary ritual, a Tiwi person might in dance stress more than one mortuary kinship relation to the deceased, perform with different categories of personnel, and thus enact a double role. Likewise, a performer might make a choice between different relationships to the deceased, acting out only one role (and even then a person who, for instance, was classified to enact a ritual worker role might be paid informally, 'outside' the ritual). The mortuary rituals encompassed an arena in which people frequently had to make choices with regard to optional kinship relationships.

The ritual exchange relations between the ritual workers and their employers were linked with the exchange of marriage partners between exogamous matriclans (*keramili*). Hart writes that the debts in death rituals 'were carried on the same mental ledgers as other debts, such as marriage debts' (Hart and Pilling 1960: 91–2). Both modes of exchange followed the same lines and were even more closely linked. It was a conventional feature of the performative role of the ritual workers to stress existing marriage debts, one way or the other. Sometimes people refused to perform as ritual workers when there had been no marriage deal effected between the respective groups or when the score was even (cf. Grau 1983: 327–32). Mortuary rituals and marriage politics were both avenues by which individual Tiwi people could acquire influence and prestige.

The participants enacted various roles that implied a breaking of ties with the deceased, and at the same time constituted a new spirit of the dead with a reconstructed biography resulting from the sequence of performances by the various categories of personnel, assembling a remodelled and distanced social personality from multiple relational angles. Before the spirit of the deceased could leave the world of the living, his or her bonds with the living had to be broken, emotionally and symbolically. The mortuary rituals provided an opportunity to reflect on the shared experiences and relationships with the deceased (and this could even be done in a form of dialogue with the deceased). The bereaved stated their loss, whereafter they were enabled to say farewell to the past. In the context of the rituals, compassionate support and protection was given to the bereaved. Collectively, leaving room for and integrating ritualised personal experiences, the situation after the death was gradually redefined, and the social order recreated. Probably, the projections of a spirit of the dead helped to mitigate the painful loss. The spirit of the deceased did not enter the other world as a nobody but as a ritually composed shadow figure, a reflection on that person when she or he was alive, so to speak. My informants said that related spirits of the dead came to the ceremonial grounds as well and carried out the rituals. It was at these times that the world of the living and the world of the dead met. After the final ritual most of the taboos were lifted because the spirit of the deceased had joined the spirits of the dead.

Tiwi mortuary rituals have much in common with Hertz's model of primary and secondary burials, although there is no actual secondary treatment of the remains (in contrast to some other Aboriginal groups, perhaps because in Tiwi eschatology there is no resurrection of the body). Hertz looks at the changing condition of the body, the soul (spirit), and the survivors in relation to the adjustment of the 'collective consciousness' to the social loss. To enable this process, a lapse of time is necessary between the funeral and post-funeral or secondary rituals. The accomplishment of the rituals, the transition of the spirit to the other world, the period of mourning for the survivors, and in Hertz's case the decomposition of the body ('when the bones are dry'), coincide (Hertz 1960). We have seen that at the conclusion of the final ritual, *iloti*, the formal period of mourning (with the accompanying *pukamani* taboos) was over, and the spirit of the deceased was supposed to have entered the other world.

In Tiwi mortuary ritual we do not have a secondary treatment of the remains but a treatment of tree trunks or poles. I was told these poles were erected at the burial or ceremonial place to keep the spirits of the dead there, to provide the spirit of the deceased with company (the best pole was usually put up at the head of the grave, if there was one). The presence of the actual grave was not necessary for the final ritual but mortuary poles were; they range from a single sapling painted white to more than twenty large elaborately carved and painted polychrome poles. In the literature hardly any explanation is given for the symbolic value of these poles, other than their being vehicles for prestige.[115] I face a problem inherent in symbolic anthropology here, because in general Tiwi themselves did not verbalise the meaning of these poles. It is clear, however, that the mortuary poles were important. Metcalf suggests 'that there are some truths that are not expressed in words, and perhaps cannot be expressed in words. Those truths are unexpressed not because they are unimportant, but because they are fundamental.' He sees it as the task of anthropologists to elicit the implicit meanings (1982: 262–3). Let me attempt an explanation.

The ritual workers, who are the only ones who may dispose of the corpse, cut trees in the area that is perceived as the deceased's country (Tiwi do not emphasise the buried corpse but the location where dead persons as spirits 'live'). The poles were preferably made from the bloodwood tree (*wuringelaka*). A red substance resembling blood flows from the stem when this type of tree is cut. The so-called Melville Island bloodwood (*Eucalyptus nesophila*) can be exceptionally large.[116] It is also a species demonstrating exceptional vitality: a sapling 'may shoot up to 2 or 3 m in a few months. Growth thereafter is usually rapid' (Hearne 1975: 61). Often spirits were connected with particular trees. The processing of the poles might be compared to the ritual processing of the bereaved; in both procedures the ritual workers were instrumental. I was told that when head-cutting was still a general practice (at least until the mid-1950s) the blood had to flow on the grave (the bloodwood trees were cut in the area surrounding the grave). Like the poles, the close relatives of the deceased went 'in fire' and were 'smoked', the fire being made by the ritual workers. The way of painting and the designs were

actually regarded as the same as those applied to the bodies of participants in the final mortuary rituals. It seemed the mortuary poles represented metaphorical bodies. In the final ritual they were held, in the
wailing, as if they were a substitute for the tactile presence of the
deceased. There was, in addition, a symbolism of lying down with the
connotation of death or sleep (e.g. in a dance movement, and in the
'lying down' during the first night of the yam ritual) in contrast to standing up. The Tiwi term for a mortuary pole is *apurununinginti*, meaning
something like 'the one that is standing up'. These poles were laid down
until the final ritual, when they were erected, and the transition of the
deceased to the world of the dead was completed. The external vitality,
or life essence, of the durable bloodwood trees seemed to be transmitted
in this symbolic way to the spirit of the deceased in the other world. After
this, the related spirits of the dead, when properly treated, promoted
good hunting, luck, protection, and health of the living.

The final rituals involved a distribution of wealth – social capital, fabrics and large sums of money – and in the past, barbed spears and ceremonial ornaments. Kan, in his study of the Tlingit potlatch, speaks of
'double obsequies' while referring to Hertz's model. The characteristics
of these post-funeral rituals include the 'erection of imposing mortuary
and memorial structures' and the distribution of wealth 'to enhance the
donors' status and prestige' (1989: 283–5). Miles (1965) amends Hertz's
model for the Ngadju-Dayak (Hertz' main ethnographic example) in
stressing the importance of economic factors and states that the timing
of post-funeral rituals is related to materialistic motives. Such economic
factors do play a role in the timing of Tiwi post-funeral rituals. In this
regard, time is needed to turn these rituals into prestigious occasions.
There is considerable variation in Tiwi final mortuary rituals; some are
more prestigious than others.

The emotional aspects are equally important (see Hiatt 1961 on
double disposals as practised by Aborigines in Arnhem Land): time is
needed to come to terms with personal loss. J. Reid (1979) argues that
Yolngu Aborigines are better able to cope with their grief because the
mortuary rituals as 'times for grieving' are alternated with 'times for living' so the bereaved can gradually adjust to ordinary life again. I believe
this makes sense for the Tiwi too. Frequently recently bereaved Tiwi persons also express their grief on ritual occasions for other deceased
people and, further, may do so at any other time when they are
reminded of the deceased.

I do not claim that emotions of grief are universal, the same everywhere. To some extent these emotions expressed in a ritual context by
Tiwi are standardised and institutionalised, even socially and culturally
desirable, but this does not necessarily imply that they are 'not really felt'

(for instance, Durkheim 1968: 397, 397n.2). Osborne notes that when an important Tiwi man dies: 'Everyone jockeys for position and no one feels any real grief, although grief is simulated' (1974: 111n.2). Hart attributes the tendency of Tiwi people to linger around when someone is about to die to 'the all-pervasive character of Tiwi opportunism' (Hart and Pilling 1960: 91, 91n.5). Both Hart and Osborne clearly understand there is something at stake in Tiwi mortuary ritual, but in their view people's attempts to achieve political goals seem to be incompatible with feelings of 'real grief'. Hart goes so far as to call the ritual workers 'non-mourners' (ibid.), notwithstanding the fact that these people perform mourning songs and wail and grieve as well. The proposition seems to be that when emotions and politics are juxtaposed in mortuary practices the emotions cannot be 'real': the grief is simulated or it is mere opportunism. I see this as stereotyping of non-Western people, suggesting they are not sincere, that emotions expressed in mortuary ritual are not really felt, for this is the connotation of the expression 'ritual grief'. Can other people be denied these feelings? How do we know? Durkheim, for instance, gives an example concerning the expression of emotion in an Aboriginal mortuary ritual:

> If, at the very moment when weepers seem the most overcome by their grief, some one speaks to them of some temporal interest, it frequently happens that they change their features and tone at once, take on a laughing air and converse in the gayest fashion imaginable. Mourning is not a natural movement of private feelings wounded by a cruel loss; it is a duty imposed by the group. (1968: 397)

As I understand it, Durkheim here infers from a sudden shift in the expression of emotion that the emotions of grief are not authentic, merely a socially desirable act. It struck me that Tiwi people could switch their expression of emotion, but this always involved a shift in focus from one significant person to another one. The emotions, however, are relational (see Lutz 1988): Tiwi stress relational contents (with the exemption of avoidance relationships) by facing the other person.[117] When in this society emotions are relational and contextual phenomena, it is plausible that the emotions involved in one relationship (for instance, to the deceased) are different from those involved in another (for instance, to a joking friend). Hence, a person in grief directed towards the deceased will change emotional expression when facing a living person.

Let me now turn to the post-funeral rituals for Tobias (June–August 1989).

*   *   *

Jerome, who had been 'put forward' by his sister Kate's children as the principal ritual worker, pressed people to go ahead with the rituals although Simon considered the time 'too early'. On the basis of his position of seniority in his patrilineage and his experience Simon would have to be consulted by Jerome concerning ritual affairs. He had nominated Jerome (his father's brother's son's son) as his successor, the person who would take over the ritual responsibilities after his death. Tobias was indebted to Jerome, according to the latter, but Tobias' daughters would become indebted to him even more.

It is important to note that Tobias' 'father', Roger Imalu, in Pularumpi, who was supposed to be the boss of the mortuary rituals of the Melville Islanders and who was expected to organise the *ilanigha* rituals, did not take up this role. Jack Munuluka, another 'father' of Tobias from Bathurst Island, became the actual boss of the joint final mortuary rituals for Tobias of the people from both islands. Jack had decided to turn the mortuary rituals into 'money business'. His involvement in the mortuary rituals for Tobias represents a good example of how a person relatively distantly related to the deceased could use mortuary rituals to acquire influence and prestige.

Shortly before the final ritual it came out as to why Roger had been so reluctant to organise the mortuary rituals. A faction in Pularumpi, dominated by Isaac, intended to hold mortuary rituals in Pularumpi separately from those at Pawularitarra, where Tobias was buried. A reason for this was that people at Pularumpi expected that some form of vengeance for Tobias' death, as was explicitly stated by the close relatives of the victim, would take place at Pawularitarra (therefore, they did not camp there during the night). There happened to be insufficient support for separate rituals, however, because a number of people on whom Isaac normally could exert influence had already committed themselves to the grand-scale ritual near Tobias' grave. Jerome, for instance, had made a huge mortuary pole. For him these rituals were an opportunity too to obtain more influence and prestige.

At the end of June, Heather telephoned Pularumpi to tell people to prepare to start the post-funeral rituals. The message had to do with 'money business'; it meant there would be enough funds to make the necessary payments. Roger was still presumed to be the boss in the mortuary rituals of the Melville Islanders for Tobias. Jack would be the boss in a separate series of rituals for the people of Bathurst Island. During the holidays, Jack camped in his country in the northwest of Bathurst Island. On a Thursday morning, 6 July, he came to Pularumpi to do his shopping and also to find out when the ceremonies were to take place. Jerome told him these would start the next Saturday. Jerome had made a phone call to his niece, Heather, urging the

Milikapiti group to come because the people in Pularumpi were ready for the axe-giving.

On Friday evening at the beer canteen Isaac performed an old song. Jerome responded with another song. He said to Isaac and other patrons that they were the only two who knew about *palingari* (the past or 'tradition') and that they were the only ones who kept it going. Jerome said that in the final mortuary ritual he would drop his loincloth like a proper widower used to do in the old days. Heather had lost some A$110 at cards, while Jerome had taken the winnings. It is very likely Heather deliberately lost the money as an informal down payment to the principal ritual worker. Jerome was getting drunk. He did not seem to take any notice of Simon, who was present at the canteen for a short period of time.

The next morning, Laura visited us. She was very nervous. Simon had growled at her because nobody had told him about the axe-giving. She had told Simon not to be angry with her because Jerome was the 'boss' and he had ordered her and her sisters to come. Heather and Laura were already there; the rest would come later. Laura thought it wrong that Simon had not been informed. He had taken care of her father, 'always fed him with beer and money'. According to Simon, it was too early to have the axe-giving; it should have been scheduled for after the holidays.

At noon, people were playing cards in the Old Camp. There was no sign of a ceremony. As the smaller rituals usually took place around this time in Pularumpi, some people believed there would be no axe-giving. Simon had gone out hunting. Jerome stated the ceremony would be later that afternoon. If Jack did not turn up, he said, Theodore (a matrilineal relative, *marauni pularti*) would replace him.

Gradually about thirty people gathered around the ceremonial ring (*milimika*) where the *kulama* had been performed. There had been an *iloti* not long before, and a sapling painted with white pipeclay was still standing in the middle of the ring. The rituals preceding the *iloti* were meant to guide the spirit of the dead to his destination: his dreaming place and his father's grave. To this ritual end, the spot had to be properly oriented. As mentioned before, facing a certain direction denoted a particular relationship with person or place. From one side of the ring one faced Tobias' little house and the place where his dead body had been found and where his spirit was still presumed to dwell; and far behind, in the central north of the island, was the location of Tobias' dreaming place (Wulintu or Nodlaw Island). The men were grouped at this side of the ring. From the other side of the ring one faced Pawularitarra, in the southwest of the island, where both Tobias and his father had been buried. The women situated themselves at that side of the ring.

Six women, Tobias' actual and classificatory daughters, painted their bodies with white clay. Two daughters also painted two axes white and put them in the middle of the ceremonial ring. As Mike had gone out hunting in the bush, looking for possums in hollow logs with a mirror, only two 'sons' (including myself) were present. Besides Jerome, twelve male and female ritual workers (Tobias' lover Jasmine among them) had come to the ceremony. At first people were waiting for Simon, but when it became clear he would not come back before the next day, the rituals began.

On this occasion, three smaller rituals – the presentation of the axe, fire, and ochres to the ritual workers – were lumped together. These were ostensibly headed by Tobias' deceased father, Kalikalini, who represented his dreaming (*irumwa*, the father's *imunga*). Nancy, a ritual worker and 'widow' (*ambaru*), was seated beside the ceremonial ring. She turned her body towards the spot where Tobias' corpse had lain and towards his dreaming place. Like Kalikalini she belonged to the Mosquito clan (*wulintuwila*) so the latter spot was also the seat of her clan (*imunga*). She, using Kalikalini's voice, sang: 'Why is everybody talking about me?' Then she stood up and, facing the township, walked back and forth in *ambaru*-fashion, singing: 'I am the man, you fellows are just rubbish (shit-people)!/Why are you talking about me, you cowards?/I am a real murderman (*kwampini*)./I am the one who killed all those people at Matalau.' These were the words of a clever politician and 'big-headed' (able) woman. In this juggling of identities Nancy was singing on behalf of Tobias' children. People in Pularumpi, including Nancy, had been talking about Kalikalini and his son (conceptually one). They pretended to be tough but in fact they were cowards. Kalikalini stressed how he dealt with such people: he killed four of Nancy's 'fathers'. What we have here is an admission of guilt, a threat of retaliation, and a display of solidarity with the bereaved children. She explained to me that she had composed the song because the people present were talking; in this way she demanded silence and respect because the rituals were about to begin. Her employing the stance of Tobias' father was another means of distancing Tobias' spirit, appropriate in this ritual context of driving the spirit of the dead away and towards his destination.

Before Nancy was finished, Theodore began performing his first song. The words were picked up by Isaac and Jerome, who were beating time with sticks on corrugated iron. Theodore told me he was singing for the bereaved children (*mamurapi*). He also took the stance of their grandfather Kalikalini: 'Get the axe and sharpen it./You cut the trees down.' The song text had a literal meaning: an axe was given to the ritual workers, and they were commissioned to make the mortuary poles and therefore had to fell some trees. The connotation of the song, in that the ritual workers had to use a sharp axe (sometimes an axe with a good handle), was that they had to do a proper job and hence would earn a lot of money. The 'daughters' danced with the high-heeled-style steps characteristic of female dancing, inside the ceremonial ring in semicircular formation, facing in the direction of their father's grave. They made movements with their arms as if they were using axes to fell trees. The formation of the dancers encompassed a highly stylised reference to jumping mullets, another of Tobias' dreamings. As we have seen, these mullets jumping out of the water indicated that Kalikalini and his companion were about to kill people at Matalau. In concerted action Nancy repeated her song outside the ceremonial ring.

After these women the 'sons' danced, also moving inward towards the centre but facing the mango tree under which Tobias' corpse had been found. The 'daughters' then danced for a second time. Heather picked up the axe. Her stepsister Ruth grabbed it and hit herself over the head with the blunt side of the blade. Heather stopped her and presented the axe to a female ritual worker from Milikapiti. This woman, Murielle, had done the same as Ruth when she was giving an axe to her (the axe-giving and the *iloti* had been held recently in this same ceremonial ring). Ruth and this woman now had come 'level'. Somewhat later, outside the ceremonial ground Ruth sat down with the blade of the axe on her head facing the mango tree. She wailed, 'giving sorry' (*nurupmiori*) for her stepfather and the money involved. Tobias' 'son', Jim, in our second dance presented the other axe to a male ritual worker, Jasmine's adoptive brother Roy Mornington.

Theodore proceeded with the next ritual, the giving of fire (*ikwoni*) to the ritual workers. He composed the following song: 'My name is Tupulu'auwungtura [another name of Kalikalini]./Take the matches and light all the grass!' Once again the symbolism of this song is intricate (the symbolic complex of bodily hair, hairy roots, and tall grass has been discussed above). The ritual workers dried the cut and skinned tree trunks above a fire and at the same time gave these a dark brown surface (from the soot) as a background for the paintings. They cleared the area around the grave and prepared the dancing grounds. Focusing on burning tall grass, Theodore indicated that the ritual workers had to do more than simply make poles; they would have to erect shades above the dancing ground to protect the performers from the heat of the sun. The dancers of both sexes performed twice. Their hand movements represented the use of sticks to produce fire. Tobias' daughter Judy gave matches to the female ritual worker from Milikapiti; Jim gave matches to a male ritual worker from Pularumpi.

For the third ritual the dancers had white clay, for their dances represented the painting of arms and faces. Theodore sang: 'Take the ochres so you got to paint up my face.' The painting of the poles was closely associated with decorating the human body with similar spectacular designs. Facial paintings were usually the most delicate, so the ritual workers had to take care that the designs painted on their poles were really striking. It was made clear that they would be paid accordingly. Tobias' 'daughter' Maud gave a piece of white clay, after Ruth had rubbed her face with it, to the female ritual worker from Milikapiti. Jim presented some to another male ritual worker from Pularumpi.

When the rituals were over, the gathering of people dispersed. Jerome stated that thirteen poles would have to be made. Nancy thereupon told me I was to give nothing to her cousin from Milikapiti, who had received the axe. 'Only [give to] us,' the ritual workers from Pularumpi, she said. At sundown, Nancy sang for Tobias' children in the beer canteen: 'Just carefully, look after your father [Sam] well because he is really drunk.'

A series of rituals called *ilanigha* would follow the rituals described above. I was told '*ilanigha* is coming up'. The first in this series (all focusing on a single theme, 'go by dreaming; father's dreaming'), was planned for the following Monday. Thereafter these rituals would continue until the *iloti* at the burial place. Roger, Tobias' classificatory father, was supposed to take the lead in these ceremonies. The axe-giving, pushed by Jerome and Heather, had been performed without him. Roger had gone off to the Safari Camp, where he worked on an irregular basis as a guide. There seemed to be a lack of commitment on his part. He once told me when Tobias was still alive that Tobias was 'nothing'; he did not appear to have liked the dead man very much.

Tobias' other 'father', Jack, informed me of his plans to have an axe-giving at Nguiu. He had his fortnightly pay day 'in the week coming up' and then following on the second pay day he would commission the ritual workers for the post-funeral rituals. 'I want to make money business of this', he explained to me, 'with my pension.'

Laura said that after this axe-giving they would have a meeting to 'ask the people' who had killed her father. Jack had no intention, as all the preceding inquests had bitterly failed, to call for such a meeting at that stage. Although most people were confident Kevin had not killed Tobias, it was still possible things hitherto unknown would be revealed in the court case. Equally important, several significant participants in the mortuary rituals had been summoned to go to Darwin to act as witnesses in court.

On 31 July, Jack had his axe-giving and the two rituals connected with it performed all 'in one go' in a ceremonial ground close to his house at the border of Nguiu (that is, in the direction of Tobias' and his father's country of origin). He had already made some payments to the four male ritual workers and pole-makers he had commissioned. These men worked and camped near Tobias' grave at the other side of Apsley Strait. To this purpose Jack had lent them his dinghy with outboard motor.

In Pularumpi, five male ritual workers were carving and painting mortuary poles to be erected at Tobias' grave. Jerome had made an exceptionally large pole. Alan Pamantari, another one of the ritual workers, commented that Roger ought to hold the *ilanigha*. Actually, he said, Roger should have done it in the week following on the axe-giving, 'but court . . . long time'. Jerome grumbled. He had told Roger several times that he was *unantani* and that he had to do it. He was the only one who could do it, Jerome said. Simon could do it eventually but he had 'other worry, other business' because his wife had died. Jerome said that therefore Roger was the only one who could do it. 'I worry', he said, that the people from Pularumpi could go to Pawularitarra without *ilanigha*; 'I'm worrying about it, we sleep there at night!' Jerome thought it dangerous to stay at the burial place unless proper rituals had been performed.

Jack had decided to have his first *ilanigha* at Nguiu on Monday, 14 August. (He would paint himself up with white clay and red and yellow ochres, he told me, because 'only white is nothing'.) On Bathurst Island these rituals were not at noon, as in Pularumpi, but at three o'clock in the afternoon, when work had been finished and the local people came to the Social Club. Under the mango trees opposite the club Jack would lead these rituals on four succeeding days, and then the Bathurst Islanders would 'finish 'em off' near Tobias' grave (on Melville Island) on Saturday morning. The theme of the rituals was Tobias' father's dreaming, the red woollybutt blossom (*mantiuloni*), because Kalikalini had 'come out' of the Woollybutt tree clan (*temeraringuwi*). The performers marked this dreaming by placing both their hands on top of their heads. Also the song lines were 'all same through', as I will discuss below.

In the week preceding the rituals at Pawularitarra *ilanighuwi* were held neither in Pularumpi nor in Milikapiti. On Tuesday, Jerome went to Milikapiti. He wanted to check with Heather because he did not want to go to the burial place 'for nothing'. Theodore was not there. He had gone to Tiwi relatives on the mainland for a funeral. The mortuary poles, however, had been made. That night Nancy and Jerome went 'wild' with Roger, who then said he would have the *ilanigha* the next day. The following evening the two men met again. Roger immediately performed a song text for an *ilanigha*. 'Alright uncle (*ilimani*, mother's father's brother's son)', Jerome said, 'you are in business'. The ritual was scheduled for the next day at noon in the Old Camp. Obviously, there would be no ritual then. Roger was too polite to make an outright refusal. The following day happened to be a pay day: people at Pularumpi were too busy playing cards to bother about a ceremony. Jerome knew this. Early in the morning he had gone to Putjamirra Safari Camp to work as a guide for the day (using this stratagem he acquired some extra money and it prevented him, given his prospective ritual 'pay day', having to 'lose' his pension money in the card games or to have to give it away to 'relations').

The heavy drinking, as usual on pay days, liberated people's tongues. It became clear why Roger had been dawdling over performing the rituals. At the instigation of Isaac, a faction of the community wanted to organise a separate *iloti* for Tobias at Pularumpi. Barry Pamantari told me Isaac had proposed it because 'us-mob' did not want to pay 'far away', to people from the other townships. Their fear of not receiving the money back, however, masked another fear. A number of people and their 'relations' in Pularumpi were afraid that the *iloti* at Tobias' grave would result in violence. As mentioned before, some men from Pularumpi had allegedly killed Tobias. Isaac's stepson told me the 'Law' required the persons to be mentioned as the killers had to be dealt with 'straight away' after the ceremony 'or at night'.

Jerome was furious about the idea of a Pularumpi faction not participating in the mortuary rituals at Pawularitarra. He had been commissioned, he argued, so this 'business' could not be stopped any more. On Bathurst Island Jack had given his orders. 'That's on', Jerome said, no one could stop it. If the dissident group at Pularumpi persevered with something else, he continued, 'we cut them off'. Jerome backed up his threat in saying he was still a 'traditional owner' (a delegate to the Tiwi Land Council). It was in Jerome's interest, being the principal ritual worker, that these people take part in the mortuary rituals.

On that Friday, I accompanied the male ritual workers from Pularumpi to Pawularitarra, where they brought the mortuary poles. Two shades had been erected above the ceremonial grounds near the grave, one for the Bathurst Islanders and one for the Melville Islanders. The male ritual workers from Milikapiti had done most of the clearing. They had also brought soft white sand for the dancing grounds and to restore the grave mound. They informed the ritual workers from Pularumpi that the mortuary poles of the Bathurst Islanders were small compared to the other ones. Jerome commented that people ought not to pay these ritual workers, only those who had made a large pole. One of the workers asked another, Alan Pamantari, if he would stay at Pawularitarra for the night. 'No', Alan replied, 'too frightened'.

More and more people at Pularumpi decided they would go on Sunday, not Saturday. Reuben, Jerome's son, thought it too dangerous to cross the strait between Nguiu and Paru when he or other people were drunk; accidents had already occurred all too often. Roger, like Isaac, also said he would go on Sunday.

Simon stated that with regard to the post-funeral rituals for Tobias, there would be a 'small one on Saturday and big *iloti* on Sunday'; on

Saturday night 'songs of sorrow' would be performed. On Saturday morning, Simon first would have a cleansing ritual of his deceased wife's house, and after that, about 11.00 am, we would go 'straight away' to Pawularitarra. Jerome lingered until he had been able to do his drinking at the beer canteen and take away a dozen cans of beer in the late afternoon. About 5 pm we left for Pawularitarra.

*   *   *

The people from Bathurst Island had performed an *ilanigha* ritual at 3 pm. Then the final rituals had been initiated by a ritual cleansing of the major participants with smoke. Most of the people had gone away to drink beer at the canteens in Milikapiti and Nguiu.

Jack was just raking away the remains of a smoking fire when we arrived. His face had been painted with red and yellow ochre. Both Jack and Jerome wore only loincloths. Jack and his wife camped on the edge of the bush to the Bathurst Island side. Jack's sister Mavis, from Pularumpi, and her husband had their campfire at some distance at the same side of the graves. There were also a number of women, including the classificatory widows of Tobias, who had also participated in the yam ritual at Myilly Point. Jerome chose a spot to make his campfire opposite Jack at the other side of the graves. In between, facing both ceremonial grounds and the graves, Tobias' 'brother' Steven Tampajani with his wife Agatha and son Harold had their campfires burning. Tobias' children would also camp at this location. Carol was the only one present at that time.

Jerome called out to her, 'All my nieces should be here!' When it had become dark he rose from his campfire and sang words of the dead man arguing with him: 'Where are your kids (female speaking, the children of his sister)?' As usual Jerome repeated the song several times. In between he called out, 'He (dead man) is worrying for his kids (male speaking)!' Somewhat later, Heather, Judy, and Ralph, among others, returned from Milikapiti. Max Tampajani, who was too drunk to stand, had come with them. He would be the cause of some trouble during the night.

Jack left his campfire, walked into the open space, and directed himself towards Tobias' grave: (Dead man saying) 'My father is sleeping with me./He (Kalikalini) is close to me./Maybe tonight I gotta sleep well!'

Jack repeated this mourning song and concluded it bewailing the loss of his 'son' Tobias. For Tiwi being with one's relatives implies a feeling that perhaps can be best translated as happiness. The singer suggested his presence appeased the spirit of the dead. At her campfire Mavis, a 'father's sister' of Tobias, wailed loudly. She stood facing his grave: (Dead man is shaking her arm, saying:) 'Hello auntie, long time to see you.'

She indicated she was not a mother-in-law (a potential relationship) to the deceased: the dead man shook her hand.

Jerome sat at his campfire and sang: (Dead man saying) 'I thought that is my brother-in-law, and he is jealous of me in the night./Maybe your kids, they might be ashamed of me swearing at you.' Jerome expressed in his song that he was sexually jealous (*tulura*) of Tobias, who had married Jerome's sister while giving no wife in return. Jerome suggested Tobias' children were ashamed of their father because he was swearing at their mother's brother.

Jerome further complained he was the only ritual worker present (he forgot about the elderly female ritual workers who camped in the bush at the other side of the graves). 'They all should be here', Jerome said. He composed a new song: (Dead man saying:) 'Why (are) you sleeping far away from me?/We should sleep together!' Jerome let Tobias speak to the people in his widow or widower category (*ambaruwi*), who ought to have been near Tobias' grave.

Jack, the boss of the post-funeral rituals, now approached and faced the grave. He performed two song verses in which the deceased asked about the axe. In this type of song, called *timatreiakuwalla*, the dead man asked his 'father' Jack about the quality of the axe (*walemani*) he had given the ritual workers. The better the axe in these songs, the more money would change hands in the ceremony, and the more prestigious the rituals would be. Jack sang: (Dead man saying:) 'I hope you gave an axe with a good handle./I hope you cleaned the axe and sharpened it with a file.' The quality of the axe given correlated with the number of ritual workers (and poles) contracted. Jack made clear he had a large amount of money to offer in mentioning a sharp axe with a new handle (*wulani*) instead of the dead man asking for a blunt axe (*tumutumunga*). He concluded his last song: (Dead man calling out:) 'Daddy come up, and sit close with me!'

Tobias' daughter Judy roasted and distributed wallaby and wild pig meat. The full moon illuminated the coloured fabrics around Tobias' grave. Max kept bothering the other people in this camp with his drunken talk. His younger brother Harold and Heather told him to 'shut up'. Max ignored their repeated requests. Harold told him to stop or he would be hit. Tobias' son Ralph awoke. He burst out crying and uttered threats of revenge for his father's death: 'Tomorrow I bust 'em up'. Thereafter, Max continued, saying he was the president of Pickataramoor (the forestry station with six inhabitants). Jerome got angry. He stood up and went to the noisy camp: 'I don't care for that, I don't care. You should have respect! What are you here for? You mob can better go! . . . Go!' Nevertheless, Max went on with his boozy talk. Then Judy took a piece of burning wood from her campfire. She walked towards Max and threw the firewood at him. She missed, fell to the ground and cried. Harold now wanted to attack his brother. Max did not stop. He said to Harold and Judy, while lifting up a can of beer: 'Oh, you want beer? Here, you have beer!' (Harold had just returned from the mainland where he had participated in a sobriety programme.) Judy fell flat onto her blanket. She cried 'Fucking beer!' – it was always beer they wanted, always beer, but she did not want beer. From his campfire Jerome called out to Max: 'You got no respect!' He warned him that they were there for 'a serious business'. Jerome moved in the direction of Tobias' grave and sang: (Dead man saying:) 'Did these people come for me?/They are talking away./Why you live with me?/Why are you living with me tonight?/You should go away!'

When a fight started between the two brothers, their father Steven took his blanket and walked away from the camp. The sick old man was followed by his wife. After a while they came back. Max's attitude had changed completely. Now he fell sprawling into the campfire. His mother tore him out of the fire. Max crashed into the fire again. Agatha pulled him out, and so it went on for some one and a half hours. Finally, Harold helped his mother carry his brother away from the campfire. Then they left him.

Now and then Jerome left his campfire. When he sang he oriented himself towards Tobias' grave. Jerome walked back and forth in *ambaru* fashion, holding up one hand in ritualised pose, fighting the spirits of the dead: (Dead man saying) 'You and me, we gonna talk tonight./But we sleep, I got tell you tomorrow morning.' Jerome employed Tobias's voice and the wording of a widower's song. The 'talk' in this type of song had the connotation of sexual intercourse; the implication in this one was that before they had sex, something had to be settled. In the next song Jerome made this clear: (Jerome asking the dead man) 'Where is your sister?' Jerome claimed a sister of the dead man for himself. He acted out the role of an *ambaru*. Sexual jealousy and proposals of fights related to women might be the conventional subject matter of the performance but that did not mean these role-attributions were entirely fictional. Jerome created trouble for Tobias because he desired a 'sister' of this brother-in-law in return. Likewise his role here was characterised by aggressive behaviour. The shark chasing its prey often represented the jealous aggressiveness of the *ambaru*. Jerome was an excellent performer of the shark dance, choreographed by his father's father's father, Kitiruta, when a shark passed his bark canoe in the 1870s (cf. Pilling 1970: 269). Kitiruta donated his name for the shark in the accompanying song to his son, who in turn passed it down to Jerome's father.

Jerome in the present type of song had to use one of his father's names instead of one of his own. He chose the name of the shark marked by Kitiruta in his song: 'I am Kitirutalimirri, cutting with my dorsal fin through the water.' (It must be noted that Tobias' dreaming in this context was not predator but prey: the mullet fish.)

Jerome told me he would sleep after he had sung a certain text a few times, but later he would start singing again. It became colder during the night (the temperature dropped about 15 degrees centigrade). Jerome was wearing only a loincloth, and tried to warm himself at his campfire. At one stage he said he saw a jungle fowl which was calling out. Jerome told the bird, his dreaming, to go away. The campfires were burning high at 3 am. It was cold. Now and then I tended our campfires. The fires were also burning high as protection against the spirits of the dead. To this end Jerome would, in addition, place a mirror behind his head.

*   *   *

At 5.40 am I awoke to Jerome's humming. He sat at his campfire, wrapped in a blanket, 'lining up' his first song of the day. He sang: 'I am Tumaturapuwi (a male jungle fowl) calling out./The dead man is getting awake./I am calling out "kurau", and shake my two wings to wake him up./ (The dead man says) "Why are you coming around and wake me up in the morning?"' Jerome 'marked' his dreaming, the jungle fowl. His task as a ritual worker was to keep the spirits of the dead at bay. First he had to awake them, starting with Tobias' spirit. The shaking of his wings represented the ritual worker's fighting pose, moving one arm above his shoulder and the other in front of him. Jerome's 'wings' here were the blades of his axes. He whispered to me that he had seen the dead man the previous night taking away the woman he was after (Tobias' clan sister). Tobias was Jerome's brother-in-law and therefore the dead man teased him in the next song-verse: (Dead man saying) 'You gammon [pretend to] dance and those fellows all are clapping for you./Maybe you will faint around the ceremonial ring (*milimika*).' Jerome considered himself to be a good dancer but he was drunk. He began and ended this mourning song, like all members of his patrilineage, with the words of warning of his great-grandfather Kitiruta at Matalau, *ninka-ninka-ninka* and pronouncing the real name of Kitiruta (which refers to a shark and at the same time to the call of the jungle fowl). He had painted his body and face with black charcoal and put a white line across his face. Jerome went around the burial place and struck the trees with his axes to chase the spirits of the dead away. He called out to these spirits: 'Hey, you!' (*awiiii*). Jack went to the grave and performed a mourning song, pretending the spirit of the dead man wanted him to support his dance early in the morning: (Dead man saying) 'Come up and clap for me!/I want to dance.' Jack cried, wailed, and called out: 'My son!'

The polemakers from Bathurst Island had produced relatively small poles, with no black background and left partially undecorated. The ritual workers from Melville Island were annoyed by this. Jerome threatened to 'cut them off' and transfer the money to those people who had made large poles (that is, to himself). The previous night he had been arguing about it with Tobias' children and with Jack. Jack now agreed with Jerome that these ritual workers had not performed a proper job. He had contracted senior men but he judged the results 'schoolboy-work'. Jerome reminded Jack that in the old days the commissioned workers who were unable to satisfy their employers were put to death with spears. Jack directed himself towards Tobias' children. He told them they had not to pay much to the Bathurst Island polemakers. Instead of 50 or 60 dollars for each of these ritual workers they ought to pay only 10 dollars, Jack said; that was enough for such work of 'little children'.

Jerome continued to go around hitting the hardwood trees at the burial place with his axes. This 'killing trees' was meant to scare off spirits of the dead. He also struck one of the remaining mortuary poles at Kalikalini's grave. Jerome was not fighting the spirits of Tobias and his deceased father, but the spirits of his competitors (his 'friends' or *mamanta*) who married into the same clan(s) as he did. Nancy commented on this performance: 'Just like they got their friend boy, that dead man and Jerome jealous of those spirits of the dead (*mopadruwi*).' Jerome, walking back and forth, lifted the axes (with the blades upright) over his head. He marked his 'father's father' who used to dance in this way, while he sang: (Jerome responding to the *mopadruwi* who asked him why he came there) 'I am Kitirutalumirri./I came all the way from Taparulukwalimili and I got two axes./I am Patingumili and I got those two axes and I came to Pawularitarra first thing in the morning to kill you, spirits of the dead.'[118]

In the camp of Steven Tampajani and Tobias' children, Agatha (*ambaru*) faced the grave and sang for her husband Steven: (Dead man saying) 'I slept well because my brother was near me.' Steven had expressed his wish to be buried next to his 'brother' Tobias (which happened a month later).

People from Bathurst Island who had crossed the sea strait were approaching the burial place. Lionel Jatukwani, one of the *ambaruwi*, came through the old settlement of Pawularitarra. He stopped every twenty metres or so, sang, and moved further in the direction of the grave, until he finally reached it. In his song-verses he expressed the notion that the spirits of his dead 'friends' were hungry to kill. He ought to go back, so he said, but being a shark he could not be scared off: 'You gotta care for yourself, maybe these spirits of the dead eat you [kill you]./You gotta go back!' (Somebody talking to him) 'You gotta go back!/People here are ready to kill!' (The singer) 'I am a shark.'

At the other side of the open space, a truckload of people from Milikapiti arrived. Jessica (*ambaru*) jumped out the back of the truck. She faced the grave of her former lover and sang: (Dead man saying to her) 'I cannot swear at you, you are still *pukamani* to me./Why you came first in the morning and sit with me?' She indicated the dead man could not make love to her because she was still under mourning taboos as her son had died the previous year. She blew kisses to Tobias' grave signifying that they had been lovers (a lover of her mother had done the same to her mother's grave). Jerome performed another song: 'I am big waves from Waru [burial place of his father's father] and these big waves go to the dead man's grave, washing it away: plruh! [sound of waves].' Dorothy Kilimirika (*ambaru*), who had camped at Pawularitarra, sang: 'Why don't you sing?/I am your sister-in-law.' Tobias had been a charmer; he liked to compose love songs. The singer stressed Tobias was dead, because he did not sing for her. Agatha (*ambaru*) sang: 'All my *mamanta* [friends] are waiting for me./They all got big sticks [to hit me].' She stated the other women of her 'moiety' would be jealous of her approaching the deceased. Her husband, Steven (*mutuni*), sang: (Dead man saying) 'What's wrong with you?/Are you sick?/Why didn't you take notice when our father Kalikalini was talking?' Steven ought to have painted himself up like a sneak attacker, and he would have to avenge his 'brother' Tobias' death, but he was ill.

The number of people at Pawularitarra rapidly increased. Many people came from Nguiu. It seemed spatial distance to the grave corresponded to people's social distance from the deceased. More coloured fabrics, mainly locally produced Tiwi designs, were put around Tobias' grave on a line alongside the mortuary poles bordering the grave area. Male ritual workers from Melville Island erected their poles in a straight line (including in it an old pole from Kalikalini's grave). A shade was made for Tobias' daughters by their menfolk. Their 'father' Bruce Kerimerini painted their faces. They also daubed themselves with white ochre and put on ceremonial paraphernalia. Simon and his family had come by car early in the morning.

Roger had come by boat. He said he had left Pularumpi the previous night but he had run out of fuel. Now the cattle truck with the other people from Pularumpi arrived as well. Nancy (*ambaru*) sang loudly: 'My clan sisters are all talking about me, listen, big mob of women talking about me: "If she comes smart in this place, well, we give her a good hiding."' She kept singing when coming from the truck and moving towards the grave. In Jerome's camp Nancy collected a black skirt and top from Jeanette, an outfit she had especially designed for her performance in the final rituals. She had also composed the next song. She first planned to sing it herself but then gave it to her half-brother Alec (*ambaru*): 'I am big waves./I came with big waves and I covered them up at Matalau./My clan sisters got all wet.' Lionel Jatukwani repeated his earlier song, facing the grave, and added: (Dead man saying) 'You and me, we have just been arguing./I might knock you down!'

Some 800 people had come to see the final mortuary rituals for Tobias. An exact count was hardly possible because people were somewhat dispersed in the bush.

First, the Melville Island group and Bathurst Island group each held cleansing rituals with smoke at some distance from the graves; this was directly followed by an *ilanigha* ritual of both groups together. This was a ritual previously conducted by the Bathurst Islanders. The subject matter of dance and song was Kalikalini's dreaming, the red woollybutt tree flower. There were a lot of woollybutt trees, blossoming red, in the area around the graves of Tobias and his father. The large group of performers depicted these flowers in the trees by putting their hands on their heads. Jack Munuluka sang: 'Red flowers, Kalikalini.' He called out, 'Kalikalini' and 'Alukutarini' (man of the Red Woollybutt Tree Flower clan, Tobias' father's father). Jack continued his song-verses: 'Lovely sunshine, making the flowers hot./Mirkutimala [Tobias' FF], the flowers are all falling down [on his grave in Tikelaru on Bathurst Island]./Two places [Melville and Bathurst Islands], all flowers are laying down./All flowers are standing up at Kalikalini's grave./Tampajani got all those flowers and he put them on his lap./Kamelatianganumau [Jack's mother's mother, who assisted Kalikalini in fights] is carrying the flowers on her lap./The flowers are all laying down at Kalikalini's grave./All flowers go to Wulintu [Tobias' dreaming place, the seat of his father Kalikalini's clan ancestress].' The accompanying dance was a slow one; it was to be followed by a quick and energetic dance in the next dance ritual.

Both groups then came together around a huge tree for a small ritual called *urukupua*. A fire was lit at the base of the tree, and one person after another held the tree and made a ritual call. Then both groups gathered at the ceremonial ring of the Bathurst Islanders, where a series of *ilanigha* rituals were held with the dance involving throwing up dirt (*kutungura*).

Finally, this series of rituals was concluded with a mock fight between (potential) spouses, called *paumati*. People were hitting each other with green boughs to 'chase the *pukamani* away'. Nancy sang: (The wives of the dead man saying) 'Why are you showing off?/What about your husband?/Why did you leave your husband behind?'

After this there was a break. A priest from the Bathurst Island Mission said mass under the shade of the Bathurst Island group. It was only attended by a handful of people. Most of the people went some way away from the ceremonial grounds to have some food. Tobias' stepdaughter Ruth had a mug of water put to her lips by her husband. Being painted up, wearing the appropriate ceremonial ornaments, and following the mourning taboos, she demonstrated she was 'really *pukamani*', seriously bereaved. In contrast to her sisters, she had not spent the night near Tobias' grave. Isaac had hung his shorts and wallet in a plastic bag on top of the shade of the Melville Island group. After this interlude, the time had come for the final grand ritual.

*   *   *

With a long honey call to greet the deceased, the men at both ceremonial grounds started the final ritual or *iloti*. The final rituals, one performed by the Melville Islanders and one by the Bathurst Islanders, were held simultaneously. Instead of treating them separately, I will follow the Melville Islanders' ritual and deal with ritual of the Bathurst Island group intermittently. In order to complicate matters as little as possible I will mention the bereavement status of the performers in brackets, without specifying their precise relationship to the deceased any further (for this see appendix 1 and 2) because this status suffices to determine their specific ritual roles.

Basil Munuluka (*unantani pulanga*) performed the first song for the Bathurst Island group: 'I wouldn't mind to flog that murderer!'

In the Melville Island ring the ritual workers lit a fire. Once again the major participants in the mortuary rituals, the actual and classificatory children of the deceased, purified themselves in the smoke. The theme of this cleansing ritual was a steamship, an allusion to the progress of Tobias' spirit on his journey to the world of the dead. Theodore (*marauni pularti*) composed the first song: 'Big steamer, a lot of smoke is coming out of its chimney!' The men called out 'poop' when they, lifting their stretched arms, denoted the firing of cannons on a man-o-war. A second song about a steamer was performed by Theodore's brother Simon (*marauni pularti*): 'They put boiling that on the boat and making coming out cheeky smoke, big thing!'

Next Tobias' children (*mamurapi turah*) danced with spears as sneak attackers. They finished their dances by pinning down the spear and calling out '*turah*' (a battle cry). Theodore sang for them: 'Maybe I don't know where he lives or sleeps (*maranukuni*) made him die!/All *mamurapi*, you fellows, want give him good hiding that man!'

Roger (*unantani pulanga*) initiated the dances of the 'fathers' and 'father's sisters'. He sang: 'I been wanna get 'em axe, and cut his neck off.' Roger then was interrupted by Jack, who gave him instructions. The dance and song ceremony (*yoi*) was stopped to give the bereaved 'children' and 'parents' an opportunity to cry at the mortuary poles. (This ritual episode is called *utruningkijerami*.) The ritual workers went ahead with sticks to chase the spirits of the dead away from the dancing ground and the poles, calling out 'hoi-hoi-hoi'. While the people were crying at the poles some of the ritual workers sang. Jerome, lifting his two axes, performed the following song: 'I am a shark and I have a big long mouth!/My throat and mouth are closing towards that grave.' Alec Adranango (*ambaru*) sang: 'I am losing my breath.' He further mentioned the burial places of his father and father's father as well as the place, Matalau, where Tobias' father killed his father's brothers.

After the men in the Melville Island group had given a long mosquito call, Theodore composed the songs for the *mamurapi turah* because he was married to Tobias' stepdaughter Ruth. Tobias' children danced with spears, representing both the spirit children and sneak attackers. Theodore sang: 'We *mamurapi* all had spears./We came a long way from Puluwarupi [Cape Fourcroy in Tikelaru, where Tobias' father's father was buried] with a bundle of spears./We knocked that tree down and made a little canoe./With the bundle of spears in the canoe we paddled across the Apsley Strait./We left the canoe here at the landing in Pawularitarra and took all the spears out of the canoe.'

Walking back and forth between the ceremonial ground and the graves, Nancy (*ambaru*) sang: (Kalikalini saying to his grandchildren) 'You fellow didn't do the same when I was young teenager (*malakaninga*).' Theodore continued: 'When I was a spirit child I lighted the fire in the shade where the Lorula ['semi-moiety' to which Tobias belonged] were camping and you fellow had all the light and make all light in the shade.'

In the Bathurst Island ring Bruce composed the first song for the *mamurapi*. It was also about the spirit children making an attack: 'You fly with machine gun on an aeroplane and shoot and bomb.' Harold (*marauni turah*) sang: 'See all the houses of these Lorula./I got the machine gun and fired at them./I went straight in and fired right in the houses./They didn't call out loud, they whispered because the machine gun was coming and all Lorula ran away.'

Colin Marshall sang for the people whose fathers belonged to Tobias' clan (*kerimerika*): 'These spirit children couldn't throw spears at them./They saw them sleeping and gave them sorry.' These people danced in the same way as the previous category of dancers but held their hands over their hearts.

In the Melville Island ring Dimitri Papuruluwi (*kerimerika* and *ambaru*) composed the songs for the *kerimerika*: 'I am a spirit child, a little boy./I throw a spear in every house./One spirit child lights the fire and he runs fast.' ('Fathers' saying) 'Who are you?' (The spirit child saying) 'I am a spirit child!' ('Fathers' saying) 'Oh, you'll be a little boy coming up.' (The singer stating) 'This spirit child put his legs aside and thrust a spear into my heart.' Dimitri acted this out with a long stick he used in walking.

In the Bathurst Island ring Roland Pamantari composed a song for the next category of patrilineal bereaved, the *kiakiae*: 'When he was born they were saying: "Oh, lovely little baby!"'

Steven (*mutuni*) sang for the *mutuni*: 'He [the dead man] spit me on my cheek'. Richard Palurati (*mutuni*) sang: 'Big stick!/He got a big stick and smashed my cheek.' Jack (*unantani pulanga*) performed a song for his clan daughter, Gay Kitiruta (*mutuni*): 'She went to Wulintu [Tobias' dreaming site, and the seat of Gay's clan ancestress] and half her face fell down on one side.' Among the Melville Islanders there were no people in this mortuary kin relationship to the deceased.

Basil (*unantani pulanga*) sang for the Bathurst Islanders of his bereavement status: 'All the women are swearing at me, saying I got big balls only.' So did Don Wangiti, who continued: 'I have sores on my balls and they smell.' And Jack: 'Somebody in Pularumpi has cut my penis, it's bleeding away./Maybe a *ningani* cut off my penis.' By suggesting a *ningani*, a (male) spirit and dreaming of the Wangiti patrilineage, had caused the death of his 'son' Tobias, Jack indirectly blamed his clan brother Kevin Wangiti. Kevin, however, did not attend the final ritual, but stayed behind in Pularumpi. He later told me he had been unable to come because he had the flu. It is likely that this inspired Jack's suspicion of him.

In the Melville Island ring Roger, who belonged to the same category of people, performed the following song: 'I am lying down and crossed my legs [sleeping].' Roger 'marked' his mother's lover, Pleipokutji, the last surviving son of Miputingkimi. Pleipokutji had composed this song for his son who had been killed at the Bathurst Island Mission: 'He plants the potatoes and all those potatoes are growing big./He gets a long stick, sharpens it, and digs the potatoes out./He brings a bag full of potatoes to the camp.' The potato is a dreaming of the Munuluka patrilineage. The song seems to be deliberately ambiguous. In 'marking', as Nancy put it, the last surviving son of Miputingkimi he indicated he was speaking about Tobias, Miputingkimi's clan brother's last surviving son. Possibly Roger alluded to the trouble related to Tobias' violent death, namely Tobias' affair with Jasmine, Andrew Munuluka's wife. The man who had been killed, for whom this song was originally composed, happened to be Andrew's father's father, and, as we have seen, grandfather and grandson are conceptually one in Tiwi perception. Andrew's grandfather had been shot while up a tree collecting mangoes by a Filipino man who mistook him for a flying fox. After the tragic incident he died (cf. C. Berndt 1950: 293; Pye 1985: 34). In his dreaming dance Andrew used to depict the picking and eating of mangoes from a mango tree. In this final mortuary ritual Roger was overruled by Jack, although he himself was senior to Jack. He covered up this blow to his prestige by putting extra emphasis on his classificatory father, who was second to Jack's father, instead of 'marking' Pleipokutji. In other words, his song proposed that the Munuluka patrilineage was more closely related to the deceased and, therefore, Roger was the second in command instead of the actual boss in this ritual.

Isaac sang for Barry (*kiakiei*): 'He (dead man) got him and put him on his lap.' Barry danced as if he were carrying a baby on his shoulders.

The next category of people to perform were the matrilineal 'children' (*mamurapi pularti*), holding their fists against their lips in their dance and ending by tipping back their heads, as if they were drinking. Simon Pamantari (*marauni pularti*) composed the following song: 'I am crying for the feeding bottle./I was crying for milk at Pularumpi and then I went on to Pawularitarra./That's the one now, that's the milk I was looking for!/That's all I had in the feeding bottle./You put it on leaves and they drank it out./I am crying for milk, again./If you don't give me milk, I put dirt on you [dance *ampikatoa*, throwing up dirt]!' He called out: '*palimpalim*' (milk) and '*mangalingari*' (milk filling up in the mother's breast).

In the following group of people this relationship with the deceased was reversed: they were 'parents giving milk' (*unantawi pularti*). These people belonged to the deceased's mother's clan and the clans his father could marry into. The subject matter of their dances, irrespective of their sex, was pregnancy, childbirth, and breast-feeding. Edmund Pamantari (*unantani pularti*) sang: 'I am nursing a little boy.' He called out: '*munkulatini*' (male foetus, that is, 'I am pregnant with a male baby'). Further he sang: 'I got baby boy!/I got baby boy laying down.' Edmund danced holding his 'breasts' in his hands. Female performers in this category wiped their abdomens and backs as if in labour. Also they were dancing as if holding babies in their hands, to be put down in the dancing ground at the conclusion of their performance. Isaac (*unantani pularti*) carried out a narrative dance about childbirth. First, he stood as if in labour in pain, using sand instead of hot ashes, to ease the abdominal pain and the pain in his back. Then he continued sitting on his heels, still in labour, striking his back. Next, he 'gave birth' to the child and sank down on his heels as if sitting on hot ashes. Isaac composed the following songs accompanying his dance: 'I am carrying, still carrying, pregnant, still baby inside./Maybe I have a baby boy inside me./I got a pain in my back./I have a male baby here and put hot ashes on my back./Hot ashes, and I sit on top of these hot ashes.'

Jerome supported his classificatory father Isaac, dancing behind Isaac's back and holding two axes. At the dancing ground of the Bathurst Islanders, Jack sang for the category of people who were clan members of the generation (in Tiwi terms) of the deceased's mother: 'They had a little boy at Wangaru./They had labour pains in Pularumpi and then they went to Pawularitarra.'

Following Jack, Bruce Kerimerini sang for the Bathurst Island maternal 'siblings' of the deceased, the *paputawi*, including himself: 'I am my leg, cut off forever./I am ashamed of this leg./I didn't watch it and then something cut my leg off.' Bruce admitted that as Tobias' elder 'brother', he should have protected him and kept him from getting into trouble.

In the Melville Islanders group it was Theodore who composed the song for these people. Like Bruce he sang about the conventional subject of an injured or lost leg, and he also made an allusion to the cause of death: 'I don't know which killer (*kwampini*) hit your leg./He stepped in the drain, fell down, and broke his leg.'

Paul Adranango (*putani*) danced the crocodile dance with a bundle of spears, in a style employed by his father. The dance depicted the Tiwi attack on the mythological crocodile-man Irekopei. He came up like a crocodile and placed the spears, each time quickly scratching his leg, in a line behind him. Moving swiftly he marked with his shoulder the spearing of his father's father Takampunga by Kalikalini. In 1975, in the *iloti* for one of Takampunga's sons, Tobias (who was a ritual worker then) had assisted Paul in a narrative dance about the killings at Matalau. Tobias in this dance replaced his father, thrusting a spear under Paul's arm, as if spearing him in the chest. Paul's dance made him square with Tobias' previous performance.

The final group of dancers were the ritual workers (*ambaruwi*). These were people either married to *mutuni* or *paputawi*. At the beginning of their dance their spouses marked this relationship by hitting their cheeks or legs. The theme of the performances was sexual intercourse, sexual jealousy and defensiveness depicted in a display of aggression (for instance, in the shark dance). In the Bathurst Island group, Lionel Jatukwani sang: 'You can't fight with me./I am a good fighter.' And Cecil Jatukwani: (Dead man saying) 'You show off to me but I gotta kill you today./All my sisters will be ashamed of me when I hit you.' Cecil had been married to Patty, a half-sister of Tobias.

At the dancing ground of the Melville Islanders, Jerome composed the first song. He made an allusion to his taking the place of his late sister as a widow, wearing a black skirt, at the funeral. Now, still dancing with the two axes, he had dropped his loincloth: 'He thought I was a girl, but he felt my genitals.' (Dead man saying) 'If you were a girl, I been want to do it right now, go straight to you.'

The other ritual workers, including Simon's sons and daughters, performed as well, making obscene dance movements. The next song was composed by Dimitri: 'He is jealous of me, all the rude words come out./I had a loincloth on, and he thinks I am a girl./He takes my loincloth off, and sees I am a boy.' His clan sister, Jasmine (*ambaru*: her actual brother and sisters performed as *kerimerika*, as they were related 'two way' to Tobias), danced as a widow, lifting her skirts, because she had been the deceased's sweetheart.

Then Jerome composed a song for Nancy: 'He tries to wave me, and he points to the mangroves.' That is to say, the dead man wanted to have sexual intercourse with her. Nancy in her dance took off her top. After her dance she performed a mourning song: (Dead man saying to her) 'I didn't know you would dance like this!' Recall that Nancy was Tobias' ex-lover.

The next phase of the mortuary ritual was the 'pay day', the giving out of money (*auwuntikra'emi*) to the ritual workers. Theodore sang: 'We are giving them man-killing spears for their pay.' Tobias' actual and classificatory daughters sat by the poles collecting the money for the payments and distributing it. Their brothers, carrying spears, danced the money to each payee. Money was contributed mainly by the *mamurapi*, the *paputawi*, and both maternal and paternal *unantawi*. It was interrupted by Isaac. Isaac showed the contents of his bag which he had taken off the roof of the Melville Island group's shelter. His wallet and money was missing. '160 [dollars], money walleti', he called out, 'pakina police [get the police], pakina police!' Simon later commented that Kalikalini's spirit had taken the money: 'He make 'em settle that.'

At the same time, the payments went on at the dancing ground of the Bathurst Islanders. Jack sang: 'Tajamini (Kalikalini's maternal brother) made the double-barbed spears and they put them in line.' Here the money was brought to each ritual worker in a dance marking a clan brother of the deceased's father. The persons who handed out the money danced, moving around in small circles while lifting both hands. The money was then dropped behind the dancer's back, at the feet of the one who was to receive it.

Isaac had kept yelling at the side of the Melville Island people, where he attracted everyone's attention. He grabbed a spear and repeated his allegations of theft. Isaac's behaviour made it difficult for anyone to remonstrate with him because he would have been able to immediately use the spear. The other suspected killers were absent (Isaac's 'brother' Oscar Pamantari had gone to Darwin, and Kevin and Rodney had not come to the ceremony because they said they were sick). Thus on this occasion nothing came of the flogging of the persons held responsible for Tobias' death.

After the payments, the poles were removed from the dancing grounds by the ritual workers and put around the grave. Jack and Roger jointly sang: 'At Cape Fourcroy [Watiutwapi], a place close by [called Kariupu, the deceased's country where his father's father is buried] the ritual workers are pushing those mortuary poles, pushing them over./They take those mortuary poles and they are waiting for a boat./A big battle ship with many sails should go to Arapi [district where Cape Fourcroy is located]./Where are they?/Prililaula [Mosquito clan, clan of Tobias' father, Jack and Roger]!'

When the poles were erected at the grave the close relatives of the deceased threw themselves at the poles and the grave mound, crying, wailing, and hitting themselves. Jack sang: (Dead man saying) 'You can't leave me alone./You stay with me.' Nancy sang: (Dead man saying) 'Let's go back home./I wouldn't mind stop my brother [Sam, Nancy's husband]./Take him home!/Maybe we will have a big fight for you.'

Following these final songs the ritual was over, and the crowd went home. Jerome and a few other ritual workers cleared the area. They had a fire burning.

I was told a few days later that Tobias' spirit no longer roamed around in Pularumpi. The possible destructive actions of the spirit had thus been neutralised, the spirit appeased. As Simon told me beforehand, the mortuary rituals for 'our friend who died in the Old Camp' would be 'something special, different', proper rituals like in the old days (*palingari*). People were also afraid of the spirit of Tobias' father, who in Tiwi tradition would have to avenge his son's death. Nancy explained, 'He is *unantani* [father bereaved of a child]. He was murderman, really murderman'. In Tiwi eschatology Tobias' spirit had to follow his father. Elaborate mortuary rituals, as in olden times, were considered necessary to appease the vengeful spirits of Kalikalini and Tobias. The disappearance of Isaac's money was attributed to the spirit of the victim's father.

Following the ceremony, arguments continued about the small poles made by the men from Bathurst Island. Heather, who said she alone had spent A\$1,380, and her sisters were all dissatisfied with a pole made by a man from Milikapiti. Tobias had made a huge pole for a final mortuary ritual for this man's father, fourteen years earlier. Tobias' children had expected him to return an equally impressive mortuary pole for their father.[119] The attendance at night did not meet the expectations of the organisers either. By and large the final mortuary rituals were enormous achievements. These rituals were the result of months of politicking. Hundreds of people from all over the islands came to look. Thousands of dollars changed hands in ritual payments. (Jerome, the principal ritual worker, was able to send his son to Darwin with his earnings from the final ritual and let him buy an outboard motor.) People put tremendous creativity and effort into it. This major event was certainly a memorable and prestigious display of the vitality of Tiwi culture.

The grand final mortuary ritual (*iloti*) for Tobias was indecisive in 'finding out' who had killed Tobias and in carrying out a ritual punishment. Nevertheless, the threat of retaliatory action had been taken seriously; it affected certain people's behaviour. The social base that had been created for the performance of the prestigious rituals might be seen as an exhibition of strength on the part of the organisers.

In theory, accusations could be raked up in any future conflict with the alleged killers. Whether the homicide eventually would have consequences for these people and in what manner an eventual retribution would take place would probably depend on a number of factors coming into play in the ongoing sociopolitical process. As Ross puts it, 'Conflicts are rooted in differences both in interests and in participants' interpretations of events and other actors' (1993: 17). The majority of conflicts revolved around strife or competition over women. Disagreements concerning men's relationships with women (unbalanced exchange of marriage partners between matriclans, maltreatment, love affairs, suspicions of infidelity, sexual jealousy, wife-snatching, rivalries between men and rivalries between women, and so forth) appeared to be the major source of conflict and violence or of the initial grievance giving rise to violence, grievous bodily harm and death, that in turn provoked retaliatory violence and killing. A 'trouble' between two individuals could in time involve many other people and be related or a 'reason' for many other troubles because the webs of relationships woven in marriage politics intersected at numerous points: this made it hard to predict the course an escalating conflict would take (cf. Hart and Pilling 1960: 86).

There were different views (plural) at any point in time and these could change over time. These views and comments might have been suggestive at times but they were certainly not conclusive. The local voices I recorded fit in with particular contexts, and as these contexts altered so did people's views: views that were taken with regard to what was known at a particular time about ill-feelings and conflict between the victim and others (a prerequisite for the credibility of accusations, cf. J. Reid 1983: 111–12), loyalties to other people (people had multiple identities and these could be negotiated, as we have seen), the prevention of possible consequences for others (and indirectly themselves and people closely related or befriended), the prevention of the embarrassment to others, and speculation with regard to uncertainties. Views might also be expressed in order to change other people's behaviour in other matters, to achieve political aims, or aimed at redirecting blame by others. Consequently, statements could not be taken at face value.

Sansom states in relation to Aboriginal fringe dwellers in Darwin that 'there are no structurally determinate consequences of homicide'. The way in which a retaliation takes place 'depends on particularities. These relate to the political status of the victim, the worth accorded to the alleged slayer by his associates, and the current state of intergroup relationships' (1980: 262–3). In the present Tiwi case I have showed that the victim had been marginalised and perhaps even outlawed, the alleged killers were protected by the reluctance of local people to speak out, and the relationships with the offended close relatives of the victim were a matter for negotiation. The victim's relatives from the other townships found themselves in a relatively weak position because they had difficulties in obtaining the necessary information about what had been going on between the victim and others in Pularumpi (e.g., the failed inquest held at the request of Tobias' children and Jack's trouble with his 'relations' who did not keep him informed about what had happened). They exerted pressure and rallied for support at the same time. One ritual after another was presented as an occasion on which the name of the killer or killers would 'come out'. In the rituals Tiwi people dealt with the homicide emotionally, cosmologically, and juridically (e.g., the songs of revenge and the treatment of allegations). There remained, however, uncertainty about who had killed Tobias. It could be argued that it had been the victim's own fault as he had forfeited his right to protection. The killing, however, was a wrong (no matter the justifications others might find) for the aggrieved party, a variety of people at different points in time, absorbing former antagonists of the victim. People's perceptions and interpretations of the homicide, taking into account both their knowledge about bad relations people had had with the victim and the current balance of mutual relations, reflected cultural possibilities. In the process of making assessments and re-assessments of the event people were caught up in a political matter; the multiple views and different targets of blame illustrated Tiwi perspectives but had to be seen in their situational contexts over time.

The Tiwi people who laid blame and the Tiwi people who were blamed all belonged to four matriclans (Stone, Mosquito, Pandanus and Fire) which between them exchanged marriage partners (Stone and Fire on the one hand, and Pandanus and Mosquito on the other). We have seen that before his death Tobias was in trouble as a result of his relationships with two women, Jasmine and Nancy. Their deceived husbands had fought him. Nevertheless, he kept annoying Nancy's husband Sam and he went on to see Jasmine, whom he started to claim as his wife. Then Tobias came into conflict with Jasmine's stepfather and others who perceived the prolonged affair as against their interests and as an infringement of their rights. The night of the killing, he allegedly gave Jasmine and Nancy beer at the club. Far from being a trivial gesture, a man handing beer to potential lovers would be construed as a prelude to a love match. Within the local cultural context this presentation of beer, openly and to unsanctioned lovers, was provocation of the worst kind.

It was people who were supposed to protect the marriages of the women mentioned who were in fact blamed for the homicide: Nancy's husband Sam, and (because Jasmine's husband was away) Jasmine's stepfather Isaac, her 'father' Oscar (also on bad terms with Tobias, possibly supporting his 'brother' Isaac), and her brothers Roy and Rodney. The charging of Kevin by the police appeared to have little credibility. Jack considered the possibility but he was cross with his 'relations' in Pularumpi who did tell him anything: Kevin belonged to his 'relations' there. It might have made him suspicious or he might have put the possibility forward in connection with the trouble with his 'relations', to remind them that he ought to be told. The mortuary rituals for Tobias and related events had resulted in a strengthening of the bonds of his children with some of his former antagonists on whom they had been dependent.

A year after the homicide a new story had gained currency: Karl Hansen who had lived with Tobias' daughter Laura in the Old Camp, had killed him. The white sailor was a different case. Not long after the killing he disappeared. It was only after some considerable time, when disturbed relationships between a number of the Tiwi people involved had been re-cemented, that he was mentioned as the alleged killer. Roger Imalu said the police had found out that it was not Kevin (his clan brother) who had done the deed but the white man: the fingerprints were 'too big'. This man might be seen as someone with a motive (he had argued with the victim) but he might also be regarded as the proverbial scapegoat. It did no one any harm, except that it weakened Laura's position vis-à-vis others (see below), to accuse this man who had left and was not able to talk or to strike back.

In 1991, two years later, new elements had been added to this story, still popular in Pularumpi. The man's Norwegian nationality had changed to German, 'police got him', and he was 'in jail for life'. As might be expected, a sergeant of police in Darwin assured me this was certainly not the case. Jerome said to me, 'They picked on that old man, [his 'father' Isaac]. But he wasn't. Was probably a white man, a German bloke.'[120] A local Aboriginal man told me about the homicide investigation by the police detectives, 'They were just not interested. They were not really interested. It is only a community of 300. Everybody knows.'

*   *   *

A death anniversary gathering for Tobias was not held a year after his death, as usual, but on the day three years after he met his death in the Old Camp. This relatively lengthy period of time was mainly due to the abruptness of his death, involving foul play. The day and night of the first anniversary, Tobias' children were on Bathurst Island. Tobias' daughter Judy said it was too early to have a commemoration. It depended on their emotions, as did the release of the taboo on the names of their dead father. On 29 October 1991, three years after Tobias' death, the time had come to lift the taboos on his names and on photographs of him.

Four days before this, Tobias' eldest daughter Laura made it known in the Social Club in Pularumpi that she would mark the anniversary of the death. An anniversary gathering at the Social Club meant the immediate family of the deceased would shout (buy for others) beer, and people would dance and perform mourning songs. A Catholic mass was to be said under the mango trees at Sam's place in the Old Camp. The news spread. 'We celebrate it', Kevin said to me, pointing towards the Social Club.

On the morning of the memorial day, photos of Tobias were shown around in the Old Camp. Every time these pictures had been looked at by a person they were turned upside down, folded into four, or hidden. In this 'open 'em up' of the pictures people gently touched them and commented on them.

A number of people were annoyed when the deacon, a non-drinker, decided he would say mass during drinking hours. About thirty people attended the mass near Laura's former hut in Sam's camp, facing the scene of the killing and also the direction of Tobias' dreaming place. Unlike Jerome and Bruce, Sam came back from the Social Club, which opened at 4 pm, for the mass at 5.30 pm. 'Leave that beer for my little brother', he said. When the deacon proceeded with the rosary, Laura and her friend, Sam and his sons, and I went off to the Social Club.

People passing through the club shook us by the hand because of the anniversary. Jasmine sat down and rubbed her eyes. Jerome, my 'drinking mate', was sitting outside. As a result of his prominent role as a principal ritual worker in the final mortuary ritual for Tobias, his prestigious performances and the exceptionally large pole he made, Tobias' daughters had become indebted to him. Jerome had been concerned about his son, Reuben, who had 'no girl', in 1989. Jack's eldest son had died in a boating accident but he had more sons, said Jerome. When his son died, he said, he would be 'finished' because he had only one son. Instead of a sister of Tobias' in return for his sister, Jerome, at last, got Tobias' daughter Laura for his son Reuben. In October 1991, he told Tobias' daughter Heather to come to Pularumpi too. Her affair with Reuben was of short duration. Laura was not amused. She threatened Reuben's sisters with a wooden club because they should have kept their brother in check. The two sisters had a fight, focused more on deterrence than a full-scale fight. Laura went around with a thin stick, not a very effective weapon. Raising the stick, she explained it was because they had 'one father'. Heather stressed they could not fight, they were sisters and daughters of the same father. Laura could have Reuben for herself again.

Outside the Social Club, Jerome made it clear that he wanted to have beer from Laura, who had had her pay day, and had announced the death anniversary for her father: 'I am the widow', he said, 'I went there with two axes'. Jerome continued, 'They should worry about me first but they only worry for themselves'. Laura, Reuben, and others were sitting inside with a large number of cans of beer. 'I gonna kick them out [of his house] tonight, kick them out', Jerome said, 'I am the widow. They are sitting there [drinking]. They should ask me in.'

While I was acting the role of go-between which had been forced upon me, Jerome had got up and was walking back and forth in the middle room of the Social Club. He kept telling people about the reason for his anger, pretending he was about to leave. When I passed on money and beer from Laura and Reuben to Jerome, and told him it was not my business, he whispered, 'I might change my mind'. He took out two dozen cans of beer before the locker closed and put them away. Next, still yelling, he entered the room where Laura and Reuben were sitting. Laura cried. Reuben sat motionless. Sam's son Mike wailed loudly. He told Jerome to go, waving him away with his hand, 'Go!' Laura cried but Jerome went on. He performed a mourning song (in *ambaru* style): (Dead man saying) 'You fellow should give him first./I am sorry for him [Jerome] at Pawularitarra.' Jerome shouted, 'You should have asked me in, not leave me there outside. I'm not a dog!' Laura countered, 'Beer, beer . . . always beer. You didn't go church, just for beer.' Jerome's body posture signalled his fierceness. He uttered a threat, 'That spirit, spirit . . .', meaning Tobias' spirit might do some harm to them if they did not treat him properly. He stood behind Laura and put his hand on her shoulder, while lifting the other hand, he sang: (Dead man saying) 'Why please yourself?/Why you fellows please yourself?/You didn't think of my brother-in-law.'

Nancy supported her 'brother' Jerome in his quarrel with Tobias' daughter. 'Far away', she said to Laura, 'It wasn't a Tiwi, *muruntani* [a white man].' She referred to the story about the killing that had gained currency in Pularumpi after the final mortuary ritual for Tobias: the white sailor who had been living with Laura in the Old Camp had knifed her father. That man now was far away (*karampi*). In other words, Laura was told that she had made the wrong decisions as to whom she was loyal. Nancy performed a mourning song (in *ambaru* style) too: (Dead man saying) 'You fellows look at my picture, remind my picture.' Photographs of Tobias could be shown again, and his names be mentioned (although I did not hear them in the following weeks).

Postscript. In September 1994, I returned to Pularumpi. Sam headed the post-funeral rituals for a young man who had died of a sickness. Nancy and other senior women urged people to come to the ceremonial grounds, calling out, 'This ceremony is more important than anything else!' At the time of the final ritual Sam made an impressive appearance: he had been painted up like Kalikalini by Laura. Sam's whole body was covered with red ochre, his back and face bore elaborate polychrome designs. Sam's presentation as Kalikalini turned his performance into a prestigious occasion. Within the ritual context he kept the memory of the killer of olden times and, implicitly, that of Tobias alive. Sam's close identification with his 'father', Kalikalini, filled the audience with awe.

In February 1994, a senior Tiwi man was stabbed to death. Two months after the event, the charge of manslaughter against the slayer, another Tiwi man, was dropped in the Northern Territory Supreme Court. The man's lawyer told the newspaper he hoped Tiwi people would accept the death as 'a tragic accident' too, for his client, who had decided to stay away from the islands, feared retaliation (*Northern Territory News*, 14 April 1994). Upon this a brother of the victim rang the paper, saying, 'It doesn't matter how long it takes me but I'm going to find him and I'm going to kill him'. 'I will do it the traditional way, not the white man way', he added. The same day the victim's brother flew to Darwin. He withdrew his threat to kill the man in question but maintained that the man would 'be punished for what he did'. In his view the state's criminal justice system had failed to mete out proper punishment by releasing the killer from jail instead of letting him 'rot there' (*Northern Territory News*, 15 April 1994). The conflict remained unsolved. The complexities of contemporary Tiwi life, including the interplay between the national law and Tiwi ways, make the course of future events rather unpredictable – not only in this case but also in the one described extensively in this book. Nevertheless, these open-ended processes carry significance and are clothed with meaning in Tiwi cultural action.

CHAPTER 9

Conclusion

At first sight a tragic event, a homicide, that occurred during my field-work seemed to be puzzling. How could this act of violence be under-stood? I have addressed the question by putting the event in context and showing how the case, composed of events that were all somehow inter-related, unfolded over time. In using a processual approach, inspired by the legacy of the Manchester school in British social anthropology, I have focused on the actions and views of individuals most directly involved in the homicide case (locally labelled 'under the mango tree'). Following Moore (1975, 1987) I attempted to do justice to the hetero-geneity and indeterminacy of Tiwi culture, considered the time of my fieldwork 'current history', and took the occurrences related to the homicide as 'diagnostic events': the homicide case served to gain insight into some aspects of the complexity of contemporary Tiwi life.

Tiwi society has seen drastic change in the twentieth century in par-ticular. At the beginning of the century the practice of killing by direct means, such as in the Tiwi institution of sneak attacks (*kwampi*), was given up, the pax Australiana established, and state law enforced on the islands. Melville and Bathurst Islands gradually became encapsulated in the Australian nation-state. The government, assisted by Catholic mis-sionaries, implemented its policies of 'protection' and subsequently 'assimilation' for Aborigines. The 'pacification' of the islands and strict supervision of their daily lives – as far as the newly-founded settlements were concerned – by mission and government authorities, however, did not prevent people from committing homicides by indirect means, the so-called poisonings. Killings were outlawed and the practice went underground, in a manner of speaking. A relaxation of patent intrusion into Tiwi internal affairs and a cultural revival (after attempts over decades to destroy Tiwi insitutions and suppress their 'pagan' rituals)

223

followed the assimilation era; but the change of government policy from 'assimilation' to 'self-determination' or 'self-government' seemed to be accompanied by a re-emergence of killings by direct means. My hypothesis is that these killings might be seen as a modern manifestation of a cultural practice that continues to be influenced by evolving, but distinctly Tiwi, tradition.

This relatively new mode of killing, however, differed from the former institution of sneak attacks on at least three points: knives replaced spears as the almost exclusive weapon, the residence of killer and victim was no longer necessarily in a different locality, and the killers employing knives, as with the 'poisonings', no longer openly revealed their identities. These modifications coincide with altered circumstances in Tiwi society: there are hardly any effective spears around in camps any more, whereas steel knives are in frequent use. People now live together in three large-scale townships, in contrast to the former relatively small bush camps spread over the islands. And although Tiwi are somewhat more at liberty to manage their own affairs, the Australian police are firmly based on the islands and the involvement of the state criminal justice system is unavoidable when someone has been stabbed to death. Protection by co-residents who may consider the homicide justified is also less effective in view of police intervention and the presence of those who have stronger ties to the victim. Possibly the killers therefore do not reveal themselves as openly as in the past (by pulling out their beards and painting their bodies with white clay).

How is it possible that people are being killed by others in this face-to-face society in which all people are related in one way or another and are supposed to show compassion? A prospective victim had committed a serious wrong or wrongs. To prevent an escalation of a conflict, a wrongdoer could move away. The person in question received warnings. A homicide was, in a phrase of Daly and Wilson, the 'most drastic of conflict resolution techniques' (1988: 10). We have seen that Tiwi killers in the past pretended not to 'know' their victims (see Pilling 1958: 236, for another example). In late twentieth-century Tiwi society the consumption of alcohol has been accepted as an excuse for 'not knowing' the victim. The aggrieved temporarily put the bonds between them and the people to whom some serious harm or a wrong had been done above their ties with the wrongdoers. After retaliation, evening the score, and their anger being diminished – or both – they might feel sorry for the (prospective) victim (cf. Myers 1986a).

Tiwi incorporated many elements of the wider society, but they adapted creatively and retained their own value and belief systems to a great extent. In a long-term historical process, numerous changes have taken place: for instance, nominal monogamy, nominal Catholicism, township life, new means of transport and communication, Western education, services, commodities and values, processed foods, the emergence of political institutionalisation. Tiwi people are still subject to the law of Australia. Since 1975 the Australian police on the islands have been responsible for maintaining law and order, although the two white police officers in the community where the homicide occurred live somewhat apart from the Tiwi population and news of many conflicts does not reach their ears. The majority of conflicts revolved around what was termed locally, by both men and women, 'woman trouble': shorthand for the whole range of troubles arising from disputed (hoped for or alleged) relationships of men with women. (The term may be somewhat misleading, for it might erroneously suggest women themselves as the source of trouble, which of course is not necessarily the case.) It was these kinds of conflicts that gave rise to lethal violence as had been the case before permanent white presence on the islands and in the intermediate period when 'poisonings' prevailed. Outright killings ('poisonings' were hardly ever detected) still were an offence according to the law of the state: in the late-twentieth-century context Tiwi people not only had to deal with the killing but also with the legal system which has been imposed. I learned of about five cases of homicide that occurred within a period of three years, in 1988–90, and in two of these cases the slayer(s) remained 'a person or persons unknown' (in other cases it was too obvious). The case of Tobias Arapi has been extensively described in the previous chapters.

The events preceding the homicide and the animosity that existed between the victim and others strongly suggest he was not killed on a whim. The case might be seen as an extraordinary one, but the underlying causes of the conflicts – of which death was a tragic result – were basic contradictions in Tiwi social organisation.

First, the ideal of an exchange of marriage partners between matriclans was not automatically realised in practice nor could it always be adhered to, as arrangements made in the past carried weight but their actualisation remained a somewhat open-ended process (their accomplishment could even stretch over generations); it took time for an exchange of partners to become even, if it was effectuated at all, and people were also unevenly distributed over the clans, in age, gender and number. Furthermore, a single clan often maintained exchange relations with more than one other clan. People's aspirations and claims in the field of marriage politics – which could be justified or unjustified from different points of view – and the unwillingness, hesitation or inability to deliver marriage partners or eventually to give compensation, as well as actions that damaged their interests in this respect, proved to be a major source of conflict and violence.

Second, brothers ideally had to cooperate and support each other, but at the same time they were competitors for the same category of women, so fraternal generosity coexisted with fraternal strife (competition tended to be more fierce between siblings who were distantly related than those who were closely related; rivalries between sisters also existed but did not take on lethal proportions). Ideally, actual and classificatory brothers ought not to fight, but in practice they frequently did fight over women.

Finally, the system of informal lover relationships, guided by the preferential rules of marriage, potentially undermined the formally acknowledged pattern of established marriages. Unsanctioned lover relationships and the possible breaking-up of marriages could have far-reaching consequences in that implicitly the clan members of the individuals concerned also tended to become involved because a particular marriage deal was always woven in a web of such arrangements: therefore the interests in marriage politics, actual and future arrangements, of quite a number of people could be at stake. The conflicts of the victim with other Tiwi people were all directly related to these contradictions.

In this small-scale society, everyone is related to all others by ties of actual or classificatory kinship. These relationships, the identity of the other, cannot be ignored under normal conditions. We have seen that 'not knowing' the other, being blinded by anger or being intoxicated, was a feature of aggressive behaviour, ranging from loudly voiced grievances to assault and death, for which people were seen as less accountable. Without denying its physical effects on the body, it must be noted that the consumption of alcohol set a context for the inflicting of violence, as the perpetrators are ascribed diminished responsibility for it, instead of being its immediate cause (cf. Brady and Palmer 1984; Myers 1986a). The infliction of physical violence (e.g., 'a good hiding') by people who were certainly not intoxicated also occurred, mostly following an acute moral wrong as perceived by the perpetrators of this violence. McKnight's thesis of an increase in violence as a result of high population and high relational density in massively enlarged Aboriginal settlements seems to be relevant here (1986). I mentioned that Tiwi perceived the township Nguiu, with a population of over 1200, as 'too big', and saw this as the main reason for the high incidence of violence there. A conventional way to avoid the escalation of a conflict or further trouble is to move away.

The Tiwi form a so-called hunter-gatherer society. In the early chapter on the research setting, I sketched the environmental features of the islands, people's ecological knowledge and spiritual attachments to the environment in conjunction with territorial affiliations, and the gender division of labour. The killing of large mobile animals appeared to be a male preserve. Likewise, all the evidence I have suggests that in the past only males committed homicides by direct means (with the exception of infanticides). The rights to use certain weapons employed in killing larger animals, such as spears and 'fighting sticks', and guns nowadays, were reserved for the men. (In the past, when introduced knives were scarce, men controlled the distribution of knives.) In different locations in this work the hunter ethos surfaced in the cosmological realm; co-operation of the spirits of the dead in hunting and gathering in the areas where these dead relatives 'lived', the laying-out of spiritual tracks in making identity claims and guiding the spirit of the deceased to the other world, magical acts to ensure the hunter's luck, and the stress on symbolic killings in rites of passage.

I have discussed Hart's analysis of 'the struggle for prestige and in-fluence', mainly in marriage politics, among Tiwi living in the bush in 1928–29 (Hart and Pilling 1960). Sixty years later, despite social trans-formation and the incorporation of many elements of modern Australian society, Hart's analysis appeared to be still valid: Tiwi indi-viduals were still striving to obtain prestige and influence. While the Roman Catholic mission succeeded in its programme to reform tradi-tional Tiwi society in bringing about a change from polygyny to monogamy and in decreasing the differences in age between marriage partners (also introducing maidenhood and prolonged widowhood as new social phenomena), the politics of marriage continued. The lengthy initiation procedures lost their previous function of keeping Tiwi males from marrying until they were at least in their twenties as a result of the situation in which young Tiwi women, age mates, could be obtained from the missionaries by men in their late teens. In past decades only a minority of the men, often already married, have undergone initiation. This new type of so-called short-cut initiation has ensured the continua-tion of the performance of the seasonal yam rituals and proved to be a breeding ground for the ceremonial leadership in the mortuary rituals.

Notwithstanding their having become nominal Catholics and nominal monogamists, Tiwi people still ideally adhered to the practice of an exchange of marriage partners between (exogamous) matriclans (*keramili*). Tiwi men had not given up their aspirations to acquire many wives. For most of the men described in these pages this was an ongoing concern. They did not actually live with all these women in a single household but the claims to them were maintained. With some of these potential spouses they could have sexual relationships. The lover rela-tionships shaped an informal pattern, cross-cutting the pattern of estab-lished marriages. Remember the woman who said that every woman must have a husband and a boyfriend. Tiwi females had their own tactics and were scheming as well, although it did not always show when they were pulling the strings. Social standing, the worth ascribed to individuals by other members of their community, was all-important. It depended on their achievements, and this could be shown in, among other things, marriage politics, reproductive success, foraging, and ritual performances. Success within these contexts enabled people to act with more relative autonomy, to put their stamp on social events, to follow their own will, pursue their own interests, and to define reality.

The point I wish to make is that too many factors are at play to predict people's future actions, as the continuous replication of a neat structure would require. The situational context left choices open to individuals. I was told by people beforehand, for instance, that they would enact a certain ritual role, but for pragmatic reasons in the end they did something different, enacting another role with other ends or not participating at all. Likewise I was told beforehand that the names of the killers would be spoken in the yam ritual, and that 'we will find out' at the time of the final mortuary ritual for the homicide victim. This did not happen. I interpreted the killing in its situational context, as previous recontextualised events made sense for the victim's opponents in their current conflicts, following on a sequence of events in which it possibly could have been settled but in which the conflict escalated instead. It did make sense in the dynamics of Tiwi politics; an individual's goal could never be reached uncompromised.

The importance of the individual in Tiwi politicking, however, is evident (cf. Myers 1986b: 139). Nothing seemed to be settled once and for all. In their social organisation such a basic social category as the clan (*imunga*) appeared to be modifiable by forceful individuals – the alignments of clans changed over time, clans amalgamated, and parts of clans split off – but new arrangements were not necessarily acknowledged by all. Currently the countries, which seemed to have become stable with the formation of the Tiwi Land Council, are being renegotiated (see pp. 24–5 above).

The Tiwi kinship system allows for a great deal of flexibility, and permits individuals considerable scope to pursue their own interests. Obtaining the compliance of relevant others, however, was a prerequisite. Tiwi people, many with strong personalities, creatively employed various stratagems, calculated as well as spontaneously improvised, in getting along and adjusting to new situations. In the ritual domain in particular, the creative potential of Tiwi people surfaced, with the stressing and reshuffling of social and cosmological identities, thriving on a web of mutual exchange relations, shaping meaning out of a common heritage and reflecting on the cherished uniqueness of the individual.

Conflicts appeared not only to be acted out between individuals but also intrapersonally. Individuals themselves had multiple identities; for instance, the disgruntled brother-in-law and strong opponent of the victim played in another context the role of the victim's widow (dressed in a skirt) who wanted to avenge his death. (I have already cited the case of a man whose mother defended him against an allegation while he himself made an admission of guilt.) The other part of the matter is that these multiple identities provided people with manifold opportunities open to individual choice.

From the beginning of my fieldwork on Melville and Bathurst Islands I was confronted with rivalries and differences of opinion in Tiwi society. Conflict and violence were an integral part of social life. The homicide case, an extended case history, enabled me to provide detailed descriptions of a number of interrelated aspects of contemporary Tiwi society and culture and history. I represented the life histories of the man who later became the victim and his father. With these I tried to connect elements in the lives of two individuals and of those associated with them with the changes that have taken place in Tiwi society from the beginning of this century onwards. New elements that were incorporated in Tiwi society (such as work, money, township life, and wives to be obtained from the missionaries) shaped their lives and movements. The victim was supposed to have inherited the character traits of his father, a man who had earned a reputation as a killer par excellence mainly as a result of his role in an ambush, in which four brothers were speared to death and a fifth escaped with a spear in his side. This was one of the last big events in which Tiwi sneak attackers (*kwampi*) operated. In time these killings, marking the end of an era, became legendary. The stories about the ambush contained much information that showed how sneak attacks were organised and demonstrated that this mode of killing was ritualised.

Afterwards the events related to the fourfold killing became the subject matter of many songs, dances and other ritual actions. I have shown that the repetitive telling of these narratives about the ambush (and ritual performances alluding to it) shortly before the victim's death could not be divorced from the situational context in which the stories were told. The narrators made selective use of events and characters of the past in their discourse about the current state of affairs. At this point it was uncertain whether the later victim would terminate his affair with a woman, married and promised to someone else; an affair a number of people in the township either disapproved of or wanted to take advantage of to promote their own interests in marriage politics. In other words, the narrations had a sociopolitical function in trying to work out an undetermined situation.

I have related the machinations of fate in the victim's life: his being expelled from his country, and the tragic deaths of his three wives, two daughters, and his own brother. His prolonged affair brought him into

serious trouble. I described the various stages in the escalation of the conflict, in the course of which more and more people turned against him.
Old grudges and grievances related to histories of disputes and killings
were brought up: but, again, these had some bearing on the current state
of affairs in marriage politics. Despite repeated warnings, the victim failed
to take the action that could have defused the mounting crisis.

Then the homicide occurred. Various possibilities were offered to
explain the death but no one seemed to be blamed openly. At this stage,
the victim's children (from the other townships) lacked the public support to bring the matter out into the open. They considered the killing
unjustified and expressed their wish to retaliate. Senior relatives from the
other island came to support them and to decide on matters. When the
results of the post-mortem were known, two detectives began investigating the homicide. They charged a man with murder, a man who according
to many local people would not have done the deed. In a mourning session people who had previously been in conflict with the victim expressed
their solidarity with his children and stressed their close relationship with
them. In a discussion about the nature of violence possibly inflicted, I suggested that it seems likely that two types of violence, moral and interpersonal, had been merged: Tiwi people had been robbed of the possibility
of executing capital punishment by the imposition of the national law. I
advanced the thesis that the culmination of a series of wrongs could, in
Tiwi terms, outlaw the wrongdoer: that is, an eventual killing, no matter by
whom, was consented to by a group of people.

An analysis of the mortuary rituals showed a further evolution of the
social drama in critical reflections on the events leading up to the homicide and on the homicide itself, as well as evaluations of its consequences. The accomplishment of the rituals involved a lot of politicking
and effort on the part of the organisers. Their indebtedness to others
could be of long duration (as the aftermath showed). Taking part in a
ritual or not taking part could be a political move, and some of the
people blamed for the homicide did not appear. The punishment of the
alleged killer(s), as was intended to take place during one ritual after the
other, did not occur: there was uncertainty, the killer(s) did not 'come
out', time was needed to 'find out' and reach an agreement about who
was to blame (the performance of one yam ritual and the final post-
funeral rituals for Tobias were postponed), white police were present,
the alleged killers absent or able to sidestep the issue, and so on. Perhaps
the threat of physical violence, and the suggestion that it was backed up
spiritually, was sufficient; it had influenced people's behaviour. Viewing
the sequence of rituals, and especially the messages ritual performances
– and song texts in particular – contained, it must be clear that these
Tiwi rituals were embedded in an ongoing social process.

The competitiveness within Tiwi society, evident in the incidence of violence and in marriage politics, is also a feature of ritual. The centrality of death-related behaviour in Tiwi cultural action, I believe, relates to the need for recurrent negotiation of social relationships. People have to live with uncertainty about the future; things cannot be put on hold, life goes on and new situations arise. A death is an emergent new situation, a loss and an occasion that provides opportunities at the same time. Following a death the social fabric has to be restored (cf. Metcalf and Huntington 1991; Bloch and Parry 1982); things can never be quite the same any more. In the ritual context, people can safely express their grief and a great many other things, as we have seen. Individuals are forced to make choices and the audience (of the living as well as the dead) bears testimony to their stand. We have seen that in this limbo context all sorts of relationships were stressed. In Tiwi eschatology the spirits of the deceased 'follow' their fathers and father's fathers. In the ritual drama the frame narrative is that of guiding the spirit of the deceased from the world of the living to the world of the dead. The participants enact ritual roles indicated by a special mortuary kinship terminology. These various roles are enacted in a certain sequence in the dance and song ceremony (*yoi*). In this sequence of performances the new spirit of the dead is constituted. Each category of personnel, enacting a particular role through conventional metaphors, contributes a part to the whole. At the same time, reflections on personal experiences relating to the deceased can be woven into these performances. The song texts are often dialogues of the performer with the spirit of the deceased and simultaneously directed at the audience.

These more personal narratives within the larger framework might be seen as reflections on the performer from the perspective of the deceased. In disconnecting or distancing the deceased from the self, as it were (e.g., the sibling who 'loses' one side of the face or a leg, symbolically representing the deceased), a relative autonomy is realised. The voice of the deceased can be employed as a rhetorical device. Mortuary rituals are avenues to obtaining prestige and influence. People who act as ritual workers are supposed to commission their employers as ritual workers when the situation is reversed. These mortuary exchange relations follow the same lines as those for the exchange of marriage partners.

For Tiwi people rituals are not bounded or discrete events; different people brought different experiences to the rituals, and these were connected by meanings and emotions and exchange relations, and the performances that alluded to many other previous occasions, although they were recontextualised and textualised every time anew. What was said and done in these rituals was closely linked to people's lives.

It was also important that in ritual action new meaning could be given to previous events. An act of killing especially tended to become recontextualised to mark significant ritual transitions. The allusions to the former killings in turn could be meaningful – could carry a hidden message – in relation to the current affairs in which performers and audience were involved as social actors.

The requirement that Tiwi singers compose entirely new songs for every occasion (unless there is a good reason to cite an old one) is in contrast to the rather fixed composition of song texts as reported from various parts of Arnhem Land (cf. C. Berndt 1950; see Berndt and Berndt 1988 for further references). The emphasis on individual creativity and orginality in Tiwi song composition is also striking, and that the creative powers are attributed to human beings ('good songwriters') instead of the beings of the Dreamtime (cf. Maddock 1986; Clunies Ross 1987). In Tiwi mortuary rituals in general there happened to be a strong emphasis in focus on deceased patrilineal relatives, such as actual and classificatory fathers and father's fathers. Tiwi people said they 'follow' them and did not mention totemic beings of the Dreamtime to me in this context, although the dreamings, as we have seen, were also important.

The rituals appeared be an arena in which skilled performers competed. These rituals were instances of 'trouble'. The arguments running through song texts, which were especially composed for each occasion, gave insight into what mattered to Tiwi from different points of view, besides showing their creativity. Not many people participated in the seasonal yam ritual (*kulama*), but its performance was still considered meaningful. It was literally stated that the yam ritual had 'to stop people from fighting'. It seems the ritualists tried to master the problems undermining their well-being. For the senior and able men it was a way to settle their disputes. Symbolic killings appeared an important element in Tiwi rituals. The rituals related to the present homicide case were interesting, for here an actual killing coincided with these symbolic killings in the ritual context. The experience of killing, which had an extra dimension for this hunting people, was carried over in the symbolism of Tiwi mortuary ritual in every type of death. Death by means of a killing is so sudden and abrupt that it could serve as a very strong image of separation and subsequent transformation (cf. Hertz 1960: 73; Burke 1974: 19–20). Rooted in this people's experience, killing or homicide appeared a major theme played upon in Tiwi ritual. The theme of killing also figured in other rituals that mark transitions, such as seasonal rituals. Given the narrative character of Tiwi ritual, actual killings exemplified this theme in the performances of participants. These killings as events were recontextualised and so gained new meanings.

In describing how the Australian criminal justice system dealt with the homicide, I have shown to be false the assumption, made on the basis of Western common sense, that no one will confess to a crime he or she did not commit. I examined how such a confession of murder in a record of interview with the police came to be made and have tried to demonstrate that too much weight was put on it. In following the court proceedings I juxtaposed Western notions of the homicide with Tiwi perceptions and interpretations. Aboriginal expertise happened not to be acknowledged as evidence in defence of the accused in the murder trial. The homicide case, unsolved by the state's criminal justice system, was by no means a clear-cut one for the Tiwi people involved, as follows from the multiple views and different targets of blame that illustrate Tiwi perspectives in their situational contexts.

Although the data revealed 'woman trouble' as a likely cultural possibility in motivating the homicide, I want to stress that it must be seen as only a possibility. In my argument and in Tiwi views over time there was no single and definite solution. Tiwi ways of dealing with the killing, especially in the yam rituals and the mortuary ritual cycle, were evidence of the originality and creativity so valued by Tiwi people and demonstrated the vitality and dynamism of Tiwi cultural action.

Mortuary Kinship Terminology*

Mortuary kinship terms	Terms for the deceased:	Kinship notation: (actual and classificatory)
mamurapi (turah)	*ringani*	F, MZH, MH
	tinganinga	FZ
	timinti	HMB, SWB, (Z)HF
	timintinga	ZSW, SW, (Z)HM, MBW
keremerika	*amini*	FF, MF, FMB, FZS
	amoa	FM, FFZ, MFZ, FZD
kiakiei	*mawanyini*	SS, BDS, maDS, ZSS, MBS
	mawana	SD, BDD, maDD, ZSD, MBD
unantawi (pulanga)	*marauni*	S, maS
	maraninga	D, maS
mutuni	*ingkalipini*	FS of different clan
	inkalipa	FD of different clan
impala	*amprinua*	(B) WM, feDHZ
	pinyua	DH, feZDH, MZH other clan
	pinyiwini	WMB, maZDH
mamurapi (pularti)	*naringa*	M, MZ, F(B)W
	ilimani	MB
	nirinua (senior to ego)	MaDH, (B)WF, FZH
unantawi (pularti)	*mworinga*	ZD, feD
	mworti	ZS, feS
	nirinua (younger than ego)	maDH, WF, FZH
paputawi	*impunga*	senior Z
	impwoka	younger Z
	juwuni	senior B
	juwani	younger B
	maningoa	MM(Z)
	angimani	MMB, much senior B
	intamiliti	feDS, ZDS
	intamilinga	feDD, ZDD
	umpurutrini	SWF, DHF
	umpuruteri	SWM, DHM
ambaruwi	*injimi*	ZH, WB, HB
	injimunga	BW, WZ, HZ
	apunai	H
	apunajina	W

Z = sister; B = brother; M = mother; F = father; D = daughter; S = son; W = wife; H = husband; fe = female speaking; ma = male speaking.
*In the compilation of this table I have also used Brandl (1971) and Grau (1983).

Mortuary Kinship Dances*

The *mamurapi (turah)* dance with (imaginary or actual) spears representing both spirit children and sneak attackers. These paternal 'children' end their dance by thrusting the 'spear' into their 'victim' (imaginary or represented by a 'father') lying down on the ground.

The *kerimerika* perform the same dance but hold one hand on their heart. These paternal 'grandparents' (given the system of alternating generations), like the 'fathers' and 'father's sisters', may have a dream about spirit children who are supposed to spear them in their heart. They are said to feel a pain in their heart when they have this dream indicating a 'baby is coming up'. At the same time, they represent the deceased's 'grandchildren' as spirit children.

The *kiakiei* dance as if they are carrying the deceased as a little child on their shoulders (a common Tiwi practice). I was told that when a child was lifted up and carried on the shoulders in a ritual context it was made 'important'. Another metaphor employed, mainly in song language, in relation to this category of people was the carrying on their shoulders of a bundle of spears that represented their 'grandchildren'.

The *unantawi (pulanga)* symbolically hold their (male) genitals during their dance and conclude this dance with 'cutting off' the penis (*tika*) with a swift movement of one hand. With this they represent their loss as the deceased's 'fathers' because they 'made' the deceased. In another dance version the performer puts a finger on the lymph nodes in his groin (*pulanga*) on each side. I was told that these glands swell up when one's legs are infected and that the *unantawi (pulanga)* feel it in this part of the body when something is wrong with one of their 'children'. The stretched forefinger here stands for a one-sided barbed spear (*tungkwaliti*), an allusion to a symbolic killing.

The *mutuni* dance holding their cheek(s), here representing the deceased in Tiwi body symbolism. They symbolically lose one side of their face. In song language it is also expressed in terms of the cheek being hurt or injured (or other metaphors might be employed, such as a boat turned on its side); and the 'lost' side of the face or healing can be found at the burial place of a paternal 'grandparent' the performers and the deceased have in common. The location happens to be a destination of the spirit of the dead. In mourning songs the names of *mutuni*, paternal 'half-siblings', are used instead of the names of the deceased. The performers hit themselves hard with their hand on one side of their face. In wailing they often do the same, or beat the side of their face against some solid object. The *mutuni* are recognisable in having their cheeks painted, either with one side painted in a colour different from the other, or with only one side of the face painted.

The *impala*. If this category of personnel is available they may enact a dance called *impala* in which they carry green boughs which they flap over their shoulders. This dance represents a bird moving its wings. At the same time it stands for the relationship between sons-in-law and mothers-in-law, who refer to each other by pointing to the shoulder (*amprinua* being the reciprocal kinship term). In song language other metaphors can be used, such as the wings of a plane, the branches of a tree, or a rope. The relationship is one of avoidance, therefore, they usually remain at a distance from the deceased. A son-in-law who is an able singer will compose mourning songs for his dead mother-in-law. These songs are conceived of as a gift. The people in this category may have their shoulders painted. A painful shoulder is said to be an indication that something is wrong with the other in this particular relationship.

The *mamurapi (pularti)* dance while holding a fist on their lips and end the dance by turning the head backwards. They are supposed to be drinking milk from the deceased's breasts. In the accompanying songs they 'cry' for the milk that has been lost, dried up, or spilled. They call out for *pularti*, breasts, *palimpalim*, milk or breast-feed, and for *mangalingari*, milk swelling up in the mother's breasts.

The *unantawi (pularti)* hold their breasts while dancing. The symbolism of nurturing is an inversion of the symbolism belonging to the previous category of bereaved. People in this category in contrast to 'drinking milk' are supposed to be 'giving milk'. But again death results in a breaking of ties and, therefore, the lack of breast-milk is for these performers the main theme of the song and dance. Labour pains and childbirth represent an alternative theme. People in this bereavement status may paint their breasts, identifying their specific relationship with the deceased. The breast(s) are the part of the body, my informants said, where they feel something is going on with a maternal 'child'.

The *paputawi* hold their leg or legs in their dance. The accompanying songs are about their injured leg or an amputated leg, a metaphor for the loss of a maternal 'sibling'. The body symbolism is derived from a myth in which a man named Purukupali fought with his younger maternal brother, Tapara, after the latter had seduced Purukupali's wife and her son had died as a result of neglect. Tapara offered to bring the child back to life but Purukupali refused the offer and said that because his son had died all people (*tiwi*) had to die. In the fight Tapara injured Purukupali's leg with a forked throwing club. The people in the *paputawi* bereavement status paint two bands with white clay on their lower legs. Their dance usually begins and ends with hitting their lower leg. A feeling in the leg indicates something is happening to a maternal 'sibling'.

The *ambaruwi* constitute a category of bereaved people consisting of, on the one hand, the actual widow or widower (*ambaru*), and on the other hand, the other *ambaruwi* from which the 'workers' who have to carry out practical and ritual tasks will be selected. The *ambaruwi* of the second type dance in fighting poses, pretending to fight off the spirits of the dead. They separate the world of the living from the world of the dead. The conventional themes of their performances are aggressiveness and sexual jealousy. In their role enactments the ritual workers show their sexual attractiveness towards the deceased and aggression towards their relations – dead or alive – who compete with them for the attention of the deceased. The religious purpose is to prepare the world of the dead for the coming of the deceased: categories of spirits of the dead are influenced, suggesting they will seduce the yet-unsettled spirit of the recently deceased.

Their sexual attractiveness towards the deceased is among the other things stressed in dance movements denoting the making of advances and sexual intercourse. For example, in one dance they 'show the knees' (*impula*) and their upper thighs by bending and opening their legs and making pelvic movements. The traditional attribute of the workers in the mortuary rituals is a piece of wood (*aruwala*), used in fights to ward off spears. Another feature of their role is the aggression of the shark (*tatuwali*), shown in the shark dance performed by ritual workers at the conclusion of the dance ceremony. It is all about sexual jealousy and the resulting fights, as in ordinary life, but is mainly directed towards the spirits of the dead. Therefore in their songs, brothers-in-law of the male deceased may jokingly exchange insults with the latter, as they do in daily life. They also emphasise eventually outstanding claims on women resulting from the exchange of marriage partners between their respective clans (*keramili*). These exchange relations parallel the exchange relations in the performance of ritual tasks (underlying these exchanges are clan exogamy and incest taboos in the first instance and *pukamani* taboos in the second). Often these *ambaruwi* were spouses of *mutuni* and *paputawi*. They could begin and end their dance by hitting their partner on the cheek or kicking on the leg respectively. Spouses or lovers of the *ambaruwi* may dance making pushing movements with their hands, representing waves crashing on the beach, a dance that has a sexual connotation for Tiwi. During the whole ceremony the second type of *ambaruwi* may dance in the background in a fighting pose, supporting their spouses, friends, and relatives.

The actual widow or widower has a slightly different style in dancing compared to the other *ambaruwi* and does not express aggressiveness. The bereaved spouse comes last. In songs and dance this person displays the features of sexual intercourse with the deceased when both were alive. The widow or widower may undress, and will ask while employing the voice of the dead partner why they no longer can have sex.

*Refer to Grau's study of Tiwi dance (1983) for further information on these dances and the dreaming dances (including a presentation of the dances in Benesh Movement Notation).

Notes

1   Under the Mango Tree

1 Only estimates are given because the resident population of the townships fluctuated. The total population of the islands was about 1900. According to the 1986 census there was an Aboriginal population of 1,651 persons (Australian Bureau of Statistics 1990: 97). This figure might not include all people of Aboriginal descent, the people who did not identify as Tiwi in particular. Altman reports that in the mid-1980s, 200 to 300 Tiwi people were thought to live on the mainland permanently (1988: 254). In 1988–89, Pularumpi was a predominantly Tiwi community of about 300, including 15 whites (sometimes a few more). Any further distinctions people made depended on context.

   My informants sometimes distinguished between Tiwi (which could include Tiwi people of mixed descent or not) and non-Tiwi, but also between 'we, black people' (*tunuwi*, including 5 non-Tiwi Aborigines), Aboriginal people of mixed descent (*pinawi*) and white people (*muruntawi*). In 1954, there was a total Tiwi population of about 950, of whom about 50 (people of mixed descent not included) lived in Garden Point (Pularumpi) and about 150 on or in the vicinity of the mainland (Hart and Pilling 1960: 107). Since then the Tiwi population has doubled. For further information see also Jones (1963) and Peterson and Taylor (1993).

2 For information on the Tiwi language see Capell (1967), Osborne (1974) and Lee (1987).

3 The kin terms in inverted commas indicate classificatory kin relationships.

4 The location of the body was later to become an issue in the murder trial in the Supreme Court. The angle from which the coroner had taken his photographs of where the corpse was situated distorted its position. Given the lack of actual measurements and technically more telling photographs, it was accepted by the court that the dead body had been lying closer to Tobias' hut than to the hut of Isaac. According to the rough measurements I took in situ, however, the corpse was lying about nine steps away from the verandah of Tobias' hut but only about three steps from Isaac's verandah.

5 At the time I understood this as an allusion to the elder brother of the deceased, as Jerome had accused Tobias at the club of having speared his

238

brother in the side. It could refer to trouble within the matrilineal clan of
the two brothers, the Stone clan.

6 See Sansom (1980: 30–4) and Langton (1988) for the social significance of
   swearing to make the style of speaking 'unwhite'.

7 In the words of Malinowski, 'The true problem is not how human life sub-
   mits to rules – it simply does not; the real problem is how rules become
   adapted to life' (1940: 127). I am aware of the problems in using a Western-
   biased concept of law in relation to Tiwi society and will use the terms connected with this concept only loosely (see also Moore 1978: 135–48; Roberts
   1979: 17–29, 1994; Rasing 1994: 36–9). See Williams (1988) for an overview
   and discussion of studies of Australian Aboriginal law.

8 Statistics here would be misleading because not only would they be incomplete but many grievances were linked to others and hard to distinguish
   singly (cf. Williams 1987: 67–8). A single dispute could go on for several
   months, involving many people and leading to a series of conflicts and
   fights between various antagonists.

9 F. Rose writes, 'The actual sexual relations between men and women were
   for the Aborigines of little consequence, and their apparent lack of sexual
   jealousy can be understood in the light of this fact' (1987: 36). As far as the
   Tiwi are concerned, I cannot agree with his assertion about the lack of sexual jealousy (*tulura* or *mantupungari*). See Burbank (1980: 85–9) for a discussion of sexual jealousy in another Aboriginal society.

10 I thank Jon Altman who helped me to clarify this point.

2   Tiwi Culture Amid Change

11 The ideal thus is a unilateral cross-cousin marriage, an asymmetrical pattern, in contrast to the Kariera system in which there is no such formal distinction between 'mother's brother's daughter' and 'father's sister's
   daughter' (to whom a single term is applied), and the preferential marriages are symmetrical bilateral cross-cousin marriages (Brandl 1971: 171).
   For a discussion of further contrasts to the Kariera system, see Hart and
   Pilling (1960: 27) and Brandl (1971: chapter 3).

12 I use 'senior' as an indication of a social status that comes with age but does
   not necessarily directly correlate to age. It is in accordance with local understanding, although in English Tiwi speak of 'old man' or 'old people'. Tiwi
   women, for instance, speak of their husband with a status of seniority as 'my
   old man' no matter that they are age mates.

13 In the past – it has become very rare nowadays – there was a ritual in which
   such an arrangement, including the successive rights in marriage of the
   mother-in-law's husband's brothers, was confirmed. This ritual (*muringelata*,
   also the female age grade term) was held at a woman's first menses.

14 To include Melville and Bathurst Islands the border of the British colony of
   New South Wales was shifted further west in 1825. Four years later all the
   land of Australia was claimed for the British Crown (Parry 1985: 1).

15 The pearlers replaced the Macassan trepangers who were officially banned
   from Australian waters in 1907 (Cense 1950: 255).

16 The anthropologists Klaatsch, Basedow, and Spencer all stayed for a short
   while at Paru as Cooper's guests. (At the time of their visits Basedow and
   Spencer had the title of Chief Protector of the Aborigines.) See Klaatsch
   (1907, 1908), Basedow (1913, 1925) and Spencer (1912, 1914, 1928).

17 The Darwin-based meat firm Vesteys took a lease on the island. Until the Great Depression a few white men worked temporarily on the island with Tiwi employees to get timber and hides (Priest 1986).

18 Nancy, one of my key informants, told me that she was sold to the priest by her stepfather for tobacco, tea, and flour when she was about eight years old. She stayed there at the convent and was educated by Catholic nuns until she was allowed to marry her husband, Sam, at an estimated age of sixteen. Nancy had been promised as a wife to an older man, but this man had died in the meantime. Sam, who used to work for the Air Force in Darwin, had two wives promised to him. Sam, from the Tiwi point of view, could marry Nancy because this marriage was a 'change 'em over' for the marriage of a woman of Sam's clan to a man of Nancy's clan in the previous generation. The couple went to live in a bush camp on Melville Island, on the other side of the strait opposite the mission.

19 Note that it took quite a number of years before the Bathurst Island Mission became a population centre of any significance. In 1923 an average of about 50 Tiwi people lived there but most of them temporarily. Two years later, 'this average had increased to about 80, including almost 20 young Christian families' (Jones 1963: 20).

3   The Victim and his Father

20 These people were Simon, Nancy, Isaac, Jerome, Ella, Bruce, Theodore, Roger, Mildred, Bill, Dimitri, and Mabel.

21 Only an actual widow (*ambaru*) or someone in this category of people (*ambaruwi*, either sex) could deliver the message, 'take licence to thing'. The person acting as messenger, of course, had relatives in the receiving camp. Sometimes, in case this person was indeed a widow, the one to whom she brought the message could marry her. The practice of using 'letter-sticks' had been adopted from mainland Aborigines, probably from the employees of the buffalo-shooter Joe Cooper who had come to Melville Island in this period.

22 This type of song was called *umpaturunumtunkkuruwatuwala.*

23 Kitiruta was described to me as a 'doctor' and 'magic man'. He could look through people's bodies, was a clairvoyant, and was the only one who dared to go into the jungle in the night.

24 One informant explained: 'They always painted all in red after that fight. That mean they got them properly [they killed them].' The homicides were considered justified. The use of the colour red (ochre) suggests a multivocal colour symbolism. It is associated with blood, danger, and mourning. When men paint their bodies with red ochres, for example during the first night of the yam ritual, it depicts them as sneak attackers (*kwampi*). In addition, red ochre (*jaringa*) identified Kalikalini, the main culprit in the accounts at the end of the 1980s, as it is closely associated with his country, Tikelaru, where it is found (cf. C. Berndt 1950: 295).

25 Nancy commented: 'He [Miputingkimi] didn't throw good. And he Kalikalini, he throwing good. He shot man one time, kill him die.'

26 Ritchie, a lay missionary, describes in great detail the rather rough way in which he, accompanied by a policeman and a medical doctor, kidnapped the old man (1934: 70–7). (The deportation of lepers was part of the government policy intended to limit the spread of the disease, considered contagious, among the Aborigines living in reserves.) The policeman fired a

shot and Ritchie 'told them that unless they brought the old man along, the policeman would take them to Darwin and put them in Fanny Bay – the jail for blacks' (ibid.: 76).

27 Pilling, however, states they went home immediately because they feared being killed by the people of the country where the ambush had been taken place. Pilling notes that in spite of the killings being justified 'there is a danger of an outbreak of violence' (1958: 329).

28 This account is based on information provided by Bruce Kerimerini, Jerome Pamantari, and Ryan Munuluka. For other accounts of this myth, see Allen (1976: 197–202) and Mountford (1958: 26–7).

29 The version recorded by Goodale (1971: 177–9) is presented in this way.

30 As Macdonald points out in relation to a Wiradjuri fight story: 'In the fight, as in the fight story, there is a transformation of the basic themes which can be discerned in social relations generally. The fight becomes the anecdotal expression of life, the ordering of reality into one symbolic event which expresses the various tensions, oppositions, contradictions and values with which people live day by day. These are relived in the stories which thus take on a timeless quality' (1988: 180).

31 Tobias recited a song of sorrow made up by his father, Kalikalini, in which he expressed how he felt sorry for his country: 'Poor country, my uncle kicked me out./ [I am] very sorry for my country./ I will be here no more/ I have only been here to look./ I miss it [my country]./ I have only been here to look./ My uncle [said]; 'go!'; 'Poor my country./ I am really sorry, my land./ I came here to look./ I am sorry, my own land.' Tobias himself composed the following song about this event: 'Look son, [the uncle said,] you got to go back./ I don't want this son, [he said,] I don't want you, you go!'

After Tobias' death, a leader of the people from Tikelaru composed a grievance song in his seasonal yam ritual saying he had never denied Tobias access to a certain part of his country (see chapter 6).

Hart (1970) reports that the people from the Tangio district in Tikelaru did not allow people from elsewhere, even Tikelaru, on their land.

32 See Hart (1974) for a vivid description of the seizure of initiates. The types of cicatrices I mention were adopted by Tiwi from mainland Aborigines in the beginning of the twentieth century. The scars (*minga*) were made with the sharp edge of a mussel shell, a piece of glass or a razor blade. For Tiwi this hostile act seems to have been associated with the way the shark's dorsal fin (also called *minga*) cuts through the water surface, a conventional sign of aggression. The shark dance, depicting this movement of the shark, is performed by brothers-in-law of the deceased in mortuary ritual.

33 As this would have been in 1971 or thereabouts I was unable to confirm it: the police station in Garden Point was founded in 1975, and the criminal records in Darwin had been (partially) destroyed by Cyclone Tracy in 1974. One might wonder if Tobias would have been employed as a police tracker a few years later if he had had a criminal record, perhaps still within memory of Darwin police officers.

4   'The Message that is Murder'

34 Childless women have no status at all in Tiwi society; they are, as Goodale puts it, 'social nonentities' (1971: 149; cf. Hart and Pilling 1960: 59).

35 On the anniversary of the death of her baby, Jasmine asked me to buy toys for my 'brother'. These toys she brought to her little son's grave.

36 (Kalikalini and Miputingkimi, talking about the people at Matalau, said) '"We got to get those men and make them die!"; I [Kitiruta] told them before, "Look out for those men [Kalikalini and Miputingkimi], watch out for their spears!"; 'Kalikalini and Miputingkimi [designated by their clan names] did not care when I said "*ninka*" ['nothing'] but they threw the spears.'

37 In the past such calls or cries were employed in fights and battles to deter opponents. I believe Tobias now clearly understood he was a man under sentence. As already noted, to avoid escalation of a conflict, Tiwi people in trouble usually move away from the place they are living.

38 Two of his daughters lived with white men; one of them was Heather's husband, a man Tobias liked very much.

39 This resembles the obtaining of an admission or the 'true story' described by Williams for the Yolngu of northeast Arnhem Land (1987: 93–4). In the previous chapter we have seen that in the past Tiwi sneak attackers admitted a killing by painting their bodies with white clay and pulling out their beards. Furthermore, Tayuni took his sons aside and asked them to tell him the 'truth', in line with the procedure I here refer to. Later, in chapter 6, I discuss the yam ritual as another context in which an offender could make such an admission, although in public, in front of an audience.

40 I was given the Tiwi term *kiritjilti* for someone who gets angry or is feeling angry. This term is also applied to food when it has a bad taste and to bad water (not dirty water in particular).

41 The fact that the cause of Tobias' death had been a stab wound to the chest Kevin might also have read in the newspaper that came in the morning prior to his so-called confession. It had been published in the 'police briefings' in the *Northern Territory News* (1 November 1988).

5   The Funeral Rituals

42 For a review of the extensive ethnographic literature on Tiwi mortuary rituals, refer to Brandl (1971: 344–404) and Grau (1983: 78–108).

43 My informants, contradicting Goodale (1971: 255), asserted that the term *pukamani* in this sense also applied to the *kulama*. The violators of a taboo become *pukamani* themselves and the same applies to food carried through a ceremonial ground.

44 In the descriptions I will use the past tense because my fieldwork was in the (recent) past. It should not be inferred that what I describe on the basis of my data no longer exists. I merely describe events that I observed in 1988–89 (and 1991).

45 I was told that in the past the deceased were wrapped in a large piece of bark, previously used to sleep on, tied with a long string. The foot tracks of the deceased would be wiped out, except in the mangrove swamps where the tide would wash them away.

46 Disagreements about the place of burial could divide immediate family members of the deceased living in different townships. I witnessed a big row over this issue in the course of which the coffin, with the corpse, had to be locked up in a police cell overnight. Influential brothers of the deceased from another township wanted to have him buried there. At first the widow agreed but then she changed her mind. A meeting was held. People, several painted up with white clay and carrying clubs, gathered around a

circular space. The brothers accused the widow of being responsible for her husband's death. Her mother spoke up for her, clapping her hands, stamping her feet, and yelling, 'She is the Queen'. The widow had a veto over all major decisions to do with the mortuary rituals. The brothers from the other township said they would not come to the funeral if the deceased were buried at the intended location. The brothers from there and a third township, however, supported the widow. She decided on her own township, whereupon the elder brothers went away. The natural father of the deceased went to them and hit himself forcefully on the head with a club. The brothers who had become angry with the others did not show up at the funeral.

47 Spencer (1914: 237) gives a description of such a dance in which the re-enactment of a sneak attack (probably the killing of Pupliangamiri which occurred before Spencer visited the islands) seems to have been merged with the conventional imagery of a spiritual conception, the father being speared by spirit children while he slept.

48 Matrilineal relatives, such as a mother and mother's brother, for example, enact the role of the deceased's mother, breast-feeding or giving birth to the deceased. ('Female speaking' and 'male speaking' in the kinship terminology also do not refer to the sex of the speaker but to the gender aspect of the relationship, for instance, the mother's brother and mother, both siblings of the same matriclan, relate to ego in the same way and employ 'female speaking' terms for ego.) See Merlan (1988) for a good discussion of gender relationships in Aboriginal societies.

49 All over the world there is a connection between percussion and transition (Needham 1967). The rhythm of foot-stamping and beating time on human flesh or with sticks on corrugated iron were part of the death rites as *rites de passage*. The great noise contrasted with the usual silence and marked the transition of the deceased from the living to the dead. Metcalf and Huntington speak of 'a purposeful noisiness' (1991: 64, 64–72).

50 Between the performances of different bereavement status there would be a small break to give everyone of a particular category of bereaved persons the opportunity to dance. Nevertheless, now and then people stirred up a fight claiming they had not been given the opportunity to dance or had not been asked to do so. Often there was also a row when certain people refused to dance. People who arrived too late, depending on their social position and relationship with the deceased, would complain and argue it should not have started without them. The people arriving when the dancing was on waited until the particular performance had ended and then went to the corpse (or bereaved close relatives of the deceased) to wail and hit themselves. Instances of serious trouble at mortuary rituals occurred when a group of people did not come and when people were accused of not having taken care of the deceased properly.

51 The widow sang: (Dead man saying) 'Oh, you sweat?/You're all wet under your pants!/Are your private parts wide or little?'

52 He sang: (Dead woman saying) 'Don't burn off the whole lot [pubic hair], because your [second] wife might growl at you.'

53 Simon told me how he 'used to go wild' in the past and with a large knife made a cut in his forehead. I was told it was not done any more because someone had died of such a cut. This aspect of mourning behaviour has changed since the 1950s (see Mountford 1958; Goodale 1971).

54 Both types of burning clothes terminated a relationship. The ritual burning of clothes of the deceased (called *amprakatika*) was, however, perceived as different from the burning of clothes of a spouse or lover (called *tupilip-iami*) to 'finish' the relationship with that person. The ritual workers burnt the clothes of the deceased. Note that in both instances it was a relationship between affines ended in this way.

55 In the past, other bodily hair of the bereaved was also removed (cf. Mountford 1958; Spencer 1914). Besides the burning of the hair on the lower legs I only saw one widow having her hair cut.

56 As one such relatively rare event happened to occur during the time of my fieldwork, I will summarise the cleansing rituals for a 'country' following this person's death. In 1989, an elderly woman who was the most senior person of the 'country' or district Imalu (in the northwest of Melville Island) died. After this the whole 'country' and adjacent sea became taboo. I was told all the greenback turtles (her dreaming), fish, and animals on the land had moved away, not allowing themselves to be caught (hunting and fishing were forbidden anyway). A special cleansing rite for the 'country' was performed at two significant places. After an elaborate cleansing rite with smoke and a series of dances and songs in the bush camp where the deceased had recently stayed, people went to the beach in front of a reef where turtles were usually harpooned. There an elaborate turtle dance was performed, concluding with a ritual washing in the sea strait. A half-brother of the deceased, while 'marking' a turtle, swam a long way into the sea. After this people went further north to a cliff with the open sea in view. Lifting one hand some men called out significant names of places along the shore in this 'country'. One of the performers explained to me it was done to tell the turtles and fish to come back. The first turtle harpooned after that was brought onto the beach in Pularumpi. The dead woman's half-brother had to cut it. He and other patrilineal relatives of the turtle dreaming performed a short turtle dance on the beach but were not allowed to eat this first turtle's meat. The widower, who participated in the cleansing rituals, told me he would not go hunting in this 'country' until the rain during the next wet season had washed all *pukamani* away. It was safe for other people, he said, but not for him. He also observed strictly the *pukamani* rules regarding himself.

57 The Aboriginal health workers complained to me that the designers of the well-equipped health clinic, containing a morgue, had given little thought to the possibility that once people had died there others would be frightened to enter the clinic to receive medical care. Though every time someone had died in the health clinic (three times during my stay) the building was ritually cleansed inside with smoke, this did not take away the fear of a number of people, especially close relatives of the deceased, regarding the spirits of the dead. Some people refused to go into the building at all, and others were reluctant to stay there for the night even when this was thought necessary for medical reasons. Some health workers said they themselves were frightened at times.

58 The Larrakia were Aborigines from the mainland who stole Tiwi wives in the 1860s. At the end of the 1980s, 'Larrakian' and 'Larrakian dog' or the Tiwi equivalent *imopungi* (female *imopunga*, derived from *mopa* or 'climbing up' the way dogs have sex irrespective of incestuous relationships) was used for a person who had illicit sex (though it was used more loosely by younger people).

6   The Yam Rituals

59 For ethnographic information on Tiwi initiations in former times, see the first-hand reports of Spencer (1914: 92–115), Fry (1949; 1950), and Hart (1928/29; 1931: 286; 1974: 349–50; Hart and Pilling 1960: 93–5). Further information based on accounts of Tiwi people has been provided by Harney and Elkin (1943: 231–2), Mountford (1958: 122–43), Goodale (1963, 1970, 1971: 204–23), and Brandl (1971).

60 In the wet season Martha Arapi frequently performed *kulama* songs just before the torrential rains. People said her singing caused the rain.

61 This seclusion of the men and hunting and the collection of yams by women did not take place in the *kulama* witnessed by Mountford and Goodale in 1954 (Goodale 1971: 184–5).

62 At the close of the wet season the wind blew the seeds of the tall spear grass (*merakati*) about. These seeds pierced the body and were said to bring sickness. Mountford was told the time for the yam ritual had come when 'the tall, annual grass was about to shed its seed' (1958: 130). Pilling notes that Merakati would punish violators of the rules and taboos during the *kulama*, especially the initial phases until the clearing of the ceremonial ground. Sickness and death resulted from the prickly seeds of the spear grass. Such a seed was called *jimanipirni*, 'he who injures or kills [me]' (1958: 159–62), a term also used for a policeman and sneak attacker alike. What we have here, I would suggest, is a symbolic killing. I was told Merakati acted upon illicit behaviour and was given an illustrative example: when sweethearts associated in the long grass, *merakati* seeds would prick into their backs.

63 Tobias' mother, Daisy, and Edmund were considered to be 'siblings' because their grandfathers were clan brothers: Edmund and Daisy were said to have one *amini*, grandfather; that is, their respective grandfathers were perceived of as conceptually one (*jinani*).

64 Brandl, however, states that Wuntherini, the mythological sea eagle who also took part in the first *kulama*, was represented here (1971: 270). But see Grau (1983: 174) who mentions the pelican too. There might be differences between the *kulama* rituals, depending on the personnel. The rituals witnessed by Grau and myself in Pularumpi were dominated by people who had the pelican as their dreaming. I found that the different indicators people used to set the time for the ritual were often (associated with) markers of their identity (e.g., dreamings). Also in everyday life people used all kinds of identity markers.

65 The singer's 'brother-in-law' and another Tiwi man went on secret missions in an American submarine to Timor, then occupied by the Japanese, during the Second World War (see also Pye 1985: 95–6).

66 As other attributes of the ritual symbol Turner mentions 'multiple meanings', 'unification of apparently disparate significata' ('interconnected by analogy or by association in fact or thought'), and 'polarization of significata' (1973: 1100). These have become clear above.

67 McCarthy remarks that 'the spear is the principal weapon of the Aborigines, and its use for the kill is the climax of many hunting methods' (cited in F. Rose 1987: 69). Rose further states, 'the animal was usually given the *coup de grâce* with the spear. In view of the economic importance of the spear, it is not surprising that its significance was recognised in the ideology and in the superstructure generally of the society' (1987: 73). He mentions Tiwi barbed spears as 'the classical examples' (ibid.: 73–4).

68 I believe the Tiwi exclamation 'finished' (*weya tua*) at the end of each ritual song and dance performance belongs to the same order of symbolic termination.

69 For a critical review see Ohnuki-Tierney (1992).

7 'Nothing but the Truth'

70 I exercised my right as a member of the public to attend the full committal hearings in the Court of Summary Jurisdiction and two weeks of the murder trial in the Supreme Court. For people involved in the case, Tiwi and white people alike, I have used pseudonyms. In my account of the proceedings I also cite from the court transcripts with permission of the accused and his counsel: Transcript of Proceedings, Court of Summary Jurisdiction, *The Police and [Kevin Wangiti]*, No. 8824150, Pularumpi, 2 February 1989 and No. 8824150, Darwin, 13 February 1989; Transcript of Proceedings, Supreme Court of the Northern Territory, *R v [Kevin Wangiti]*, S.C.C. No. 186 of 1988, Darwin, 24 July – 11 August 1989.

71 Statement to the police, 1 November 1988. This statement and other statements to the police cited below were exhibits at the trial and were read out in court.

72 Transcript of Proceedings, Supreme Court of the Northern Territory, ibid., 1 August 1989, 439–41.

73 Transcript of Proceedings, Supreme Court of the Northern Territory, ibid., 24 July 1989, 28–9.

74 Note that Laura did not mention the alleged axe fight, which would have indicated a more serious matter. She might not have known about it. Sam's representation of his fight with Tobias (a fight with large clubs) as fist fighting, however, suggests it was probably considered unwise to tell about such fights with weapons because of the consequences it could have for the persons involved when it came to the ears of white authorities. In the past, boxing had been introduced by the missionaries to change people's way of fighting. Consequently, fist fighting might have come to be seen as something more likely to be acceptable to outsiders.

75 Transcript of Proceedings, Supreme Court of the Northern Territory, ibid., 25 July 1989, 157.

76 For discussions of the problems of communication between Aborigines and the police see Strehlow 1936; Elkin 1947; Eggleston 1976; Liberman 1981, 1985; Coldrey 1987; Foley 1988; Ligertwood 1988. Foley (1988) presents a good overview of the relations between Aborigines and the police, and their historical background.

77 'The tricking of a criminal into an admission of his crime is applauded in many famous detective stories', Elwin writes with regard to the Maria of India. 'It is probable that unless some such methods were used a majority of Maria criminals would go unconvicted' (1977: 177). The status of a confession to a crime as evidence, however, is disputed even in Western societies: suspects appear to admit crimes they did not commit to get attention, to protect others or as a result of pressure exerted by the police, among other reasons (Wagenaar in *NRC Handelsblad*, 4 February 1993 and 9 March 1993, see also Ginzburg 1992). W.A. Wagenaar holds that a confessional record of interview should be 'an agenda for research' instead of the conclusion of an investigation (personal communication).

78 When Kevin stood trial in the NT Supreme Court, the Crown prosecutor said in his summing up to the jury that it was 'a matter of common sense' and 'just contrary to human experience that anybody says: "Yes, I did this" when this is a serious thing which he or she appreciates will affect them seriously. The more serious the matter is, the more reluctant people are to confess. It's also a fact of life . . . that we accept almost as a matter of course that when people do confess to fault of any sort, that what they say is true' (Transcript of Proceedings, Supreme Court of the Northern Territory, ibid., 9 August 1989, 819).

79 Ethnographers, as Clifford makes clear, have come to realise that they (too) are working in a political context with power relations and ingrained ways of representing others that cannot be completely kept in check, so that, at the most, 'partial truths' can be presented (1986: 7; see also Burridge 1973; Marcus and Cushman 1982; Marcus and Fisher 1986).

80 The Law Reform Commission, reporting on its inquiry into the recognition of Aboriginal customary laws, recommends, 'A customary law defence should not be available in cases of homicide, or of life-threatening assault' and '[a] partial customary law defence should be created, similar to diminished responsibility, reducing murder to manslaughter' (1986: 88–9).

81 Statement to the police, 29 October 1988; Transcript of Proceedings, The Supreme Court of the Northern Territory, ibid., 26 July 1989, 191.

82 I was told that Kevin and his Mosquito clan brother were competitors for a woman of the Stone clan. This suggests the brother might have had an axe to grind with Kevin. Hence his statement, directing suspicion towards Kevin – at least in the perception of the police detectives – must be treated with circumspection. Moreover, at the time the detectives made a reconstruction of his movements on the night of the killing, the names of his putative father, his 'grandfather' and his girlfriend (all of the Stone clan) were on the CIB detectives' shortlist of suspects. These names, among others, were written up on a board at the police office.

83 Kevin was at liberty to stay in the Old Camp as far as the police were concerned. It was not until Monday morning, about ten o'clock, that the police ordered the people living in the Old Camp to leave the area temporarily.

84 Question marks were omitted throughout this written declaration of the detective in charge, typed up more than a month after the date of the interrogation.

85 Transcript of Proceedings, Supreme Court of the Northern Territory, ibid., 25–26 July 1989, 155, 197, 199.

86 Note that both Nancy and Sam made a statement to the police that when they came from the club they walked home. They did not mention, as follows from the statement of their son Mike, they got supper at their daughter's place, located just on the other side of the main road from the Old Camp (that is, in Tiwi perception, on their way home, to the south).

87 Transcript of Proceedings, Supreme Court of the Northern Territory, ibid., 25–6 July 1989, 155, 199.

88 At their request my wife Jeanette, for instance, was on watch (for she could stop white women) while the female Tiwi witnesses went to the toilet in the Supreme Court building, so they could leave the door open and keep in touch.

89 This is not to say that Aborigines, including Tiwi, are never physically assaulted by police officers. Powers the police, as representatives enforcing

the state law, still have (e.g., drunken people, at the discretion of police officers, may be locked up in the cells overnight), and the grim historical experiences of Aborigines in relations with the police, cannot be put aside but
contribute to the fears – justified or not – of Aborigines questioned or held
by police officers.

90 It is also in the nature of interaction between Aboriginal speakers that they
tell what they already know and enter into an exchange of information. Part
of the story thus first has to be told before additional information can be
elicited from the other person (Foley 1988: 170).

91 See Von Sturmer for a discussion of silence as a sign of disapproval (1981:
17). Liberman remarks that silence may be 'utilized mostly when the initia-
tive of the scene has been handed over to the Aborigine and the Aborigine
is unwilling to risk exercising it. The silence constitutes a period of holding
during which a local order may develop without the Aboriginal person having to initiate it' (1981: 250–1). Here, if we rule out contradiction, silence
was the only option left to Kevin.

92 Transcript of Proceedings, Supreme Court of the Northern Territory, 25
July 1989, 119.

93 Transcript of Proceedings, Court of Summary Jurisdiction, ibid., 13
February 1989, 34; Transcript of Proceedings, Supreme Court of the
Northern Territory, ibid., 25 July 1989, 120, 147.

94 Record of Interview between Detective Constable [Owen Berman] and
[Kevin Wangiti] at the Pularumpi Police Station, 1 November 1988, 1. In
Aboriginal societies, according to Sansom, the witness is a kind of trouble-
helper (1980: 240 ff.). Note that the 'prisoner's friend' was Jasmine's eldest
brother.

95 Record of Interview, ibid., 2.

96 Ibid.

97 Ibid., 4. Note the question mark; the detective repeatedly made these kinds
of Freudian typing errors: e.g., question 177 on page 10: 'Why did you stab
that dead person?' Answer of the suspect: 'Because he was trying to kill me?'
I admit the task of an interrogating detective is extremely difficult. The difficulties of language, the lack of comprehension on both sides, unfamiliarity with the suspect's cultural background, and the readiness of the
Aboriginal suspect in general to say what he or she seems to want to hear,
might drive the interrogating detective easily into despair. A police detective under cross-examination once told the court about his method of interrogation: 'It is probably a habit to suggest an answer that is logical'
(Eggleston, cited in Liberman 1981: 248).

98 Ibid., 10.

99 Transcript of Proceedings, Court of Summary Jurisdiction, ibid., 2 February
1989, 18.

100 Transcript of Proceedings, Court of Summary Jurisdiction, ibid., 2 February
1989, 24–5.

101 Transcript of Proceedings, ibid., 29.

102 Transcript of Proceedings, Court of Summary Jurisdiction, 13 February
1989, 31–9.

103 Transcript of Proceedings, ibid., 41.

104 Transcript of Proceedings, ibid., 42.

105 The Chamberlain case has been front page news in Australia from 1981
onwards. Lindy Chamberlain was charged with murder after the disappearance of her baby at Ayers Rock (Uluru) in the Northern Territory. She

claimed a dingo had taken the baby (see Bryson 1986; Chamberlain 1990). Kevin's case was hardly covered by the media but there are some striking resemblances and overlaps, not only in personnel and setting but also in the workings of criminal investigation and the production of evidence to criminal courts in the Northern Territory.

106 Out of the court, he asked me why they kept him in Darwin all that time for such nonsense while on Melville Island his wife was lying on her death-bed. When this was made known to the Crown prosecutor Simon was able to go off to Pularumpi immediately after he had given evidence in court.

107 Transcript of Proceedings, Supreme Court of the Northern Territory, ibid., 24–31 July 1989, 6–327.

108 Ligertwood notes that, as a result of this, 'only rarely will defence counsel call an Aboriginal accused to testify in his defence' (1988: 203).

109 Transcript of Proceedings, ibid., 31 July–11 August 1989, 344–985.

110 This time he was not sworn in but affirmed because the judge was not satisfied he understood the swearing in on the bible (Transcript of Proceedings, ibid., 1 August 1989, 396).

111 Transcript of Proceedings, ibid., 2 August 1989, 504.

112 Transcript of Proceedings, ibid., 508.

113 It is admitted even in cases concerning Aborigines (e.g., Wilson 1982: 115). See Biernoff (1984) for a discussion of the problems involved in the application of psychiatric notions developed in a non-Aboriginal tradition to Aborigines, especially when there is disregard of the subjective reality of Aboriginal people. With regard to the Tiwi, see Reser (1991) versus Robinson (1990).

114 Transcript of Proceedings, ibid., 9 August 1989, 816–7.

8 The Post-Funeral Rituals

115 According to Hart, however, 'Tiwi grave posts are a specialised method of satisfying the need, which all societies feel, for every individual in a society to give public proof of his sorrow at the death of any member of that society' (1932: 18). And Goodale writes, 'The poles . . . symbolize the status and prestige of the deceased, as well as those of his surviving close kin. These symbols are necessary to facilitate the transfer of the deceased from the world of the living to the world of the *mobuditi* [*mopadruwi*] with the same relative status and prestige' (1971: 310).

116 'This species, found naturally on Melville and Bathurst Islands, parts of Cobourg and Cape York Peninsula, . . . naturally grows 17 to 28 m, but specimens 35 m tall and 1 m in diameter have been recorded' (Hearne 1975: 61).

117 Myers states that among the Pintubi Aborigines 'kin status is largely a matter of feeling' (1986a: 104).

118 Depending on the context, the blades figured as birds' wings, shark fins, shark teeth, the sharp edges of waves producing cliffs at the coastline, or the fluttering wings of a butterfly.

119 My data do not support Goodale's statement that in contrast to interactions in daily life 'the obligations acquired during a *pukamani* [post-funeral rituals] end immediately thereafter' (1971: 317).

120 In Tiwi songs and views Germans, alluding to films about the Second World War they have seen over the years, were the bad guys, so to speak. In contrast, Americans were the heroes.

Glossary

For Tiwi kinship and mortuary kinship terminology, refer to appendix 1, 2.

ajipa   polychrome, stage of the seasonal yam ritual
ambaru song   type of mourning song
aminiyarti   one 'grandfather' group
amputji   spirit, the Rainbow Snake
aramipi   'relations' (not marriageable), members of related clans
arawuringkiri   spear with barbs on two sides
arini   tough man
arntukuni   coward

big-headed   skilled song composer
big mob   a lot, many
billabong   Australian–English for a blind creek, backwater or pool
boss   ceremonial leader

camp   dwelling place, hut, group of houses
cheeky   disrespectful of authority (Sansom 1980: 26)
corroboree   Australian–English for an Aboriginal ceremony
country   territorial affiliation, also surroundings of ancestral burial place

deaf   unable to understand in both senses (*orimi*)
dreaming   an affiliation with a location, environmental feature or natural species inherited patrilineally (Brandl 1971: 544)
dreaming dance   dance marking a 'dreaming'
dreaming place   location representing the seat of the mythological ancestress of father's and father's sister's clan

Esky   brand name of a cool box

gammon   pretence

(to) humbug   to court, or to be nasty

ilanigha   mortuary ritual
ilanighi   first initiate

250

iloti	final mortuary ritual (literally, 'forever')
imanka	spirit, shadow, reflection, photograph, film
imunga	'skin group' or matriclan, also sun and breath
irumwa	'dreaming'
jamparipari	spirit
keramili	exchange of partners in marriage between matriclans
(to) kill	to kill, hit or injure
kruti	fruit (e.g., mangoes)
kulama	seasonal yam ritual
kwampi	sneak attacks, sneak attackers (male singular: *kwampini*)
letterstick	message carved in a stick
mamanukuni song	type of mourning song
mantawi	friends (male singular: *mantani*; female singular: *mantanga*)
merekati	spirit connected with long grass
miarti	pandanus (mother-in-law of *jamparipari* and *amputji*)
milimika	ceremonial ring, cleared dancing ground
mob	loosely structured group
moluki	(ritual) bath or washing
mopadruwi	spirits of the dead (*mopaditi*; *mopadringa*)
moyla week	'nothing' week, that is, a week without a pay day
muringelata	ritual for a young woman's first menses
muruntika	ritual at the beginning of the wet season
muruntawi	white people (*muruntani*; *muruntaka*)
naga	loincloth
nemara	talk, trouble, meeting
ngirramini	story, talk, word, argument, trouble
ningawi	small spirits living in the mangroves
old man	father or husband (senior man)
old people	senior people of the past
palingari	the (unspecified) past
paumati	a post-funeral ritual mock fight between (potential) spouses
pay day	pay day or time of ritual payments
pemenua	small spirit
plekuti	crying
pongkini	male peace maker, mostly a senior man
promise	person with whom a marriage has been arranged
pukamani	taboo or taboo-related
putaputuwi	spirit children
putuputu	sorrow
relations	members of related clans (*aramipi*) [note that these clans do not exchange partners in marriage]
shade	windbreak, ceremonial hut or shelter
skin group	matriclan (*imunga*)
smoking	cleansing ritual with smoke
songwriter	song composer
sugar bag	Australian–English for wild honey

tapara	the moon
taringini	poisonous snake
tilamara	paint, ochres
tiwi	(living) people (*tini; tinga*)
tokwainga	goose-feather ball
tucker	food
tungkwaliti	spear with barbs on one side
walemani	axe
word	song text, message, argument
worker	person who performs services in mortuary ritual (*ambaru*)
yoi	dance and song ceremony

References

Allen, L.A. 1976 *Time before morning: Art and myth of the Australian Aborigines.* Adelaide: Rigby.

Altman, J.C. 1988 *Aborigines, tourism, and development: The Northern Territory experience.* Darwin: Australian National University North Australia Research Unit.

Ariès, P. 1983 (1977) *The hour of our death.* Harmondsworth: Penguin Books.

Australian Bureau of Statistics 1990 *Aboriginal people in the Northern Territory.* Darwin: Australian Bureau of Statistics.

Basedow, H. 1913 Notes on the natives of Bathurst Island, north Australia, *Journal of the Royal Anthropological Institute* 43, 291–323.

Basedow, H. 1925 *The Australian Aboriginal.* Adelaide: F.W. Preece and Sons.

Bell, D. 1988 Exercising discretion: Sentencing and customary law in the Northern Territory, in B.W. Morse and G.R. Goodman (eds) *Indigenous law and the state.* Dordrecht: Foris Publications, 367–411.

Berndt, C.H. 1950 Expressions of grief among Aboriginal women, *Oceania* 20, 286–332.

Berndt, R.M. 1965 Law and order in Aboriginal Australia, in R.M. Berndt and C.E. Berndt (eds), *Aboriginal man in Australia.* Sydney: Angus and Robertson, 167–206.

Berndt, R.M. and Berndt, C.H. 1988 (1964) *The world of the first Australians* [revised edition]. Canberra: Aboriginal Studies Press.

Biernoff, D. 1982 Psychiatric and anthropological interpretations of 'aberrant' behaviour in an Aboriginal community, in J. Reid (ed.), *Body, land and spirit: Health and healing in Aboriginal society.* Brisbane: University of Queensland Press, 139–53.

Bloch, M. 1975 Introduction, in M. Bloch (ed.), *Political language and oratory in traditional society.* London: Academic Press, 1–28.

Bloch, M. 1992 *Prey into hunter:The politics of religious experience.* Cambridge: Cambridge University Press.

Bloch, M. and Parry, J. (eds) 1982 *Death and the regeneration of life.* Cambridge: Cambridge University Press.

Blok, A. 1991 Zinloos en zinvol geweld, *Amsterdams Sociologisch Tijdschrift* 18, 189–207.

253

Bohannan, P. 1967 Patterns of homicide among tribal societies in Africa, in M.E. Wolfgang (ed.), *Studies in Homicide*. New York: Harper and Row, 211–37.

Boissevain, J. 1974 *Friends of friends*. Oxford: Basil Blackwell.

Borofsky, R. 1987 *Making history: Pukapukan and anthropological constructions of knowledge*. Cambridge: Cambridge University Press.

Borsboom, A.P. 1982 Van assimilatie tot zelfbeschikking: Analyse van een Aboriginal emancipatiebeweging in Arnhem Land, noord- Australië, *Sociaal Antropologische Cahiers* I, Nijmegen: ICSA.

Borsboom, A.P. 1987 Koloniale geschiedenis van Australische Aborigines, in A. Borsboom and J. Kommers (eds), *Processen van kolonisatie en dekolonisatie in de Pacific*. Nijmegen: Centrum voor Studies van Australië en Oceanië.

Brady, M. and Palmer, K. 1984 *Alcohol in the outback: Two studies of drinking*. Darwin: Australian National University North Australia Research Unit.

Brandl, M.M. 1970 Adaptation or disintegration?: Changes in the kulama initiation and increase ritual of Melville and Bathurst Islands, Northern Territory of Australia, *Anthropological Forum* 2, 464–79.

Brandl, M.M. 1971 Pukumani: The social context of bereavement in a north Australian Aboriginal tribe. PhD thesis, University of Western Australia, Perth.

Brogan, T. 1990 *The Garden Point mob*. Darwin: Historical Society of the Northern Territory.

Brown, H.Y.L. 1906 *Northern Territory of South Australia, north-western district. Reports (geological and general) resulting from the explorations made by the government geologist and staff during 1905*. Adelaide: C.E. Bristow.

Bryson, J. 1986 *Evil Angels*. Melbourne: Penguin Books.

Burbank, V.K. 1980 Expressions of anger and aggression in an Australian Aboriginal community. PhD. thesis, Rutgers University, New Brunswick.

Burbank, V.K. 1988 *Aboriginal adolescence: Maidenhood in an Australian community*. New Brunswick: Rutgers University Press.

Burke, K. 1974 (1950) *A rhetoric of motives*. New York: University of California Press.

Burridge, K. 1973 *Encountering Aborigines: Anthropology and the Australian Aboriginal*. New York: Pergamon Press.

Campbell, J. 1834 Geographical memoir of Melville Island and Port Essington, on the Cobourg Peninsula, northern Australia; with some observations on the settlements which have been established on the north coast of New Holland, *Journal of the Royal Geographical Society* 4, 129–81.

Capell, A. 1967 The analysis of complex verbal forms, with special reference to Tiwi (Bathurst and Melville Islands, north Australia), in C.G. von Brandenstein; A. Capell and K. Hale, *Papers in Australian Linguistics* 2, Canberra: Australian National University, 43–62.

Cense, A.A. 1952 Makassaars-Boeginese prauwvaart op Noord-Australië, *Bijdragen tot de Taal-, Land- en Volkenkunde* 108, 248–65.

Chamberlain, L. 1990 *Through my eyes*. Melbourne: Mandarin Australia.

Chisholm, R. and Nettheim, G. 1984 *Understanding law: An introduction to Australia's legal system*. Melbourne: Butterworths.

Clifford, J. 1986 Introduction: Partial truths, in J. Clifford and G.E. Marcus (eds), *Writing culture: the poetics and politics of ethnography*. Berkeley: University of California Press, 1–26.

Clunies Ross, M. 1987 Research into Aboriginal songs: The state of the art, in M. Clunies Ross, T. Donaldson and S. Wild (eds), *Songs of Aboriginal Australia*. Sydney: Oceania Monograph 32, 1–13.

Coldrey, J. 1987 Aboriginals and the criminal courts, in K.M. Hazlehurst (ed.), *Ivory scales: Black Australia and the law*. Sydney: New South Wales University Press/Australian Institute of Criminology, 81–92.

Collman, J. 1979 Social order and the exchange of liquor: A theory of drinking among Australian Aborigines, *Journal of Anthropological Research* 35, 208–24.

Comaroff, J.L. and Roberts, S. 1981 *Rules and processes: The cultural logic of dispute in an African context*. Chicago: University of Chicago Press.

Cummings, B. 1990 *Take this child: From Kahlin compound to the Retta Dixon's children's home*. Canberra: Aboriginal Studies Press.

d'Abbs, P. 1987 *Dry areas, alcohol and Aboriginal communities: A review of the Northern Territory restricted areas legislation*. Darwin: Darwin Institute of Technology.

Daly, M. and Wilson, M. 1988 *Homicide*. New York: Aldine de Gruyter.

Darnton, R. 1985 (1984) *The great cat massacre*. Harmondsworth: Penguin Books.

Davis, N.Z. 1985 *The return of Martin Guerre*. Harmondsworth: Penguin Books.

Durkheim, E. 1968 (1912) *The elementary forms of the religious life*. New York: Free Press.

Elkin, A.P. 1947 Aboriginal evidence and justice in north Australia, *Oceania* 17, 173–210.

Elkin, A.P. 1964 (1938) *The Australian Aborigines* [third edition]. New York: Natural History Library/Doubleday Anchor.

Elwin, V. 1977 (1943) *Maria Murder and Suicide* [second edition]. Bombay: Oxford University Press.

Fallon, J. 1991 The good old days, *Nelen Yubu* (48), 12–16.

Fisher, M. and Hennessy, P. 1988 Aboriginal customary laws and the Australian criminal law in conflict, *Law and Anthropology*, Internationales Jahrbuch für Rechtsanthropologie, 3. Wien: VWGÖ-Verlag/Klaus Renner, 83–102.

Flinders, M. 1814 *A voyage to Terra Australis*. London: Nicol.

Foelsche, P. 1882 Notes on the Aborigines of north Australia, *Transactions and proceedings and report of the Royal Society of South Australia* 5, 1–18.

Foley, M. 1988 (1984) Aborigines and the police, in P. Hanks and B. Keon-Cohen (eds), *Aborigines and the law*. Sydney: Allen & Unwin, 160–90.

Freud, S. 1983 (1913) *Totem and taboo*. London: Ark/Routledge and Kegan Paul.

Fry, H.K. 1949 A Bathurst Island mourning rite, *Mankind* 4, 79–80.

Fry, H.K. 1950 A Bathurst Island initiation rite, *Mankind* 4, 167–8.

Gale, F., Bailey-Harris, R. and J. Wundersitz 1990 *Aboriginal youth and the criminal justice system*. Cambridge: Cambridge University Press.

Gee, L.C.E. 1907 Notes of a cruise round Melville and Bathurst Islands, *Australasian Association for the Advancement of Science*, Report 11, 539–47.

Geertz, C. 1973 Thick description: Toward an interpretative theory of culture, in *The interpretation of cultures*. New York: Basic Books, 3–30.

Geertz, C. 1983 Common sense as a cultural system, in *Local knowledge*. New York: Basic Books, 73–93.

Geertz, C. 1986 Making experiences, authoring selves, in V.W. Turner and E.M. Bruner (eds), *The anthropology of experience*. Urbana: University of Illinois Press, 373–80.

Ginzburg, C. 1982 (1976) *De kaas en de wormen*. Amsterdam: Bert Bakker.

Ginzburg, C. 1984 Beweise und Möglichkeiten, In N.Z. Davis, *Die Wahrhaftige Geschichte von der Wiederkehr des Martin Guerre*. München: Piper, 185–213.

Ginzburg, C. 1988 Morelli, Freud, and Sherlock Holmes: Clues and scientific method, in U. Eco and T.A. Sebeok (eds), *The sign of three: Dupin, Holmes, Pierce*. Bloomington: Indiana University Press, 81–118.

Ginzburg, C. 1992 *De rechter en de historicus*. Amsterdam: Bert Bakker.

Goodale, J.C. 1962 Marriage contracts among the Tiwi, *Ethnology* 1, 452–66.

Goodale, J.C. 1963 Qualifications for adulthood: Tiwi invoke the power of a yam, *Natural History* 72, 10–17.

Goodale, J.C. 1970 An example of ritual change among the Tiwi of Melville Island, in A.R. Pilling and R.A. Waterman (eds), *Diprotodon to detribalization. Studies of change among Australian Aborigines*. East Lansing: Michigan State University Press, 350–66.

Goodale, J.C. 1971 *Tiwi wives. A study of the women of Melville Island, north Australia*. Seattle: University of Washington Press.

Goodale, J.C. 1982 Production and reproduction of key resources among the Tiwi of north Australia, in N.M. Williams and E.S. Hunn (eds), *Resource managers: North American and Australian hunter-gatherers*. Canberra: Australian Institute of Aboriginal Studies, 197–210.

Goodale, J.C. and Koss, J.D. 1971 The cultural context of creativity among Tiwi, in C.M. Otten (ed.), *Anthropology and art*. New York: Natural History Press, 182–200.

Grau, A. 1983 Dreaming, dancing, kinship: The study of *yoi*, the dance of the Tiwi of Melville and Bathurst Islands, north Australia. PhD thesis, The Queen's University, Belfast.

Gsell, F.X. 1956 *'The bishop with 150 wives': Fifty years as a missionary*. Sydney: Angus and Robertson.

Hall, R.A. 1989 *The Black Diggers: Aborigines and Torres Strait Islanders in the Second World War*. Sydney: Allen & Unwin.

Harney, W.E. 1965 (1957) *Life among the Aborigines*. London: Robert Hale.

Harney, W.E. and Elkin, A.P. 1943 Melville and Bathurst Islanders: A short description, *Oceania* 43, 228–34.

Harrison, L. 1986 Diet and nutrition in a Tiwi community. A study of factors affecting the health status of under-threes at Milikapiti, north Australia. PhD thesis, Australian National University, Canberra.

Hart, C.W.H. 1928/29 Unpublished fieldnotes. 10 vols. [held by Dr. N. Peterson, Department of Archaeology and Anthropology, Australian National University, Canberra].

Hart, C.W.H. 1930 The Tiwi of Melville and Bathurst Islands, *Oceania* 1, 167–80.

Hart, C.W.H. 1931 Personal names among the Tiwi, *Oceania* 1, 280–90.

Hart, C.W.H. 1932 Grave posts of Melville Island, *Man* 32, 18.

Hart, C.W.H. 1954 The sons of Turimpi, *American Anthropologist* 56, 242–61.

Hart, C.W.H. 1970 Some factors affecting residence among the Tiwi, *Oceania* 40, 296–303.

Hart, C.W.H. 1974 (1955) Contrasts between prepubertal and postpubertal education, in G.D. Spindler (ed.), *Education and cultural process*. New York: Holt, Rinehart and Winston, 342–60.

Hart, C.W.H. 1979 (1970) Fieldwork among the Tiwi, 1928–1929, in C.W.M. Hart and A.R. Pilling, *The Tiwi of north Australia* [fieldwork edition]. New York: Holt, Rinehart and Winston, 114–35.

Hart, C.W.M. and Pilling, A.R. 1960 *The Tiwi of north Australia*. New York: Holt, Rinehart and Winston.

Hart, C.W.M., Pilling, A.R. and Goodale, J.C. 1988 *The Tiwi of north Australia* [third edition]. New York: Holt, Rinehart and Winston.

Hearne, D.A. 1975 *Trees for Darwin and northern Australia*. Canberra: Australian Government Publishing Service.

Hertz, R. 1960 (1907) A contribution to the study of the collective representation of death, in *Death and the Right Hand*. Glencoe: The Free Press, 25–86, 117–71.

Hiatt, L.R. 1961 Mortuary rites and practices in central Arnhem Land. Unpublished typescript.

Hiatt, L.R. 1965 *Kinship and conflict. A study of an Aboriginal community in northern Arnhem Land.* Canberra: Australian National University.

Hiatt, L.R. 1985 Maidens, males, and Marx: Some contrasts in the work of Frederick Rose and Claude Meillassoux, *Oceania* 56, 34–46.

Hingston, J.P. 1938 Exploration of Melville Island [1877], *Royal Australian Historical Society Journal and Proceedings* 24, 157–63.

Horton, D. (general ed.) 1994 *The encyclopædia of Aboriginal Australia*. vol. 2. Canberra: Aboriginal Studies Press.

Jones, F.L. 1963 *A demographic survey of the Aboriginal population of the Northern Territory, with special reference to Bathurst Island Mission.* Canberra: Australian Institute of Aboriginal Studies.

Kan, S. 1989 *Symbolic immortality: The Tlingit potlatch of the nineteenth century.* Washington: Smithsonian Institution Press.

Kapferer, B. 1986 Performance and the structuring of meaning and experience, in V.W. Turner and E.M. Bruner (eds), *The anthropology of experience*. Urbana: University of Illinois Press, 188–203.

Keen, I. 1977 Ambiguity in Yolngu religious language, *Canberra Anthropology* 1, 33–50.

Keen, I. 1982 How some Murngin men marry ten wives: The marital implications of matrilateral cross-cousin structures, *Man* 17, 620–42.

Keen, I. 1988 Twenty-five years of Aboriginal kinship studies, in R.M. Berndt and R. Tonkinson (eds), *Social anthropology and Australian Aboriginal studies.* Canberra: Aboriginal Studies Press, 79–123.

Kertzer, D.I. 1988 *Ritual, politics, and power.* New Haven: Yale University Press.

King, P.P. 1827 *Narrative of a survey of the intertropical and western coasts of Australia performed between the years 1818 and 1822 (by Captain Phillip King).* 2 vols. London: John Murray.

Kirk, R.L. 1983 (1981) *Aboriginal man adapting: The human biology of Australian Aborigines.* Melbourne: Oxford University Press.

Klaatsch, H. 1907 Schlussbericht über meine Reise nach Australien in den Jahren 1904–1907 (Mai 1906 bis April 1907: Nordwest Australien, Nord-Territorium, Melville-Island, Tasmanien), *Zeitschrift für Ethnologie* 39, 635–90.

Klaatsch, H. 1908 Some notes on scientific travel amongst the black population of tropical Australia in 1904, 1905 and 1906, *Report on the 11th meeting of the Australasian Association for the Advancement of Science held at Adelaide, 1907,* Adelaide, 557–92.

Kriewaldt, M.C. 1960 The application of the criminal law to the Aborigines of the Northern Territory of Australia, *University of Western Australia Law Review* 5.

Kuschel, R. 1992 Killing begets killing: Homicides and blood feuds on a Polynesian outlier. Unpublished paper presented at the First European Colloquium on Pacific Studies, Nijmegen.

Lakoff, G. and Johnson, M. 1980 *Metaphors we live by.* Chicago: University of Chicago Press.

Langton, M. 1988 Medicine Square, in I. Keen (ed.), *Being black: Aboriginal cultures in 'settled' Australia.* Canberra: Aboriginal Studies Press, 201–25.

Law Reform Commission 1986 *The recognition of Aboriginal customary laws: Summary report.* (Report No. 31) Canberra: Australian Government Publishing Service.

Lee, J. 1987 *Tiwi today: A study of language change in a contact situation.* Pacific Linguistics, Series C – No. 96. Canberra: The Australian National University.

LeVine, B.A. 1982 Gusii funerals: Meaning of death and life in an African community, *Ethos* 10, 26–65.

Liberman, K.B. 1981 Understanding Aborigines in Australian courts of law, *Human Organization* 40, 247–55.

Liberman, K.B. 1985 *Understanding interaction in central Australia: An ethnomethodological study of Australian Aboriginal people.* Boston: Routledge and Kegan Paul.

Ligertwood, A. 1988 (1984) Aborigines in the criminal courts, in P. Hanks and B. Keon-Cohen (eds), *Aborigines and the Law.* Sydney: Allen & Unwin, 191–211.

Loorham, C. 1982 A NT record of interview: Kumajay's case, *Aboriginal Law Bulletin* (3), 3–4.

Lutz, C.A. 1988 *Unnatural emotions: Everyday sentiments on a Micronesian Atoll and their challenge to Western theory.* Chicago: The University of Chicago Press.

Macdonald, G. 1988 A Wiradjuri fight story, in I. Keen (ed.), *Being black: Aboriginal cultures in 'settled' Australia.* Canberra: Aboriginal Studies Press, 179–99.

Macknight, C.C. 1976 *The voyage to Marege: Macassan trepangers in northern Australia.* Melbourne: Melbourne University Press.

Maddock, K. 1986 (1972) *The Australian Aborigines: A portrait of their society* [second edition]. Melbourne: Penguin Books.

Maddock, K. 1988 (1984) Aboriginal customary law, in P. Hanks and B. Keon-Cohen (eds), *Aborigines and the law.* Sydney: Allen & Unwin, 212–37.

Malinowski, B. 1940 (1926) *Crime and custom in savage society.* London: Kegan Paul, Trench, Trubner & Co.

Marcus, G.E. and Cushman, D. 1982 Ethnographies as texts, *Annual Review of Anthropology* 11, 25–69.

Marcus, G.E and Fischer, M. 1986 *Anthropology as a cultural critique.* Chicago: University of Chicago Press.

McKnight, D. 1981 Sorcery in an Australian tribe, *Ethnology* 20, 31–44.

McKnight, D. 1986 Fighting in an Australian Aboriginal supercamp, in D. Riches (ed.), *The anthropology of violence.* Oxford: Blackwell, 136–63.

Meggitt, M.J. 1986 (1962) *Desert people: A study of the Walbiri Aborigines of central Australia.* London: Angus and Roberston.

Merlan, F. 1988 Gender in Aboriginal social life: A review, in R.M. Berndt and R. Tonkinson (eds), *Social anthropology and Australian Aboriginal studies.* Canberra: Aboriginal Studies Press, 17–76.

Metcalf, P. 1982 *A Borneo journey into death: Berawan eschatology from its rituals.* Philadelphia: University of Pennsylvania Press.

Metcalf, P. and Huntington, R. 1991 *Celebrations of death: The anthropology of mortuary ritual.* [second edition]. Cambridge, Mass: Cambridge University Press.

Miles, D. 1965 Socio-economic aspects of secondary burial, *Oceania* 35, 161–74.

Moore, S.F. 1975 Epilogue: Uncertainties in situations, indeterminacies in culture, in S.F. Moore and B. Myerhoff (eds), *Symbol and politics in communal ideology.* Ithaca: Cornell University Press, 210–39.

Moore, S.F. 1978 *Law as process: An anthropological approach.* London: Routledge and Kegan Paul.

Moore, S.F. 1987 Explaining the present: Theoretical dilemmas in processual ethnograpy, *American Ethnologist* 14, 727–36.

Morphy, H. 1984 *Journey to the crocodile's nest*. Canberra: Australian Institute of Aboriginal Studies.

Morony, R. 1991 The Community Development Employment Projects (CDEP) scheme, in J. Altman (ed.), *Aboriginal employment equity by the year 2000*. Canberra: Academy of the Social Sciences in Australia/Centre for Aboriginal Economic Policy Research, 101–6.

Mountford, C.P. 1956 Expedition to the land of the Tiwi, *The National Geographic Magazine* 109, 417–40.

Mountford, C.P. 1958 *The Tiwi, their art, myth and ceremony*. London: Phoenix House.

Mulvaney, D.J. and Calaby, J.H. 1985 *So much that is new: Baldwin Spencer 1860–1929*. Melbourne: Melbourne University Press.

Myers, F.R. 1986a *Pintubi country, Pintubi self: Sentiments, place, and politics among Western Desert Aborigines*. Washington/Canberra: Smithsonian Institution Press/Australian Institute of Aboriginal Studies.

Myers, F.R. 1986b The politics of representation: Anthropological discourse and Australian Aborigines, *American Ethnologist* 13, 138–53.

Northern Territory Police Force 1990 *Annual report of the Police Force of the Northern Territory: For the year ended 30 June 1989*. Darwin: Police Headquarters.

Ohnuki-Tierney, E. 1992 Vitality on the rebound: ritual's core? *Anthropology Today* 8, 17–20.

Osborne, C.R. 1974 *The Tiwi language*. Canberra: Australian Institute of Aboriginal Studies.

Peacock, J.L. 1989 (1986) *The anthropological lens: Harsh light, soft focus*. Cambridge: Cambridge University Press.

Peterson, N. 1993 Demand sharing: Reciprocity and the pressure for generosity among foragers, *American Anthropologist* 95, 860–74.

Peterson, N. and Taylor, J. 1993 Tiwi population dynamics, 1929–1991. Unpublished paper presented to the Seventh International Conference on Hunting and Gathering Societies, Moscow, August 1993.

Petri, H. 1954 *Sterbende Welt in Nordwest-Australien*. Braunschweig: Albert Limbach Verlag.

Pilling, A.R. 1958 Law and feud in an Aboriginal society of north Australia. PhD thesis, University of California, Berkeley.

Pilling, A.R. 1962 Statistics, sorcery, and justice, *American Anthropologist* 64, 1057–9.

Pilling, A.R. 1965 An Australian Aboriginal minority: The Tiwi see themselves as a dominant majority, *Phylon* 26, 305–14.

Pilling, A.R. 1968 Predation and warfare, in R.B. Lee and I. DeVore (eds), *Man the hunter*. Chicago: Aldine, 157–8.

Pilling, A.R. 1970 Changes in Tiwi language, in A.R. Pilling and R.A. Waterman (eds), *Diprotodon to detribalization: Studies of change among Australian Aborigines*. East Lansing: Michigan State University Press, 256–74.

Pilling, A.R. 1978 A socio-cultural approach to homicide. Unpublished manuscript. Wayne State University, Detroit.

Pilling, A.R. 1988 Sneak attacks, in W.C.M. Hart, A.R. Pilling and J.C. Goodale, *The Tiwi of north Australia* [third edition]. New York: Holt, Rinehart and Winston, 93–5.

Priest, C.A.V. 1986 *Northern Territory recollections*. Victoria: C. Priest.

Pye, J. 1985 (1977) *The Tiwi Islands* [third edition]. Darwin: Coleman/Catholic Mission Headquarters.

Rasing, W.C.E. 1994 *'Too many people': Order and nonconformity in Iglulingmiut social process*. PhD dissertation. Series Recht en Samenleving, nr. 8. Nijmegen: Katholieke Universiteit, Faculteit der Rechtsgeleerdheid.

Reid, G. 1990 *A picnic with the natives. Aboriginal-European relations in the Northern Territory to 1910*. Melbourne: Melbourne University Press.

Reid, J. 1979 A time to live, a time to grieve: Patterns and processes of mourning among the Yolngu of Australia, *Culture, Medicine and Psychiatry* 3, 319–46.

Reid, J. 1983 *Sorcerers and healing spirits: Continuity and change in an Aboriginal medical system*. Canberra: Australian National University Press.

Reser, J.P. 1991 The cultural context of Aboriginal suicide: Myths, meanings, and critical analysis, *Oceania* 61, 177–84.

Riches, D. 1986 The phenomenon of violence, in R. Riches (ed.), *The anthropology of violence*. Oxford: Basil Blackwell, 1–27.

Riches, D. 1991 Aggression, war, violence: Space/time and paradigm, *Man* 26, 281–98.

Ritchie, P.H. 1934 *North of the never never*. Sydney: Angus and Robertson.

Robert, W.C.H. 1973 *The Dutch explorations of the north and northwest coast of Australia, 1605–1756*. Amsterdam: Philo Press.

Roberts, S. 1979 *Order and dispute: An introduction to legal anthropology*. Harmondsworth: Penguin Books.

Roberts, S. 1994 Law and dispute processes, in T. Ingold (ed.) *Companion encyclopedia of anthropology*. London: Routledge, 962–82.

Robinson, G. 1990 Separation, retaliation and suicide: Mourning and the conflicts of young Tiwi men, *Oceania* 60, 161–77.

Rosaldo, R. 1986 Ilongot hunting as story and experience, in V.W. Turner and E. Bruner (eds), *The anthropology of experience*. Urbana: University of Illinois Press, 97–138.

Rosaldo, R. 1989 *Culture and truth: The remaking of social analysis*. Boston: Beacon Press.

Rose, D.B. 1992 *Dingo makes us human: Life and land in an Australian Aboriginal culture*. Cambridge: Cambridge University Press.

Rose, F.G.G. 1987 *The traditional mode of production of the Australian Aborigines*. London: Angus and Roberston.

Ross, M.H. 1993 *The management of conflict: Interpretations and interests in comparative perspective*. New Haven: Yale University Press.

Roth, P. 1989 How narratives explain, *Social Research* 56, 449–78.

Rowley, C.D. 1986 (1970) *The destruction of Aboriginal society*. Melbourne: Penguin Books.

Sansom, B. 1977 Aborigines and alcohol: A fringe camp example, *Australian Journal of Alcoholism and Drug Dependence* 4, 58–62.

Sansom, B. 1980 *The camp at Wallaby Cross: Aboriginal fringe dwellers in Darwin*. Canberra: Australian Institute of Aboriginal Studies.

Searcy, A. 1905 *In northern seas*. Adelaide: W.K. Thomas.

Searcy, A. 1909 *In Australian tropics* [second edition]. London: Robertson & Co.

Seremetakis, C.N. 1991 *The last word: Women, death, and divination in inner Mani*. Chicago: The University of Chicago Press.

Shore, B. 1982 *Sala'ilua: A Samoan Mystery*. New York: Columbia University Press.

Simpson, C. 1954 Island of Yoi, In *Adam in ochre: Inside Aboriginal Australia* [third edition]. Sydney: Angus and Robertson, 130–62.

Sowden, W.J. 1882 *The Northern Territory as it is: A narrative of the South Australian parliamentary party's trip, and full descriptions of the Northern Territory; its settlements and industries.* [Reprint by the History Unit of the University Planning Authority, Darwin, n.d.] Adelaide: W.K. Thomas.

Spencer, W.B. 1912 An introduction to the study of certain native tribes of the Northern Territory, *Bulletin of the Northern Territory* No. 2 (April 1912, Melbourne).

Spencer, W.B. 1914 *Native tribes of the Northern Territory of Australia.* London: Macmillan.

Spencer, W.B. 1928 *Wanderings in wild Australia.* vol. 2. London: Macmillan.

Spencer, W.B. and Gillen, F.J. 1968 (1899) *The native tribes of central Australia.* [Unabridged republication of the work originally published by Macmillan & Co.] New York: Dover.

Stanner, W.E.H. 1979 Durmugam: A Nangiomeri (1959), in *White man got no Dreaming: Essays 1938–1973.* Canberra: Australian National University Press, 67–105.

Stanner, W.E.H. 1989 *On Aboriginal religion.* Sydney: Oceania Monograph 36.

Stevenson, P.M. n.d. The seasons and seasonal markers of the Tiwi people of north Australia. Unpublished manuscript.

Stevenson, P.M. 1985 Traditional Aboriginal resource management in the wet-dry tropics: Tiwi case study, In M.G. Ridpath and L.K. Corbett (eds) Ecology of the Wet-Dry Tropics, *Proceedings of the Ecological Society of Australia* 13, 309–15.

Strehlow, T.G.H. 1936 Native evidence and its value, *Oceania* 6, 323–35.

Sutton, P. and Rigsby, B. 1982 People without politicks: Management of land and personnel on Australia's Cape York Peninsula, in N.M. Williams and E.S. Hunn (eds), *Resource Managers: North American and Australian hunter-gatherers.* Canberra: Australian Institute of Aboriginal Studies, 155–71.

Swaardecroon, H. and Chastelijn, C. 1856 Verslag eener reis naar de Noordkust van Nieuw-Holland, in 1705, *Bijdragen tot de Taal-, Land- en Volkenkunde van Nederlandsch Indië* [nieuwe volgreeks, eerste deel], 193–202.

Thompson, E.P. 1979 *Folklore, anthropology, and social history.* Brighton: Noyce.

Tonkinson, R. 1988 One community, two laws: Aspects of conflict and convergence in a Western Australian Aboriginal settlement, in B.W. Morse and G.R. Goodman (eds) *Indigenous law and the state.* Dordrecht: Foris Publications, 395–411.

Turner, V.W. 1957 *Schism and continuity in an African society.* Manchester: Manchester University Press.

Turner, V.W. 1973 Symbols in African ritual, *Science* 179, 1100–5.

Turner, V.W. 1974 *Dramas, fields and metaphors: Symbolic action in human society.* Ithaca: Cornell University Press.

Van Velsen, J. 1967 The extended-case method and situational analysis, in A.L. Epstein (ed.), *The Craft of Social Anthropology.* London: Tavistock Publications, 129–49.

Van Gennep, A. 1960 (1909) *The rites of passage.* Chicago: University of Chicago Press.

Venbrux, E. 1993a 'You can't win': Australian Aborigines and the Anglo-Australian criminal justice system, in H. Driessen (ed.) *The politics of ethnographic reading and writing: Confrontations between Western and indigenous views.* Saarbrücken/Fort Lauderdale: Breitenbach Publishers, 40–64.

Venbrux, E. 1993b Les politiques de l'émotion dans le rituel funéraire des Tiwi d'Australie, *L'Ethnographie* 89, 61–77.

Venbrux, E. 1993c Under the Mango Tree: A case of homicide in an Australian Aboriginal society. PhD thesis, University of Nijmegen, Nijmegen.

Von Sturmer, J. 1981 Talking with Aborigines, [reprint] *Australian Institute of Aboriginal Studies Newsletter*, new series, No. 15, 1–19.

Von Sturmer, J. 1987 Aboriginal singing and notions of power, in M. Clunies Ross, T. Donaldson and S.A. Wild (eds), *Songs of Aboriginal Australia*. Sydney: Oceania Monograph 38, University of Sydney, 63–76.

Warner, W.L. 1931 Murngin Warfare, *Oceania* 1, 457–94.

Warner, W.L. 1958 (1937) *A black civilization: A social study of an Australian tribe* [revised edition]. n.p. [New York]: Harper and Brothers.

Williams, D. 1981 *Exploring Aboriginal kinship*. Canberra: Curriculum Development Centre.

Williams, N.M. 1987 *Two laws: Managing disputes in a contemporary Aboriginal community*. Canberra: Australian Institute of Aboriginal Studies.

Williams, N.M. 1988 Studies in Australian Aboriginal law 1961–1986, in R.M. Berndt and R. Tonkinson (eds), *Social anthropology and Australian Aboriginal studies*. Canberra: Aboriginal Studies Press, 191–237.

Wilson, P.R. 1982 *Black death, white hands*. Sydney: Allen & Unwin.

Index

263